BIOCENTRISM AND MODERNISM

Examining the complex intersections between art and scientific approaches to the natural world, *Biocentrism and Modernism* reveals another side to the development of Modernism. While many historians have framed this movement as being mechanistic and "against" nature, the essays in this collection illuminate the role that nature-centric ideologies played in late-nineteenth to mid-twentieth-century Modernism.

The essays in *Biocentrism and Modernism* contend that it is no accident that Modernism arose at the same time as the field of modern biology. From nineteenth-century discoveries, to the emergence of the current environmentalist movement during the 1960s, artists, architects, and urban planners have responded to currents in the scientific world. Sections of the volume treat both philosophic worldviews and their applications in theory, historiography, and urban design. This collection also features specific case studies of individual artists, including Raymond Duchamp-Villon, Paul Klee, Wassily Kandinsky, and Jackson Pollock.

Oliver A.I. Botar received his Ph.D. in Art History from the University of Toronto and is Associate Professor of Art History in the School of Art at the University of Manitoba, in Winnipeg, Canada.

Isabel Wünsche studied Art History and Archaeology in Berlin, Moscow, Heidelberg, and Los Angeles, and completed her Ph.D. dissertation at Heidelberg University. She is Professor of Art and Art History at Jacobs University in Bremen, Germany.

Biocentrism and Modernism

Edited by Oliver A.I. Botar and Isabel Wünsche

ASHGATE

Published by
Ashgate Publishing Limited
Wey Court East
Union Road
Farnham
Surrey, GU9 7PT
England

Ashgate Publishing Company
Suite 420
101 Cherry Street
Burlington, VT 05401-4405
USA

www.ashgate.com

British Library Cataloguing in Publication Data
Biocentrism and modernism.
1. Modernism (Aesthetics) 2. Art and biology. I. Botar, Oliver A. I. (Oliver Arpad Istvan), 1957– II. Wünsche, Isabel.
700.1'08–dc22

Library of Congress Cataloging-in-Publication Data
Botar, Oliver A. I. (Oliver Arpad Istvan), 1957–
Biocentrism and Modernism / Oliver A.I. Botar and Isabel Wünsche.
pages cm
Includes bibliographical references and index.
ISBN 978-1-4094-0050-9 (hardcover : alk. paper)
1. Modernism (Art) 2. Nature (Aesthetics) 3. Human ecology in art. I. Wünsche, Isabel. II. Title.

N6465.M63B68 2011
709.04—dc22

2010044257

ISBN 9781409400509 (hbk)

MIX
Paper from responsible sources
FSC® C018575
FSC
www.fsc.org

Printed and bound in Great Britain by the MPG Books Group, UK

Contents

Illustrations

Color plates

1 Paul Klee, *Nekropolis* [Necropolis], 1929/91, oil on muslin on plywood, 63 × 44 cm. Staatliche Museen zu Berlin, Nationalgalerie, Museum Berggruen, Berlin, Germany. © 2009 Artists Rights Society (ARS), New York/VG Bild-Kunst, Bonn. Photo: Bildarchiv Preussischer Kulturbesitz, Berlin/Art Resource, New York

2 Paul Klee, *Flüchtiges auf dem Wasser* [Fleeting on the Water], 1929/320 pen and watercolor on paper on cardboard, 26 × 30.5 cm. Private collection, Italy. © 2009 Artists Rights Society (ARS), New York/VG Bild-Kunst, Bonn

3 Peter Blake, "Ideal Museum" for Jackson Pollock's work, 1949. Original model lost. Replica fabricated by Patrick Bodden, with sculptures by Susan Tamulevich, 1994–95. Reconstructed model in landscape. Made possible by a grant from the Graham Foundation for Advanced Studies in the Fine Arts. Photo: Jeff Heatley. Collection of the Pollock-Krasner House and Study Center, East Hampton, NY

4 Jackson Pollock, *The Key*, 1946, oil on linen, 149.8 × 208.3 cm. Unframed. Through prior gift of Mr. and Mrs. Edward Morris, 1987.261, The Art Institute of Chicago. Photography © The Art Institute of Chicago. © The Pollock-Krasner Foundation/Artists Rights Society (ARS), New York

5 Jackson Pollock, *Summertime: Number 9A, 1948*, 1948, oil, enamel and house paint on canvas, 84.8 × 555.0 cm. Tate Gallery, London. Photo: Tate, London/Art Resource, NY. © The Pollock-Krasner Foundation/Artists Rights Society (ARS), New York

Figures

1 Defining Biocentrism

1.1 Photographer unknown, Ernst Haeckel meets Wilhelm Ostwald on the occasion of a meeting of the Monist League, n.d. [c. 1906–15], silver gelatine copyprint, 17.7 × 12 cm. Ostwald Papers, Berlin-Brandenburgische Akademie der Wissenschaften, Berlin

1.2 Designer unknown, cover for Ernst Haeckel, *Die Welträtsel* [1899] (Leipzig: Alfred Kröner, 1908). Private collection

1.3 Photographer unknown, *Portrait of Hans Driesch*, n.d. [c. 1900], silver gelatine print. Courtesy of Besitznachweis Universitätsbibliothek Leipzig, Nachlass 250:6.2, Foto Nr. 44

1.4 Photographer unknown, *Portrait of Ludwig Klages*, n.d. [c. 1900–1910], silver gelatine print. Courtesy of Deutsches Literaturarchiv, Marbach am Neckar, Germany

Contributors

Allan Antliff is Research Chair in Modern Art at the University of Victoria, Canada, and author of *Anarchist Modernism: Art, Politics, and the First American Avant-Garde* (2001), *Art and Anarchy: From the Paris Commune to the Fall of the Berlin Wall* (2007), and editor of *Only a Beginning: An Anarchist Anthology* (2004). He serves as art editor for the UK-based journal *Anarchist Studies* and is a frequent contributor to *Canadian Art* and *Galleries West*.

Mark Antliff is Professor of Art History at Duke University and the author of numerous studies of European modernism, including *Inventing Bergson: Cultural Politics and the Parisian-Avant-Garde* (1993), *Avant-Garde Fascism: The Mobilization of Myth, Art and Culture in France, 1909–1939* (2007), and, with Patricia Leighten, *A Cubism Reader: Documents and Criticism, 1906–1914* (2008).

Vivian Endicott Barnett is an independent art historian specializing in the work of Wassily Kandinsky. As Curator of the Solomon R. Guggenheim Museum in New York, she worked on three exhibitions devoted to Kandinsky, and she wrote the essay "Kandinsky and Science" (reprinted here in abridged form) for *Kandinsky in Paris: 1934–1944* (1985). She has since prepared *Kandinsky Watercolours: Catalogue Raisonné* (1992, 1994) and more recently *Kandinsky Drawings: Catalogue Raisonné* (2006, 2007). Ms. Barnett is the author of *Kandinsky at the Guggenheim* (1983), *Vasily Kandinsky: A Colorful Life. The Collection of the Lenbachhaus, Munich* (1995), and *The Blue Four Collection at the Norton Simon Museum* (2002) as well as numerous exhibition catalogue essays. She is a member of the Société Kandinsky in Paris and Consulting Director of the Hans K. Roethel-Jean K. Benjamin Archive at the Guggenheim.

Oliver A.I. Botar received his Ph.D. in Art History from the University of Toronto and is Associate Professor of Art History in the School of Art at the University of Manitoba, in Winnipeg, Canada. His specialties include early twentieth-century Central European Modernism; László Moholy-Nagy; "Biocentrism" and Modernism in early to-mid twentieth-century art, architecture, and photography; Modernist art in alternative media; and

Canadian Modernism. He has worked as a curator, organizing exhibitions in Budapest, New Brunswick, New York, Toronto, and Winnipeg on Moholy-Nagy and on Hungarian and Canadian modern art, and is non-resident curator of The Salgo Trust for Education in New York. He is the author of numerous publications, including *Technical Detours: The Early Moholy-Nagy Reconsidered* (2006; in Hungarian, 2007) and *A Bauhäusler in Canada: Andor Weininger in the 50s* (2009).

David Haney received his master's degree in Architectural History and Theory from Yale in 1995, his Ph.D. from the University of Pennsylvania in 2005, and has been a lecturer in Architecture at Newcastle University in the United Kingdom since that time. His dissertation on the German Modernist landscape architect Leberecht Migge (1881–1935) was recently published as *When Modern Was Green* (2010). This study documents ecological concepts within German Modernism, for the first time in depth. His current and future research work is directed towards rethinking conventional architectural and landscape history, identifying ecological strategies and developments as a means of readdressing typical narratives.

Sara Lynn Henry is Professor Emerita of Art History and National Endowment for the Humanities Distinguished Teaching Professor of Humanities, Emerita, at Drew University, Madison, NJ. She is also active as an independent curator and art writer. Her Ph.D. dissertation "Paul Klee, Nature and Modern Science, the 1920s" (University of California, Berkeley, 1976) is a seminal work in Klee studies. She has both published extensively on and curated exhibitions concerning the relationship of art to nature and science. The dialogue of contemporary American art with Asian practices and aesthetics has also been a preoccupation in her writings.

Elizabeth L. Langhorne is Associate Professor at Central Connecticut State University, where she teaches Modern and Contemporary Art History. She has taught at the University of Richmond, where she was also Director of the Marsh Gallery, at the University of Virginia, and at Tulane University. Her 1977 Ph.D. dissertation for the University of Pennsylvania, "A Jungian Interpretation of Jackson Pollock's Art through 1946," sparked a scholarly discussion with William Rubin in the pages of *Art in America*. In the fall of 1986 she became an Ailsa Mellon Bruce Visiting Senior Fellow, National Gallery of Art, Center for Advanced Study in the Visual Arts. She has published several articles on Jackson Pollock and has recently completed the book manuscript *Portrait and a Dream: Jackson Pollock's Search for Meaning*. Dr. Langhorne is a member of the Vieques Historic Conservation Trust and a board member of the Hamden Land Conservation Trust.

Jennifer Mundy is Head of Collection Research at the Tate Gallery in London, and is responsible for developing research initiatives on the collection at the Tate. After studying Modern History at Oxford, she completed a Ph.D. dissertation on the subject of Biomorphism at the Courtauld Institute of Art, and has published widely in the area of Dada, Surrealism, and abstract art. As a curator at the Tate, she has organized many exhibitions, notably, "Surrealism: Desire Unbound" (2001) and "Duchamp, Man Ray, Picabia" (2008). She is editor of the online research journal *Tate Papers* in which she recently published articles on Cornell, Hartung, and Duchamp. She is currently preparing a volume of Man Ray's writings on art for Getty Publications.

Spyros Papapetros is Assistant Professor in the School of Architecture and the Program in Media and Modernity at Princeton University. He is an art and architectural historian and theorist whose work focuses on the historiography of art and architecture, the intersections between architecture and the visual arts, as well as the relationship between architecture, psychoanalysis, and the history of psychological aesthetics. He has published many articles and reviews, as well as book chapters in edited anthologies on architecture and Surrealism, the work of Gordon Matta-Clark and Josiah McElheny. He has completed a book manuscript on the role of animation in early twentieth-century art and architectural historiography and avant-garde practice, and is currently working on a second book manuscript on the revival of cosmological discourses in the art and architecture of the twentieth century.

Elke Sohn studied Architecture and Urban Planning at the University of Fine Arts in Hamburg, where she completed her doctorate in the Theory and History of Architecture with the thesis *Zum Begriff der Natur in Stadtkonzepten – anhand der Beiträge von Hans Bernhard Reichow, Walter Schwagenscheidt und Hans Scharoun zum Wiederaufbau nach 1945* (2008). She is currently Assistant Professor at the University of Applied Sciences, Saarbrücken, where she teaches History and Theory of Art and Architecture. She has published on modern and post-war architecture and urban planning and, with Hartmut Frank, edited a series on the contemporary theory of architecture.

Monika Wucher is an art historian who lives and works in Hamburg, Germany. She studied Art History and Cultural Anthropology in Tübingen, Budapest, and Hamburg. Her work focuses on research projects and transcultural initiatives in Central and Eastern Europe on topics ranging from Modernism to the life sciences and social criticism in the art of the twentieth and twenty-first centuries. Her publications include articles on Will Grohmann, Hans (János) Mattis-Teutsch, Martin Munkácsi, and the Cologne Progressives.

Isabel Wünsche is Professor of Art and Art History at Jacobs University in Bremen, Germany. She studied Art History and Classical and Christian Archaeology in Berlin, Moscow, Heidelberg, and Los Angeles, and completed her Ph.D. dissertation on the Organic School of the Russian Avant-Garde at Heidelberg University in 1997. Her field of expertise is European Modernism and the historic avant-garde movements, particularly the Russian avant-garde, German Expressionism, and the Bauhaus. Her books include *Galka E. Scheyer & The Blue Four: Correspondence 1924–1945* (German and English editions, 2006), *Kursschwankungen: Russische Kunst im Wertesystem der europäischen Moderne* (2007, together with Ada Raev), and *Harmonie und Synthese. Die russische Moderne zwischen universellem Anspruch und nationaler kultureller Identität* (2008).

Introduction: Biocentrism as a constituent element of Modernism

Oliver A.I. Botar and Isabel Wünsche

Global warming, mass extinction of animal and plant species, desertification of enormous tracts of land, the destruction of rainforests and boreal forests, and the death of the coral reefs are pressing issues of our time. Since the period of the waning of Modernism over the past forty years, we have become increasingly aware of the advent of an environmental crisis of almost unimaginable proportions. Given also the breathtaking advances in biology, particularly genetics, over the past few decades, and hotly debated political issues such as the ethics of stem-cell research, we are increasingly reminded of issues of the definition and control of life and the central role played by the life sciences. With the requirement, therefore, to rethink our relationship with what we have since the Enlightenment termed the "natural," the editors think it imperative that we gain a better understanding of the ways in which attitudes towards "nature" and "life" shaped our culture and in which ways they helped form modernity and engender Modernism. It is widely assumed that Modernist culture had little interest in or even awareness of this looming crisis, or even of "nature" as such. Yet a closer examination of almost any genre of Modernist artistic and cultural production reveals an active interest in the categories of "life," the "organic," and even the destruction of the environment in modernity. While as citizens, we might take an active role in dealing with today's environmental problems, as historians, it is not necessarily our job to address them, but it *is* our role to address the history of the developing awareness of these crises. Clearly, the closely related histories of biology and the life sciences on the one hand, and of environmentalism on the other, are central to this task. However, cultural history, including its components such as visual studies, art and architectural history and the history of urban planning, also has an important role to play in this regard, particularly within a context in which there has been such wilful ignorance of an aspect of our common cultural inheritance. A denial of an awareness of our place in "nature" among the Moderns may act as a justification for a continued disavowal of such concerns. Or it may result in the unfair characterization of Modernist culture as having been somehow "against" nature, and therefore as having been merely a part of the problem and never of its possible solutions. What we now know is that many members of the various Modernist cultural movements were early adherents of the emergent environmental consciousness that permeated *fin de siècle* culture.

In this anthology, we look at some aspects of a largely neglected field of Modernist studies: the role played by nature-centric ideologies of the late nineteenth to mid-twentieth centuries, that is, the years after the rise of the science of biology during the nineteenth century, up to the period just before the emergence of the current environmentalist movement during the 1960s. Indeed, there is a serious lack in cultural history, which, by virtually ignoring the *fin de siècle* discourse around nature and the participation of important figures in it, has insufficiently contextualized Modernist culture. When not ignoring the interconnections between nature-centric ideology and Modernism, historians were denying it, emphasizing, instead, its anti-natural, so-called "mechanistic" aspects. In defining "nature-centrism" or "Biocentrism," what we have done is to identify a series of discourses which, while differing from each other in certain respects, shared a set of themes, attitudes, and topoi relating to nature, biology, and epistemology. While distinguishable from each other, these discourses held in common a set of tenets that included a belief in the primacy of life and life processes, of biology as the paradigmatic science of the age, as well as an anti-anthropocentric worldview, and an implied or expressed environmentalism. Indeed, the turn of the nineteenth–twentieth centuries was characterized by a revival of aspects of Romanticism, among them an intuitive, idealistic, holistic, or even metaphysical attitude towards the idea of "nature" and the experience of the unity of all life. The German philosopher Max Scheler described the revival in 1913 as "groups of movements that, without or with ties to the great reactionary movement of Romanticism, wish to renew the *Gestalt* of the human heart."[1]

It is our contention that it is impossible to fully comprehend Modernist culture without properly framing the nature-centric worldview in early twentieth-century Europe. However, such a frame or category has traditionally not been in use within the field of cultural history. In 1998, Oliver Botar proposed the use of the German term *Biozentrik* or Biocentrism for its designation.[2] This term was used principally during the first half of the last century by the German philosopher Ludwig Klages and by the Austro-Hungarian biologist and popular scientific writer Raoul Heinrich Francé, both of whom had a significant effect on many cultural figures in Central Europe.[3] The term is employed in contemporary English by deep ecologists such as Arne Naess in approximately the same sense. This, coupled with the fact that its early twentieth-century usage within the crucial German-speaking context gives it historical legitimacy, induced us to adopt it for our purposes in this anthology. Stated succinctly "Biocentrism" is Nature Romanticism updated by the Biologism of the mid- to late nineteenth century.[4] As the essays in this volume demonstrate, it is, however, important to note that the relative proportions of these two components varied between individuals, between countries, and over time. For example, the artistic approaches of the members of the early Russian avant-garde in St. Petersburg were predominantly shaped by organic models that resulted from the artists' nature-centric worldviews, which were based on Nature Romanticism updated by recent discoveries in the life sciences along with a strong interest in metaphysical inquiry, while the French discourse of the same time was more dominated by Bergsonism and Biocentric Anarchist ideas. While László Moholy-Nagy, the Hungarian artist and theorist active in Germany, England, and the United States, represented an almost entirely biologistic viewpoint—that is, one largely devoid of metaphysical or Romantic positions[5]—an artist such as Wassily Kandinsky, active during his career within the Russian, German, and French artistic contexts, represented a prominent case in which an artist moved from a more metaphysical worldview towards a more biologistic position.

The interconnectedness between the development of biology as a science and nature-centric positions in philosophical and intellectual thought was, as George Rousseau put it in 1992, intimately associated with the rise of Modernist culture during the second half of the nineteenth century:

> It is hardly accidental that ... modernism ... arises ... simultaneously with modern biology. The two viewed in tandem ... offer the most substantial proof for the unity of cultural development and pose a significant challenge to those who claim that large concurrent cultural movements usually have little impact on each other. And it is ... the vitalism inherent in early modern biology that must concern us if we hope to grasp why modernism has emerged at a particular moment under specific cultural conditions.[6]

It is therefore not surprising that our research has indicated a pervasive interest on the part of many early to mid-twentieth-century Modernist visual cultural practitioners in this particular set of ideas. Artists and theorists as varied and as central to the Modernist cultural project as Hans Arp, Constantin Brancuşi, Raymond Duchamp-Villon, Max Ernst, Pavel Filonov, Naum Gabo, Barbara Hepworth, Paul Klee, František Kupka, Franz Marc, Joan Miró, Henry Moore, Mikhail Matiushin, Vladimir Tatlin, László Moholy-Nagy, Georgia O'Keeffe, Jackson Pollock, and Władysław Strzeminski; photographers such as Ansel Adams and Edward Weston; designers, including Roberto Burle-Marx, Charles and Ray Eames, Russel Wright, and Eva Zeisel; architects such as Antonio Gaudí, Ludwig Mies van der Rohe, and Frank Lloyd Wright; and the art critics Ernő Kállai and Herbert Read, all pursued Biocentric approaches in their work.

Many, though by no means all, of these artists and designers worked in the style of "Biomorphic Modernism," that is, in a style characterized by its evocative swells, curves and arabesques. Echoing the forms of cells, organelles and fetuses, it was in some sense seen by artists to figure the conceptions of "life," "origins," and "nature." While these are all themes and motifs that refer to the life sciences or to concepts current within the Biocentric discourses, when it comes to Biocentrism as a worldview espoused by some artists, there is no *necessary* connection between ideological background and style. Thus, other artists such as László Moholy-Nagy, Lazar El Lissitzky, and Ludwig Mies van der Rohe followed Raoul Francé in regarding all technologies, including human ones, as part of the larger complex of "nature," and therefore they did not feel compelled to work in a biomorphic style. They felt justified in working in more technologically or geometrically oriented styles while espousing nature-centric views.

This stylistic heterogeneity is only one indication of the fact that Biocentric cultural practitioners formed neither a coherent school nor a movement. They formed, rather, a broad-based trend that, while not usually conscious of itself, reflected a wider intellectual current within the culture of modernity. But this was the case even with regard to this wider intellectual movement. Rather than describing a self-conscious movement, we see the term "Biocentrism" as a concept, or a frame that enables us to take note of phenomena or aspects thereof that would otherwise go unnoticed. It is a historical construct, then, rather than a term describing some putative or "rediscovered" aspect of historical reality. Like many useful frames, the more one looks, the more one sees; the more one moves it about while looking, the more one sees. Looking through the frame of "Biocentrism", then, we see work to be done in the fields of the histories of the visual, of art, architecture and landscape architecture, of design, photography, and urban planning, as well as of aesthetics, throughout Europe and the Americas, and perhaps beyond, and at all points along the traditional left–right political spectrum.

While there is a comparatively large body of literature on nature-centrism and particular artists such as Hans Arp, Arthur Dove, Antonio Gaudi, and Paul Klee; on Biomorphic Modernism in art, on design and architecture; and on organic ideology in modern architecture and urban planning, no comprehensive studies on the connection between Biocentrism and modernity or Biocentrism and Modernism exist. The basic references in this regard remain Lancelot Law Whyte's anthology *Aspects of Form*, George Rousseau's anthology *Organic Form: The Life of an Idea,* and Frederick Burwick's anthologies *Approaches to Organic Form* and (with Paul Douglass) *The Crisis in Modernism: Bergson and the Vitalist Controversy*.[7] Other important precedents in the field of cultural history include books by Eva Barlösius, Anna Bramwell, Donna Jean Harraway, Anne Harrington, Elenor Jain, Jackson Lears, Ulrich Linse, David Pepper, and Jürgen Wolschke-Bulmahn.[8] Some literary scholars, among them Maike Arz, Monika Fick, and Gunter Martens, have also explored the discourses from their perspective.[9] In art history, there have been a few dissertations written on related subjects, including those of three contributors to this volume,[10] as well as a number of works that have broached the wider subject of nature, organicism, and Modernism.[11] Another publication in German, Annette Geiger, Stefanie Hennecke and Christin Kempf's anthology *Spielarten des Organischen*, published while the present volume was in preparation, is along the same lines as our own endeavor and attempts to offer a wider view of the connection between organicism and Modernist art, architecture, and design.[12] The time seems ripe to examine this expanding field in English.

This anthology consists of three thematic sections. The first three essays concentrate on the philosophical worldviews and cultural concepts of Biocentrism, *Bioromantik*, and Biomorphism, as well as their emergence and influence upon artistic production of the late nineteenth and early twentieth centuries. Focusing on philosophical problems of meaning and ontology, particular emphasis is placed on the various ways in which organic metaphors and models derived from the life sciences shaped the cultural and artistic discourse of the period.

Adopting the German term *Biozentrik*, Oliver A. I. Botar views Biocentrism as a worldview of the late nineteenth and early twentieth centuries that thoroughly informed Modernist art, architecture, product design, urban planning, and landscape design. Shaped by the *Lebensphilosophie* of Friedrich Nietzsche, Henri Bergson, William James, Georg Simmel, and Ludwig Klages on the one hand, and influenced by the work of scientists with philosophical pretensions, such as Ernst Haeckel, Hans Driesch, Raoul Francé, and Ernst Mach, on the other, Biocentrism also includes aspects of the Neo-Romanticist revival, among them an intuitive, idealistic, Holistic, and even metaphysical attitude towards the idea of nature and the experience of the unity of all forms of life. Botar examines a wide array of nature-centric discourses and beliefs, including Neo-Vitalism, Organicism/Holism, the Monist League, *Lebensphilosophie*, Neo-Lamarckism, the *Neue Naturphilosophie*, biologism, and the *Reformbewegung*, and emphasizes that, while the groupings did not hold identical bundles of concepts in common, they did hold in common the privileging of biology as the source for the paradigmatic metaphor of science, society, and aesthetics; a consequent, biologically based epistemology; an emphasis on the centrality of "nature," "life," and life-processes rather than "culture"; an anti-anthropocentric *Weltanschauung*; the self-directedness and "unity" of all life; a valorization of the quasi-mystical feeling of unity with all nature, what Simmel termed the *kosmovitalen Einsfühlung*; a stress on flux and mutability in nature rather than stasis; and a concern for "wholeness" as opposed to reduction at all levels. Thus, he defines Biocentrism as *Naturromantik* updated by nineteenth-century biologism.

Monika Wucher extends Botar's discussion through a critical examination of *Bioromantik* (Bioromanticism), a term coined by the Hungarian art critic Ernő [Ernst] Kállai at the beginning of the 1930s. Convinced that psychological and biological factors would have a greater effect on art than supposed rationality and objectivity, Kállai believed that *Bioromantik* would "lead the intellect … to the primary sources and basic drives of life." Wucher demonstrates that Kállai's specific approach of linking art and popular scientific knowledge offered an opportunity to mediate between ideologies, conflicts, and opposing standpoints. In examining Kállai's fictitious discussion with Adolf Behne about Berlin's new commercial boulevards, she points out that, although

Behne emphasized that sensations were evoked by certain impressions—most vividly when tension was given form—Kállai held that they were *optische Erlebnistriebe* (forces of optical receptivity) that had to be stimulated in some way because he saw the potential of art in the evolution of "rightful resistance against the mechanistic works of ... capitalistic-utilitarian civilizations."

Jennifer Mundy discusses the origin and early use of the term "biomorphic" and examines the reasons why the term has not gained wide acceptance within art history. Originally used as an etymologically logical term for designs in late nineteenth-century anthropology, the term "biomorphism" was coined in 1935 by Geoffrey Grigson to characterize a new, vital type of abstraction that combined geometrical designs with the exercise of the memory and the emotions. Grigson used the term to promote "a resynthesising of intellect with emotion, of form with matter, of geometric with organic." Alfred H. Barr, first director of the Museum of Modern Art in New York, used it to contrast the two main trends in non-figurative art: "the shape of the square" with "the silhouette of the amoeba." In presenting contemporary art in terms of the rectilinear and rational versus the organic and emotive, Barr was attempting to match the diverse developments of modern art with the conceptual schemas of Wölfflinian formalism in art history. Maintaining that there were two types of art: representational works and abstract compositions, he viewed biomorphism as a form of near-abstraction. Although the term biomorphism was revived in the 1960s by Lawrence Alloway and William Rubin, it never was used to identify a particular artistic movement, but only to describe the fluid, organic shapes in the work of artists as diverse as Hans Arp, Constantin Brancusi, Jean Hélion, Wassily Kandinsky, Joan Miró, Henry Moore, Yves Tanguy, and others.

The second set of essays explores the application of nature-centric worldviews and organic models to art and architectural historiography, urban planning and design, as well as Modernist art theory. Exploring interpretative models developed through the implementation of biological concepts in art and design theory, the authors demonstrate that such strategies not only serve to reinterpret human history and to redefine the relationship between humanity and nature, but they can acquire particular social, cultural, and/or political meanings.

Tracing the intersections between the natural science investigations of the latent energy of inorganic matter and the historiographies of art and architecture in early twentieth-century German art history, Spyros Papapetros looks at the animation of the inorganic in the artistic and architectural discourses of the time in a discussion of Alois Riegl's crystalline rotundas, Ernst Haeckel's living crystals, Wilhelm Worringer's strapwork ornaments, and Aby Warburg's Monist psychology of art. While Darwin's diagrams of "stimulus movement" influenced Riegl's distinction between the kinetic qualities of the basilica and the non-kinetic features of the rotunda, Haeckel's radiolaria and Lehmann's liquid crystals provided the Monist proof that the distinction between the organic and the inorganic did not exist and that all matter was animate.

In his 1907 doctoral dissertation *Abstraktion und Einfühlung,* Worringer coined the phrase "the animation of the inorganic." In contrast to Haeckel's Monism, Worringer's scheme is not a dialectical synthesis between the animate and the inanimate, the organic and the inorganic; for him, the animation of the inorganic is a permanent reaction, an irresolvable contradiction between two opposite states: abstraction and empathy, fear and attraction, resistance and extension. Inspired by the publications of Haeckel, Roberto Benzoni, and Johannes Schlaf, Warburg created what he called "dynamic psychomonism," an attempt to compensate between two polarities, such as subject and object, empathy and distance, and the identification of magic and the division of logic.

Exploring analogies between natural and artistic design, David Haney and Elke Sohn discuss the concept of the city as an organism in twentieth-century gardening and urban planning in Germany. With the emergence of the Reform Movements, garden and city were no longer seen in isolation, but in interaction with the larger environment: soil, landscape, and cosmos. The discourse on the *Siedlung* as an organism focused on autonomy, vitality, self-determination, natural growth, cultural improvement, and economic and intellectual rootedness in the region. "Natural methods" derived from the natural sciences and nature-oriented philosophies, including Neo-Lamarckism, Monism, biologism, and organicism, were used as models for organic garden- and city-planning structures. Nutrition, hygiene, and fresh air and light were some of the themes that were particularly emphasized by the reformers. Building upon the opposition of city versus country, the reform movements developed a variety of approaches reaching from explicit anti-urbanism to determined efforts to redesign the city as an holistic entity embedded in the surrounding environment. Urban concepts such as the *Gartenstadt,* the *Stadt-Land-Kultur,* the *Stadtlandschaft,* and the *Stadt-Land-Stadt* reflected the widespread desire to wed settlements and green spaces. The authors demonstrate the strong belief in the interrelatedness of urban settlement and agriculture that was incorporated into the full spectrum of political and social reform movements, ranging from conservative and racist, to communist and anarchist.

Isabel Wünsche examines the holistic worldviews and organic approaches to art that were particularly prominent among the members of the prerevolutionary avant-garde in St. Petersburg. Rather than viewing artistic activity as a passive imitation of nature, these artists saw it as an active expression of the relationship between the artist and the natural environment, calling for a new, absolute art based on the universal laws and organic principles of nature rather than being mere copies of it. Their understanding of the active role of the artist and the crucial position of the work of art in the overall process of human evolution was shaped by evolutionary theory, particularly the Lamarckian tradition of a teleological development toward increasing perfection. The artists' preoccupation with the basic elements, fundamental principles, and creative processes that constitute the work of art found its reflection in the discussion of *faktura,* a term describing the "texture" of the work of art—that is, the physical properties and energetic potential of the materials and the organic principles and natural laws inherent in the creative process—thus embodying the fundamental difference between the Russian focus on the artistic process and the Western European focus on the stylistic results of pictorial invention. Investigating the role that the life sciences played in providing organic metaphors and biological models for art and design in early twentieth-century Russian culture, Wünsche demonstrates that, contrary to the commonly held view that the Russian avant-garde was a modernist movement in the Cubist-Constructivist tradition, the works of artists such Pavel Filonov, Nikolai Kulbin, Mikhail Matiushin, Vladimir Tatlin, and even Kazimir Malevich were shaped by nature-centric worldviews and organic principles.

Approaching Biocentrism in art from a political perspective—that is, at the intersection between art and politics—Allan Antliff explores Herbert Read's concept of Modernism with which he defended abstract art and Surrealism in the name of an organicist politics of anarchism. An admirer of the Russian anarchist Peter Kropotkin, whose writings he published in 1942, Read brought not only abstract art but also Surrealism under the umbrella of Biocentrism and defended both against British Communist Party assertions that realism was the only revolutionary art form. He maintained that Capitalism fragmented the social organism and repressed artistic activity in the process, but that Soviet Communism and Fascism were equally damaging because they both subordinated all aspects of society, including the arts, to the central control of the state. In *Art and Industry* (1935), Read defended abstract art for keeping "the formal essence of all art" alive; in *Art and Society* (1937), he wrote that Surrealism's goal was to unify our psyche with our social life in recognition that, at present, there was a profound lack of "organic connection" between the two. However, in *Poetry and Anarchism* (1938), Read predicted that artists would continue creating art attuned to the unconscious, inspired as they would be by the "natural freedom" permeating an anarchist society. Thus, Surrealism, like abstraction, would transcend its condition under capitalism and be integrated into the social organism.

The last four essays present specific case studies on the work of individual artists, among them Raymond Duchamp-Villon, Paul Klee, Wassily Kandinsky, and Jackson Pollock. The concern here is to explore the ways in which these artists have employed Biocentric ideas as inspiration for and/or as explanations of their artistic practice and to consider their significance for metaphysical meaning and historical significance.

Acknowledging that in recent years the structuralist methodology has dominated the study of Cubist collage, Mark Antliff sets out to consider the role of organicist metaphors in the art and art criticism of the so-called Puteaux Cubists, particularly focusing on the work of Raymond Duchamp-Villon. He argues that the Puteaux Cubists simultaneously embraced Bergsonian paradigms and failed to fully grasp the "postmodernist" implications of a philosophy that ultimately transcended the "closure" usually imputed to organicist conceptions. Duchamp-Villon, whose organicism differed greatly from that of his Cubist colleagues (who rejected the decorative altogether), asserted that his sculptural reliefs could exist both as autonomous, organic wholes and as rhythmic voices in a larger decorative chorus. To his mind, the rhythm of a decorative ensemble does not become overly "simple" or extensive by virtue of the surface covered, but retains its organic, living quality; each sculpture in an ensemble is an organism subsumed within the larger collective rhythm of a new organism. Antliff demonstrates that Duchamp-Villon thus could claim that his sculpture was both closed and open—that is, in a condition of physical being and of durational becoming in the artistic imagination. The synchronic arrangement of sculptures in a decorative ensemble allowed for both their organic integrity and their ability to meld into the greater organic form that constitutes the decorative program.

Sara Lynn Henry looks at the impact of modern geology and meteorology on the structure and iconography of Paul Klee's pictorial language. Examining a body of his work, she traces Klee's scientific curiosity, particularly by looking at his explorations of geological life, the movement of water, and the weather. Identifying phenomena such as the diagrammatic use of signs, geological layering, botanical proliferation, and rhythmic wave patterns, she stresses the artist's ability to abstractly symbolize and structure nature according to its principles and according to his own imagination. For Klee, science was not a limitation in order to achieve accurate representation, but rather an opening to freedom and mobility; the realization of the continuous genesis of new forms gave him a certain freedom to invent new forms—"images of nature's potentialities." The result was an undermining of the Romantic nineteenth-century sense of scale and place of the human within the everyday landscape. As a twentieth-century artist in the Neo-Romanticist tradition, Klee thus found himself between the poles of "natural law" and the irrational self.

To highlight the ways in which the artistic œuvres of individual artists changed over time, the editors choose to include Vivian Endicott Barnett's 1985 classic essay on Wassily Kandinsky's work of his Parisian period. Although it is well known that Kandinsky's early work was strongly shaped by metaphysics and the Occult, it is less known that by the 1930s his thinking was more biologistic which, combined with his deeply rooted Nature Romanticism, resulted in what was essentially a Biocentric position. Thus, Barnett focuses on the introduction of biological images into the artist's œuvre. She demonstrates that Kandinsky's newly awoken preference for abstraction, which had its origin in the natural forms of organic life, can be linked to both the influence of artists such as Hans Arp, Max Ernst, and Joan Miró, all of whom he met in Paris, and Kandinsky's interests in the natural sciences. Tracing his biological motifs back to the illustrations of single-celled organisms, embryos, plants and animals in publications such as Ernst Haeckel's *Kunstformen der Natur*, Karl Blossfeldt's *Urformen der Kunst*, the encyclopedia *Die Kultur der Gegenwart*, and scientific journals such as *Die Koralle*, Barnett outlines the degree to which Kandinsky's paintings of his early Parisian period were influenced by biomorphic forms and motifs derived from microbiology.

Examining Jackson Pollock's 1949 collaboration with Peter Blake to create a model for an Ideal Museum, Elizabeth Langhorne sees in Abstract Expressionism an attempt to leave tradition behind in favor of what can be called a Biocentric approach. While the "oneness" with nature has been dismissed in modern and postmodern discourse, she demonstrates that, in leaving panel painting behind, Pollock was struggling to make "life" or "nature" rather than the human subject the center of his art. Blake's Ideal Museum allowed Pollock to leave behind the optical Renaissance tradition within which Clement Greenberg, Michael Fried, and Pepe Karmel have placed Pollock's art. Langhorne emphasizes that, to the degree that Pollock's mimesis of nature invites the viewer's bodily participation, his art goes beyond the old anthropocentrism—centered on the viewer as the seeing, knowing subject—to a new Biocentrism. Thus, the dream of an opening to nature embodied in the Ideal Museum offers an alternative to the scientific approach, with its detachment from and sense of control over nature that underlies the Renaissance paradigm of painting.

While the contributions to this anthology include a wide range of media and topics, the publication does not cover all areas of Modernist cultural practice. Nature-centrism and architecture is an exceedingly rich field of inquiry, and there exists already a fairly plentiful literature on this subject, so we have consciously emphasized other aspects of cultural history over it.[13] Designers such as Charles and Ray Eames, László Moholy-Nagy, Vladimir Tatlin, Russel Wright, Alvar Aalto, Tapio Wirkkala, and Eva Zeisel self-consciously invoked natural analogies and larger environmental frameworks in their works—a thorough study of their design practices could, regrettably, not be included in this book. Photographers have, ever since the invention of the medium, focused their viewfinders on aspects of nature, and some of them, such as Ansel Adams and Edward Weston, became pioneer environmental activists.[14] Indeed, the first organized environmentalist movement, the Sierra Club, established a photographic collection as early as 1925, in which Adams played an important role.[15] Meanwhile, photography was put to use imaging scientific phenomena, aspects of nature invisible to the unaided human eye, and Modernists such as Moholy-Nagy were eager to harness such discoveries to their practice.[16] We look forward to future publications for a treatment of this important theme. Thus, we see this anthology as the beginning of a more widespread process of the re-examination of our Modernist cultural heritage in all its medial, ideological, and geographic heterogeneity, and throughout its historical run.

Notes

1 Max Scheler, *Wesen und Formen der Sympathie* (1913), 2nd ed. 1922 (Berne: Francke, 1973), 104.

2 Oliver A.I. Botar, "Prolegomena to the Study of Biomorphic Modernism: Biocentrism, László Moholy-Nagy's 'New Vision' and Ernő Kállai's *Bioromantik*," Ph.D. dissertation, University of Toronto, 1998.

3 Ibid., Chapter 2.

4 Ibid., 7.

5 On Moholy-Nagy and Biocentrism, see Oliver A.I. Botar, "The Roots of László Moholy-Nagy's Biocentric Constructivism," in Eduardo Kac, ed., *Signs of Life: Bio Art and Beyond* (Cambridge, MA: The MIT Press, 2007), 315–44.

6 George Rousseau, "The Perpetual Crises of Modernism and the Traditions of Enlightenment Vitalism: With a Note on Mikhail Bakhtin," in Frederick Burwick and Paul Douglass, eds., *The Crisis in Modernism: Bergson and the Vitalist Controversy* (Cambridge: Cambridge University Press, 1992), 20.

7 Lancelot Law Whyte, ed., *Aspects of Form: A Symposium on Form and Nature in Art* (1951). Preface by Herbert Read (Bloomington, IN and London: Indiana University Press, 1961); George S. Rousseau, ed., *Organic Form: The Life of an Idea* (London and Boston: Routledge and Kegan Paul, 1972); Frederick Burwick, ed., *Approaches to Organic Form: Permutations in Science and Culture* (Dordrecht: D. Reidel, 1987); Frederick Burwick and Paul Douglas, eds., *The Crisis in Modernism: Bergson and the Vitalist Controversy* (Cambridge: Cambridge University Press, 1992).

8 Eva Barlösius, *Naturgemäße Lebensführung: Zur Geschichte der Lebensreform um die Jahrhundertwende* (Frankfurt am Main and New York: Campus, 1997); Anna Bramwell, *Ecology in the 20th Century: A History* (New Haven, CT: Yale University Press, 1989); Götz Großklaus and Ernst Oldemeyer, eds., *Natur als Gegenbegriff: Beiträge zur Kulturgeschichte der Natur* (Karlsruhe: Leopar, 1983); Donna Jeanne Haraway, *Crystals, Fabrics, and Fields: Metaphors of Organicism in Twentieth-Century Developmental Biology* (New Haven, CT: Yale University Press, 1976); Anne Harrington, *Reenchanted Science: Holism in German Culture from Wilhelm II to Hitler* (Princeton, NJ: Princeton University Press, 1996); Elenor Jain, *Das Prinzip Leben: Lebensphilosophie und ästhetische Erziehung* (Frankfurt am Main: Peter Lang, 1993); T.J. Jackson Lears, *No Place of Grace: Antimodernism and the Transformation of American Culture 1880–1920* (New York: Pantheon, 1981); Ulrich Linse, *Ökopax und Anarchie. Eine Geschichte des ökologischen Bewegungen in Deutschland* (Munich: DTV, 1986); David Pepper, *The Roots of Modern Environmentalism* (London: Croom Helm, 1984); Jürgen Wolschke-Bulmahn, *Auf der Suche nach Arkadien: Zur Landschaftsidealen und Formen der Naturaneigniung in der Jugendbewegung und ihrer Bedeutung für die Landespflege* (Munich: Minerva, 1990).

9 Maike Arz, *Literatur und Lebenskraft: Vitalistische Naturforschung und bürgerliche Literatur um 1800* (Stuttgart: M. & P. Verlag für Wissenschaft und Forschung, 1996); Monika Fick, *Sinnenwelt und Weltseele: Der psychophysische Monismus in der Literatur der Jahrhundertwende* (Tübingen: Max Niemeyer, 1993); Gunter Martens, *Vitalismus und Expressionismus: Ein Beitrag zur Genese und Deutung expresionistischer Stilstrukturen und Motive* (Stuttgart: W. Kohlhammer, 1971).

10 Botar, "Prolegomena"; Jennifer Virgina Mundy, "Biomorphism," Ph.D. dissertation, University of London, 1987); Isabel Wünsche, "Das Kunstkonzept der Organischen Kultur in der Kunst der russischen Avantgarde," Ph.D. dissertation, Heidelberg University, 1997 (Ketsch: Mikroform Dissertation, 1997).

11 Mark Antliff, *Inventing Bergson: Cultural Politics and the Parisian Avant-Garde* (Princeton, NJ: Princeton University Press, 1993); Hartmut Böhme, "Verdrängung

und Erinnerung vor-moderner Natur-Konzepte. Zum Problem historischer Anschlüsse der Naturästhetik in der Moderne," *Kunst Nachtrichten* (Zurich) 24, no. 1 (February 1988): 35–47; Yves-Alain Bois and Rosalind E. Krauss, *Formless: A User's Guide* (New York: Zone Books, 1997); Thomas Brandt, "Von der Reduktion zum Wachstum. Vom Wandel geometrischen Formen in den 30er Jahren," in *1937. "... und nicht die leiseste Spur einer Vorschrift"—Positionen unabhängiger Kunst in Europa um 1937* (exh. cat.) (Düsseldorf: Kunstsammlung Nordrhein-Westfalen, 1987); Charlotte Douglas, "Evolution and the Biological Metaphor in Modern Russian Art," *Art Journal* 44, no. 2 (Summer 1984): 153–61; Hartmut Eggert, Erhard Schütz, and Peter Sprengel, eds., *Faszination des Organischen. Konjunkturen einer Kategorie der Moderne* (Munich: Iudicium, 1995); Hubertus Gaßner, ed., *Élan Vital oder das Auge des Eros. Kandinsky, Klee, Arp, Miró, Calder* (exh. cat.) (Munich: Haus der Kunst, 1994); Günter Feuerstein, *Biomorphic Architecture: Human and Animal Forms in Architecture* (Stuttgart, London: Edition Axel Meyers, 2002); Jürgen Fitschen, ed., *Die organische Form: Bildhauerkunst, 1930–1960* (exh. cat.) (Bremen: Gerhard-Marcks-Haus, 2003); David Kinmont, "Vitalism and Creativity: Bergson, Driesch, Maritain and the Visual Arts, 1900–1914," in Martin Pollock, ed., *Common Denominators in Art and Science* (Aberdeen: Aberdeen University Press, 1983), 69–77; Christoph Kockerbeck, *Ernst Haeckels "Kunstformen der Natur" und ihr Einfluß auf die deutsche bildende Kunst der Jahrhundertwende* (Frankfurt am Main: Peter Lang, 1986); Michael Kröger, "'... gleichsam biologische Urzeichen ...' Die Erfindung biomorpher Natur in Malerei und Fotografie der dreissiger Jahre," *Kritische Berichte* 18, no. 4 (April 1990): 3–87; Christa Lichtenstern, *Die Wirkungsgeschichte der Metamorphosenlehre Goethes. Von Philipp Otto Runge bis Josef Beuys* (Weinheim: VCH, 1990) and *Metamorphose vom Mythos zum Prozessdenken. Ovid-Rezeption, Surrealistische Ästhetik, Verwandlungsthematik der Nachkriegskunst* (Weinheim: VCH/Acta Humanora, 1992); Beate Manske, ed., *Die organische Form: Produktgestaltung, 1930–1960* (exh. cat.) (Bremen: Wilhelm-Wagenfeld-Stiftung 2003); Gert Mattenklott, *Karl Blossfeldt 1865–1932. Das photographische Werk* (Munich: Prestel, 1981); Jennifer Mundy, "Form and Creation: The Impact of the Biological Sciences on Modern Art," in *Creation: Modern Art and Nature* (exh. cat.) (Edinburgh: Scottish National Gallery, 1984), 16–23; Karin Orchard and Jörg Zimmermann, eds., *Die Erfindung der Natur: Max Ernst, Paul Klee, Wols und das surreale Universum* (exh. cat.) (Freiburg im Breisgau: Rombach, 1994); Lisa Phillips, ed., *Vital Signs. Organic Abstraction from the Permanent Collection* (exh. cat.) (New York: Whitney Museum of American Art, 1988); Phillip C. Ritterbush, *The Art of Organic Forms* (exh. cat.) (Washington, DC: Smithsonian Institution Press, 1968); Caroline van Eck, *Organicism in Nineteenth-Century Architecture: An Inquiry into its Theoretical and Philosophical Background* (Amsterdam: Architectura and Natura Press, 1994); Annika Waenerberg, "Das Organische in Kunst und Gestaltung: Eine kurze Geschichte des Begriffs," in Annette Geiger, Stefanie Hennecke and Christin Kempf, eds., *Spielarten des Organischen in Architektur, Design und Kunst* (Berlin: Dietrich Reimer, 2005), 20–35; Siegfried Wichmann, *Jugendstil Art Nouveau: Floral and Functional Forms* (Boston, MA: Little Brown, 1984); Isabel Wünsche, "Naturerfahrung als künstlerische Methode: Organische Visionen in der Kunst der klassischen Moderne," in Elke Bippus and Andrea Sick, eds., *Industrialsierung und Technologisierung von Kunst und Wissenschaft* (Bielefeld: transcript, 2005), 86–108, and "Lebendige Formen und bewegte Linien: Organische Abstraktionen in der Kunst der klassischen Moderne," in *Floating Forms: Abstract Art Now* (exh. cat.) (Bielefeld: Kerber, 2006), 10–22.

12 Annette Geiger, Stefanie Hennecke, and Christin Kempf, eds., *Spielarten des Organischen in Architektur, Design und Kunst* (Berlin: Dietrich Reimer, 2005).

13 The literature on Frank Lloyd Wright should serve as an example in this regard; but in a more unexpected vein, see also, for example, Detlef Mertins, "Living in the Jungle: Mies, Organic Architecture, and the Art of City Building," in Phyllis Lambert, ed., *Mies in America* (New York: Henry N. Abrams 2001), 590–641. See also van Eck, *Organicism in Nineteenth-Century Architecture.*

14 Adams was an active member of the Sierra Club as early as 1919.

15 http://sierraclub.org/history/timeline.asp. See also Ansel Adams and John Muir, *Yosemite and the Sierra Nevada,* ed. Charlotte E. Mauk (Boston, MA: Houghton Mifflin Company, 1948).

16 See Oliver A.I. Botar, "László Moholy-Nagy's 'New Vision' and the Aestheticization of Scientific Imagery in Weimar Germany," in: Linda D. Henderson, ed., "Modern Art and Science," special issue, *Science in Context* 17, no. 4 (2004): 525–56.

1

Defining Biocentrism

Oliver A.I. Botar

In some remote corner of the universe ... glittering in innumerable solar systems, there once was a star on which clever animals invented knowledge. That was the haughtiest and falsest minute of [so-called] "world history"—yet only a minute. After nature had drawn a few breaths the star grew cold, and the clever animals had to die.

(Nietzsche, 1873)[1]

The brief period of a few thousand years ... of civilization is an evanescently short episode in the long course of organic evolution, just as this, in turn, is merely a small portion of the history of our planetary system; and as our mother-earth is a mere speck in the sunbeam in the illimitable universe, so man himself is but a tiny grain of protoplasm in the perishable framework of organic nature.

(Haeckel, 1900)[2]

The biocentric way of thinking seems not any more to be merely one possible way, it is, rather, the only possible way to order experience, i.e. nature; to make it usable. Stated briefly: it is the only possible way to live.[3] The age of biological thinking has ... just begun.

(Francé, 1923/1928)[4]

These passages reflect the biologistic Neo-Romanticism (what I will propose we term "Biocentrism") which characterized a worldview of the late nineteenth and early twentieth centuries.[5] This Neo-Romanticism was a reaction to what was seen as the excessive positivism and materialism of nineteenth-century science. It was expressed through the *Lebensphilosophie* [philosophy of life] of, inter alia, Friedrich Nietzsche, Henri Bergson, William James, Georg Simmel, and Ludwig Klages, and the work of scientists with philosophical pretensions such as Ernst Haeckel, Hans Driesch, Raoul Francé, Ernst Mach, Élissée Reclus, Peter Kropotkin, and Patrick Geddes.[6] Because this Neo-Romanticism informed much important Modernist art, architecture, landscape design, product design, urban planning, and other fields, it is important to examine it.

Framing this biologistic Neo-Romanticism—even in a preliminary, sketchy fashion such as I am able to undertake here—is a challenging task, for the picture is complex. While historians of ideas have studied some components of this complex discourse, others have received little or no attention, and the ill fit of these elements into the prevailing historiographic framework is largely unexamined.[7] Most importantly—and this is where the proposed category of Biocentrism comes into play—despite hints and near-misses, no adequate attempt has yet been made to define a category in the history of ideas broad enough to be useful to cultural historians concerned with the expression of attitudes towards nature through art in this period, and yet sufficiently specific to reflect the concerns of the architects, artists, designers and planners. In other words, it would be useful to have a category coherent enough to have use-value, yet permeable enough to allow for the multiple views of the individuals who would comprise it. As a cultural/art historian delving into the field of intellectual history, there is bound to be a degree of superficiality, indeed naïveté in such an undertaking, and I readily admit this. Nevertheless, in this chapter I will attempt to reframe these views as a coherent, if open intersection of discourses. Because my own research is focused on the German cultural sphere, the paradigmatic one when it comes to biologistic Neo-Romanticism, I have adopted a term from early twentieth-century German usage: *Biozentrik* or Biocentrism.[8]

The turn of the century was characterized by a revival of aspects of Romanticism, among them an intuitive, idealistic, Holistic, even metaphysical attitude towards the idea of "nature," of the experience of the unity of all life, what Max Scheler referred to as *Vitalmystik* and its *kosmovitale Einsfühlung*; what Ernst Bloch ironically termed *Hurrapentheismus*.[9] Nietzsche referred to this unity of life as *All-Leben*, while in a more scientific vein, the influential Austro-Hungarian biologist and popular scientific writer Raoul Heinrich Francé referred to it as *Plasma*.[10] It is these two impulses, *Vitalmystik* and biologism, that characterize the phenomenon most succinctly. It is to be located in what intellectual historian Niles Holt has termed "the decline of materialistic and mechanistic interpretations in Europe in the decade and one-half after 1900," as Kurt Bayertz phrases it, "the broad spectrum of biologistic thought at the turn of the century," as Ernst Bloch saw it, in the transmutation of the mechanistic into the pantheistic, and as Max Scheler saw it in the 1920s, "the pan-Romantic conception of man that we now find among many thinkers in different scientific disciplines."[11] It is within this context that Holt places the work of *Lebensphilosophen* and biologists such as Henri Bergson, Hans Driesch, Eduard von Hartmann, and Ernst Haeckel.[12]

The primarily philosophical component of nature-centric Neo-Romanticism was the biologistic wing of *Lebensphilosophie*, a philosophical variety which, based on the results of *Naturphilosophie* and of nineteenth-century science (especially biology), attempted to rethink philosophical categories such as "life" and "nature," as well as epistemology, ethics, and morality. In his history of German philosophy in the modern period, Herbert Schnädelbach reminds us of the general import of the concept of "life" in modernity, of its role in the anti-Modernist cultural critique which suffused the *fin de siècle*. As he writes:

> It is important that the term "life" in this connection does not refer primarily to anything biological. In fact, "life"' is a concept ... which ... led the attack on ... a civilization which had become intellectualistic and antilife, against a culture which was shackled by convention and hostile to life, and for a new sense of life ... in general for what was "authentic", for dynamism, creativity, immediacy, youth. "Life" was the slogan of the youth-movement, of the Jugendstil, neo-Romanticism, educational reform and the biological and dynamic reform of life. The difference between what was dead and what was living came to be the criterion of cultural criticism, and everything traditional was summoned before the "tribunal of life" and examined to see whether it represented authentic life, whether it "served life", in Nietzsche's words, or inhibited and opposed it.[13]

As British environmental historian Anna Bramwell formulates it: "Life-philosophy was a response to the revolutionary idea that man and world and nature were one ... and the resulting implication that man's intellect was not autonomous."[14]

The most influential representative of this philosophical position was Friedrich Nietzsche. Neither on the Left nor the Right, more than any other philosopher, Nietzsche's biologically-based system of ideas decentered the human species and inspired a rethinking of traditional Judeo-Christian morality and ethics.[15] A *Lebensphilosoph* such as Nietzsche "implicitly places the affirmation of life at the centre of man's being."[16] Besides Nietzsche, Arthur Schopenhauer, Eduard von Hartmann, Bergson, Hermann Keyserling, the later Georg Simmel, Theodor Lessing, Oswald Spengler, Ludwig Klages, Wilhelm Dilthey, Eduard Spranger, and the American "Pragmatists" William James and John Dewey were all counted as *Lebensphilosophen*.[17]

At its height, *Lebensphilosophie* intertwined with Neo-Vitalism[18] and the Monism of the *Monistenbund* [Monist League], both of which—though rooted in contemporary science and promoted by scientists—focused on philosophical issues. "Vitalism" has been defined in opposition to "Mechanism" as "a miscellany of beliefs united by the contention that living processes are not to be explained in terms of the material composition and physico-chemical performances of living bodies."[19] Vitalism is characterized by "the belief that forces, properties, powers or 'principles' which are neither physical nor chemical are at work in, or are possessed by living organisms, and ... any explanation of the distinctive features of living organisms which did not make references to such properties, forces, powers or principles [such as Mechanism] would be incomplete."[20] Continued in various forms from the time of Aristotle through Spinoza to the present, Vitalism—like Occultism and Neo-Catholicism—re-emerged in the late nineteenth century as a reaction to, or an attempt to mitigate, what were seen to be the excesses of materialism, mechanism, and positivism. Around the turn of the century a new, more sophisticated kind of Vitalism developed, what has been termed "Neo-Vitalism" and what Mikhail Bakhtin and others since have referred to as "Critical Vitalism."[21] Philosophers usually classified as Neo- or Critical Vitalists (though they are sometimes termed *Lebensphilosophen*) include Nietzsche, Bergson, Driesch, Klages, and Johannes Reinke.[22] Wolfgang Krabbe sees Vitalism as having been the "conventional ideology" of the Lebensreform movement.[23] In the introduction to their anthology on Neo-Vitalism Burwick and Douglass discuss the emergence of this philosophy:

> Gilbert Ryle scorned [Vitalism] ... Still, "critical vitalism" ... has deserved more careful assessment than Ryle allows. This vitalism emerged in the nineteenth century transition from matter-based physics to an energy-based physics; it was an emergence noted by artists, philosophers, and scientists alike, which began early in the century ... Whereas naive vitalism had posited a substance (archeus, vital fluid) in order to fit the evidence of a materialist ontology, critical vitalism focussed on process and dynamic impulse in the context of an ontology of energy and idea. German *Naturphilosophie* was joined by the critical vitalisms of Bergson and Driesch, and the aesthetic and social vitalism of Nietzsche. There can be no doubt that, as the century closed, the vitalist tradition was being powerfully reinterpreted by some of the most celebrated intellectuals in the West.[24]

While I can only touch on this topic—which awaits fuller treatment in that history of Neo-Vitalism urgently in need of being written[25]—the possible Vitalist solutions to the Mechanist–Vitalist debate were diverse. They included Driesch's revival of the Aristotelian *Entelechie,* based on his observations of the regenerative capabilities of dissected sea-urchin blastomeres; the Baltic-German biologist Johann Jacob von Uexküll's related *Gen,* which he felt harmonized with *Entelechie*; Francé's "psychovitalistic" and biologistic amalgam of a pervasive life-substance, a kind of super-organism he termed *Plasma*; the more poetic and speculative Bergsonian *élan vital* and Klagesian *kosmogonen Eros*; the quasi-metaphysical Haeckelian *Seele*; and the physics-based Ostwaldian *Energetik*.[26] As we have seen, the more pantheistic of these systems, those characterized by what he termed *kosmovitale Einsfühlung,* Max Scheler labeled *Vitalmystik*. Scheler saw as "ein zweifelloser Fortschritt" [an undeniable step forward] Bergson's and Driesch's concept of the unity of organic life over what he termed the "alten Monismus" [old Monism] of Hegel, Schopenhauer, Schelling and von Hartmann.[27]

There was no coherent Neo-Vitalist ontology or epistemology, and there is little agreement about the varieties of Neo-Vitalism or the distinctions between Neo-Vitalism, Organicism, Holism, mysticism, and even mechanism.[28] There was certainly no self-aware "Neo-Vitalist" group and Driesch was one of few philosophers designated as "Neo-Vitalist" to embrace the term.[29]

More coherent as a social grouping, equally diverse intellectually speaking, and based on contemporary scientific research just as Driesch's thinking, was early twentieth-century Germanic "Monism." In general, Monism is defined as "a metaphysical system based on the assumption of a single ultimate principle or kind of being instead of two or more; [one which is] opposed to dualism and pluralism ...".[30] This definition begs the question of what that single ultimate principle is and suggests the multiplicity of possible Monisms. "Monism" was introduced in its current sense as opposed to "Dualism" in the early nineteenth century and was adopted by German biologist and Darwin popularizer Ernst Haeckel, Francé's boyhood hero and Driesch's professor and early mentor (Fig. 1.1).[31]

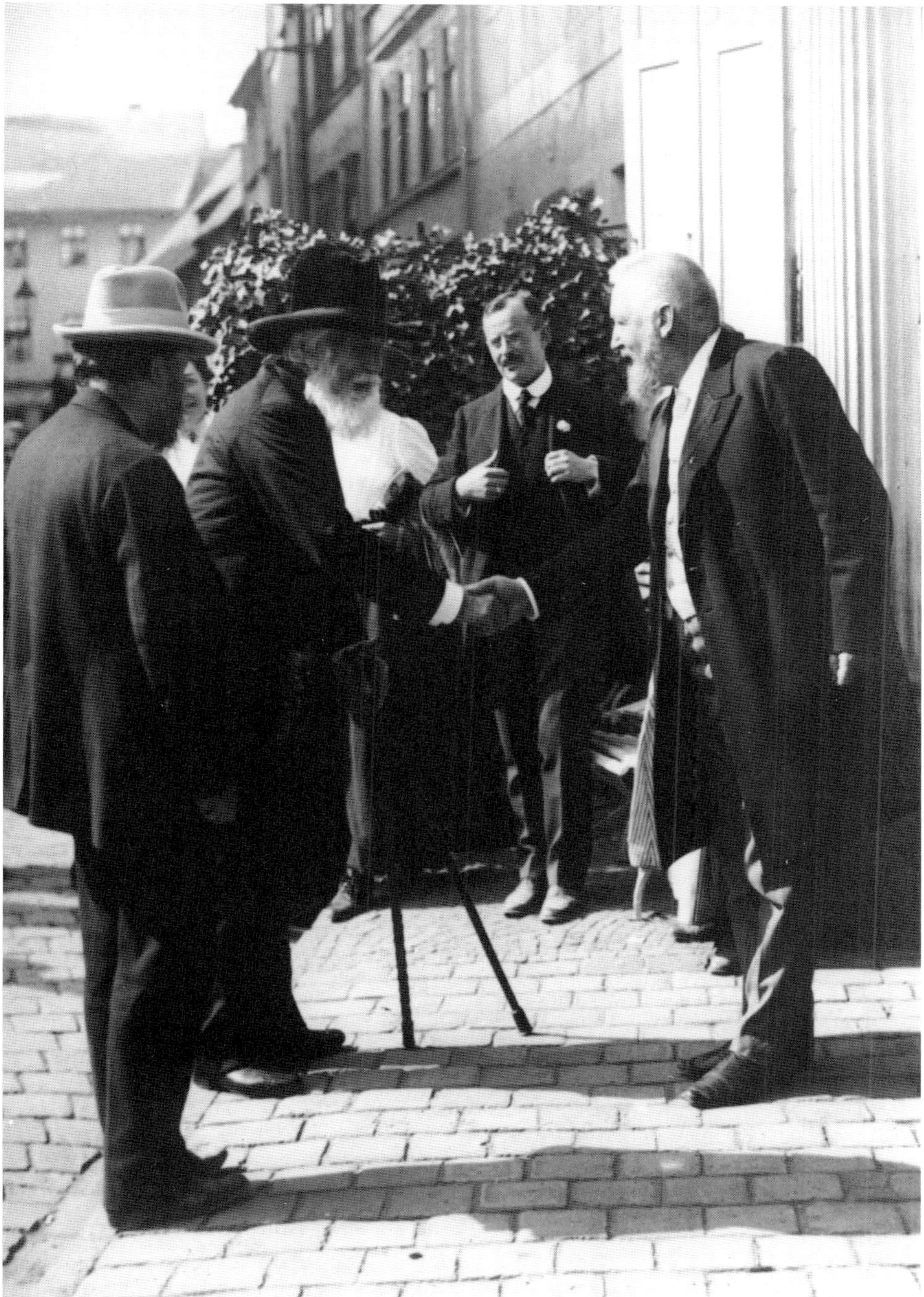

1.1 Photographer unknown, Ernst Haeckel (left), meets Wilhelm Ostwald (right) on the occasion of a meeting of the Monist League, n.d. [c. 1906–15], silver gelatine copyprint, 17.7 × 12 cm. Ostwald Papers, Berlin-Brandenburgische Akademie der Wissenschaften, Berlin

Haeckel's usage of the term "Monism", beginning in 1863, marked a decided shift in the nature of the debate around Monism and Dualism.[32] Rather than operating within the discourse of metaphysics, as the Monist-Dualist debate had done previously, Haeckel removed it to that of natural science. Rollo Handy sees him as being "convinced of the essential unity of organic and inorganic nature, and argued that the simplest protoplasmic substances arose from inorganic carbonates through spontaneous generation ... [rather than] a miraculous origin ...".[33] His "confidence that 'consciousness, thought and speculation' are 'functions of the ganglionic cells of the cortex of the brain,' his 'hard' determinism, his mechanism, his complete rejection of the supernatural, and his enthusiasm for science, all inclined his contemporaries to classify him as a materialist."[34] With what Bloch cleverly calls "sonnige Banalität" [cheerful banality], he wished to reduce "the 'riddles of the universe'," as he termed scientific unknowns, to one "riddle," that of the nature of substance, and he claimed that his Monism did this. He saw Darwin's theory of natural selection as a materialist mechanism to explain organic life, its origins and its changes. In 1868 he wrote: "Evolution is now the magic word with which we will solve all of the riddles around us, or at least be on the way to solving them."[35] Haeckel himself defined Monism simply as "that unifying conception of nature as a whole."[36]

While this position seems materialist and mechanist—and Haeckel certainly appeared as such to Christians and other idealists (whom he attacked mercilessly throughout his career), as Bloch points out, there was an ambivalence in Haeckel's own thinking from the start, a substrate of pantheistic vitalism rooted in German Nature Romanticism, a quasi-animist belief that, as Rollo Handy puts it, "both matter and ether possess sensation and will in the lowest grade."[37] For much of his career, Haeckel's ontology pendulated like some gestalt figure with two possible sense-configurations between a materialist Monism and this other, Vitalist kind of Monism, what Bloch referred to as "eine pantheistelnd gemachten Mechanik" [a mechanism made pantheizing], before becoming lodged permanently in the configuration which signified "Vitalist" towards the end of his career. As Kelly writes in *The Descent of Darwin*:

> his Monism seemed to assert that everything was unified because everything was matter ... in his *Riddle of the Universe*, where he summarized his ideas, Haeckel vehemently denied that he was a materialist because his system, unlike materialism, did not see matter as dead. Rather, Haeckel placed himself in what he thought was the tradition of Spinoza and Goethe. These thinkers, he believed, saw nature as a single universal substance that was both matter and spirit—a universe of animated matter.[38]

Given such a multifaceted position, Haeckel's views were received in different ways during his long career. Niles Holt writes that "Haeckel clashed with clericals and scientific colleagues, political figures and philosophers. Like a many-sided geometrical figure, Haeckel—zoologist, popularizer of

Darwinism, and polemicist for his own Monism—excited varying images in the minds of rivals and admirers."[39] While this was the way he was seen, during most of his career Haeckel in effect sought a mediate position; he was anxious to differentiate his Monism from both materialistic and idealistic Monisms. According to Gienapp, Haeckel's "Monism was neither the elaboration of a new atheistic materialism based on Darwinian evolution nor the unfounded fanciful speculation of a nature philosopher," both accusations commonly leveled at him. "Rather it was a romantically based view of nature in which the materialistic tendencies inherent in this point of view were fully elaborated."[40] As with Francé later on, the mediate location of Haeckel's Monism between the reductive materialism of positivist scientific thinking, and of idealist religious or esoteric systems of thought, was what made it so appealing to those artists who sought such a position themselves: a synthesis of hard science and metaphysics.[41]

His popular Monist manifesto, *Die Welträtsel* [The Riddle of the World] appeared in 1899, and, translated into at least 23 languages by 1912 including Hebrew and Japanese, became a worldwide best-seller, read by many of the generation who were growing up around the turn of the century (Fig. 1.2).[42] Strongly evident in *The Riddle of the World*, Haeckel's ambivalence tilted increasingly towards the Vitalist, indeed *vitalmystische*, end of the spectrum during his career, and by 1904 he had drawn up plans to transform Monism into a scientifically based, in effect Neo-Vitalistic, "Monistic Religion" as an alternative to the traditional religions.[43] In his thirty "theses of Monism" of 1904, Haeckel planned the Monist League as the basis for a "potential 'compromise' church, as the 'link' between science and religion," based on the precepts of early Christianity, the philosophy of Spinoza, and the writings of Goethe.[44] The Monist League was founded in 1906 by Haeckel, Wilhelm Ostwald and Ernst Mach to promote the development of such a "religion," though it has also been seen to be a typical organization of the *Reformbewegung*.[45] The artist Franz von Stuck, Raoul Francé, and the scientific writer and novelist Wilhelm Bölsche were also founding members of the Monist League, Bölsche propounding a view of the sex drive ("love") as the vital force.[46] In 1911, Ostwald—by then a Nobel Prize winner in chemistry—assumed the presidency of the Monist League, which he held until 1915 (see Fig. 1.1).[47] Ostwald's Monism was based on his "Energetism,"[48] the idea that, as Holt phrases it, "energy is the substrate of all phenomena and ... all observable changes can be interpreted as transformations of one kind of energy."[49] As Holt has pointed out, "Ostwald ... regarded his Energism as the ultimate monism, a unitary 'science of science' which would bridge not only physics and chemistry, but the physical and biological sciences as well."[50] Ostwald's Energetism offered a more scientific nomenclature than Haeckel's emphasis on the naturally occurring "soul" as the animating force,[51] a factor which may account for Ostwald's greater influence on the general public, including artists, by the early twentieth century.[52] Mach, meanwhile, took a radically biologistic, or, in Pauline Mazumdar's terms, a "biological positivist" approach to Monism.

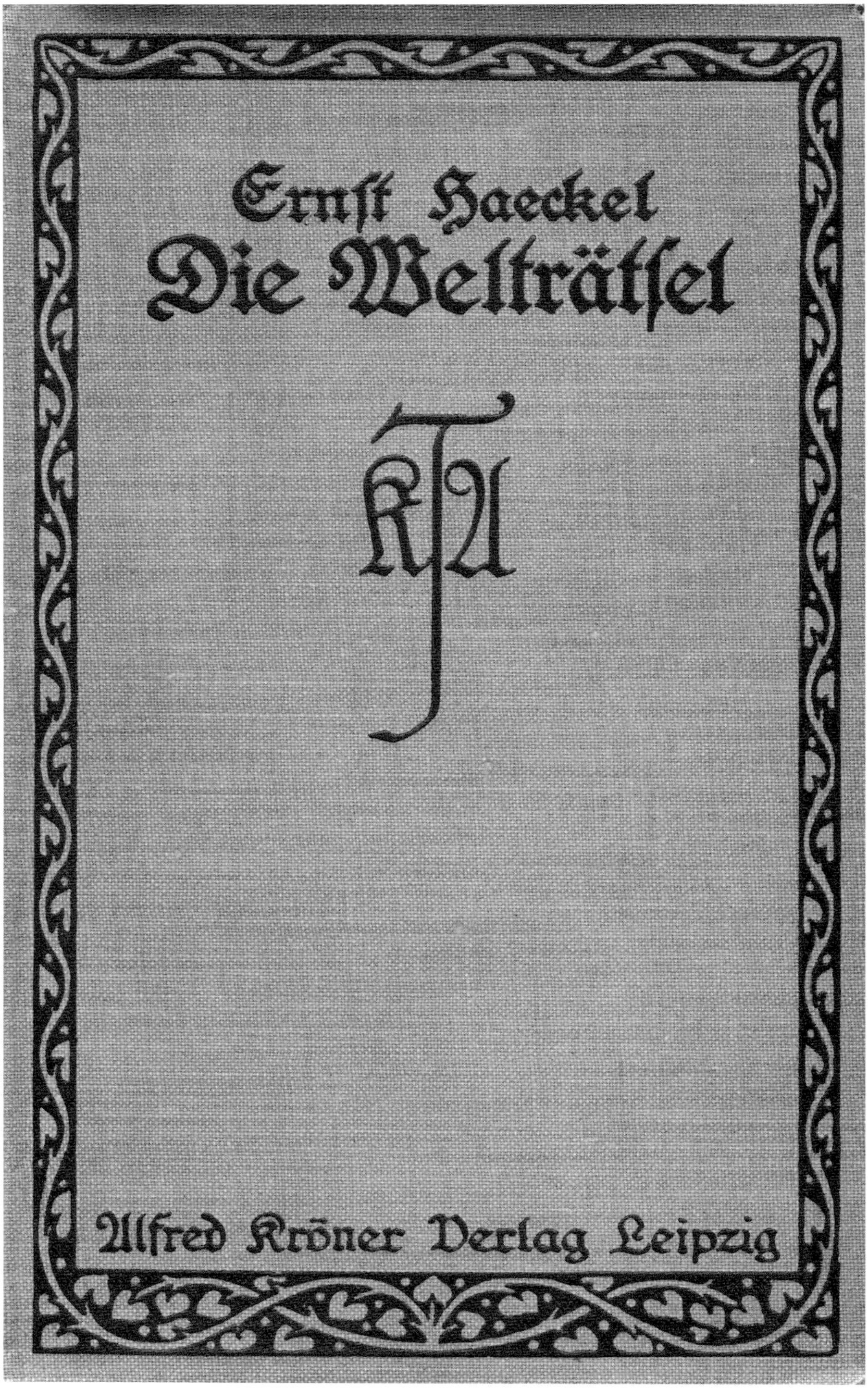

1.2 Designer unknown, cover for Ernst Haeckel, *Die Welträtsel* [1899] (Leipzig: Alfred Kröner, 1908). Private collection

For Mach, only a biological phenomenology was possible, a knowledge based on the *Vorstellung* of sense impressions.[53] Despite disagreements amongst the Monists, Haeckel's status as both the spiritual father of the Monist League and as an important Neo-Vitalist late in his life, and the *au fond* Vitalist nature of both Ostwald's "Energetist Monism" and Francé's *Plasmatik*, demonstrate the extent to which Neo-Vitalism and Monism were interlinked, indeed could scarcely be disentangled, even if Mach's positivistic Monism was also present.[54]

Returning to the question of the relationship between Neo-Vitalism and the philosophy of life, Fellmann writes of the determinant role Neo-Vitalism played in the development of *Lebensphilosophie*.[55] Some historians, such as Anna Bramwell, simply assume the identity of Neo-Vitalism (including Monism) and *Lebensphilosophie*.[56] Philosophers such as Bergson, Klages, Dilthey, and Simmel are alternately listed as being *Lebensphilosophen* and neo-Vitalists. *Lebensphilosophie*, Neo-Vitalism, and the Monist League were so closely linked, as to be parts of a single philosophical current.

The second component of turn-of-the-century nature-centric Neo-Romanticism, that of the "New Biology," is equally complex. Science historians have written of the bona fide "neo-idealist" scientific perspectives, mainly within the field of biology, such as Neo-Lamarckism, Organicism, and Holism, which were to varying degrees in revolt against the prevailing reductivist-mechanistic, instrumental, and positivistic scientific practices of the time.[57] Paul Weindling writes that during this *fin de siècle* "theology ... had been shaken by historical scholarship. Biology, however, promised to extend the idea of social progress to the history of life ... A vast new market ... had emerged for Haeckel's organicist synthesis."[58]

As we have seen, Haeckel was a complex figure whose work was received variously: arch-materialist and arch-mechanist as well as arch-idealist, arch-Vitalist, even arch-mystic. While his philosophical orientation was grounded in German *Naturromantik*, from Darwin Haeckel adopted the rejection of a teleological understanding of evolution, seeing instead—in a decidedly proto-Bergsonian manner—"the world as an eternal evolution of substance, and man as part of that evolution."[59] However, since he believed in the inheritability of acquired characteristics, Haeckel was also Lamarckian. In fact, Haeckel and Herbert Spencer were crucial to the rise of a Neo-Lamarckian reaction to the theory of natural selection which happened simultaneously with the popularization of Darwinism in the late nineteenth and early twentieth centuries,[60] an apparently contradictory process which Alfred Kelly—who skillfully avoids the question of Neo-Lamarckism in his book—has described as the "descent of Darwin."[61] Indeed, this "Eclipse of Darwinism," as Julian Huxley termed it, or "Non-Darwinian Revolution," as Bowler refers to it, and its Neo-Lamarckian aspect was widespread.[62] While not all Neo-Vitalists and members of the Monist League were Neo-Lamarckians, the three most important neo-Vitalists, Haeckel, Driesch, and Bergson were—as were Francé, von Uexküll and the anarchist geographers Reclus and Kropotkin, the latter of whom was so important to the Weimar German artistic avant-garde.[63]

Inevitably Neo-Vitalism and Neo-Lamarckism are closely associated and by around 1907–1908 Neo-Lamarckism, or "psychobiology" as Francé termed it, had formed into a "movement."[64]

However contradictory, Haeckel's attempt to synthesize the Mechanist with the Vitalist, the scientific with the "religious" or "mystical," the material with the ideal and the Darwinian with the Non-Darwinian, was precisely what many saw as necessary to combat a perceived degeneration of society and the alienation of the public from science at the turn of the century. This "organicist synthesis" is what Francé was referring to when he wrote of "die neue Naturphilosophie" in the *fin de siècle*.[65]

It was out of the turn-of-the-century Neo-Nature Philosophy, especially as elaborated by Driesch, and out of Neo-Lamarckism[66] that the scientifically more respectable Organicism and Holism developed as part of the anti-mechanistic, systems-based approach to biology in the early part of the century (Fig. 1.3).[67] Despite the rhetoric—both then and now—to the contrary, it is impossible to separate this phenomenon, emergent from the Neo-Vitalist and Monist circles of Haeckel and Driesch, from Neo-Vitalism and Monism, though Holism and Organicism came to the fore after the First World War, at a time when Neo-Vitalism and Monism had gone out of fashion.[68] The Germans have referred to this phenomenon as "die Neue Biologie" [the New Biology], a term which—as Michael Kröger's usage of it indicates—is employed in a historical sense in Germany, while in North America it is in use for an analogous phenomenon as it exists today.[69]

It is not necessary here to unravel or resolve the debates around this "New Biology" concerning natural selection versus Neo-Lamarckian and teleological views of evolution, materialism versus idealism, Monism versus dualism, mechanism versus Organicism, Neo-Vitalism or positivism, and reductivism versus Holism. The current state of science history is one of confusion—both terminological and conceptual—concerning these matters. Rather than argue for an airtight category with firm boundaries, what I will do is focus on the commonalities of what I see as the interlocking complex of Organicism and Holism. Thus, though—like Neo-Vitalism and Monism—it was not necessarily anti-materialistic, and—like Neo-Vitalism and Holism—it did not always eschew mechanistic explanations, the New Biology shared ground with the romantically derived, neo-pantheistic, almost mystical focus on the problematic of life and Becoming of *Lebensphilosophie*, the Monist League, and Neo-Vitalism.[70]

A comparison of the definitions of Organicism and Holism from *The Harper Collins Dictionary of Philosophy* should make clear that Holism is largely subsumable under sense no. 2 of Organicism:

> Organicism: 1. any theory that explains the universe on the basis of an analogy to a living organism. 2. any theory that explains the universe as the function of a whole causing and coordinating the activities of the parts. Compare with Animism, Holism, Vitalism. Opposed to Mechanism.[71]

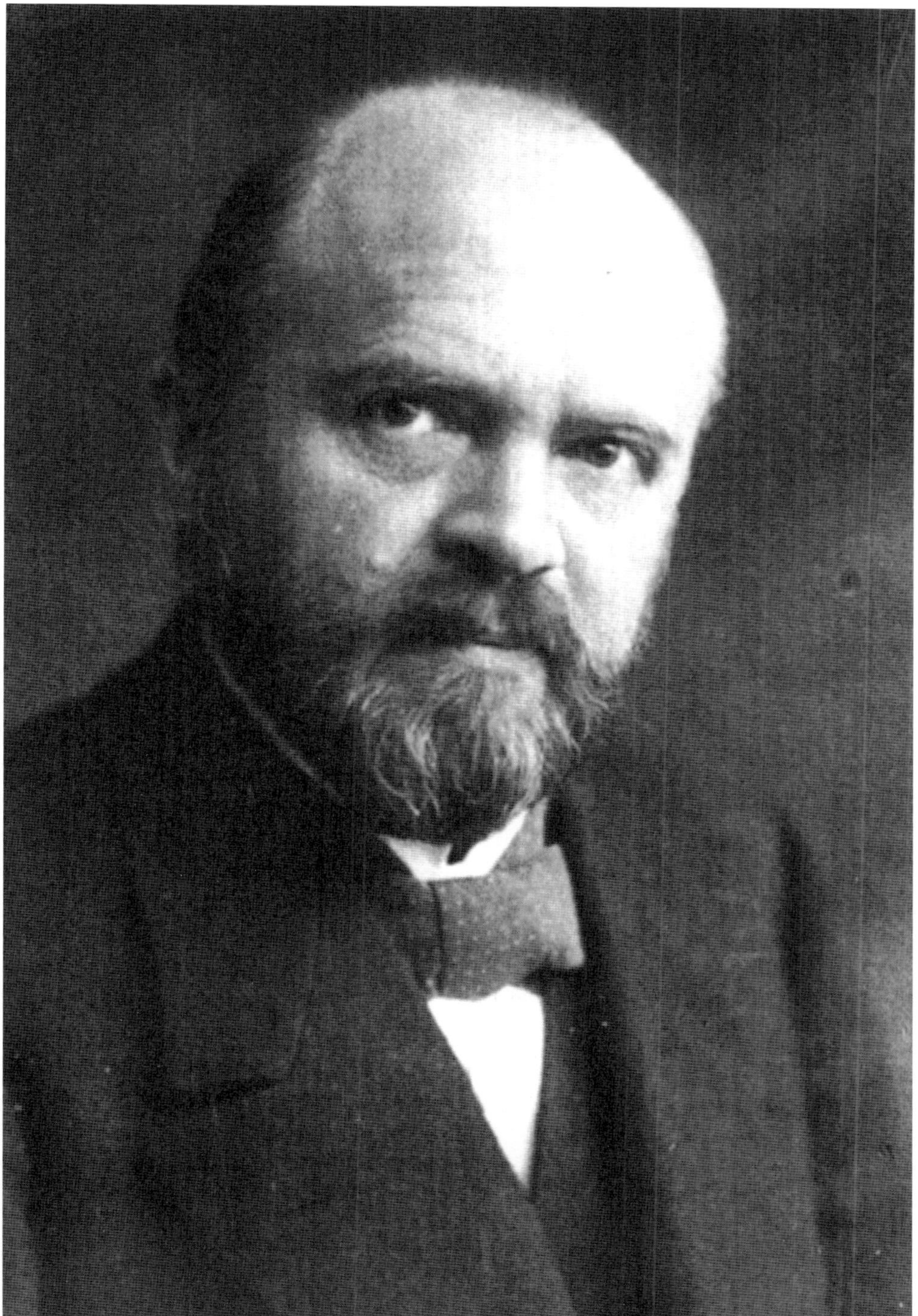

1.3 Photographer unknown, *Portrait of Hans Driesch*, n.d. [c. 1900], silver gelatine print. Courtesy of Besitznachweis Universitätsbibliothek Leipzig, Nachlass 250:6.2, Foto Nr. 44

> Holism: The theory that there is a real, fundamental, and irreducible difference between living and nonliving, between organic and inorganic activity. The parts of living (organic) wholes function differently within the whole from the way they do outside it. Organic wholes must be studied as wholes ...[72]

In other words, Holism is an Organicist theory of living things. The commonality is the idea that entire systems must be studied in order to understand both the system and its components. As Isabel Wünsche has phrased it, "the parts of such complex, nonmechanical systems cannot be independently analyzed without destroying their very essence ... Every organic theory, therefore, views the world as a complex entity of integrated parts, that is, as an organism."[73] Thus it is not surprising that the terms "Organicist" and "Holist" (and their variations) are often used interchangeably.[74]

More recently there have been serious attempts by historians to define Organicism and Holism as categories in the history of science: Donna Jean Haraway's construction of Organicism as a new Kuhnian paradigm engendered by a shift from the use of the machine metaphor (by both Mechanists and Vitalists) in nineteenth-century biology to the metaphor of the organism, and Anne Harrington's definition of Holism as part of a cultural response—as expressed through science—to the perceived mechanization of society and thought.[75] Both Haraway and Harrington construct complex models of Organicism and Holism. Haraway's model involves groups among German-speakers, Americans, the British, and the Soviets in which she privileges their rhetorical anti-Vitalism.[76] Harrington's model of an anti-mechanistic science of "Holism," meanwhile, invokes Neo-Lamarckism as a common feature.[77] While Harrington limits her discussion to germanophone Central Europe, and so her category is not strictly speaking comparable to Haraway's, it shares features with Haraway's "organismic paradigm." An obvious intersection is Gestalt theory, which comprises much of Harrington's construction, and forms a major part of the German component of Haraway's. More crucial is the common origin of Haraway's and Harrington's categories in the work of Hans Driesch,[78] establishing both Organicism and Holism as—historically at least—varieties of a sort of neo-Neo-Vitalism. Thus, though Haraway's perspective is international while Harrington is specific to Central Europe; and Haraway defines her category via a shift in the prevalent metaphor, while Harrington identifies Holists by their conceptual commonalities and common social response, they are describing aspects of a single category, a kind of Organicist/Holist complex.

Because of its common origin in the work of Driesch, moreover, this complex intersects extensively with Neo-Vitalism, Monism and *Lebensphilosophie*. As mentioned, in the minds of many writers, Organicism and Vitalism are equivalent or very closely linked. Not only does Harrington cite Driesch as the founder of German Holism, she names among its important representatives Driesch's friend von Uexküll—a pairing recognized by Heidegger himself.[79] When the Driesch scholar Horst Freyhofer discusses Driesch and von Uexküll (along with Klages and Bergson) as "Vitalists," and even Heidegger as "Organicist," we begin to realize the extent to which *Lebensphilosophie*, Organicism, Holism and Neo-Vitalism are interlinked.[80]

While Haraway is anxious in her book to distinguish between the organismic paradigm and Neo-Vitalism, others such as Hilde Hein have argued for their essential identity. That this distinction between Organicism and Vitalism is problematic, however, is suggested by Haraway's own usage of the term "nonvitalist organicist," as well as by Hilda Hein's materialist view.[81]

An analogous controversy exists within the discussion around whether Holism is a variety of materialism or not. Garland Allen distinguishes between "mechanistic materialism" and "Holistic materialism" or simply "Holism," implying that Holism is by nature always materialist.[82] Golley, on the other hand, writes of both materialist and idealist Holists.[83] While some have been anxious to emphasize the distinctions between Holism and Neo-Vitalism,[84] the same arguments linking Organicism to Neo-Vitalism hold in the case of Holism and Neo-Vitalism: The Holist/Organicist complex emerged from the *Neue Naturphilosophie* [new Nature Philosophy] to form a "New Biology," part of the nature-centric Neo-Romantic cultural current of the *fin de siècle*.

A critique of modernity was inherent in biologistic Neo-Romanticism.[85] In America, James' and Bergson's ideas combined with neo-Transcendentalism into what Jackson Lears has termed "anti-Modernism."[86] In German this is referred to as *Kulturkritik*, a critique of rampant urbanization, industrialization, internationalization, and the instrumentalist view of nature. *Kulturkritik* was expressed through the network of reformist impulses, which in German is referred to as *Lebensreform* [life reform], as well as the ecological wing of the *Jugendbewegung* [Youth Movement]. In Germany, one of the manifestations of this on the Left was the commune movement linked to the anarchism of Gustav Landauer and Peter Kropotkin and the Activism of Kurt Hiller. *Kulturkritik* emerged from the central problem of *Lebensphilosophie*: the distinction between *Geist*, that is intellect, and *Seele*, or soul, which is the locus of life. The unconscious is valorized as the authentic self, a self which must be accessed to ensure authentic expression.

As Bloch suggests, the deeper, unconscious self along with its impulses, the "Dionysian" self, is in this system valorized as the "authentic" self, the self which should be consulted (through "intuition," for example) to ensure authentic expression. The transposition of the scientific debate to the metaphysical plane and the search for authentic expression was most famously and most radically carried out by Klages in his 1929 magnum opus, *Der Geist als Wiedersacher der Seele* [Intellect as the Enemy of Soul] (Fig. 1.4).[87] Following the critiques of Bloch and Georg Lukács, Klages' book was received variously as a John the Baptist-like preparing-of-the-way for Hitler's messianic anti-rationalism, or alternatively, it was praised as a searing critique of the instrumentalist modern consciousness before even Heidegger engaged in it.[88] As Fellmann has pointed out, a more nuanced view of Klages and his thought would be helpful.[89] Klages scholar Richard Hinton Thomas explains the thesis of the book:

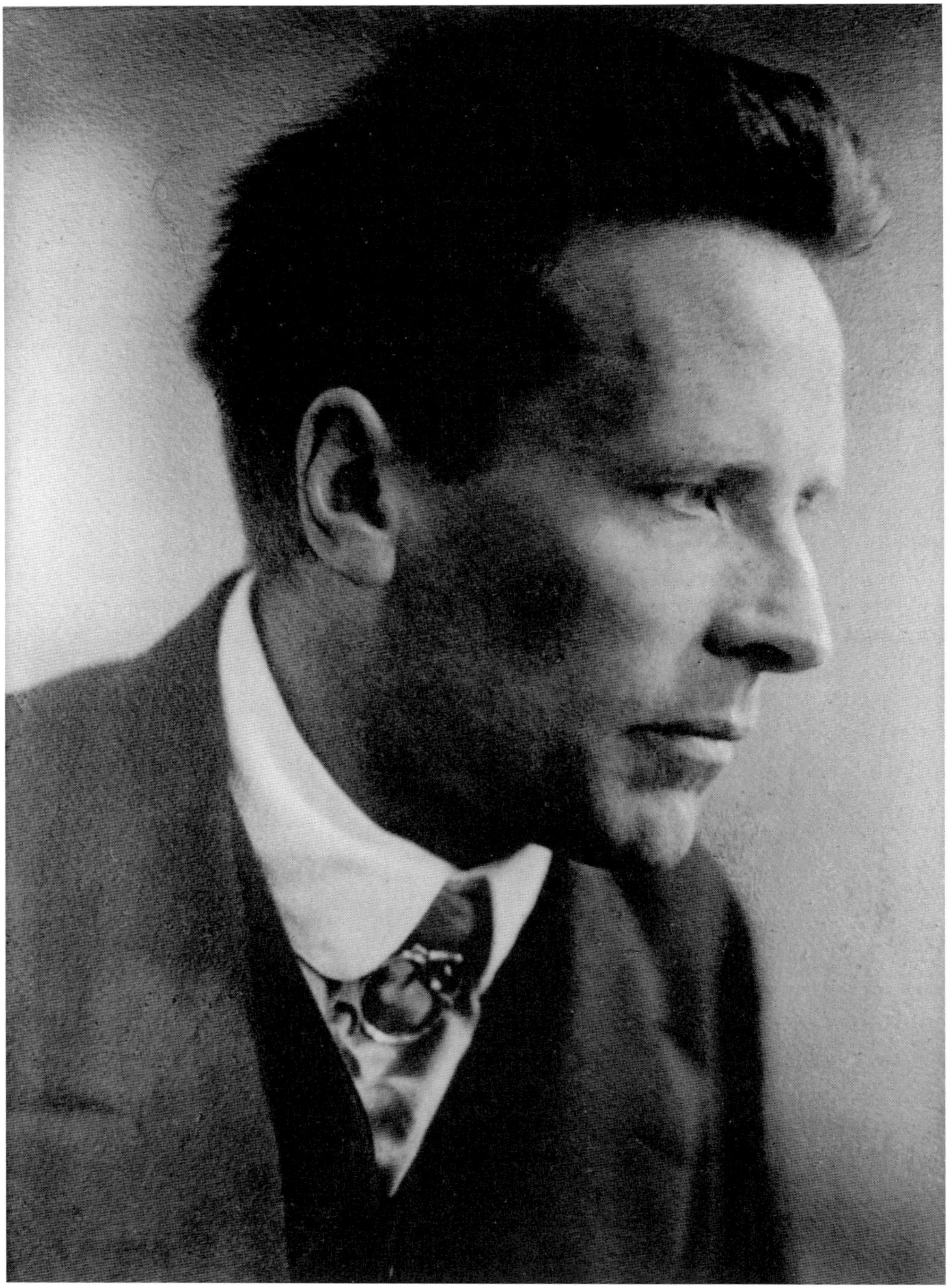

1.4 Photographer unknown, *Portrait of Ludwig Klages*, n.d. [c. 1900–1910], silver gelatine print. Courtesy of Deutsches Literaturarchiv, Marbach am Neckar, Germany

> If on the one view "Geist" is an ennobling, liberating aspect of life, for Klages it is not part of life at all. It is a sort of space-invader from another world, from "outside life." The emphasis is always on the destructiveness of "Geist". It is destructive of peace, of nature ... of organic bonds, of "life". It is "Geist" that thinks up the instruments—industrialization, technology and so on—of what we deceptively call progress, and wherever the idea of progress has held sway, man in his arrogance has "scattered the seeds of murder all around and the horror of death."[90]

The search for authenticity in the *Seele* underlies the pervasive "primitivism" of the Modernist project.[91] It comes then as no surprise that the psychologist Hans Prinzhorn, the crucial interwar theorist of primitivism as it relates to the art of children and the mentally ill, was one of Klages' most devoted disciples, and that Ernst Fuhrmann, the self-described *Biosoph* and anarchist nature-centric theorist,[92] was also deeply affected by his thought.[93] Indeed, Furhmann's views were deeply anti-anthropocentric:

> The people of today refuse to understand their entire higher manifestations of life in the context of the image of nature and in their identity with nature ... they are made up of nothing but nature and ... nothing in them supercedes nature.[94]

Humanity and its cultural manifestations were seen by him to be akin to plants and animals, and worthy of the same kind of analysis, a kind of nature-centric phenomenology.

The critique of environmental degradation was closely associated with this anti-rationalist discourse, particularly among the relevant philosophers between the wars. As part of *Kulturkritik*, von Uexküll, Francé, and Fuhrmann and the philosophers Spengler, Klages, Heidegger, and Lessing wrote on this subject.

Inasmuch as his thinking accorded with that of Kropotkin, Francé was related to Klages, who, as we have seen, has been compared to Landauer. However, unlike Klages, he was no anti-Semite,[95] and unlike Spengler, Francé was no *Kulturpessimist* [cultural pessimist] with respect to technology; he was—like Fuhrmann—not against technology per se (Fig. 1.5).[96] For Francé, "the Law of the World ensures that, in the end, the technology of the organic and the technology of humans, are identical."[97] Just like non-human technology, our technology is built up of combinations of seven basic "technical forms" or *Grundformen*.[98] If human technology is a subset of organic ("natural") technology, then it is not something foreign to or necessarily destructive of our ecosystems. Just as we stand to profit from observing the workings of *Biozönose* [ecosystems] in nature, we stand to benefit from our observation of naturally occurring technologies. Technologies of all kinds, including non-human ones, and our ability to learn from them, Francé termed *Biotechnik*, a predecessor of today's "bionics" or "biotechnology."[99] Indeed, Francé supported himself in part from patents he took out on technologies adapted from "nature."

The constructive counterpart to *Kulturkritik* was biologism, a "popular Darwinian" *Weltanschauung* that privileged biology among the sciences, applying biological concepts to other spheres of knowledge.[100] Social Darwinism, which attempted a biological legitimation of capitalist competition and

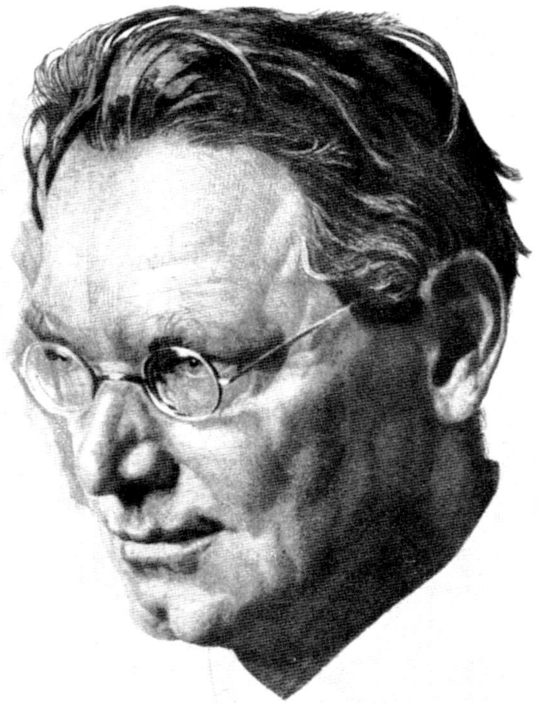

1.5 Sigmund Lipinsky (1873–1940), *Portrait of Raoul H. Francé*, n.d. [c. 1920–21], etching, dimensions unknown. After: Frontispiece for Raoul H. Francé, *Bios: Die Gesetze der Welt* (Munich: Franz Hanfstaengl, 1921). Copyscan by Allen Paterson. Private collection

Kropotkin's Anarchism that wished to justify altruistic cooperation employing analogies from "nature,"[101] represented ideological poles based on biological observation that pervaded Western culture in the *fin de siècle*.[102] Kropotkin's friend and Bergson's admirer, the Leftist Scottish biologist and urban theorist Patrick H. Geddes, saw the biological concept of evolution as applicable to all fields of knowledge:

> Changing order, orderly change, and this everywhere—in nature inorganic and organic, in individual and in social life—for this vast conception, now everywhere diffusing, often expressed, rarely as yet applied, we need some general term—and this is Evolution.[103]

Geddes applied the principles of "mutual aid" to a "dynamic, holistic vitalist and unitary" conception of human settlement, influencing many urban theorists and architects, including Lewis Mumford.[104] While there was a powerful component of National Socialism which was biologistic, it is crucial to realize that there was a biologistic stream on the Left as well. Biologism and *Kulturkritik* fed as easily into the Nazi ideology of Blood and Soil as they did into Anarchism and Socialist utopianism.

Klages' philosophy elicited loyalty just as well from Prinzhorn and Fuhrmann,[105] who became associated with Nazism in the early 1930s, as from Walter Benjamin, who became a Klages devotee after he heard his environmentalist lecture given in 1913 to the *Freideutsche Jugend* [Free German Youth]:

> Horrible are the effects that "progress" has had on the aspect of settled areas. Torn is the connection between human creation and the earth, destroyed for centuries, if not for ever, is the ancient song of the landscape ... The reality behind the facade of "utility," "economic development" and "*Kultur*", is the destruction of life,

thundered Klages.[106] But just as some National Socialists admired Klages' philosophy and his anti-Semitism, the principal Nazi ideologue Alfred Rosenberg was one of Klages' most vicious critics:

> These disciples of Klages refer to themselves as the "biocentric" school, and they regard it as their sacred mission to do battle with the so-called "mechanistic" philosophy; the far greater danger that I believe confronts us today is, rather, the biocentric philosophy itself, which must not be permitted to infect with its false teachings the scientific doctrines espoused by the National Socialist Movement.[107]

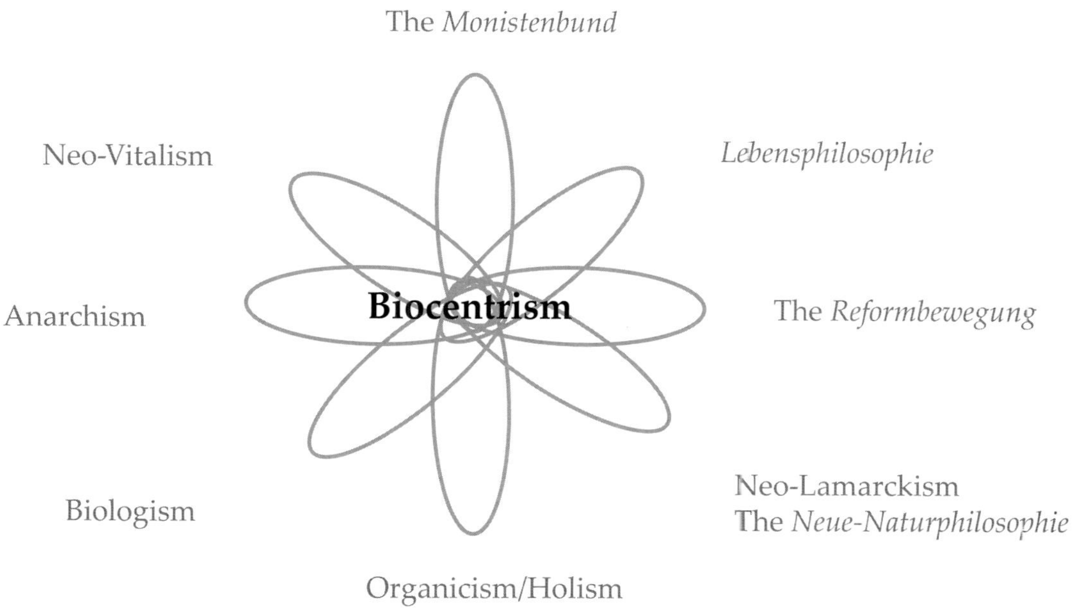

1.6 Conceptual model of Biocentrism. Graphics by Liv Valmestad, University of Manitoba, Architecture and Art Library

Anna Bramwell has suggested that to deal with the slippage of ecological thinkers between Left and Right, historians employ a third fundamental political category, that of "ecologism."[108]

While I have been focusing on the commonalities, one could equally well enumerate a list of differences between the constituents of this *fin de siècle* nature-centric Neo-Romanticism. Indeed, because of these differences, it is problematic to conceive of it as a single category in the history of ideas. It might be more useful to think of these constituent discourses (such as Neo-Vitalism, Organicism/Holism, the Monist League, *Lebensphilosophie*, Neo-Lamarckism, the *Neue Naturphilosophie*, Biologism, the *Reformbewegung*) as sets containing arrays of concepts and beliefs. While the arrays of concepts and beliefs within each set are not identical, there is a degree of commonality between them—that is, the sets intersect (Fig. 1.6). The intersection I am concerned with here consists of an array of closely related concepts—the privileging of biology as the source for the paradigmatic metaphor of science, society and aesthetics; a consequent biologically based epistemology, indeed psycho-biology; an emphasis on the centrality of "nature," "life," and life-processes rather than "culture;" an anti-anthropocentric *Weltanschauung*; the self-directedness and "unity" of all life; a valorization of *kosmovitale Einsfühlung*; a stress on flux and mutability in nature rather than stasis; a concern for "whole-ness" as opposed to reduction at all levels—which were present to a significant degree in all these categories. It is to refer to this biologistic, Organicist, nature-centric (that is, anti-anthropocentric), *vitalmystisch*, psycho-biological, Vitalistic-Monist and holistic aspect of the components of turn-of-the-century Neo-Romanticism, specifically their intersection in this respect, that I revive a German term employed by Klages, Francé, and their followers: *Biozentrik*.[109]

Biozentrik, then, is here constituted as a commonly held bundle of concepts, theories, beliefs, practices, and prescriptions that privileged *Leben* over *Geist*, that foregrounded the concept of our inseparability from and dependence on nature, and that had their origins in Romantic *Naturphilosophie*, biologism, and neo-Lamarckism. If we mentally reconstruct, in turn, other epistemological fields in the intellectual world of the time—for example, empiricism/positivism, Marxism/Socialism, and *Biozentrik*'s Neo-Romantic sibling, the turn-of-the-century Occultist revival—as we have *Biozentrik* (that is, as the intersection of groups of concept-bundles or discourses)—and if we take into consideration the fact that individuals change their views over time, indeed that they hold conflicting views simultaneously—then we begin to understand how it is that a single discourse such as Neo-Vitalism can contain within itself both materialist and idealist views, both mechanism and Vitalism, or how the Monist League could include Haeckel and Ostwald as well as the arch-Positivist Mach.[110] If we think, finally, of the fact that the synchronic structure outlined above also changes diachronically—with the period around the First World War and its aftermath constituting a particularly salient rupture— then we begin to understand how complicated history can be, and why it is crucial to keep individual differences and life-stories as well as changes over time in mind while trying to understand the "big picture" through reductive modeling.

Biozentrik can perhaps best be characterized as Naturromantik—including both its scientific and metaphysical baggage—updated by nineteenth century biology. In its usage by Klages, *Biozentrik* was contrasted with both logocentrism and anthropocentrism.[111] *Biozentrik* rejected anthropocentrism, decentering the human species in favor of "nature" and "life." Since humanity was seen to be part of these larger wholes of life and nature, everything humans do and produce is also part of nature for Biocentrics, and hence explicable in its terms. As Haeckel and others had before him, the English Organicist philosopher Alfred North Whitehead wrote of the realization that "human beings are merely one species in the throng of existences. These are animals, the vegetable, the microbes, the living cells, the inorganic physical activities."[112]

The inevitable ethical dimension of this realization has led to environmentalism. Indeed it is no accident that the science of ecology emerged from *Biozentrik*: Haeckel coined the term *Oecologie* in 1866, in his magisterial *Generelle Morphologie*,[113] and the Neo-Vitalist Holist von Uexküll coined the term *Umwelt* (environment) in 1909.[114] Francé, building on his version of the ecosystem concept, *Biozönose*, carried out groundbreaking work in the field of soil ecology. As we have seen, Francé was also an early environmentalist, and Klages' *Mensch und Erde* [Man and Earth] is recognized by the German Greens as the original environmentalist manifesto: it was typical for *Biozentriker* to be engaged in both the descriptive (scientific) and normative (environmentalist, political) varieties of ecological study just as Haeckel's intentions were scientific, normative, ethical and aesthetic. With this in view it is less surprising that we should find Biocentrically minded individuals in the Anarchist, Socialist, and Fascist camps.

As I have hinted, there was a rupture within German Biocentrism around 1919. While Monism had been out of fashion since the War, the final blow was Haeckel's death in 1919. After this Francé, who had been distancing himself from Haeckel, manifested ambitions to replace Haeckel as the leading Monist. In 1920, at the meeting of the Schopenhauer Society, Francé announced his "Objective" or "Biocentric" Epistemology. This was more practical, biologistic, and functionalist than pre-war Monism had been. It was also less Romantic; it claimed for itself objectivity or *Sachlichkeit* to a greater extent. Inspired by his own pioneering work on soil ecosystems, Francé constituted nature as *Bios*, "a holistic system consisting of parts which are ordered with respect to one another." This prescient, indeed pioneering, "systems" view of the phenomenal world, saw it as a nested hierarchy of integrated ecosystems which strove for an optimal state of balance or harmony driven by the "Law of the Optimum," which saw every process exerting the least effort to arrive at the form which was necessary for its function. But as a response to the chaos after the War, Francé saw the harmony of nature not only as a descriptive model, but also as a normative principle. "There is only one means," he wrote in 1920, "to distance oneself from suffering, and that is to know the laws of the world in which we live, and to be able to keep oneself in harmony with them!"[115]

Another way in which postwar Biocentrism differed from its pre-war variety was that it found itself in a highly charged political field. After the collapse of the German empire in 1918, society was polarized, and, as science historian Harrington has put it, "holism often spoke with a political accent." Like the rest of German society, Biocentrically minded intellectuals had to make choices. While Klages (despite his anti-Semitism) and Driesch resisted the National Socialist temptation, Heidegger did not; while Francé, Prinzhorn, and Fuhrmann were ambivalent at best. Thus, it is important to keep the political dimension of Biocentrism in mind, but it is equally important to not dismiss Biocentrically minded individuals, be they artists, designers, scientists or philosophers, because of their presumed politics.[116]

Notes

1 Friedrich Nietzsche, "On Truth and Lie in an Extra-Moral Sense" (1873), in Walter Kaufmann, transl. and ed., *The Portable Nietzsche* (Harmondsworth, England: Penguin, 1968), 42.

2 Ernst Haeckel, *The Riddle of the Universe* (1900), trans. Joseph McCabe (Buffalo: Prometheus Books, 1992), 14.

3 Raoul Francé, *Die Welt als Erleben: Grundriss einer objektiven Philosophie* (Dresden: Alwin Huhle, 1923), 24.

4 Raoul Francé, *Der Organismus. Organisation und Leben der Zelle* (Munich: Drei Masken, 1928), VII.

5 In 1984 Edward O. Wilson coined the term "biophilia" to refer to the "innate tendency [of humans] to focus on life and life-like processes." (Quoted in Stephen R. Kellert's introduction to the volume of essays edited by him and by Edward O. Wilson, *The Biophilia Hypothesis*, Washington DC: Island Press, 1993, 20.) Kellert goes on: "The biophilia hypothesis proclaims a human dependence on nature that extends beyond the simple issues of material and physical sustenance to encompass as well the human craving for aesthetic intellectual, cognitive, and even spiritual meaning and satisfaction [deriving from nature]." Given this definition, the term "biophilia" could well be applied to turn-of-the-century life-centric intellectual tendencies.

6 Niles R. Holt, "Ernst Haeckel's Monistic Religion," *Journal of the History of Ideas* 32, no. 2 (April–June 1971): 267. As Driesch himself wrote of his relations with Bergson after having met him and spoken with him in 1911, "in many things we had the same view, even if I had reservations with respect to his indeterminism." Hans Driesch, *Lebenserinnerungen* (Basel: Ernst Reinhardt, 1951), 146. On the French geographer and Anarchist Reclus's ideas as Biocentric, see Serena Keshavjee, "Natural History, Cultural History and the Art History of Élie Faure," *Nineteenth-Century Art Worldwide*, 8, no. 2 (Fall 2009) at http://19thc-artworldwide.org/index.php/autumn09/natural-history-cultural-history-and-the-art-history-of-elie-faure.

7 For example, Anne Harrington comments: "The history of science is still waiting for some systematic comparative analysis of twentieth-century Holism in the life and mind sciences that would both clarify larger unifying patterns across cultural and national contexts and also tease apart salient distinctions." Harrington, *Reenchanted Science: Holism in German Culture from Wilhelm II to Hitler* (Princeton, NJ: Princeton University Press, 1996), xxii. On Holism as a component of Biocentrism, see below.

8 Oliver Botar, "Prolegomena to the Study of Biomorphic Modernism: Biocentrism, László Moholy-Nag's 'New Vision,' and Ernő Kállai's *Bioromantik*," Ph.D. dissertation, University of Toronto, 1998 (Ann Arbor, MI: UMI, 2001).

9 Max Scheler, *Wesen und Formen der Sympathie* (1913), 2nd ed. 1922 (Berne: Francke, 1973), 82–104. Ernst Bloch, "Über Naturbilder seit Ausgang des Neunzehnten Jahrhunderts" (1927), in Bloch, *Literarische Aufsätze* (Frankfurt am Main: Suhrkamp, 1965), 453. Scheler cites Hans Driesch as the thinker to see this "cosmic sympathy" as a "sign of a wholeness that transcends personality" [Zeichen überpersonaler Ganzheit] (p. 82), a "subjective index of consciousness ... of the metaphysical state of unity of all living things" (p. 85). On Scheler see Elenor Jain, *Das Prinzip Leben: Lebensphilosophie und ästhetische Erzhiehung* (Frankfurt am Main: Peter Lang, 1993), 120–21.

10 Raoul Francé, *Plasmatik: Die Wissenschaft der Zukunft* (Stuttgart: Walter Seifert, 1923).

11 While he sees Ludwig Klages as being "primarily responsible for providing the philosophical foundation" for this Pan-Romantic conception, the other examples he gives are "Edgar Dacqué, Leo Frobenius, C.G. Jung, Hans Prinzhorn, Theodor Lessing, and, to a certain extent, Oswald Spengler." Max Scheler, *Man's Place in Nature*, trans. and ed. Hans Meyerhoff (New York: The Noonday Press, 1961), 85. This essay was originally published in 1928 as *Die Stellung des Menschen im Kosmos*.

12 Holt, "Ernst Haeckel's Monistic Religion," 267. Scheler (and others) would include Simmel on this list as well (*Wesen und Formen der Sympathie*, 85).

Kurt Bayertz, "Biology and Beauty: Science and Aesthetics in *Fin-de-siècle* Germany," in Mikulás Teich and Roy Porter, eds., *Fin de siècle and its Legacy* (Cambridge, MA: Cambridge University Press, 1990), 291.

13 Herbert Schnädelbach, *Philosophy in Germany 1831–1933,* trans. Eric Matthews (Cambridge: Cambridge University Press, 1984), 139. Schnädelbach's a-biologistic characterization of *Lebensphilosophie* tends to depend on Dilthey's approach, rather than on the more biologistic variants of life-philosophy. See, for example, ibid., 147. Wilhelm Dilthey is usually included among the *Lebensphilosophen* (see, for example, Ferdinand Fellmann, *Lebensphilosophie: Elemente einer Theorie der Selbsterfahrung* (Reineck bei Hamburg: Rowohlt, 1993), 108ff.) However, as Plantinga points out, Dilthey's "choice of the term 'life' does not ... reflect the widespread interest in biological matters that is typical of the late nineteenth century. Dilthey, in fact, manifested no special interest in biology and did not use the term 'life' in a biological sense." Theodore Plantinga, *Historical Understanding in the Thought of Wilhelm Dilthey* (Toronto: University of Toronto Press, 1980), 74.

14 Anna Bramwell, *Ecology in the 20th Century: A History* (New Haven, CT and London: Yale University Press, 1989), 177.

15 On Nietzsche's anti-anthropocentrism, see especially Luc Ferry, *The New Ecological Order*, trans. Carol Volk (Chicago, IL: The University of Chicago Press, 1995), 79. On his thinking being neither Right nor Left, see Henning Ottmann, "Anti-Lukács: Eine Kritik der Nietzsche-Kritik von Georg Lukács," *Nietzsche Studien* 13 (1984): 576.

16 Joan Stambaugh, *The Other Nietzsche* (Albany, NY: State University of New York Press, 1994), 9.

17 For a listing of *Lebensphilosophen*, see Jain, *Das Prinzip Leben*, 20. On Raoul Francé's views of Eduard von Hartmann, see Francé, *Die Welt als Erleben*, 8, 12, 51–52, 166. On von Hartmann as Haeckel's opponent, see David deGrood, *Haeckel's Theory of the Unity of Nature* (Amsterdam: B.R. Grüner, 1982), 5. On Simmel, see, for example, Fellmann, *Lebensphilosophie*, 124ff, and Jain, *Das Prinzip Leben*, 47–48. On Lessing, see Franz Sawicki, "Die Lebensphilosophie," in *Lebensanschauungen moderner Denker*, vol. 2, *Die Philosophie der Gegenwart* (Paderborn: Ferdinand Schöningh, 1952), 214 and Jain, *Das Prinzip Leben*, 49–50, 65–8, *et passim*. On Keyserling, see Ute Gahlings, *Sinn und Ursprung: Untersuchungen zum philosophischen Weg Hermann Graf Keyserlings* (Sankt Augustin: Academia Verlag, 1992) and Jain, *Das Prinzip Leben*, 113–17. For an account of what one could dub Keyserling's metaphysical Biocentrism, see his "Der natürliche Wirkungskreis," in *Der Weg zur Vollendung. Mitteilungen der Gesellschaft für freie Philosophie, Schule der Weisheit, Darmstadt*, no. 10 (1925): 1–17. On Keyserling and *Lebensphilosophie*, see Paul Feldkeller, "Bücherschau," *Der Weg*, no. 5 (1923): 100–105. On Keyserling's lecture series on "Mensch und Erde" (of which the eighth lecture was to be given by Hans Prinzhorn), see "Chronik der Schule der Weisheit," *Der Weg*, no. 12 (1926): 18. Despite the obvious reference to Klages in the title of this lecture series, for Keyserling's mixed views on Klages, see "Bücherschau," *Der Weg*, no. 5 (1923): 84–90. For von Uexküll's praise of Keyserling, see Johann Jacob, Baron von Uexküll, *Bausteine zu einer biologischen Weltanschauung. Gesammelte Aufsätze*, ed. Felix Gross (Munich: F. Bruckmann, 1913), 50. On Spengler as *Lebensphilosoph*, see Thomas Kluge, *Gesellschaft, Natur, Technik. Zur lebensphilosophischen und ökologischen Kritik von technik und Gesellschaft* (Opladen: Westdeutscher Verlag, 1985). On Spranger, see Jain, *Das Prinzip Leben*, 197ff.

18 On this relationship, see Schädelbach, *Philosophy in Germany 1831–1933*, 146–47.

19 *The Harper Dictionary of Modern Thought* (New York: Harper & Rowe, 1988), 898.

20 E. Benton, "Vitalism in Nineteenth-Century Scientific Thought: A Typology and Reassessment," *Studies in the History and Philosophy of Science* 5, no. 1 (1974): 18.

21 See Bakhtin, "Contemporary Vitalism" (1927) in Frederick Burwick and Paul Douglass, eds., *The Crisis in Modernism: Bergson and the Vitalist Controversy* (Cambridge: Cambridge University Press, 1992), 80. Bakhtin distinguished traditional Vitalism from the more sophisticated Vitalism of the *fin de siècle*. He called the latter "critical Vitalism," and distinguished it from the uncritical Vitalism of the late eighteenth and early nineteenth centuries. In his essay Bakhtin sought to prove, however, that a truly critical Vitalism was impossible, that all Vitalisms are by nature dogmatic, that the basic tenets of Vitalism—even its critical variety—must be accepted on faith. Morton O. Beckner, in his article on Vitalism for Paul Edwards, ed., *The Encyclopedia of Philosophy* (New York: MacMillan, 1967), 254, also employs Bakhtin's term "critical Vitalism," including principally Aristotle and Driesch in this category. More recently Michael A. Weinstein has proposed a "Critical Vitalist" philosophy in his book *Structure of Human Life: A Vitalist Ontology* (New York: New York University Press, 1979), ix.

22 On Driesch, see, for example, Bramwell, *Ecology in the 20th Century*, 54ff. On Reinke as a Neo-Vitalist philosopher, see for example, Sawicki, *Moderne Denker*, vol. 2, 308–9.

23 Wolfgang R. Krabbe, *Gesellschaftsveränderung durch Lebensreform: Strukturmerkmale einer sozialreformerischen Bewegung im Deutschland der Industrialisierungsperiode* (Göttingen: Vandenhoeck & Ruprecht, 1974), 108; see also p. 172. The definitive work on *Lebensreform* is Kai Buchholz, Rita Latocha, Hilke Peckmann, and Klaus Wolbert, eds., *Die Lebensreform. Entwürfe zur Neugestaltung von Leben und Kunst um 1900*, 2 vols. (Darmstadt: Häusser, 2001). See especially Wolfgang Krabbe, "Biologismus und Lebensreform," vol. 1, 79–81.

24 Burwick and Douglass, Introduction, *Bergson and the Vitalist Controversy*, 1.

25 Before 1982 Freyhofer wrote: "Any intellectual history of the last hundred years will remain incomplete if it does not include an account of vitalism." Intellectual history continues to remain incomplete in this regard. Horst H. Freyhofer, *The Vitalism of Hans Driesch. The Success and Decline of a Scientific Theory* (Frankfurt am Main and Bern: Peter Lang, 1982), 13.

26 On von Uexküll's harmonization of *Entelechie* and *Gen*, see von Uexküll, *Bausteine zu einer biologischen Weltanschauung*, 99. On the *Plasma* see Francé, *Plasmatik*. For Francé's critique of some of these concepts as opposed to his own *Plasma*, see *Plasmatik*, 125.

27 Scheler, *Wesen und Formen der Sympathie*, 84.

28 Benton attempts to taxonomize the Vitalist-Mechanist continuum in "Vitalism in Nineteenth-Century Scientific Thought": 18. In discussing typologies in this connection, Rousseau refers to Timothy Lenoir's category of "vital materialism" and notes the breakdown of easy categorizations in the debate. (George S. Rousseau, "The perpetual crises of modernism and the traditions of Enlightenment vitalism: with a note on Mikhail Bakhtin," in Burwick and Douglass, eds., *The Crisis in Modernism*, 45.) The difficulty of taxonomization reflects not only the general confusion as far as the types of Vitalisms are concerned, but also the extent to which Vitalism is distinguishable from Mechanism, and the degree to which Vitalism is identical to varieties of

Organicism and Holism. For example, Max Verworn distinguishes three kinds of Vitalism, one of which, "Mechanistic Vitalism," is essentially identical to some Organicisms, and certainly to Holism. He described Mechanistic Vitalism as "the view that ... the life processes rest basically on physico-chemical factors, but the conditions in the living organism are so complex, that they have up to now not been elucidated. These complex conditions which are peculiar to living organisms in contrast to inorganic nature, may for the present call (sic) the life force." Quoted in Pauline M.H. Mazumdar, "The Antigen-Antibody Reaction and the Physics and Chemistry of Life," *Bulletin of the History of Medicine* 48, no. 1 (Spring 1974): 16. Recognizing the overlap between some kinds of Vitalism and systemic-organicist-mechanist views, rather than to mechanism, J.A. Schmoll opposes Vitalism to "Morbidity." (He opposes mechanism to transcendentalism.) Reported by Roger Bauer in his Preface to Roger Bauer, et al., eds., *Fin de Siècle. Literature und Kunst der Jahrhundertwende* (Frankfurt am Main: Vittorio Klostermann, 1977), X–XI. On Mechanism and Vitalism Rousseau writes: "The point is that both philosophies—Mechanism and Vitalism—developed hand in hand, and it is difficult to separate them during the Enlightenment. When one faded, the other blossomed; but neither waned for very long." Rousseau in Burwick and Douglass, eds., *The Crisis in Modernism*, 32.

29 It was not embraced by his friend Jacob von Uexküll. For examples of the use of the term "Neo-Vitalism" early in the century, see Karl Bräunig, *Mechanismus und Vitalismus in der Biologie des neunzehnten Jahrhunderts* (Leipzig: Wilhelm Engelmann, 1907), 64ff, and Hans Haustein's "Biologie" column written for the *Sozialistische Monatshefte* of Berlin during the mid-1920s: for example, vol. 63, no. 3 (March 1926), 180. On this relationship, see Schnädelbach, *Philosophy in Germany 1831–1933*, 146–47.

30 *Oxford English Dictionary*, 2nd ed., vol, 9 (Oxford: Clarendon Press, 1989), 1001.

31 For a history of the concept of Monism, see Horst Hillermann, "Zur Bergriffsgeschichte von 'Monismus'," *Archiv für Begriffsgeschichte* 20 (1976): 215–35.

32 Ibid., 229.

33 Rollo Handy, "Ernst Heinrich Haeckel," in Edwards, ed., *The Encyclopedia of Philosophy*, 399. See also Jürgen Sandmann, "Ernst Haeckels Entwicklungslehre als Teil seiner biologistischen Weltanschauung," in Eve-Marie Engels, ed., *Die Rezeption von Evolutionstheorien im 19. Jahrhundert* (Frankfurt: Suhrkamp, 1995): 329–31.

34 Ibid., 400.

35 Quoted in Alfred Kelly, *The Descent of Darwin: The Popularization of Darwinism in Germany, 1860–1914* (Chapel Hill, NC: University of North Carolina Press, 1981), 24.

36 Ernst Haeckel, *Monism as Connecting Religion and Science. The Confession of Faith of a Man of Science* (London: Adam and Charles Black, 1894), 3.

37 Handy, "Ernst Heinrich Haeckel," 399. On Haeckel's ambivalence, see Ruth G. Rinard, "The Problem of the Organic Individual: Ernst Haeckel and the Development of the Biogenetic Law," *Journal of the History of Biology* 14, no. 2 (Fall 1981): 249–75; Holt, "Haeckel's Monistic Religion," 267; and Kelly, *The Descent of Darwin*, 27–28. On his pantheism, Norbert Elsner, "'Natur und Geist—spricht man so zu Christen?' Ernst Haeckel oder die theologische Versuchung eines Naturforschers," in Ulrich Mölch, ed., *Europäische Jahrhundertwende. Wissenschaft, Literatur und Kunst um 1900* (Wallstein Verlag, n.d. [1998]), 35–65.

38 Kelly, *The Descent of Darwin*," 27.

39 Holt, "Haeckel's Monistic Religion," 266.

40 Ruth Anne Gienapp, "The Monism of Ernst Haeckel" (Ph.D. dissertation Cornell University, 1968), 198.

41 On the materialist/idealist binary, see Garland E. Allen, Introduction, *Life Science in the Twentieth Century* (New York: John Wiley & Sons, 1975), xx.

42 Haeckel, *Die Welträtsel* (Leipzig: Alfred Kröner, 1899). Simplified *Taschenausgabe*, 1908. The list of languages into which the book was translated is from a document written in his own hand, on display at the Ernst Haeckel Haus, Jena, Germany, 1999.

43 Holt discerns four stages in the development of Haeckel's thinking ("Haeckel's Monistic Religion," 267–68), while Kelly sees one course of change, from materialism and mechanism towards Vitalism and even religiosity (*The Descent of Darwin*, 25). Note, however, that in Kelly's opinion, despite this evolution, "the public Haeckel is most accurately represented when his work is considered ... as a single unified system" (p. 25).

44 Holt, "Ernst Haeckel's Monistic Religion," 277. Also Handy, "Ernst Heinrich Haeckel," 401.

45 Holt, "Ernst Haeckel's Monistic Religion," 277. On the founding of the Monist League, see John T. Blackmore, *Ernst Mach. His Work, Life and Influence* (Berkeley, CA: University of California Press, 1972), 192–94. On the Monist League as an organization of the "Gebildeten-" or "Kultur-Reformbewegung" see Krabbe, *Gesellschaftveränderung durch Lebensreform*, 131. On a central topos of the *Reformbewegung* as a holistic, anti-dualistic/Monistic conception of humanity's "unity with nature," see 167, 171–2.

46 On Francé, see Joachim Wolschke-Bulmahn, *Auf der Suche nach Arkadien* (Munich: Minerva, 1990), 84. Bölsche, like Francé, was a popular and radically Biocentric writer on natural questions, a convinced Haeckelian, and a member of the Monist League. Together, Francé and Bölsche produced the "Kosmos" series of popular scientific publications which enjoyed enormous success in early twentieth-century Germanophone Europe. Bölsche's greatest success was his *Liebesleben in der Natur* of 1898–1902 (*Love-Life in Nature. The Story of the Evolution of Love*, trans. Cyril Brown (New York: Albert and Charles Boni, 1926). Because of Bölsche's enormous influence and output (his books had sold 1.5 million copies by 1914), further study is called for concerning his effect on the Biocentric discourse as artists participated in it. On Bölsche, see Kelly, *The Descent of Darwin*, Chapter 3: "Erotic Monism: The Climax of Popular Darwinism," and Fritz Bolle, "Wilhelm Bölsche: Der Mensch und das Werk," Preface to Bölsche, *Das Liebesleben in der Natur* (Hannover: Fackelträger-Verlag, 1955). For a bibliography of his writings, see Bölsche, *Die naturwissenschaftlichen Grundlagen der Poesie*, ed. Johannes J. Braakenburg (Tübingen: Max Niemeyer and DTV, 1976).

47 Niles Holt, "A Note on Wilhelm Ostwald's Energism," *Isis* 61, no. 208 (Fall 1970): 388.

48 While Holt uses the term "Energism," Milič Capek employs "Energetism" in his article "Wilhelm Ostwald" in Edwards, ed., *The Encyclopedia of Philosophy*.

49 Ibid., 5.

50 Holt, "A Note on Wilhelm Ostwald's Energism": 386.

51 On this, see Friedrich Niewöhner, "Zum Begriff 'Monismus' bei Haeckel und Ostwald," *Archiv für Begriffsgeschichte* 24, no. 1 (1980): 125; and Paul Weindling, "Ernst Haeckel, Darwinismus and the secularization of nature," in James R. Moore, ed., *History, Humanity and Evolution. Essays for John C. Greene* (Cambridge: Cambridge University Press, 1989), 324.

52 On Ostwald and Ernst Mach, see also Pauline Mazumdar, *Species and Specificity: An Interpretation of the History of Immunology* (Cambridge: Cambridge University Press, 1995), 69. The Russian polymath Alexander Bogdanov based his organicist *Tektologiia*, the science of organization, in Ostwald's Energism. It was of enormous influence on the Russian Constructivists and is now regarded as the most important forerunner of Systems Theory. See Oliver A.I. Botar, *Természet és technika: Az újraértelmezett Moholy-Nagy 1916–1923* [Nature and Art: Moholy-Nagy Reconsidered 1916–1923] (Budapest: Vince Kiadó, 2007), 192 ff.

53 Mazumdar, *Species and Specificity*, 169–70.

54 The term "Energeticist Monism" is cited by Capek in "Wilhelm Ostwald," 5.

55 Fellmann, *Lebensphilosophie*, 27–28. See also Fellmann, "Die Lebensreformbewegung im Spiegel der deutschen Lebensphilosophie," in Buchholz et al., eds., *Die Lebensreform*, vol. 1, 151–56.

56 Bramwell, for example, equates Vitalism and *Lebensphilosophie*, in *Ecology in the 20th Century*, 177.

57 See, for example, D.C. Phillips, "Organicism in the Late Nineteenth and Early Twentieth Centuries," *Journal of the History of Ideas* 31, no. 3 (July–September 1970): 424–27.

58 Weindling, "Ernst Haeckel, *Darwinismus* and the secularization of nature," 315.

59 Handy, "Ernst Heinrich Haeckel," 400. See Kelly, *The Descent of Darwin*, 24–25, for an account of the origin of Haeckel's Monism in Darwinism.

60 Bramwell, *Ecology in the 20th Century*, 47, and Peter J. Bowler, *The Non-Darwinian Revolution: Reinterpreting a Historical Myth* (Baltimore, MD: The Johns Hopkins University Press, 1988), 84. The American scientist Alpheus Packard coined "Neo-Lamarckian" in 1885. See Peter J. Bowler, *The Eclipse of Darwinism. Anti-Darwinian Evolution Theories in the Decades around 1900* (Baltimore, MD: The Johns Hopkins University Press, 1983), 55, 60. For an acknowledgment of this embedded in an attack on Haeckel as a "fanatical materialist and mechanist," see Adolf Wagner, *Geschichte des Lamarckismus: Als Einführung in die Psycho-Biologische Bewegung der Gegenwart* (Stuttgart: Franckh'sche Verlagshandlung, nd [1909]), 135.

61 Kelly, *The Descent of Darwin*. On this phenomenon, see also Timothy Lenoir, *The Strategy of Life. Teleology and Mechanics in Nineteenth Century German Biology* (Dordrecht: D. Reidel, 1982); Emanuel Rádl, *The History of Biological Theories (1905–09)* (London: Oxford University Press, 1930), 271ff.; and Arthur Koestler, *The Case of the Midwife Toad* (New York: Vintage, 1971).

62 On Huxley's term, see Bowler, *The Eclipse of Darwinism*, 5. Peter Bowler has described the Neo-Lamarckian movement within the popularization of Darwinism in "Lamarckism," Chapter 4 of *The Eclipse of Darwinism*. See also Robert Proctor, *Racial Hygiene: Medicine under the Nazis* (Cambridge, MA: Harvard University Press, 1988), 31. For a contemporary view, see the Francé-enthusiast Adolf Wagner's *Geschichte des Lamarckismus.*

63 Bowler, *Eclipse of Darwinism*, 55–58, and Keshavjee, "Natural History, Cultural History and the Art History of Élie Faure."

64 On "Psychobiology" being coined by O. Kohnstamm, and for the definition of the term, see Wagner, *Geschichte des Lamarckismus*, 169. On Kohnstamm's ideas, see ibid., 178–81. For Francé's version of "Psychobiology," see his *Der Weg zu mir: Die Lebenserinnerungen, erster Teil* (Leipzig: Alfred Kröner, 1927), 179–80, 186–7, and *Die Welt als Erleben*, 118. On the development of Francé's Psychobiology and the "school" that developed around it in Munich early in the century, see Francé, *Zoesis: Eine Einführung in die Gesetze der Welt* (Munich: Franz Hanfstaengl, 1920), 19. Adolf Wagner sees the "psycho-biologische Bewegung" as a second, higher stage of "die heutigen lamarckistischen Bewegung" in his *Geschichte des Lamarckismus,* 169; on Francé in this book, see ibid., 199–209. According to Sulloway, Freud's thinking was also "psychobiological." Frank J. Sulloway, *Freud, Biologist of the Mind: Beyond the Psychoanalytic Legend* (New York: Basic Books, 1979), 4. For a more contemporary understanding of the term "psychobiology" as "the discipline which studies the biological sources, the biological characteristics and functions of the psyche," see George G. Haydu, "Psychobiology and the Theories of Being and Becoming," *Man and World* 12, no. 4 (1979): 486–97; the quotation is on p. 486. Haydu does not refer to Francé in his article.

The close relation of Neo-Vitalism and Neo-Lamarckism is the case even if, as Bowler writes, "Driesch, the most prominent vitalist of his day, was only a lukewarm advocate of Lamarckism." On the complex relationship between Neo-Lamarckism and Vitalism, see Bowler, *The Eclipse of Darwinism,* 80. On Bergson as Lamarckian, see Harrington, *Reenchanted Science*, 90–91. On Francé, as Neo-Lamarckian, See Francé, *Zoesis*, 19, as well as Wagner, *Geschichte des Lamarckismus*. On Neo-Lamarckism as a Neo-Vitalist (as opposed to old Vitalist) position, see Wagner, 14–19.

65 Francé would have known of Ostwald's *Naturphilosophie*, vol. 1 of *Bücher der Naturwissenschaft* (Leipzig, 1900); in English: *Nature Philosophy*, trans. T. Seltzer (New York: Holt, 1919).

66 Bowler, *The Eclipse of Darwinism*, 105.

67 Allen, Introduction, *Life Science in The Twentieth Century*, xix.

68 On the reticence of Holists and Organicists to acknowledge their Neo-Lamarckian ideas, and of Smuts' "explicit use of Lamarckism in [his] attack on mechanistic biology," see Bowler, *The Eclipse of Darwinism*, 105.

69 See, for example, Robert Augros and George Stanciu, *The New Biology: Discovering the Wisdom in Nature* (Boston, MA: The New Science Library, 1987). On the revival of Neo-Lamarckian ideas currently underway, see also Bowler, *The Non-Darwinian Revolution*, 201. See Michael Kröger, "'... gleichsam biologische Urzeichen ...' Die Erfindung biomorpher Natur in Malerei und Fotografie der dreissiger Jahre." *Kritische Berichte* 18, no. 4 (April 1990): 84, note 8.

70 On the neo-pantheistic background of *Lebensphilosophie*, see Otto Friedrich Bollnow, *Die Lebensphilosophie* (Berlin: Springer, 1958), 101–12 and Gudrun Kühne-Bertram, *Aus dem Leben—zum Leben: Entstehung, Wesen und Bedeutung populärer Lebensphilosophien in der Geistesgeschichte des 19. Jahrhunderts* (Frankfurt am Main: Peter Lang, 1987), 86–89. On the animism which underlies Driesch's Neo-Vitalism, see Freyhofer, *The Vitalism of Hans Driesch*.

71 Peter A. Angeles, *The Harper Collins Dictionary of Philosophy*, 2nd ed. (New York: Harper Collins, 1992), 216.

72 Ibid., 127.

73 Isabel Wünsche, "Organic Visions and Biological Models in Russian Avant-Garde Art," Chapter 6 in this volume. See also Isabel Wünsche, "Naturerfahrung als künstlerische Methode: Organische Visionen in der Kunst der klassischen Moderne," in Elke Bippus and Andrea Sick, eds., *Industrialsierung und Technologisierung von Kunst und Wissenschaft* (Bielefeld: Transcript, 2005), 87, and "Lebendige Formen und bewegte Linien: Organische Abstraktionen in der Kunst der klassischen Moderne," in *Floating Forms: Abstract Art Now* (exhib. cat.) (Bielefeld: Kerber, 2006), 10.

74 For example, Parascandola writes of Henderson's "Holistic, organismic approach" as a single trend in the biological science of the early twentieth century. John Parascondala, "Organismic and Holistic Concepts in the Thought of L.J. Henderson," *Journal of the History of Biology* 4, no. 1 (Spring 1971): 64. See also the single list of books on "organismic, holistic views in twentieth-century science and philosophy" in note 4 on page 64.

75 See Haraway's "Conclusion" for a summary of her arguments in Donna Jean Haraway, *Crystals, Fabrics, and Fields: Metaphors of Organicism in Twentieth-Century Developmental Biology* (New Haven, CT: Yale University Press, 1976), 188–206. It should be noted that Haraway does not feel fully successful in having demonstrated such a paradigm shift (ibid., 195–206).

76 Ibid., 38–9.

77 See Harrington, *Reenchanted Science*, 89, xvii.

78 Haraway, *Crystals, Fabrics, and Fields*, 22–23; Harrington, *Reenchanted Science*, 46–54.

79 On this friendship and mutual support, see Harrington, *Reenchanted Science*, 48–54. On von Uexküll's son's denial that his father was a "Vitalist" despite his close association with Driesch, and despite his public image as a Vitalist, see 52–53, 228, note 74. On von Uexküll's praise of Driesch's work as being "of basic importance," see von Uexküll, *Bausteine zu einer biologischen Weltanschauung*, 36. Harrington feels it possible that von Uexküll's concept of *Umwelt* may have contributed to Heidegger's concept of Being-in-the-World (*Reenchanted Science*, 53–54).

80 Freyhofer, *The Vitalism of Hans Driesch*, 167. On von Uexküll as Vitalist, see also Adolf Behne, "Biologie und Kubismus," *Die Tat* (1916): 699. On Heidegger and Klages, see Hans Kunz, *Martin Heidegger und Ludwig Klages. Daseinsanalytik und Metaphysik* (Munich: Kindler, 1976). See also Jack Burnham, *Beyond Modern Sculpture. The Effects of Science and Technology on the Sculpture of this Century* (New York: George Braziller, 1968), 76.

81 Haraway, *Crystals, Fabrics, and Fields*, 17, 23; and Hilde Hein, *On the Nature and Origins of Life* (New York: McGraw-Hill, 1971), 74.

82 Allen, *Life Science in the Twentieth Century*, xxi.

83 Frank Benjamin Golley, *A History of the Ecosystem Concept in Ecology: More Than the Sum of the Parts* (New Haven, CT: Yale University Press, 1993), 25–29.

84 Allen, *Life Sciences in the Twentieth Century*, xxi–xxii.

85 See Hans-Joachim Lieber, *Kulturkritik und Lebensphilosophie* (Darmstadt: Wissenschaftliche Buchgesellschaft, 1974).

86 See Jackson Lears, *No Place of Grace: Antimodernism and the Transformation of American Culture 1880–1920* (New York: Pantheon Books, 1981). While some aspects of Lears' construction, especially the "martial ideal" and the Catholic revival, have absolutely nothing to do with what is being discussed here, others, such as educational reform and anti-industrialism, do. As Sherrye Cohn notes, "Transcendentalism is Romanticism in its American guise." Cohn, *Arthur Dove: Nature as Symbol* (Ann Arbor, MI: UMI Research Press, 1985), 2. On the German Romantic origins of American Transcendentalism, see ibid., 11; and Octavius Brooks Frothingham, *Transcendentalism in New England: A History* (New York: Putnam & Sons, 1876).

87 Ludwig Klages, *Der Geist als Wiedersacher der Seele* [1929], 3rd ed. (Munich: Barth, 1954).

88 Most famously in his 1953 lecture "The Question Concerning Technology, "in Heidegger, *Basic Writings*, ed. David Farrell Krell (New York: Harper & Rowe, 1977). For positive valuations of Klages, see the journal devoted to Klages studies, *Hestia*, published in Bonn, and (English) John Claverley Cartney's Klages websites, neither of which really deal with the problem of Klages' anti-Semitism.

89 Fellmann, *Lebensphilosophie*, 155.

90 Richard Hinton Thomas, "Nietzsche in Weimar Germany—and the Case of Ludwig Klages," in Anthony Phelan, ed., *The Weimar Dilemma: Intellectuals in the Weimar Republic* (Manchester: Manchester University Press, 1985), 79–80.

91 For a good discussion of the origins of "primitivism" in Modernism, see Gill Perry, "Primitivism and the Modern," Part One of Charles Harrison, Francis Frascina, and Gill Perry, *Primitivism, Cubism, Abstraction: The Early Twentieth Century* (New Haven, CT: Yale University Press, 1993), esp. 34–36.

92 On Fuhrmann's politics as Anarchist, see Gert Mattenklott, Vorwort in Ernst Fuhrmann, *Neue Wege*, vol. 10 in *The Collected Works* (Hamburg: Ernst Fuhrmann Archiv, 1983): V, VIII.

93 This is evident, for example, in Fuhrmann's discussion of the rhythm of breath as "the highest principle of life." Indeed, by the mid-1920s, Fuhrmann sought personally to cooperate with the philosopher. Fuhrmann, *Der Sinn im Gegenstand* (Munich: Georg Müller, 1923): 18. Cf. various texts by Klages from 1913 on, published as *Vom Wesen des Rythmus* (Kampen auf Sylt: Niels Kampmann, 1934). Fuhrmann's two letters sent to Klages during the mid-1920s offer cooperation, and display intense admiration. (Deutsches Literaturarchiv, Marbach, Klages Papers). For a summary of Fuhrmann's philosophy, see Volker Kahmen, "Ernst Fuhrmann—Photographs of Plants" in *Ernst Fuhrmann* (exhib. cat.) (Rolandseck: Bahnhof Rolandseck, 1979).

94 Quoted in Volker Kahmen, "Ernst Fuhrmann—Photographs of Plants," 47 (trans. Ciarán A. Mulhern).

95 For clear (and shocking) statements of Klages' anti-Semitism, see his *Rhythmen und Runen* (Leipzig: Barth, 1944). The complex nature of this anti-Semitism is indicated by the fact that his closest childhood friend was the German-Jewish philosopher Theodor Lessing and his intellectual mentor and close friend was the Hungarian-Jewish philosopher Menyhért (Melchior) Palágyi. Given that his second wife, Annie Francé Harrar was half-Jewish, it is not surprising that Francé's writings reveal philo-Semitic rather than anti-Semitic tendencies despite the fact that some of his writings were attractive to some Nazis, and that late

in life (probably for existential reasons) he joined the National Socialist Party. I spoke on "Raoul Francé and National Socialism: A Problematic Relationship" at the Fifth International Congress of Hungarian Studies, held at Jyväskylä, Finland, in August 2002, and have plans to publish this paper.

96 See his critique of Spengler's idea of the "Decline of the West": Raoul Francé, *Die Kultur von Morgen: Ein Buch der Erkenntnis und der Gesundung* (Dresden: Reissner, 1922), 139. See Oswald Spengler, *The Decline of the West. Form and Actuality* (1918), trans. Charles Francis Atkinson (New York: Alfred A. Knopf, 1927). Though he criticized it in many respects, Francé considered Spengler's *Der Untergang des Abendlandes* to be important because of its attempt to found a "biologisches Geschichtwissenschaft" (Francé, *Zoesis*, 21–23). On Spengler's critique of technology, see Kluge, *Wissenschaft, Natur, Technik*, Part 1.

97 Francé, *Die Pflanze als Erfinder* (Stuttgart: Kosmos, 1920), 72. Interestingly—and tellingly—enough Francé does not discuss Klages in his books; they must have seen each other as rivals. On Spengler's position concerning technology as a "Faustian" pact, see Ingeborg Güssow, "Kunst und Technik in den 20er Jahren," in Helmut Friedel, ed., *Kunst und Technik in den 20er Jahren: Neue Sachlichkeit und Gegenständlicher Konstruktivismus* (Munich: Städtische Galerie im Lenbachhaus, 1980), 34. On Spengler, the conservative critique of technology in Weimar Germany, and its later confluence with National Socialism, see Kluge, *Gesellschaft, Natur, Technik*.

98 Ibid.

99 For an account of Francé's pioneering role in the development of biotechnology, what we would now refer to as "bionics" (one of the few areas in which a secondary literature has developed on him), see R.R. Roth, "The Foundation of Bionics," *Perspectives in Biology and Medicine* 26, no. 2 (Winter 1983): 229–42; and Robert Bud, *The Uses of Life: A History of Biotechnology* (Cambridge, MA: Cambridge University Press, 1995), 60–63. Note that Francé acknowledges Ernst Kapp as one of the forerunners of *Biotechnik*, though he criticizes him for having misguided the conception of *Biotechnik* towards the "metaphysical concept of organ projection" (Francé, *Bios. Die Gesetze der Welt* (Munich: Franz Hanfstaengl, 1921), vol. 2, 128). On Kapp, see Wünsche's chapter in this anthology (Chapter 6).

100 See Fellmann, *Lebensphilosophie*, 29–30.

101 Kropotkin's *Mutual Aid* was written in England as a series of articles between 1890 and 1896. On Kropotkin's importance to the emergence of the environmental movement, see Steven G. Marks, *How Russia Shaped the Modern World* (Princeton, NJ and Oxford: Princeton University Press, 2003): 54–56.

102 On this, see Kelly, *The Descent of Darwin*, Chapter 6 ("Social Darwinism and the Popularizers), and Bowler, *The Non-Darwinian Revolution*, Chapter 7 ("Social Darwinism").

103 Geddes and J. Arthur Thomson, Introduction to *Evolution* (London: Williams & Norgate, 1911), ix. Quoted in Wojtowicz, *Lewis Mumford*, 11.

104 B.T. Robinson quoted in Bramwell, *Ecology in the 20th Century*, 77–80. On Geddes and Kropotkin, see Volker M. Welter, "The Geddes Vision of the Region as City: Palestine as a 'Polis'," in Jeannine Fiedler, ed., *Social Utopias of the Twenties: Bauhaus, Kibbutz and the Dream of the New Man* (Dessau: Bauhaus Dessau Foundation and Tel Aviv: Friedrich-Ebert Foundation, 1995), 72–79. See also Stalley, ed., *Patrick Geddes*.

105 Thanks to David Haney for pointing out to me Fuhrmann's Nazi sympathies during the early 1930s.

106 Klages, "Mensch und Erde," in Klages, *Mensch und Erde. Elf Abhandlungen* (Stuttgart: Alfred Kröner, 1973), 10, 12.

107 John Claverley Cartney, web-page editor, *Rosenberg Contra Klages*. Excerpts from Alfred Rosenberg's address, "Gestalt und Leben" (1938), trans. Cartney. www.revilo-oliver.com/Writers/Klages/Rosenberg_contra_Klages.html (accessed November 3, 2002).

108 For a more detailed discussion of Bramwell's category, see Botar, *Prolegomena to the Study of Biomorphic Modernism*, Chapter 2.

109 Note that Francé referred mainly to a *Biozentrische Erkenntnistheorie* or Biocentric epistemology as the basis for what he referred to as *Objektive Philosophie*; see, for example, *Zoesis*, 10, *Die Welt als Erleben*, 11 and esp. 14. Note however, that he stated that he might as well have termed his *Objektive Philosophie* as *Biozentrische Philosophie*. Francé, *Die Welt als Erleben*, 17. He also referred to it simply as *Biozentrik*; see, for example, *Bios*, vol. 1, 31. In his *Wörterbuch der philosophichen Begriffe*, Johannes Hoffmeister cites only the publications of Francé and Klages in his entry on "biozentrisch" (2nd ed. Hamburg: Felix Meiner, 1955), 128, although there was at least one other author Rudolf Goldscheid, who employed the term "biozentrische Weltanschauung" as early as 1911 in his *Höherenentwicklung und Menschenökonomie. Grundlegung der Sozialbiologie* (Leipzig: Werner Klinkhardt, 1911), 659ff.

110 Another way to conceptualize this phenomenon is to think in terms of Wittgenstein's "open set" theory.

111 See Ernst Hoferichter, "Ein Erforscher und Künder des Lebens," in Herbert Hönel, ed., *Ludwig Klages. Erforscher und Künder des Lebens. Festschrift zum 75. Geburtstage des Philosophen am 10 Dez. 1947* (Linz: Ost Verlag für Belletristik und Wissenschaft, 1947), 17; and Konrad Eugster, "Anthropozentrisches und nichtanthropozentrisches Weltbild: Versuche zu Begründungen," *Hestia* (1990–91): 56–74.

112 Alfred North Whitehead, *Modes of Thought* (1938) (New York: The Free Press, 1968), 112. The cognate English form of *Biozentrik*, "biocentrism" has a history of usage: The 1933 edition of the *Oxford English Dictionary* defines "biocentric" as "treating life as a central fact," while in his introduction to Klages-disciple Hans Prinzhorn's study of the art of mentally disabled people, *Bildnerei der Geisteskranken*, James L. Foy writes that "Biocentrism provides an outlook on man through a new kind of recognition of man's intimate and inescapable kinship with, and dependence upon, the self-regulating animal, vegetable and inorganic worlds". William Little, et al., eds., *Shorter Oxford English Dictionary* (1933), 3rd ed. (Oxford: Clarendon Press, 1959), 180. James L. Foy, Introduction to Hans Prinzhorn, *Artistry of the Mentally Ill* [1922] (Berlin: Springer, 1972), X. Wolfgang Geinitz writes that, after his first visit to Klages late in 1920, Prinzhorn "then became a fanatical and uncompromising representative of Klages' biocentric *Lebenslehre*." Given the above discussion, it comes as no surprise that the dominant usage today in English is an environmentalist one, but one that is cognate with earlier uses. Thus, environmental ethicist Paul Taylor employs the term to refer to the view that "the living things of the natural world have a worth that they possess simply in virtue of their being members of the Earth's Community of Life," ideas which echo those of Francé and other Weimar Biocentric thinkers unknown to Taylor. See Taylor, *Respect for Nature*, Chapter 3:

"The Biocentric Outlook on Nature." For contemporary usage, see also Donald Worster, *Nature's Economy. A History of Ecological Ideas*, 2nd ed. (New York: Cambridge University Press, 1994).

113 Bramwell, *Ecology in the 20th Century*, 39.

114 Bramwell, *Ecology in the 20th Century*, 56 and Harrington, *Reenchanted Science*, 34–48. On von Uexküll's current popularity amoung bio-semioticians (as the founder of their field), see Kalevi Kull, "Biosemiotics in the Twentieth Century: A View From Biology," *Semiotica* 127, no. 1/4 (1999), 385–414; and among post-Modernists, see Sandford Kwinter, *Architects of Time: Toward a Theory of the Event in Modernist Culture* (Cambridge, MA: MIT Press, 2001), 135ff.

115 Francé, *Zoesis*, 58.

116 For a more detailed discussions of this topic, see Chapter 2 of Botar, *Prolegomena to the Study of Biomorphic Modernism*.

2

Rereading Bioromanticism

Monika Wucher

Among the life science-oriented conceptions of artistic practice put forward in early twentieth-century Europe, what the Hungarian critic Ernst (Ernő) Kállai (1890–1954)[1] termed *Bioromantik* [Bioromanticism] is one of the less self-explanatory. Tracing its development and context is useful as it does more than simply add another term to the roster of artistic concepts related to the era's variants of *Lebensphilosophie*;[2] it serves to elucidate an important moment in cultural history. The aim of this essay is to clarify the notion of *Bioromantik* and to contextualize it within Kállai's œuvre. Special attention will be paid to the role that Kállai's ideas played with respect to debates concerning modern art and culture in Germany during the 1920s and early 1930s.

Kállai introduced the term *Bioromantik* after he had been living in Germany for ten years, a decade during which he was intimately involved in discussions around the Constructivist art scene in Berlin, primarily in the circle of the Galerie der Sturm, and the Hungarian artistic immigrants' circle that included László Moholy-Nagy, László Péri and Alfréd Kemény (Durus). From these starting points, he pursued his interest in the question of how contemporary art and life were interrelated. Like many others of his time, he based his approach on an art that he saw as possessing the same principles as contemporary philosophical theories concerned with the life sciences which discerned these principles as operating in both nature and society. However, his specific approach of linking art and popular scientific knowledge presented an opportunity to mediate between ideologies, conflicts, and opposing standpoints. The search for a counterweight to the dominant forces is all the more evident in Kállai's work when it comes to the discussion of imbalances or of hegemonic claims in society and art. Because they were seen to be comparable structures shared by both art and nature, laws, processes, and forms provided the preconditions for the envisioned reconciliation. The three scenarios discussed here will not only demonstrate that Kállai's thinking was essentially a manner of processing knowledge about life, they provide insight into his specific interpretation of the characteristics of nature and above all into their strategic application in contemporary discussions. They are examples of the controversies that culminated in the concept of Bioromanticism at the beginning of the 1930s.

First scenario

During his early years of involvement with the Constructivist debates in Berlin, Kállai began to formulate the idea of a connection between modern life and art. His first attempt to articulate this kind of link terminologically resulted in the Hungarian expression *életkonstrukció* [lifeconstruction].[3] This neologism is one of several original linguistic inventions of the Hungarian Constructivist circle.[4] The new term represented the highest ambitions of art. The ideal of a "construction" was combined with the features of "life," a fusion that entailed artistic solutions not only for the aims of the Constructivists—achieving analytical consciousness, consideration of the quality of materials, economy in all aspects of work—but also for dealing with the many conditions that cannot initially be analyzed, organized, or directed.[5] Among them, Kállai mentioned "current events in the life of society" and sudden shifts towards politically revolutionary situations. To him, other forces that disrupted the work of "construction" were rooted in human psychology. It is the "imperfections and imponderables, tragic instincts and volitions"[6] of people that—aside from political incidents—provided wide-ranging arguments against the belief that art and society were exclusively a matter of engineering. Art that is capable of including such uncertainties would, "with respect to society," establish "a veritable lifeconstruction."[7]

Kállai's demand for completeness also addressed the differences between the relative standpoints of concurrent Constructivist ambitions. In his "Correction (to the attention of 'De Stijl')" of 1923, he once again argued for a complete *lifeconstruction*.[8] Coming from Leiden, where *De Stijl* was founded, Theo van Doesburg arrived in Germany at the end of 1920 with his journal in his luggage. As the representative of *De Stijl,* he first established personal contacts with the international art world in Berlin, the city which "de facto became to him a window to Central Europe."[9] His efforts met with a lot of interest from members of the Hungarian avant-garde. *Ma,* the periodical edited by Lajos Kassák for which Kállai wrote most of his Hungarian-language articles during those years, advertised *De Stijl*[10] and published writings by van Doesburg[11] as well as reproductions of his works. A collaborative project of *De Stijl* and *Ma* was to print the reports and declarations of participants of the 1. Kongress der Union internationaler fortschrittlicher Künstler [1st Congress of the Union of International Progressive Artists], held in Düsseldorf from 29 to 31 May 1922, as well as an additional statement by members of the *Ma* circle (including Kállai), who had been unable to send a representative to the conference.[12]

The result of this cooperation was that *De Stijl* "found a respectful understanding but no true sympathy" among the Hungarians.[13] Kállai might have attended van Doesburg's talk held in Berlin during the spring of 1922, or he might have read van Doesburg's two-part article "Der Wille zum Stil" [The will to style], based on that talk.[14] The topic must have been extraordinarily interesting to the Hungarian critic of Constructivism, since van Doesburg's subheading announced the "re-forming of life, art and technology." In the second part of his statement that placed *De Stijl,* as an epoch-making artistic movement, at the forefront of cultural development, van Doesburg elucidated how he saw a new unity of art and life: "The new intellectual understanding of art not only found the machine to be beautiful, but it immediately recognized its unlimited expressive possibilities in art."[15] According to this vision, art formed a bond with technology regarding aesthetics, production methods and their area of influence. Their combined efforts were meant to aid progress in achieving "independence from nature" on the broadest scale. Thus they fulfilled tasks such as "collectively tackling entire urban districts, skyscrapers and aeroplane stations." All this was introduced as the consequence of an otherwise unquestioned "need," "demand," or "general aspect of today's life."[16]

Kállai must have substantially disagreed with this vision. His reply proves that explanations such as van Doesburg's were the focal point of all contemporary tendencies covered by the term *Constructivism.*[17] Kállai's "Correction"[18] became a fundamental critique of any Constructivist art that claimed to correspond with something it asserted as a general determinant beyond human nature.

> The essence of art lies not in some ultimate truth that exists without reference to any kind of human consciousness and independently of concrete time and space, but in its usefulness for the study of life, in its power to set things in motion.[19]

he emphasized. As a consequence, he pointed out that psychological and biological factors would have a greater effect on art than supposed rationality and objectivity. Accordingly, his call for *lifeconstruction* was meant to relate artistic demands to the political and cultural circumstances of their time, to outline a counter-plan to their seemingly timeless validity. His reference to psychological and biological conditions allowed him to combine Constructivism with unpredictable factors that to him were arguments which supported his view that artistic constructions are dependent on their time—his own era having been one that Kállai perceived as being not merely dazzling and rational. As he articulated it, these artworks were rooted in "fleeting time, contingencies, doubts and catastrophes."[20]

Second scenario

Ideas of vitality played a decisive role in the question of how the life impetuses could be transferred—not only from nature to art, but also from the artwork to the recipient. In his early writings in Hungarian, Kállai had already coined another term, *életesség* [literally: life-likeness, a paraphrase of vitality], to ascribe to an artwork the qualities of *élet* [life].[21] These qualities contained opportunities to mediate between art and the general public. Accordingly, examinations of visual perception became a focus of attention in the mid-1920s. Due to the different ambitions of contemporary critics, however, the understanding of vital or life processes such as seeing and perceiving could easily develop into controversies about what would be the most relevant visual experiences.

What constituted relevant visual experiences had already been a problem for some time. In 1926, the German art historian Adolf Behne pointed out society's lack of interest in contemporary art. This caused him to directly address artists, especially painters, in an article he wrote for the Berlin monthly *Sozialistische Monatshefte*. Behne tried to explain the behavior of the general public. To him, the stimulation of an individual's sensory perception is clearly the result of physiological reactions. Interest from crowds of visitors expressed as curiosity or enthusiasm were psychological reflexes caused by intense stimulation from "life, vigour, activity."[22] In other words, public attention was considered to have its source in the laws of nature. In 1926—the year of Behne's article—aside from sports events, it was the Berlin Motor Show at Kaiserdamm, Berlin's exhibition center, that made the strongest impression of vitality on Behne. Accordingly, he gave the following advice:

> Frankly speaking, the creators of these automobiles and motors posit a new standard for artistic values. The artist has only one way to escape from his hopeless defensive actions. And that is to achieve an equally intense or even more intense vigour and vitality in works of art.[23]

Clearly Behne believed art to be based on psychological effects—on the influence of forms that, to him, promised energy, tension, verve, and potential.

Kállai intervened when Behne compared vitality with tension, suspense, raciness, and the like. In a later issue of *Sozialistische Monatshefte*, he wrote an article on the relevance of painting and new media, which made reference to Behne's statement.[24] His starting points were similar to Behne's: Kállai also assumed that visual perception, especially the visual curiosity of the general public, was based on *Triebkräfte* [driving forces]. He therefore thought that natural, physiological processes are responsible for the desire to see. He agreed that there are optical stimuli that appeal to human nature strongly.

The difference in the two critics' views related to the question of the role that spectacle had in society and the function of art within the vital processes of seeing. According to Behne, sensations were evoked by certain impressions most vividly when tension was given form. According to Kállai, there were *optische Erlebnistriebe* [forces of optical receptivity] that had to be stimulated in some way. But, instead of concentrating on which images and forms might satisfy the desire to see, he wrote about something he called *optische Erlebnisäquivalente* [optical equivalents of experiences]. By this he meant that the public searches for images that correspond most closely to its social and economic realities—and so these "optical equivalents" would inspire the greatest degree of interest. Unlike Behne, Kállai did not play painting off against other media to make his argument, however. In his view, the diverse visual art disciplines were all components of certain experiences of reality. It therefore seemed reasonable to him to see photography and film as providing the most compelling visual argument:

> Pictures already exist in which standardized, mechanized people, forced into restlessness by capitalistic working conditions, reach the fulfilment of their visual desires ... It is the photographs in the illustrated magazines, the splendid scenery in revues, and above all the sensations in cinemas that nowadays attract the main groups of perceivers.[25]

According to this understanding, there are no appealing pictures per se, but rather diverse social experiences that lead to corresponding visual preferences. The general public was characterized by Kállai as hunted, restless, and busy, forced into economic constraints, into commercialization and communication. To him, these factors left their marks on people's behavior and their way of looking at things. At the same time, these circumstances were responsible for contemporary society's hunger for spectacles. Floods of rapidly changing pictures, an abundance of contradictory moments, and long periods of tension in film revealed themselves as being in perfect accord with this media phenomenon.

Kállai's idea of a congruence between visual attractions and social reality became an even more significant issue during the years following. In some of his major articles, for example, he evaluated the fate of Bauhaus-inspired works. His point was that clever, business-minded fellow travelers had already exploited Bauhaus principles. But he also asked how this could have happened and found the main reason in tendencies that stylized formal elements of Bauhaus products, so that they could easily become symbols of a sophisticated life of luxury.[26] To Kállai, the magazine *Das neue Berlin* was an example of those undertakings that actively encouraged this boom:

> The exhibition of cold splendour is back again. It has just been rejuvenated, has exchanged the historical robe for a sort of ... raciness ... *Das neue Berlin* despises the swollen marble and stucco showiness of the "Wilhelmian" [*sic*!] public buildings and churches, but it revels in the hocus-pocus of megalomaniacal motion-picture palaces, department stores, automobile "salons" and gourmets' paradises with their shrieking advertisements.[27]

From Kállai's point of view, *Das neue Berlin* adapted to the prevailing political and economic realities rather than to the requirements of a more complete understanding of life which included not only its physiological state but also conditions even more complex, or those that were as yet unclear. Kállai's article "Kunst liegt auf Straße" [Art lies on street] is an imagined discussion with Behne about Berlin's new shopping streets.[28] What if the façades of the department stores, the shop windows with their displays, the billboards and neon signs, the fashionable dress of pedestrians, and the design of cars passing by really served as pioneering models for art? Behne, on the other hand, wrote in "Kunstausstellung Berlin" [Berlin Art Exhibition] about the modern shopping street as the most beautiful show on display, and one that is even offered for free.[29] To his mind, it taught the general public about modern design and creative principles in a way that art itself would never be capable of. To Kállai, the Kurfürstendamm was more an example of "commercial democracy's road of victory"—an avenue on which no attempt was made to face urgent social challenges such as unemployment, the housing shortage, corruption, the rise of National Socialism, and national rearmament.

The debate concerning visual perception had led to a standoff. Kállai did not suggest that the medium of film showed more vitality than did painting, as Behne had done with design and architecture. He saw the potential of art in the evolution of "righteous resistance against the mechanistic works of … capitalistic-utilitarian civilisation."[30] Behne had called for the cultivation of tension, in line with his understanding of vitality. Kállai demanded quite the reverse: the "reduction of tension"—as a necessary counterbalance to contemporary profit-orientated exertions. To him, this was an expression of vitality in tune with its time.

Third scenario

Around 1930, Kállai introduced another neologism. After having been concerned with the interrelation of art and life processes since the start of his critical practice, and having tested his arguments in debate, the new term *Bioromantik* was an attempt to update his viewpoint against the background of intensifying struggles, not the least in the sphere of art. He must have been aware that his *Wortgebilde* could be misunderstood, or was at least open to mockery.[31] Nevertheless, it was the right term for him to "lead the intellect … to the primary sources and basic drives of life,"[32] a strategy to activate potentials that in his view comprised art's actual reserves.

As in *lifeconstruction*, the components of the new term referred to nature and art. However, *Bioromantik* had undergone significant modifications: its foci had shifted towards scientific ambitions on the one hand and genealogical or historic perspectives on the other. Employing *Romantik*, Kállai made reference to a venerable art historical category to which he linked some contemporary art: "One must go far back in the history of art, to Caspar David Friedrich and Blechen and to the Old Masters, before one finds works with a similarly deep sense of nature and harmony,"[33] he pointed out in his first article in *Forum*, the German- and Hungarian-language art and architecture journal published in Bratislava, a few months before he wrote about "Bioromanticism" in the same magazine. On the other hand, the *Bio* component of the new term realigned a discussion that had previously focused on contemporary mass perception and society, towards natural scientific models such as biochemistry[34] and biology. In fact, in Kállai's article "Bioromantik"[35] the reader may detect a couple of concrete scientific discoveries of the era.

The strongest hints are contained in the many remarks connected to visualization and research-derived imagery such as scientific illustrations, photography or film. In particular, the text draws on microbiological and medical images by describing "the objectivity of aquatic animals and plants,"[36] "the physiognomies of spermatozoons, hili and ovaries,"[37] "primitive cell formations and the activity of hidden organs,"[38] all this in analogy to abstract and Surrealist artworks. When Kállai stressed the patterns of motion in these visualizations, when he was attracted by "spontaneous, meaningful-rhythmic mobility,"[39] he was clearly making reference to scientific films in particular. How popular such motion pictures were—not least thanks to the *Kulturfilm* genre in contemporary German cinema—may be ascertained from Kállai's own reviews in the "Bewegungskunst" [motion art] section of *Sozialistische Monatshefte*. Between 1930 and 1933, he was the editor of this section[40] in which he briefly but enthusiastically reviewed films such as those made by the French scientific filmmaker Jean Painlevé, screened at Berlin's Urania cinema in the spring of 1930.[41] While Kállai did not name the films he had seen, they were more than likely part of Painlevé's more popular œuvre, produced in parallel to his scientific films. By the time of the Berlin screening, short films such as *La Pieuvre* [The Octopus], *L'Oursin* [The Sea Urchin], or *Hyas et sténorinques* [Hyas and Stenorhynchus] were his most popular productions.[42]

Though not immediately mirrored in any of Kállai's articles before his return from Germany to Hungary,[43] further exposure to scientific films corroborated his art-philosophical approach to life sciences. At the time of his return, he had been working on the subject of Bioromanticism for more than two years,[44] and he had just published his article on the subject. Of this he later wrote that he "had created the new term to signify the common intellectual perspective and mental shift revealed in the various tendencies of modern painting and sculpture."[45] With these advanced ideas in mind, late in 1932 he attended a presentation of microscope and X-ray films by the prominent immunologist Wilhelm Kolle.[46] Kállai paid particular attention to the analogies suggested by the motion and formations of cells and organs depicted in the films. Recalling the experience years later, he emphasized that "the optical similarity" between the pulsating movements in the live cultures and the streets of big cities, for example, "was startling enough."[47] From there it was a short leap to include artworks in the structural comparison.

Another scientific source for Kállai was the endocrinologist Selmar Aschheim's demonstration of sex hormone in fossilized plants. It was in a little-known article on the former Bauhaus student Fritz Winter that Kállai first used the metaphor of "coal and seed conjoining"[48] in order to allude to the painter's symbolic exploration of subterranean spheres. He later returned to this particular image of a correlation between inorganic and germinating, organic nature, when he reviewed one of Winter's works in his essay "Zeichen und Bilder" [Signs and Images].[49] In this text, he argued that the sign which the picture represented was in fact a "collective sign of life" which opened up amazing perspectives on interconnections in nature:

> *Coal and seed join together*. Whoever denies the existential meaning of such artistic fantasies will maybe learn a thing or two when they hear that a researcher has unmistakably identified the same sex hormone in human, animal, and vegetative organisms as in coal. What awesome expanses of space and time, what a fantastic interweaving of the being and fate of terrestrial life crowds together in this scientific perception![50]

Only a few newspaper clippings kept by Kállai reveal that the coal-and-seed metaphor with its artistic dimensions concerning correlations in nature goes back to Aschheim's sensational research.[51]

It is necessary to keep in mind that contemporary scientific activities such as the examples identified here were incorporated into the "bio" concept not because natural sciences were the chief concern of Kállai and his artistic circles. Nor was it solely a matter of unguessed-at philosophical and aesthetic dimensions opening up in the realms of research, particularly regarding the production of scientific images. Despite all his enthusiasm, the art critic was aware that his Bioromanticism was a retreat and a refuge. He explained it as an attempt "to go back to the last remaining reserves and reservoirs of power."[52] But what exactly was the threat to which Bioromanticism reacted? Some of the artworks Kállai spoke of were seen by him as plain representations of the current dangers art had to face. For example, Hans Arp's reliefs were to him "signs of the purest metaphysical angst, of the personality's fear for its intellectual room to maneuver given that it has been reduced to the absolute minimum and fatally engulfed by the masses."[53]

When the conception of Bioromanticism assumed clear outlines, its borrowing from life processes was more than a search for persuasive arguments against dominant economic and hegemonic forces. The "new organicism"[54] was meant to facilitate the formation of a counterweight to these developments. Therefore, its greatest opportunities were seen in the potential to provide a common ground for the fragmented and isolated contemporary art community. The vision was that a united, collective power of art could grow on these foundations. In fact, Kállai directed most of his energy towards bringing stylistically opposed art tendencies together under one roof. His main attempts were the exhibitions "Vision und Formgesetz" [Vision and the Law of Form] which he organized at the Galerie Ferdinand Möller in Berlin,[55] and "Kunst und Wirklichkeit" [Art and Reality] which he proposed to the Leipzig art gallery, though the project remained unrealized.[56] His writings and lectures about "Zeichen und Bilder" [Signs and images][57] in particular came out firmly in favor of an art unified by knowledge about life.

This common knowledge was meant to help face the demands made on art by economics and technology, by political parties, and by the general public. If the deadly constrictions of art Kállai spoke of were not just the rhetoric of an eloquent art critic, if both contemporary rejection and utilization of art resulted in angst, the meaning of *Bioromatik* as a refuge is all the more noteworthy. Around 1930, threat is tangible in Kállai's texts. He described his considerations concerning art's limited role in society: "Art must be a compliant and inexpensive stooge of the immediate everyday social practices and of their emergency decrees. Utilitarian art with a registered syndicate stamp or trademark."[58] He warned about the "reasons for conflict which … accumulate and will let us stumble with our eyes wide open into new world wars."[59] He provided no concrete example that illustrated the reasons for this atmosphere of threat, however.

Nevertheless, it is a remarkable coincidence that the formulation of *Bioromatik* paralleled Kállai's consideration of *gesellschaftsfremd* [alien to society][60] as a term of reproach against art.[61] In fact, the "bio" concept can be understood as the critic's defense against such accusations—an "antidote"[62] as he referred to the action of psychological-biological connotations in art. There were a few opportunities to test the effectiveness of this defense. In November 1932, an exhibition of the Nassauischer Kunstverein opened at the Neues Museum in Wiesbaden, which, according to a contemporary newspaper review, had received its motto from the title of Ernst Kállai's opening lecture and the "book on modern art named 'Zeichen und Bilder' he had written."[63] The press response to the exhibition was mixed. To one critic of the *Wiesbadener Zeitung*, the artworks on show were "either caricature or abstract distortion and violation." And he continued by posing the question "is this really meant to be artistic expression of our time?"[64] An even stronger reproach of *Gesellschaftsfremdheit* [isolation from society] met the exhibition from the critic of the *Essener Anzeiger* after it had traveled to the Folkwang Museum in Essen in February 1933:

> Where is the abstract art of 1932/33 heading? From pedantic, cubic geometry it has turned into a blob-like miasma. Its spirit spreads out like a coloured stew. Minor borrowings from much-maligned Nature have to help give the concoction a face … For years, positive art criticism has never tired of pointing out the lack of contact this "art" has with the people. What is on display here as "Zeichen und Bilder" is no less than an … isolation cell of artistic thinking.[65]

In Germany at the beginning of the 1930s, modern life sciences and Kállai's explanations were apparently not enough to legitimize the artistic tendencies presented in "Zeichen und Bilder."

Notes

For his thorough proofreading I wish to thank Jonathan Long, Berlin.

1 For biographical details see Éva Forgács, "Bevezető", in Ernő Kállai, *Művészet veszélyes csillagzat alatt. Válogatott cikkek, tanulmányok* (Budapest: Corvina Kiadó, 1981), 9–35; Tanja Frank, "Nachwort", in Ernst Kállai, *Vision und Formgesetz. Aufsätze über Kunst und Künstler von 1921 bis 1933* (Leipzig, Weimar: Gustav Kiepenheuer Verlag, 1986), 251–73; Csilla Markója, "Nachwort", in Ernst Kállai, *Schriften in deutscher Sprache, 1920–1925*, vol. 2 of *Gesammelte Werke/Összegyüjtött írások* (Budapest: Argumentum Kiadó and MTA Művészettörténeti Kutató Intézet [1999]), 169–77.

2 An idea of the number of attempts to "reorganize life and art" as an inseparable whole in German, other European, and American art communities since the turn of the twentieth century is given in Kai Buchholz et al., eds., *Die Lebensreform. Entwürfe zur Neugestaltung von Leben und Kunst um 1900*, vols. 1 and 2 (Darmstadt: Haeusser-Media/Verlag Häusser and Institut Mathildenhöhe Darmstadt, 2001).

3 Ernő Kállai, "A konstruktív művészet társadalmi és szellemi távlatai," *Ma* 7, no. 8 (1922): 59; and Ernő Kállai, "Korrekturát (a 'De Styl' figyelmébe)," *Ma* 8, nos. 9–10 (1923): 16. Reprinted in Ernő Kállai, *Magyar nyelvű cikkek, tanulmányok, 1912–1925*, ed. Árpád Tímár, vol. 1 of *Összegyüjtött írások/Gesammelte Werke* (Budapest: Argumentum Kiadó and MTA Művészettörténeti Kutató Intézet, 1999), 40 and 63.

4 Another example is the term *képarchitektúra* which was used by the Hungarian avant-garde figure Lajos Kassák. Regarding this concept, Éva Forgács claimed that its translation should also mirror the original usage and therefore suggests "picturearchitecture." See Éva Forgács, "Between Cultures. Hungarian Concepts of Constructivism", in Timothy O. Benson, ed., *Central European Avant-Gardes: Exchange and Transformation, 1910–1930* (exhib. cat., Los Angeles County Museum of Art, Haus der Kunst Munich, Martin-Gropius-Bau Berlin) (Cambridge, MA: The MIT Press, 2002), 163.

5 See Kállai's description of these perspectives, in Kállai, "Korrekturát (a 'De Styl' figyelmébe)."

6 Ibid.

7 Ibid. Éva Forgács's argument in "Between Cultures" concerning the creation of "picturearchitecture" can support "lifeconstruction" as well. Other translations such as "life-construct" (see *Between Worlds. A Sourcebook of Central European Avant-Gardes, 1910–1930*, ed. Timothy O. Benson and Éva Forgács (Cambridge, MA: The MIT Press, 2002), 443) do not take the conceptual nature of the original term *életkonstrukció* into account.

8 Kállai, "Korrekturát (a 'De Styl' figyelmébe)."

9 Sjarel Ex, "'De Stijl' und Deutschland 1918–1922. Die ersten Kontakte", in Bernd Finkeldey et al., eds., *Konstruktivistische Internationale, 1922–1927. Utopien für eine europäische Kultur* (exhib. cat. Kunstsammlung Nordrhein-Westfalen, Düsseldorf, et al.) (Stuttgart: Verlag Gerd Hatje, 1992), 77.

10 See *Ma* 8, no. 1 (1922), and *Ma* 9, no. 1 (1923).

11 Theo van Doesburg, "Az építészet mint szintetikus művészet," *Ma* 7, no. 7 (1922): 35 and Theo van Doesburg, "Az ideális esztétikától a materiális megvalósítás felé," *Ma* 9, no. 1 (1923): [4–5].

12 See the participants' reports and declarations published in German with a Dutch introduction, *De Stijl* 5, no. 4 (1922): 49–64, and the statement of *Ma*, *De Stijl* 5, no. 8 (1922): 125–28 (German repr. in Finkeldey et al., *Konstruktivistische Internationale, 1922–1927*, 300–306). The compilation was published and introduced in Hungarian under the headline "A haladó művészek első nemzetközi kongresszusa," *Ma* 7, no. 8 (1922): 61–64. However, diverging views appear from these documents. *Ma*'s "Statement" varies in the two publications and, regarding its attitude, it decisively differs from the "Report of the Dutch Stijl group." A critical comparison of these texts is still lacking, although the differences have been addressed by Júlia Szabó, *A magyar aktivizmus művészete 1915–1927* (Budapest: Corvina Kiadó, 1981), 125–27, and Krisztina Passuth,

"Ungarische Künstler und die Konstruktivistische Internationale", in Finkeldey et al., *Konstruktivistische Internationale, 1922–1927*, 240.

13 Mariann Gergely, "The Dutch De Stijl Group and Hungary," in *De Stijl csoport 1917–1931* (exhib. cat. Magyar Nemzeti Galéria) (Budapest 1986), n.p.

14 Theo van Doesburg, "Der Wille zum Stil (Neugestaltung von Leben, Kunst und Technik)," *De Stijl* 5, no. 2 (1922): 23–32, and 5, no. 3 (1922): 33–41.

15 "Die neue geistige Kunstauffassung hat nicht nur die Maschine als Schönheit empfunden, sondern sie hat ihre unendlichen Ausdrucksmöglichkeiten für die Kunst sofort anerkannt." (Van Doesburg, "Der Wille zum Stil," 34; trans. MW).

16 Ibid.

17 Depending on the context, van Doesburg counted himself among the Constructivists. See his signature under "Erklärung", the statement by the Internationale Fraktion der Konstruktivisten [International Faction of Constructivists], *De Stijl* 5, no. 4 (1922): 64 (repr. in Finkeldey et al. *Konstruktivistische Internationale, 1922–1927*, 304).

18 Kállai, "Korrekturát (a 'De Styl' figyelmébe)."

19 "A művészet lényege nem egy minden emberi tudatbeli vonatkozástól függetlenül is megálló, konkrét időhöz és térhez nem kötött igazságban, hanem élettani használhatóságában, lendítő erejében rejlik." (Kállai, "Korrekturát (a 'De Styl' figyelmébe)," 14; trans. MW).

20 Kállai, "Korrekturát (a 'De Styl' figyelmébe)," 16.

21 In his early article "Új művészet," *Ma* 6, no. 8 (1921): 115 (repr. *Magyar nyelvű cikkek*, 12), Kállai connected *életesség* to an "opening up to cosmic spheres" in Albert Gleize's pictures. In "A kubizmus és a jövendő művészet," *Ma* 7, no. 2 (1922): 27 (repr. *Magyar nyelvű cikkek*, 21), *életesség* is explained in the paintings of Fernand Léger as "irrestible dynamism". In an article on Ivan Puni, the *életesség* of the artist's work is described as a "psychic" quality sprung from the "problematic human character." See Ernő Kállai, "Iwan Puni," *Ma* 7, no. 3 (1922): 35 (repr. *Magyar nyelvű cikkek*, 29). To László Moholy-Nagy's art Kállai attributed an "almost organic vitality." See Péter Mátyás [Ernő Kállai], "Moholy-Nagy," *Ma* 6, no. 9 (1921): 119 (repr. *Magyar nyelvű cikkek*, 15). For a detailed analysis of the topos in relation to Moholy-Nagy's work of the years 1920 to 1925, see Monika Wucher, "Attribute des Konstruktivismus", in Hubertus Gaßner et al., eds., *Die Konstruktion der Utopie. Ästhetische Avantgarde und politische Utopie in den 20er Jahren* (Marburg: Jonas Verlag, 1992), 194–95.

22 Adolf Behne, "Worin besteht die Not der Künstler?," *Sozialistische Monatshefte* 32, no. 1 (1926): 37.

23 Ibid. (trans. MW).

24 Ernst Kállai, "Malerei und Film," *Sozialistische Monatshefte* 32, no. 3 (1926): 164–68. Reprinted in Monika Wucher, ed., *Ernst Kállai. Schriften in deutscher Sprache, 1926–1930*, vol. 4 of *Gesammelte Werke/Összegyüjtött írások* [hereafter GW 4] (Budapest: Argumentum Kiadó and MTA Művészettörténeti Kutató Intézet, 2003), 9–14.

25 Kállai, "Malerei und Film," 165 (trans. MW).

26 Ernst Kállai, "Zehn Jahre Bauhaus," *Die Weltbühne* 26, no. 4 (1930): 135–39 (repr. GW 4, 153–58).

27 Kállai, "Zehn Jahre Bauhaus," 135 (trans. in Benson and Forgács, *Between Worlds*, 637). As Behne was the editor of *Das neue Berlin*—though indirectly—his debate with Behne is being reopened here.

28 Ernst Kállai, "Kunst liegt auf Straße, lächelt Dr. Behne an. Das neue Berlin, happy-end, keep smiling," *Das Kunstblatt*, 13 (1929) 12: 373–74 (repr. GW 4, 147–49).

29 Adolf Behne, "Kunstausstellung Berlin," *Das neue Berlin*, 1 (1929) 8: 150–52; repr. in Haila Ochs, ed., *Adolf Behne. Architekturkritik in der Zeit und über die Zeit hinaus, Texte 1913–1946* (Basel et al.: Birkhäuser Verlag, 1994), 153–55.

30 Kállai, "Malerei und Film," 168 (trans. MW).

31 "Witzigen Gedankensprüngen zu 'Biochemie', 'Biomalz' und ähnlichem sei hiermit von vorneherein jeder Spielraum gern gegönnt." Ernst Kállai, "Bioromantik," *Forum. Zeitschrift für Kunst, Bau und Einrichtung* [Bratislava] 2, no. 10 (1932): 271. Reprinted in Monika Wucher et al., eds., *Ernst Kállai. Schriften in deutscher Sprache, 1931–1937*, vol. 5 of *Gesammelte Werke/Összegyüjtött írások* [hereafter GW 5] (Budapest: Argumentum Kiadó and MTA Művészettörténeti Kutató Intézet, 2006). A shorter version of this article was published in *Sozialistische Monatshefte* 39, no. 1 (1933): 46–50. Another version was published in *Pester Lloyd* [Budapest], 15 November 1939, 3–4.

32 Kállai, "Bioromantik," 271 (see note 31).

33 "Man muß weit zurückgehen in der Geschichte der Kunst, zu Caspar David Friedrich und Blechen und den alten Meistern, bis man Werke einer gleich tiefen Naturempfindung und Harmonie finden kann." See Ernst Kállai, "Kunst und Technik," *Forum. Zeitschrift für Kunst, Bau und Einrichtung* [Bratislava] 2, no. 7 (1932): 187; trans. MW. A slightly different version of this article was published in *Kölnische Zeitung*, 9 February 1932; repr. GW 5). An exemplary case illustrating Kállai's manner of reinforcing contemporary art with Romanticism is his article on Lyonel Feininger: "Romantik heute wie vor hundert Jahren," *Die neue Linie*, 3, no. 12 (1932): 22–23 (repr. GW 5).

34 Kállai mentioned this example in his essay "Zeichen und Bilder II," *Forum. Zeitschrift für Kunst, Bau und Einrichtung* [Bratislava] 3, no. 5 (1933): 150 (repr. GW 5).

35 Kállai, "Bioromantik."

36 Ibid., 272.

37 Ibid., 273.

38 Ibid.

39 Ibid.

40 For an overview of Kállai's "Bewegungskunst" reviews, see their complete reprint (see GW 4 and GW 5).

41 Ernst Kállai, "Film," *Sozialistische Monatshefte* 36, no. 5 (1930): 510 (repr. GW 4, 175). On the same page, Kállai commended an Ufa production, a short film entitled "Das Geheimnis der Eischale" [The Secret of the Eggshell], "with beautiful scientific shots."

42 See Andy Masaki Bellows and Marina McDougall, eds., with Brigitte Berg, *Science is Fiction. The Films of Jean Painlevé* (Cambridge, MA: The MIT Press and San Francisco, CA: Brico Press 2000).

43 Kállai returned to Budapest in the summer of 1935.

44 Kállai had prepared a talk on Bioromanticism as early as 1930. In a letter to Naum Gabo, he mentioned two lectures he was dealing with: "'Gesellschaftsfremde Kunst' und 'Bioromantik'". Although the letter is undated, it must have been written during the first half of 1930, because at that time Kállai was living in Berlin-Steglitz, Bismarckstraße, the address given in the letter (Bauhaus Archiv, Berlin, inv. no. 3653/16).

45 "Bióromantika: … ezt az új fogalmat … magam alkottam, hogy vele a modern festészet és szobrászat különböző irányaiban mutatkozó, közös szellemi távlatot, lelki célzatot megjelöljem." See Ernő Kállai, *A természet rejtett arca* (Budapest: Misztótfalusi, 1947), 15; trans. MW.

46 For a detailed examination of Kállai's and Kolle's contact, see Oliver A.I. Botar, "Ernő Kállai and Wilhelm Kolle. Science and Art in Weimar Germany," *Acta Historiae Artium Academiae Scientiarum Hungaricae* 37 (1994–95): 273–77.

47 Ernő Kállai, *A természet rejtett arca*, 13; trans. MW. A German version of the passage concerning the experience of the films from Kolle's research institute in Frankfurt am Main is included in Kállai's typescript for a book on "Zeichen und Bilder." The fragment of the typescript is preserved in the Kállai file at the Archive of the Institute of Art History, Hungarian Academy of Sciences, Budapest, inv. no. MTA-MKI-C-I-11/589, 1–16.

48 Ernst Kállai, "Zu den Arbeiten von Fritz Winter," *Die neue Stadt*, May 1932, 43 (repr. GW 5).

49 Kállai, "Zeichen und Bilder II."

50 "*Kohle und Samen verbinden sich.* Wer den existenziellen Sinn solcher Künstlerphantasien bestreitet, wird vielleicht doch eines besseren belehrt, wenn er hört, daß ein Forscher das gleiche Geschlechtshormon im menschlichen, tierischen, pflanzlichen Organismus—und in der Steinkohle einwandfrei festgestellt hat. Welch ungeheure Weite von Räumen und Zeiten, welch phantastische Verflechtung von Wesen und Schicksalen des Erdenlebens drängt sich in dieser wissenschaftlichen Erkenntnis zusammen!" (Kállai, "Zeichen und Bilder II," 150; trans. MW).

51 The clippings are preserved in the Kállai file at the Archive of the Institute of Art History, Hungarian Academy of Sciences, Budapest, inv. no. MTA-MKI-C-I-11/uncatalogued material. There is one article from a Berlin daily (according to the advertisements on the back) entitled "Der Motor der Sexualfunktionen" which emphasized that the hormone "can be found not only in animal organisms, but also in plants. Aschheim was able to prove this even in peat, coal and petroleum." (no source, no date; trans. MW). Among the clippings, a similar reference is given in an article by C.O., "Sexualhormone der Pflanzen," *Unterhaltungsblatt der Vossischen Zeitung*, 14 July 1933.

52 Kállai, "Bioromantik," 274.

53 "[Arps Bilder] sind Zeichen der nacktesten metaphysischen Daseinsangst. Es ist die geistige Raumangst, der bis aufs letzte eingeschrumpften, von der Masse tötlich umstellten Persönlichkeit." (Kállai, "Bioromantik," 273; trans. MW).

54 Ernst Kállai, "Malerei und Film," *Die Weltbühne* 27, no. 22 (1931): 807 (repr. GW 5).

55 Ernst Kállai, "Vision und Formgesetz," *Blätter der Galerie Ferdinand Möller* 8 (1930); 1–10 (repr. GW 4).

56 Ernst Kállai, "Ideen- und Organisationsentwurf zu einer internationalen Ausstellung moderner Kunst im Leipziger Museum", typescript, dated 13 May 1931. The 13-page typescript is preserved in the Kállai file at the Archive of the Institute of Art History, Hungarian Academy of Sciences, Budapest, inv. no. MTA-MKI-C-I-11/573.1–13. A first analysis of the exhibition draft was formulated by Gábor Pataki, "Technoromantik," in Gaßner et al., eds., *Die Konstruktion der Utopie*, 203–8.

57 Ernst Kállai, "Zeichen und Bilder," *Die Weltbühne* 28, no. 38 (1932): 444–45 (repr. GW 5); Ernst Kállai, "Zeichen und Bilder," *Forum* 3, no 4/5 (1933): 122–23, 150–51 (see note 34); and Ernst Kállai, "Zeichen und Bilder," *Pester Lloyd* [Budapest], 6 March 1938. "Zeichen und Bilder" was also the topic of a book project of which parts are preserved at the Archive of the Institute of Art History, Hungarian Academy of Sciences, Budapest (see note 47). A first attempt to frame the project was undertaken by Gábor Pataki, "'Zeichen und Bilder'. Ein Rekonstruktionsversuch des letzten theoretischen Werks von Kállai," *Acta Historiae Artium Academiae Scientiarum Hungaricae*, 36 (1993): 232–35.

58 "Die Kunst hat ein fügsamer und billiger Handlanger der zunächstliegenden sozialen Tagespraxis und ihrer Notverordnungen zu sein. Eine Gebrauchskunst mit eingetragenem Zweckverbands- oder auch Warenzeichen." (Ernst Kállai, "Kunst und Wirklichkeit," *Sozialistische Monatshefte* 37, no. 10 (1931): 999, trans. MW; repr. GW 5).

59 Ernst Kállai, "Grenzen der Technik," *Die Weltbühne* 27, no. 14 (1931): 505 (repr. GW 5).

60 Kállai, "Bioromantik," 272.

61 See the two lectures he was working on in 1930 (see note 44).

62 Ernst Kállai, "Kunst und Technik," *Sozialistische Monatshefte* 37, no. 11 (1931): 1102 (repr. GW 5).

63 W.W., "Nassauischer Kunstverein," *Wiesbadener Tagblatt*, 14 November 1932, 4. This report suggests that Kállai's book "Zeichen und Bilder" already existed at least in manuscript form. However, it remained a publishing project throughout his life (see note 57).

64 [No author], "Zeichen und Bilder," *Wiesbadener Zeitung—Rheinischer Kurier*, 17 November 1932, [4].

65 "Aber wohin geht die abstrakte Malerei von 1932/33? ... Sie verwandelt sich aus pedantischer Geometrie des Kubischen in quallige Miasmen. Der Geist läuft wie ein farbiger Brei auseinander. Kleine Anleihen bei der geschmähten Natur müssen aushelfen, dem Elaborat ein Gesicht zu sichern ... Seit Jahren wird die positive Kunstkritik nicht müde, auf den mangelnden Kontakt solcher 'Kunst' mit dem Volk hinzuweisen. Was man hier als 'Zeichen und Bilder' zeigt, ist gerade eine artistische Isolierzelle des künstlerischen Denkens ..." ("Abstraktion und Einordnung," *Essener Anzeiger*, 26 February 1933; trans. MW).

3

The naming of Biomorphism

Jennifer Mundy

Styles are not usually defined in a strictly logical way. As with languages, the definition indicates the time and place of a style or its author, or the historical relation to other styles, rather than its peculiar features. The characteristics of style vary continuously …

(Meyer Schapiro, 1966)[1]

Biomorphism is a term that sits uneasily in the lexicon of modern art movements. There was no biomorphist school or movement, no biomorphist manifesto and no obvious leader or spokesman for the trend. The meaning of the term is not widely agreed upon and the various interpretations of it that exist tend to reflect particular national critical and literary traditions. Although the term has a certain resonance, for example, in Germany due to its evocation of Romantic and Vitalist traditions strongly rooted in Germanic philosophy, it has almost no currency in French criticism to this day. Invented in 1935 by an Englishman to describe a trend in contemporary Continental art, and then given fresh impetus by an American, the style label was very much the product of an Anglo-Saxon perspective on international art, a perspective that was, at the very least, one step removed from the events, personalities and critical traditions of the Parisian avant-garde it sought to label. Was this perspective, however, correct or, more aptly expressed, a *useful* way of describing the fluid, organic shapes in the art of such diverse figures as the Russian pioneer of abstraction Wassily Kandinsky, the Swiss abstract artist Hans Arp, the Catalan Joan Miró who joined the Surrealist movement in 1925, the French Surrealist Yves Tanguy, and the British sculptor Henry Moore who self-consciously straddled abstraction and Surrealism? What were the gains and what were the losses in this way of picturing the interwar art scene? And what is involved in our use of this term today?

In focusing on the origins and early use of the term biomorphism, this essay will underscore a salient but often forgotten truth about all such labels. In the accounts of the groups and movements that have structured so much writing on the history of art, the value and justification of art-isms often appear self-evident and immutably fixed. However, the naming of a style always reflects a particular response to issues of contemporary debate, a championing of one perspective upon these issues amid other possible views. The survival of that perspective within subsequent discussion is less evidence of its accuracy than of its persuasiveness and of its compatibility with the systems of thought and priorities brought to bear upon the writing of the history of art. Noting that style was not something tangible, the writer George Kubler once compared the "seeing" of style, or the acceptance of a significant relatedness of certain works of art, to seeing a rainbow: "It is a phenomenon of perception governed by the coincidence of certain physical conditions. We can see it only briefly while we pause between the sun and the rain and it vanishes when we go to the place where we thought we saw it."[2] This essay aims to trace the somewhat curious constellation of conditions that made it possible for the term to be coined and to suggest the reasons why the neologism has failed to win general acceptance within art history and art criticism.

Geoffrey Grigson: Between idea and emotion

A poet and friend of many of the leading artists of the day, Geoffrey Grigson (1905–85) introduced his concept of biomorphism in a short article called tellingly "Comment on England." This was published in January 1935 in the first issue of *Axis*, a magazine that aimed to create a new forum for discussion of the latest trends in modernist art. Generally favorable to abstraction, *Axis* nonetheless challenged some of the critical language surrounding the movement. Its young editor, Myfanwy Evans, began her introductory essay by stating plainly, "Abstract is an inadequate and misleading term;"[3] and she proceeded to analyze the ways it had been confused with simplification, generalization, mechanical imagery and the idea of progress. Her intention was not to slim down the range of works to which the term could properly be applied; she wanted, rather, to explore its many variations, "moving sometimes towards a suggestion of Surrealism, in Miró's work for instance, keeping traces of the object in Julio González' or Graham Nash's."[4]

Grigson began his article by criticizing geometric abstraction. It established an order on its material, he wrote, by withdrawing from life, by negating the evidence of the senses and emotions; its goal was to reduce everything to an "intellective type, to 'art itself'." Then, with a few swift steps, he outlined a new and individual vision of the potential of abstract art. Referring to anthropological discussion of the meaning of so-called "primitive" ornament, Grigson called for a new, vital type of abstraction that combined geometrical designs with the exercise of the memory and the emotions:

> Abstract art at this time needs (but actually and not only in fancy) to be bodied out in such a way; to be penetrated and possessed by a more varied affective and intellective content. Only so can it answer to the ideological and emotional complexity of the needs of human beings with their enlarged knowledge of the widened country of self.[5]

Grigson claimed that some younger artists were beginning to practice this type of affective abstraction: "abroad Picasso, Brancusi, Klee, Miró, Hélion; in England Wyndham Lewis and Henry Moore." Between the "new preraphaelitism" of the Surrealist group and the "unconscious nihilism" of abstract art, between the poles of representation and abstraction, between a rational and an emotional approach to art, lay an art permeated with life. He explained:

> Abstractions are of two kinds, geometric, the abstractions which lead to the inevitable death; and biomorphic. The biomorphic abstractions are the beginning of the next central phase in the progress of art. They exist between Mondrian and Dalí, between idea and emotion, between matter and mind, matter and life.[6]

In coining this new term, Grigson's purpose, it should be noted, was essentially polemical rather than descriptive; his eye was fixed on not what was, but what he felt should be, the direction of modern art. He predicted that this would be the main trend in future years. "The practice of painting and sculpture is gaining new rotundity of purpose and achievement," he wrote, and cited the words of the French painter Jean Hélion, "For the idea of element, brought too much forward, must be substituted the idea of plurality. For the idea of machine, must be substituted the idea of being."[7] However, Grigson could name only a handful of artists who were biomorphist; and he was not always consistent in his identification of what was biomorphist about their work. His notion of biomorphism was still very much an idea, and one that was only just beginning to make itself manifest in works of art.[8]

Grigson wrote more extensively about his likes and dislikes in an essay in a volume entitled *The Arts Today*, published later in 1935. Much of the essay is given over to a wide-ranging discussion of the principles of art and its formal language, under such headings as "Art, Is It?," "Abstraction—Creation," "Caves—Picasso," and "Puritans and Impure." Here Grigson revealed his very particular vision of the "virtue of synthesis, and the virtue of the necessary half-abstraction." He claimed that the current division of contemporary art into the two camps of opposed form and spiritual principles, abstraction and Surrealism, was inimical to the well being of art as a whole, and called for a "new synthesis of the two ways, the idealist way and the way of Surrealism, a resynthesising of intellect with emotion, of form with matter, of geometric with organic."[9]

In his battle against the new "puritanism" in avant-garde art, Geoffrey Grigson looked to the disciplines dealing with the study of man for evidence that subject matter played a crucial role in art. Rather than the "cold comfort" of an ordered, mechanical aesthetic, art, he felt, had to address what he described in his unpublished notebooks of the 1930s as the "discomfort of the half-known caves of the mind." These notebooks, in which he mapped out arguments and copied sections of texts he admired, show him to have studied specialist volumes on modern literature, psychology, and anthropology. In looking to these particular fields in his attempt to make sense of new trends in the arts, Grigson was by no means unusual. By the mid-1930s, the main lines of the debate about the aesthetic status of "savage" art, prehistoric art, and child art, and the links between these types of art and avant-garde work, were well established. Grigson went one step further than most contemporary critics, however, in drawing direct comparisons between contemporary art and a quite specific type of prehistoric art. The identity of the trend he labeled biomorphism was bound up in his understanding of the stages of development in the very earliest art; and to understand this it is necessary to trace the origins of the term itself.

The prehistory of biomorphism

The terms "biomorph" and "biomorphic" were coined by Alfred Cort Haddon, a leading figure in the study of anthropology at Cambridge, in his book *Evolution in Art. As Illustrated by the Life-History of Designs* (1895). As the title suggests, Haddon applied to the study of primitive ornament a biologist's conception of the stages of life: he wrote about the development of particular designs as a record of early vitality, succeeded by a move towards complexity and maturity, followed by decline and decay. A biologist by training with a passion for classification, Haddon coined the word "biomorph" as an etymologically logical term for designs derived from an animate source. He explained it was to be a generic term for patterns related to men, animals, and plants, currently known as anthropomorphs, zoomorphs, and phyllomorphs:

> All three terms have references to living beings, hence the appropriateness of classing them under the general designation of "biomorph." The biomorph is the representation of anything living in contradistinction to the skeuomorph, which ... is the representation of anything made, or of the physicomorph which is the representation of an object or operation in the physical world.[10]

Through Haddon's book, the term "biomorph" entered the language of anthropology and prehistory as an uncontroversial, though not particularly common, term. Significantly, it was used during the 1910s and 1920s in reference to the mysterious petroglyphs found in the caves of the Mas d'Azil—and it was the discussion concerning the petroglyphs' symbolism that, as he made plain in *The Arts Today*, inspired Grigson to use the term.

In this book, Grigson acknowledged that he based his understanding of biomorphist art upon recent discussion of the meaning of designs on Azilian pebbles. He did not specify the source of his term, and cited only in this connection the writings of a British prehistorian, Miles Burkitt:

> The Azilian culture, regarded as a culture of decay, comes after the Magdalenian culture, and it produced instead of such magnificent work, only numbers of these pebbles painted with vital designs in red ochre. "The motive for painting these river pebbles", Mr. Miles Burkitt declares, "and their use is unknown," but I do not think

that any acute painter of our day would doubt that an essential motive in making them (whatever their "use") was an art-motive.[11]

However, in his volume *Our Early Ancestors*, published in 1926 and cited in a footnote by Grigson, Burkitt did not use the word "biomorphic." A more probable source was Hans Obermaier's standard work on the subject, *Fossil Man in Spain*, published in England in 1924, in which two types of markings on Azilian pebbles were discussed—one with "conventionalised human forms" and the other with "symbolic, biomorphic signs; that is to say, with totem pictures."[12] Echoing this formulation, Grigson noted that the designs on Azilian pebbles had been divided "by an anthropologist" into two classes: "designs produced by the more or less obvious abstraction of natural forms (such as the human figure) and 'biomorphic shapes'." He wrote of the "vital designs" found on Azilian pebbles:

They are paintings in which an organic-geometric tension is very well obtained. Many of their forms are almost certainly "degraded," as orthodox anthropologists would say, from organic forms which came nearer nature. Some forms are further from any originals, and these have been described as "biomorphic," which is no bad term for the paintings of Miró, Hélion, Erni and others, to distinguish them from the modern geometric abstractions and from rigid surrealism.[13]

Grigson alighted on this comparison of the schematic markings on Azilian pebbles and the forms of contemporary art partly because he noted the visual affinities between, on the one hand, the mesolithic dot and line symbols found painted on the stones and, on the other, the "hieroglyphs" in Miró's pictures. In this he was echoing a growing awareness among critics that Miró's imagery was related in spirit and form to prehistoric art. However, for Miró's work as a whole there are more obvious sources in prehistoric art—notably, the petroglyphs on the human figure found on cave walls in Spain—than this minor, and relatively obscure, type of art, if such it was, found on Azilian pebbles. The purpose of Grigson's comparison, however, was not primarily visual; rather, he had been struck by a parallel between the history of prehistoric art and the development of modern art in its shift away from representation towards a reduced form of mark-making:

Abstract art first, then figured art, then a new move to abstraction by tightening in on the forms of the figured art—that seems to have been the earliest course of things. The first abstract art may be compared with the extreme geometric abstractions of our own day, the great cave paintings with the masterpieces from Giotto to the last century bodied out in visual language, the half-abstract art, which followed the cave paintings, with Cubism, and with the new painting of such artists as Miró and Hélion which seems to be going back to figured forms through a new semi-abstraction.[14]

Prehistory offered parallels with modern art, Grigson thought, and also pointed to the importance of an emotional basis and ultimately realist basis for art in addressing man's psychological needs. However, though Grigson used the language of visual form, he was somewhat indifferent to the look of the art in question. For this reason, there were a number of anomalies in his list of biomorphist artists. Could Hélion's work really be placed in the same category as that of Moore's? Grigson fudged the issue. He noted that Hélion had recently abandoned the path of pure geometry and had moved towards an "ideographic" imagery which appeared more and more organic, he insisted, even if not *as* organic as other biomorphist artists. What was important for Grigson in the work of Hélion (and, indeed, in that of Brancusi and Wyndham Lewis, artists not nowadays seen as biomorphist) was its articulation of the idea of synthesis and balance. Indifferent to the visual aspect of art on anything other than on a metaphoric level, he had sought to define an attitude, and, ultimately, a set of aesthetic qualities. This relative lack of interest in the look of art, however, could not survive long within the predominantly formalist terms of reference of mainstream discussion of contemporary art.

Alfred Barr: Silhouette of the amoeba

The writings and adventurous exhibition program of Alfred Barr, director of the Museum of Modern Art in New York from 1929 to 1948 and director of collections thereafter, had an enormous impact on modern art history in America. Barr made his mark early in his career when he organized in 1935–36 two major survey exhibitions of recent art, *Cubism and Abstract Art* and *Fantastic Art, Dada and Surrealism*. Bringing to the American public an extraordinarily rich selection of works by the leading artists of the early twentieth century, these shows marked a turning point in perceptions of modern art. What had seemed difficult or outlandish was presented in these exhibitions as a logical development of certain long-standing trends; and even still active movements such as abstraction and Surrealism were presented as rooted in the past. With the comprehensiveness of the exhibitions, and the sheer clarity of the accompanying catalogues, Barr made an extraordinarily powerful contribution to the study of the history of what was very much contemporary art. Even Meyer Schapiro, a lecturer at Columbia University and critic of Barr's formalism, described the catalogue of *Cubism and Abstract Art* as "the best ... that we have in English on the movements now grouped as abstract art."[15]

It was in this catalogue that Barr elaborated his vision of "biomorphic abstraction." While Grigson had used the term "biomorphic" to describe the work of a handful of artists, and a complex, essentially polemical, understanding of the nature of art, Barr used it to describe one of the two main trends in non-figurative art: "The shape of the square," he wrote, "confronts the silhouette of the amoeba."[16]

Barr saw the work of artists such as Mondrian and Ben Nicholson, on the one hand, and, on the other, Arp and Moore, as the latest manifestation of a long-standing dualism of form and meaning in the history of modern art. In their dependence upon the forms of geometry and the processes of logic and calculation, artists such as Mondrian and Nicholson were heirs to the tradition of Seurat and Cézanne; while the current represented by the work of Arp and Moore had its source in the work of Gauguin, the Fauvists and German Expressionists. This second tradition, by contrast with the first, was, "intuitional and emotional rather than intellectual; organic or biomorphic rather than geometric in its forms; curvilinear rather than rectilinear, decorative rather than structural, and Romantic rather than classical in its exaltation of the mystical, the spontaneous, and the irrational."[17] Barr even predicted that biomorphist art would soon become the dominant trend in modern abstract art:

> At the risk of generalising about the very recent past, it seems fairly clear that the geometric tradition in abstract art ... is in the decline. Mondrian, the ascetic and steadfast champion of the rectangle, has been deserted by his most brilliant pupils, Hélion and Domela, who have introduced in their recent work various impurities such as varied textures, irregularly curved lines and graded tones. Geometric forms are now the exception rather than the rule in Calder's mobiles. The non-geometric biomorphic forms of Arp and Miró and Moore are definitely in the ascendant. The formal tradition of Gauguin, Fauvism and Expressionism will probably dominate for some time to come the tradition of Cézanne and Cubism.[18]

Barr does not seem to have thought his attribution of an identity and an importance to biomorphist art was at all controversial. Grigson's article and essay are listed in the bibliography of the catalogue, but Barr used the terms "biomorph" and "biomorphic abstraction" without any form of explanation. Perhaps, over the space of the year between Grigson's and Barr's writings, the term had entered the language of private conversations about contemporary art. Or perhaps, the epithet "biomorph," or "shape of life," seemed so self-evidently appropriate for the works in question that Barr did not pause to consider the origins or significance of the new term. In any event, Barr's use of the word in what became a primer for a generation of those interested in modern art helped determine later interpretations of the term.

Like many writers of the period, Barr associated form in art with certain emotional and, ultimately, psychological dispositions which lay at the root of different types of expression in the arts. He had first developed his vision of the cultural implications of the formal language of modern art while teaching at Wellesley College in the late 1920s. His preparatory notes for his lectures show that he contrasted the impulse towards the absolute and the pure revealed in Cubism and early abstraction with the return to figuration and the new interest in the imagery of dreams and the art of children, the mad, and so-called primitive tribes of the 1920s. "Conclusion:" he wrote in his lecture notes, "Descartes versus Rousseau."[19]

Reason versus emotion, the ascetic versus the sensual, the classical versus the Romantic, the mechanistic versus the primitive: the implications of the opposition of the "shape of the square" and the "silhouette of the amoeba" were potentially wide-ranging. Barr did not hesitate: "Apollo, Pythagorus and Descartes watch over the Cézanne-Cubist-geometric tradition," he proclaimed in his catalogue essay in 1935, "Dionysius (an Asiatic god), Plotinus and Rousseau over the Gauguin-Expressionist-non-geometric line."[20]

An impure abstraction

Barr aimed to present the various stories of the development of modern art in an easily comprehensible manner; but, as his critics were to point out, the cost of this clarity was perhaps an over-confident disregard for the complexities associated with interpreting development and change in art. He wrote, for example, that the Surrealist painter Yves Tanguy "took the flat, organic, biomorphic shapes of Arp and Miró, and, about 1927, painted or drew them in the round,"[21] but he did not attempt to explain why Tanguy should have done so, or to comment on the meaning of his mysterious images. He wrote a great deal about what he called, "the modern masters of abstract art associated with Surrealism;" yet, though he was correct to point out that in certain instances the philosophical differences between abstraction and Surrealism were not accompanied by marked differences in imagery, the simplicity of his formulation suggests that he was not fully aware of the controversial nature of his statement. What many had hinted at, but declined to put so baldly, he expressed in categorical terms when he wrote that certain works by André Masson and Tanguy, "whatever their Surrealist significance may be, are even more abstract than Picasso's *collages* and may be considered one of the results of the early 20th century impulse towards abstract design."[22]

Inevitably, Barr's categorizations aroused criticism. "Mr. Barr has engaged himself in placing each artist in his right pigeon-hole," wrote a reviewer in *Axis*, "but he is apt to give the impression that by doing so he has done all that is necessary to explain the artist's existence."[23] "He gives us, it is true, the dates of every stage in the various movements, as if to enable us to plot a curve, or to follow the emergence of the art year by year," wrote Meyer Schapiro, "but no connection is drawn between the art and the conditions of the moment."[24]

Many factors influenced Barr's approach, including a personal predilection for classification and definition (he was an amateur ornithologist) and, no doubt, the pressures imposed by the perceived need to convey a clear story to the general public. An important factor, however, was undoubtedly his idea of what an account of trends in modern art should be; and this was formed in some measure by his exposure to current art historical orthodoxies in his years as a student in Princeton. In particular, his view of the history of modern art as the history of contrasting form types recalls—surely consciously—the polarities established by the father of the discipline of art history, Heinrich Wölfflin. In presenting recent art in terms of an opposition between, on the one hand, the rectilinear and rational and, on the other, the organic and emotive, Barr was attempting to match the confusing and diverse developments of recent art with the conceptual schemas of art history—a goal that reflected the influence of Wölfflinian formalism on his outlook and that of many of his generation of scholars in America.[25]

Although he occasionally used descriptive phrases such as "silhouette of the amoeba" and "water-worn stone" to describe the shapes, Barr was noticeably reluctant to discuss the meaning or subject matter of biomorphist art. For him, biomorphism was a form of near-abstraction. He explained that there were two types of art: representational works, in which recognizable objects exist in three-dimensional space; and abstract compositions, made of shapes and colors which, at least in the artist's conception, are independent of the appearances of the material world. Related to this second type of art were near-abstract works, or "compositions in which the artist, starting with natural forms, transforms them into abstract or nearly abstract forms." The artist "approaches an abstract goal but does not quite reach it."[26] Cubism and, he suggested, biomorphist art fell into this second category.

Behind Barr's formulation lay the idea that representation and abstraction were two poles of artistic expression, linked by a sliding scale of degrees of abstractness or reference to the appearances of the world. For Barr, the "Arp 'shape"' was a soft, irregular curving silhouette, "half-way between a circle and the object represented."[27] Grigson had voiced a similar view when he described abstraction as "the extreme withdrawal from the 'real' forms of nature, from representation, to and beyond the real forms of art."[28]

This notion of the polarity of the representational and the abstract was central to the ideology of modernism. The story of the succession of movements and -isms that made up the history of art since the days of the Impressionists was presented as a revolutionary break with tradition: the concerns of modern art were not simply different from, but opposed to those of the past. Abstraction versus representation; the autonomy of the plastic language of art versus illusionism; creativity versus slavish reproduction: the rhetoric of modern art endlessly multiplied the dualisms that defined its own novelty. Crucially, popular taste versus elitism was another—and perhaps the most difficult for defenders of modern art to confront—of the dualisms entrenched in discussion about contemporary art.

In this climate of polarized positions many felt there was little choice but to be for Modernist art or against it. Those who were sympathetic to the new had no desire to appear to join the ranks of the philistines, or to risk being branded insensitive or unenlightened by submitting the theories of modern artists to analysis. Consequently, there was little sustained debate about the premises and value of these theories, and even their most irrational and improbable aspects passed unchallenged in the camp of the supporters of modern art. Barr, and before him, Grigson, were among this broad category of commentators whose support for avant-garde art curtailed, it seems, the areas which they were willing to address. They saw their role as that of explaining and justifying the modern movement to a public that was largely ignorant of trends in art of the last twenty years. At a time when the revived fortunes of abstract art had given a new edge to the long-standing popular and official hostility to modern art, neither man wanted to criticize what they felt needed to be defended. It is perhaps in this context that the reluctance of both men to press home criticisms of current shibboleths should be seen. Grigson condemned Mondrian and Nicholson for believing that there could be such a thing as a "pure" art, but he himself used a similar sort of language in defining biomorphist art as "impure" art. Equally, Barr wrote that the elimination of the connotations of subject matter and the pleasure of easy recognition in "pure" abstract painting constituted a "great impoverishment" of art; but, shunning polemic, the only comment he offered on this was that certain artists preferred impoverishment to adulteration. He chose to slip the term "biomorphic abstraction" into the sequence of modern art movements without explanation or justification. Defining it as a type of "near abstraction," akin in type to Cubism, he introduced the new -ism with a minimal disturbance to the received view of the history of modern art.

Grigson's and Barr's notion of a half-abstract art was based on a compromise. It appeared to leave intact the so-called purity of the imagery of an artist like Mondrian, while at the same time recognizing the existence of a range of works that, whatever the expressed intentions of the artists, in some measure resembled the appearances of the natural world, evoking analogies with cells, pebbles, clouds, buds, breasts, and hips. The revived fortunes of abstract art in the early 1930s, and the warring stances of the publicists of the abstract and Surrealist groups in Paris, had made the idea of the non-representational purity of the plastic language of art highly sensitive and difficult to challenge. The notion of an impure abstraction reflected the latest thinking on the subject within these confines; but, although innovative in itself, it was perhaps not radical enough.

In 1937, Meyer Schapiro, the critic whose views had been footnoted by Barr, responded to *Cubism and Abstract Art* with a critique that has lost little of its force today. He praised Barr's text for its comprehensiveness and its willingness to address basic questions concerning the nature of abstraction, but he complained that Barr had written about abstract art as if it had arisen simply because artists had "grown bored with painting facts," and as if it were an art of pure form without content. It was the weaknesses of these two assumptions, widespread in contemporary writing on modern art, that Schapiro set out to expose in his essay "The Nature of Abstract Art," published in a left-wing periodical, *Partisan Review*.

Schapiro pointed out that the idea of the purity of abstract art rested on the assumption that representational art was a passive mirroring of things, and was therefore essentially non-artistic, and implied that abstract art was a purely aesthetic activity unconditioned by objects and based on its own eternal laws. He wrote:

> These views are thoroughly one-sided and rest on a mistaken idea of what a representation is ... All renderings of objects, no matter how exact they seem, even photographs, proceed from values, methods and viewpoints which somehow shape

the image and often determine its contents. On the other hand, there is no "pure" art, unconditioned by experience; all fantasy and formal construction, even the random scribbling of the hand, are shaped by experience and by non-aesthetic concerns.[29]

If there was no "pure" art, then, by extension, there could hardly be an "impure" art; and Barr's definition of Cubist and biomorphist art was fatally flawed. It is significant that, from the late 1930s, the hesitation shown by both Barr and Grigson regarding the question of what biomorphist art resembled (and hence what it could be said to mean) disappeared, as commentators—and a number of artists—began to use more straightforwardly descriptive terms to characterize biomorphic forms. It was Schapiro's throwaway comment that biomorphic abstraction expressed a collapse of faith in the ethos of the machine,[30] rather than Barr's seemingly non-interpretative description "halfway between the object and the thing represented" that indicated the path followed by later discussion of biomorphist art. Henry Moore's comment in 1937—very different in tenor from his statements of the early 1930s—reflected a new approach:

It might seem from what I have said of shape and form that I regard them as ends in themselves. Far from it. I am very much aware that associational psychological factors play a large part in sculpture. The meaning and significance of form itself probably depends on the countless associations of man's history. For example, rounded forms convey an idea of fruitfulness, maturity, probably because the earth, women's breasts and most fruits are rounded.[31]

1960s reprise

The term biomorphism was exhumed from decades of critical silence in America in the 1960s. Lawrence Alloway, a British critic then living in New York, raised the question of the existence of a distinctive biomorphist style or idiom in his article "The Biomorphic Forties," published in *Artforum* in 1965. He did not identify the source for his use of the term in his article but, as he acknowledged later, he borrowed the term directly from Barr.[32] He began with an etymological analysis of the word:

Bio: "a combining form denoting relation to, or connection with, life, vital phenomena, or living organisms."

Morpology: "the features, collectively, comprised in the form and structure of an organism or any of its parts."[33]

His subject was the soft, fluid shapes in the paintings of such American painters as Arshile Gorky, Jackson Pollock, William Baziotes and Mark Rothko. But he placed this imagery firmly in the context of the work by such earlier European artists as Hans Arp, Joan Miró and Wassily Kandinsky—artists associated with abstraction and Surrealism and, he argued, with traditions that predated both. This current of organic imagery—with its evocation of "seeding, sprouting, growing, loving, fighting, decaying, rebirth"—may not have been recognized or acknowledged at the time, but was nonetheless real and potent, supported, he wrote, by "clusters of ideas about nature, automatism, mythology and the unconscious."[34]

In the following year, William Rubin, chief curator at the Museum of Modern Art in New York, took up this idea of a biomorphic current, recasting it as a "post-cubist morphology." Like Alloway, but unlike Barr or Grigson, Rubin presented biomorphism as allied to Surrealism rather than abstraction. Writing in *Artforum*, Rubin traced biomorphism back to the organic, nature-based decorative motifs of Art Nouveau, the dominant style of the childhood of Surrealist artists and, he said, an "unquestionable" influence upon them. Like Alfred Barr (his predecessor at the Museum of Modern Art), he saw the first hint of a pictorial biomorphism in the allusions to a human presence in Marcel Duchamp's mechanomorphic paintings of the early 1910s. These were followed by the biomorphism proper of the reliefs of Hans Arp, and later such Surrealist artists as Miró, Masson, and Tanguy. Biomorphic shapes infiltrated much Surrealist art but were not noted by writers at the time:

> the biomorphic or organic form, perhaps too plastic an element to appeal to the Surrealist poet-critics, was passed over in silence ... And yet it represents a major common denominator—perhaps the only one—which allows us to draw together the stylistic innovations of the surrealist years. If there is a characteristic formal element that runs like a *leitmotif* through the stylistic innovations of 1915-47, it is surely this biomorphology.[35]

Rubin's article was republished a few years later in his magisterial study of the art of this period, *Dada and Surrealist Art* of 1969. That the concept of biomorphism survived, albeit only just, in art historical use is perhaps largely due to the prominence that Rubin accorded it in what was one of the most important and certainly the most lavishly illustrated overviews of the subject to date.

However, once again the term failed to secure a niche in the lexicon of modern art terms. The list, for example, of dictionaries of art terms, in which the word does *not* figure, is long—and comprehensive. No other writers have taken up the cudgels on behalf of the concept; and where the adjectives "biomorphic" or "biomorphist" are used to describe the imagery of, say, Arp or Miró, it has been without discussion or speculation about what exactly links the work of these two artists and so many others who used similar types of imagery. Does the term refer to a style or a morphology, a set of significantly related themes or was it simply a feature of the art of the period that in itself had no particular importance? And whose is the deciding judgment—artists and critics of the interwar and immediately postwar period or art historians today?

The answers to these questions depend very much on the nature of the priorities and concepts that are brought to bear on the issue. Given their silence on this question, it could be assumed that, for the vast majority of artists in question, and of writers and critics then and later, the idea of biomorphism was not crucially important or relevant. The artists lived and worked in an environment in which attention focused on the complex and contentious issues associated with the causes of late Cubism, abstraction or Surrealism. Much of the critical commentary of the period and also many statements by artists focused on defining positions in relation to the already well-established movements, and this textual material inevitably determined to a large extent the parameters of subsequent discussion.

For a period in the 1930s, artists and writers saw the art of their time in terms of two rival camps—Surrealism and, particularly following the 1931 launch of the international grouping *Abstraction-Création*, non-figurative art. This polarization led perhaps inevitably to a call for some sort of synthesis,[36] and to a more nuanced consideration of the position of artists like Arp and Moore who produced works that could be described as neither fully abstract nor Surrealist. Not fully supported by many leading artists, this consideration, however, was not far-reaching enough in its critique of existing positions to overturn the orthodoxies of the day. Notwithstanding the interesting history of the concept of biomorphism—and the cultural status and undeniable influence of such figures as Barr and Rubin—the term still has only an uncertain status and meaning even today within the fields of modern art history and art criticism. Its origins in a discourse about the historical origins of art and the emotional needs of man are forgotten, and it is now used to denote simply (and facilely) an irregularly curvilinear form language that evokes the patterns of organic nature and the shapes of a few recognizable objects such as pebbles and amoebae.

Notes

1 Meyer Schapiro, "Style," in A. Kroeber, ed., *Anthropology Today: An Encyclopedic Inventory* (Chicago, IL: Chicago University Press, 1966), 288.

2 George Kubler, *The Shape of Time* (New Haven, CT and London: Yale University Press 1968), 129.

3 Myfanwy Evans, "Dead or Alive," *Axis* (January 1935): 3.

4 Ibid., 4.

5 Geoffrey Grigson, "Comment on England," *Axis* (January 1935): 8.

6 Ibid.

7 Ibid., 10.

8 Of Hans Arp, arguably the principal biomorphist artist, there is not a word in Grigson's article in *Axis*, and this despite the fact that Arp, along with Wadsworth and Hepworth, was represented in the first issue of the magazine with what are now seen as classic interpretations of the biomorphist idiom. What linked these artists (and distinguished them from, for example, Henry Moore) was the fact that they were members of *Abstraction-Création*. Grigson had been to Paris at the suggestion of Ben Nicholson to see an exhibition by the group, and knew that the majority of its members practiced a straight-line, "pure" abstraction of the sort he disliked so strongly. He seems not to have appreciated the differences of style and approach within this loosely knit group,

and associated Wadsworth, Hepworth, and, in particular, Arp, a founder member of the group, with "pure" abstraction. In a postcard to Ben Nicholson dated June 1934 (Tate Gallery Archive), Grigson reported that he had been able to meet Hélion, Mondrian, and Brancusi in Paris, but "hadn't time to get out to the Arps" (Hans Arp and Sophie Taueber-Arp lived at Meudon on the outskirts of Paris). It is not clear if Grigson ever met Arp or had much opportunity to see his work (having just resigned from the group, Arp was not represented in the *Abstraction Création* exhibition Grigson would have seen in Paris), and, if not, this might explain his curious silence about the latter's work.

9 Geoffrey Grigson, "Painting and Sculpture," in *The Arts Today* (London: Bodley Head, 1935), 87.

10 A.C. Haddon, *Evolution in Art. As Illustrated by the Life History of Designs* (London: W. Scott, 1895), 126.

11 Grigson, "Painting and Sculpture," 80–81.

12 Hans Obermaier, *Fossil Man in Spain* (New Haven, CT: Yale University Press 1924), 331.

13 Grigson, "Painting and Sculpture," 81.

14 Ibid., 80.

15 Meyer Schapiro, "The Nature of Abstract Art," in *Modern Art: 19th and 20th Centuries. Selected Papers* (London: Chatto & Windus, 1978), 187.

16 Alfred Barr, *Cubism and Abstract Art* (exhib. cat.) (New York: Museum of Modern Art, 1936), 19.

17 Ibid.

18 Ibid., 20.

19 Irving Sandler and Amy Newmans, eds., *Defining Modern Art: Selected Writings of Alfred Barr, Jr.* (New York: Abrams, 1986), 67.

20 In citing Apollo and Dionysius in his list of the attributes of the two trends, Barr made appeal to a cliché of contemporary psychology. The nineteenth-century German philosopher and poet Friedrich Nietzsche had given currency to these terms in his account of the development of ancient Greek drama, *The Birth of Tragedy* (1872). Become a literary commonplace, these terms were invested with a modern currency when adopted by the psychologist Carl Jung: in *Psychological Types* (1922), he related these Nietzschean types of artistic expression to innate psychological tendencies, in particular, to extroverted and introverted responses to the outer world. The American anthropologist Ruth Benedict provoked renewed interest in the theme of the Apollonian and the Dionysian in *Patterns of Culture*, published in 1932. In this she contrasted the Apollonian measured sobriety of South-West Pueblo Indians with the Dionysian spirit of the neighboring, but alien, culture of the Plains Indians. Although criticized for its impressionistic handling of the evidence in anthropological circles, Benedict's book proved an immensely popular work (it was cited, incidentally, by Grigson in *The Arts Today*), and it lent topicality to Barr's characterization of the two types of abstract art. Classical versus Romantic, however, was perhaps the dualism most obviously related to the visual arts of the polarities listed by Barr. Whether revered, parodied, or expressing the desire to integrate the old within the new, the classical tradition was very much alive in "return to order" movements in Europe of the late 1910s and early 1920s. Later, the Surrealists, who fiercely opposed the new emphasis on order and restraint in the arts,

as well as all questions of aesthetic quality, championed the cause of the irrational and emotive; while the small group of Neo-Romantic painters looked back to the "poetry" of Picasso's works of the Blue and Rose periods. So current was the cliché of classical versus Romantic as applied to contemporary art that Barr was able to associate the evocative quality of biomorphist art, in particular, its suggestion of the swelling, budding forms of nature, with a Rousseau-type Romanticism: organic, emotive, mystical, anti-rational, the adjectives flowed one from the other as Barr sketched the parameters of the stereotype of Romantic expression in the arts.

21 Barr, *Cubism and Abstract Art,* 186.

22 Ibid., 179.

23 J. Richards, untitled review, *Axis* (July 1936): 31.

24 Schapiro, "The Nature of Abstract Art," 187.

25 See J. Ackerman, R. Carpenter, C. McCorkel, and C. Eisler, "Kunstgeschichte American Style," in Donald Fleming and Bernard Bailyn, eds., *The Intellectual Migration: Europe and America, 1930–1960* (Cambridge, MA: Belknap Press, 1969), 544–629; C. McCorkel, "Sense and Sensibility: An Epistemological Approach to the Philosophy of Art History," *Journal of Aesthetics and Art Criticism* 34, no. 1 (Fall 1975): 35–50.

26 Barr, *Cubism and Abstract Art,* 13.

27 Ibid., 186.

28 Grigson, "Painting and Sculpture," 72.

29 Schapiro, "The Nature of Abstract Art," 200.

30 Ibid., 195–96.

31 Henry Moore, "Notes on Sculpture," in Myfanwy Evans, ed., *The Painter's Object* (London: Gerald Howe, 1937), 28–29.

32 In a letter to the author dated 19 November 1988, Lawrence Alloway wrote: "Yes, I know Alfred Barr used BIOMORPHISM in the 1930s. I knew it then and I am sure that's where I got the term from. The fact is I was not content with the formalising effects of modern art theory in general and Biomorphism seemed a way of defining an art redolent of organic meaning … I don't think the term Biomorphism was much used at the time I wrote."

33 Lawrence Alloway, "The Biomorphic Forties," *Artforum* (September 1965): 18.

34 Ibid., 20.

35 William Rubin, "Toward a Critical Framework: 3. A Post-Cubist Morphology: Preliminary Remarks," *Artforum* (September 1966): 46.

36 See, for example: *Thèse, synthèse, antithèse* (exhib. cat.) (Lucerne: Kunstmuseum Lucerne, 1935), 11–12.

4

On the biology of the inorganic: Crystallography and discourses of latent life in the art and architectural historiography of the early twentieth century

Spyros Papapetros

From Edward Tylor's ethnographic descriptions of tribesmen attributing souls to bamboo trees in his *Primitive Culture* to Charles Darwin's story of his dog barking at an open parasol in his *Descent of Man*, late nineteenth-century anthropologists were bewildered by the attribution of life to inanimate objects in motion.[1] Conversely, contemporary Monist scientists such as Ernst Haeckel, Wilhelm Ostwald, and Ernst Krause unambiguously conferred life on so-called inanimate nature. Transitional organisms precariously situated between the organic and the inorganic—or between animal, vegetal and mineral conditions—were particularly privileged objects of scientific inquiry. From the circular schedules of climbing tendrils to the irritable movements of insectivorous plants, and from the imperceptible growth of coral to the copulating amalgamations of so-called "living crystals": as long as it could be excited, every object was deemed to be animated and to have will, sensation, and a soul of its own.[2] Yet between ethnographic animism and scientific Monism there were specific differences. While the primitive *anima* of the bamboo tree was divined by external movement, the soul of the crystal was internal, immobile, invisible, and noticeable only through the microscope. The animation of the tree was subjective, created by the illusions of the deceived spectator; the internal life of the crystal was allegedly objective, resting on the qualities of matter itself. This ineffable type of animation, resting half on metaphysics and half on physics, is the animation of the inorganic: a living contradiction, a conceptual amoeba extending its pseudopodia over the bodies of several artistic modernisms and the histories that precede them.

This essay traces the intersections between the natural sciences investigating the latent energy of inorganic matter and the historiographies of art and architecture motivated by a similar curiosity for inert objects that could ostensibly be energized. Early twentieth-century German art history presents us with two contrasting models of such vivification. First, the external animation of *äussere Beweglichkeit* [moving forms] detected by Aby Warburg in fluttering hair, billowing draperies, and meandering snakes; and second, the inner life of *innere Lebendigkeit* [immobile forms] examined by Alois Riegl and Wilhelm Worringer in vegetal and crystalline ornaments. This latter silent mode of animation can be intuited, but cannot be seen. It is an imperceptible vibration, more *geistig* [spiritual] than *sinnlich* [sensory]. It has less to do with movement than with the repository of energy accumulated in stillness. The following notes from early twentieth-century art historiography and science attempt to make explicit the impact of this covert energy.

Animal basilicas and vegetal rotundas

In a note from an unpublished lecture of 1898, which preceded the publication of his *Late Roman Industry*, Alois Riegl discusses certain typological distinctions in early Christian architecture:

> The centralized building is related to the plant which lacks a will and stands even closer to the crystalline qualities (*Krystallinismus*) of inorganic material. In contrast, the longitudinal building takes view of the spiritual as it externalizes itself in the animal in distinction with the plant. The Christian devotional building is meant to be interior space (*Innerraum*).[3]

Initially, Riegl's note seems incomprehensible (no wonder it did not make it to the published text). Why is the rectangular basilica like an animal and the circular rotunda like a crystal or a plant? According to nineteenth-century morphological discourses the reverse should be true: the organic was circular and the inorganic polygonal or cubic.[4] The issue is clarified when Riegl later states that a basilica has *Bewegungsmachung* [kinetic qualities] as opposed to the *Beruhigung* [non kinetic repose] of the rotunda.[5] Therefore the basilica of old St. Peter's behaves as if it contained an animal running along its horizontal axis, while Santa Constanza (to choose two of the contemporaneous examples from Rome illustrated in Riegl's book) stands quietly in space like a crystal or a plant.

One might be tempted to dismiss all this as plain formalism—artificial subtleties of late nineteenth-century *Kunstwissenschaft* about buildings merely on the basis of photographs. But Riegl's distinctions are significant, for not only do they reiterate a shift in the focus of art and architectural history from façade and elevation to typology and plan, but they also presage an imminent transition from external form to the psychological qualities of *Innerraum* [interior space]. The basilica of old St. Peter's is like an animal not because it looks like an animal, but because it moves, feels, behaves, and even *thinks* like an animal—this is why the basilica partakes of the *das Geistige* [spiritual], as Riegl notes.[6] External morphology no longer matters. What counts is internal intensity, rhythm, what Riegl calls *Bewegungsmachung*—that is, movement-in-the-making, an energy more potential than active, more intuitive than seen.

While working on these lectures, Riegl was reading St. Augustine and his commentators.[7] If the basilica moves and thinks, then it has the two highest degrees of the soul originally described by Aristotle and reconfigured by St. Augustine in his *De Anima*. These two qualities are self-propelled movement (found in animals and humans) and intellect (found only in man). And yet the Rotunda is animated by a different type of soul; it has the soul of a plant, what Riegl and Schopenhauer, following medieval scholastic interpreters of Aristotle, would call *anima vegetativa*.[8] Buildings, like plants, partake of this vegetal soul; both organisms have no external movement of their own, yet they are permeated by an impervious will impelling them to expand upwards and defy gravity.[9]

One could detect a similar transition from external animal movement to internal vegetal impulse in Riegl's earlier work on ornamentation in his *Stilfragen* [Questions of Style] of 1893. From the hard immobility of the Egyptian lotus to the spiraling vivacity of the Mycenean tendril, and from the rhythmic balance of the Attic acanthus to the naturalist exuberance of Greco-Roman vine motifs, Riegl traces the diagrammatic development of these ornamental motifs from stillness to animation.[10] However, Riegl's ornamental plants do not come from the ground; they are inorganic. By increasingly distancing themselves from their vegetal origin, they become intellectual patterns. In fact, Riegl's mental "plant-motifs" are doubly inorganic. They are never attached to the ground, and they transform while perpetually migrating from one region to another. Their only approximation of nature is in their perpetual movement away from it (Fig. 4.1).

While Riegl refuted the naturalist origins of so called "plant motifs," the essential characteristics of such ornaments ostensibly replicate the plants' external movements. In their continuous gyration, the spiral ornaments examined by the art historian ostensibly simulate Charles Darwin's diagrams of the *Reizbewegungen* [stimulus movements] of plants. Recording the various positions of climbing plants during the course of a day, Darwin proved that tendrils move in a circular fashion, which he termed *circumnutation*.[11] In the diagrams illustrating Darwin's experiments, the perpetual spiraling of the tendril was abstracted into an angular network of points, arrows, and dotted zigzag lines (Fig. 4.2). The graceful curvature of the tendril turned into a polyhedral surface—something that looked more like a crystal than a spiraling stem. It is as if the drawing process diagrammed the conceptual crystallization of plant life. Darwin's circumnutating diagrams are ultimately fossils of movement substituting motion by a series of arrests.

The primary characteristic of this (almost) suspended animation was its slowness. "It takes hours for the leaves to turn towards the light; it takes minutes perhaps a quarter of an hour, for the tendrils to twine around their support; even a snail moves more quickly," Gustav Theodor Fechner had remarked in his *Soul of Plants*.[12] Yet, however slow or coy, movement was definitely present. Human anticipation enhanced this invisible form of animation.

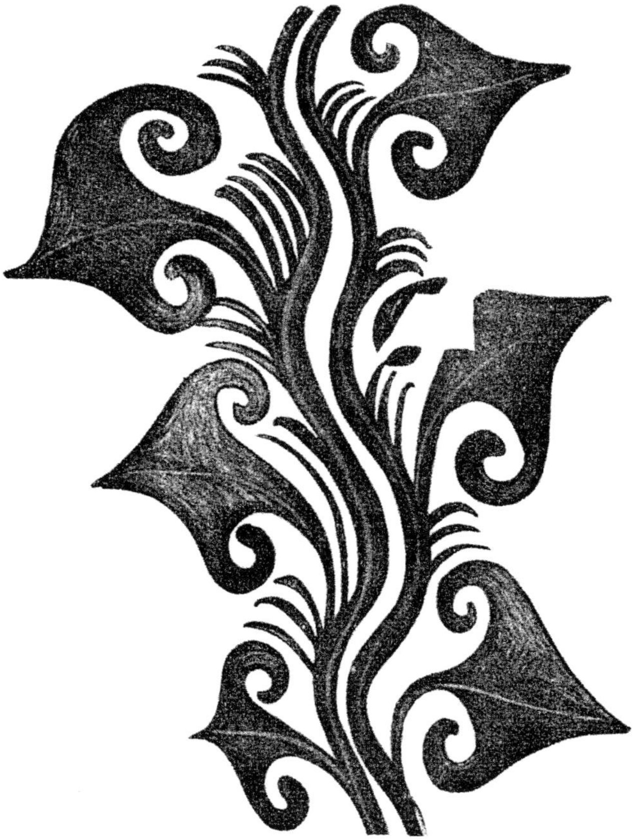

4.1a Mycenian tendril, bands with vegetal ornaments from Alois Riegl, *Stilfragen* (Berlin: G. Siemens, 1893)

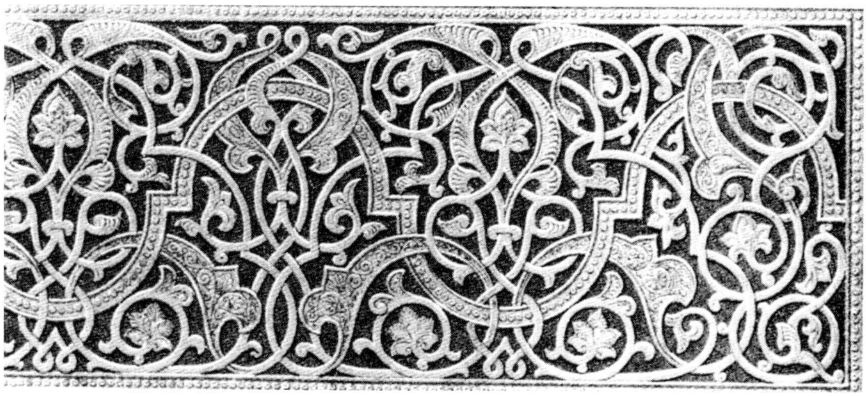

4.1b Arabesque—Egypt, bands with vegetal ornaments from Alois Riegl, *Stilfragen* (Berlin: G. Siemens, 1893)

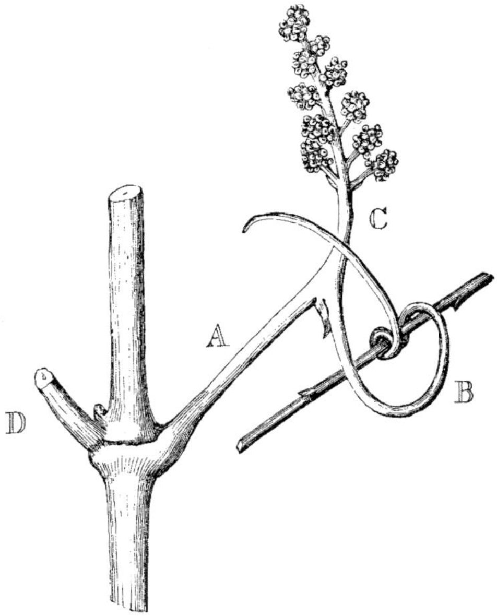

4.2a Diagram of plant movement (circumnutation) from Charles Darwin, *The Power of Movement in Plants* (London: John Murray, 1880)

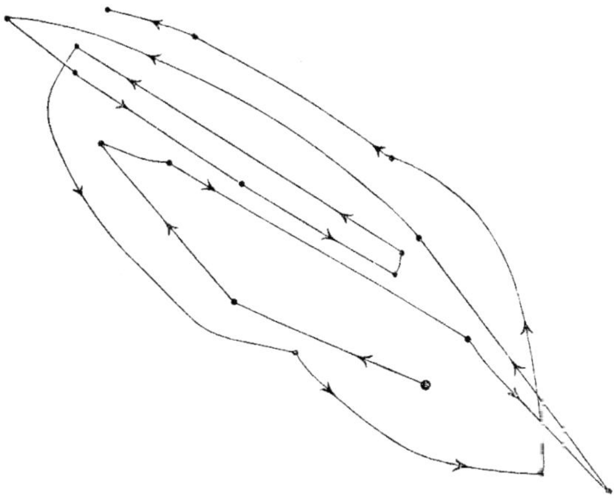

4.2b Diagram of plant movement (circumnutation) from Charles Darwin, *The Movement and Habits of Climbing Plants* (New York: D. Appleton & Co., 1876)

Just as Darwin's climbing tendrils turn into petroglyphs, so do Riegl's meandering ornaments ultimately transform into crystals. The final stage of this crystallization process is the *arabesque*, a synthesis between the lively animation of the tendril and the geometric regularity of the crystal (Fig. 4.2b). This tangle of lines is a continuous fabric, simultaneously animate and inorganic. It is a crystal with a soul—a form of soul denunciated by Aristotle, yet acknowledged by pre-Socratic philosophers and rediscovered by Riegl's contemporary Monist natural philosophers. Vitalistic impulses accumulated inside the rigid vessels of minerals and crystals. Miraculously, the inorganic walls start to bend and a new form of matter comes to life—a crystal warped by the very rigidity that had coerced its formation.

Living crystals and mineral snakes

In 1904, the crystallographer Otto Lehmann made a discovery that radically transformed contemporary scientific opinions on crystals. Lehmann's ostensible triumph was the analytic description of "liquid" or "flowing" crystals (*flüssige* or *fliessende Kristalle*]. As a tribute to Heraclitus, who 2,500 years earlier had declared that *ta panta rhein* [everything flows], including stones, Lehmann also called these objects *rheocrystals*. By using a specially formulated microscope and through the application of polarized light, Lehmann managed to measure changes in extension and contraction of rheocrystals under heat and cold, which allowed him to argue that these minerals had significant plastic qualities. Lehmann published his findings in several books, including *Die neue Welt der flüssigen Kristalle* [The New World of Flowing Crystals] of 1911, in which he emphasized the connections between the science of crystals and biology.[13]

Like the *biocrystals* discovered by Haeckel in 1872, liquid crystals were a mixture of mineral substances, such as calcite or flint, with organic plasma. Yet rheocrystals also had the ability to form a skin through which they appeared to breathe like living organisms. Moreover, these flowing crystals, although sexless, could multiply by means of a peculiar form of copulation. For example, when two spindle-form rheocrystals came into contact, their skins would combine and the substance of one crystal would flow into the other until their bodies merged into a single new longer crystal (Fig. 4.3a). In fact, when Haeckel reproduced Lehmann's drawing in his publications, he expanded the width of the new combined crystal to make it look bigger and fatter, as if this visual enhancement would increase the fertile effect of the crystals' reproductive union (Fig. 4.3b).[14] As Haeckel wrote, this form of reproduction was basically a "homophagy" of inorganic bodies, a crystal cannibalism: "They grow by eating one another. It is usually the stabile form that eats the labile one."[15] This was but one more sign of the advantages of immobility over movement, in fact a perfect example of how immobility can become "pregnant" with potential.

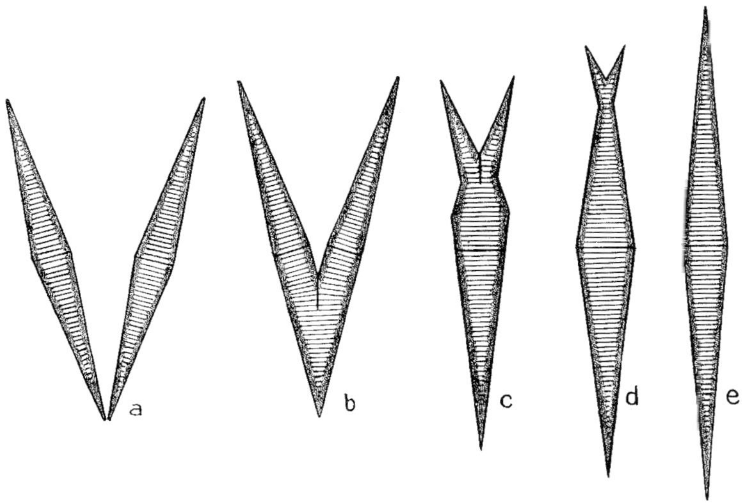

4.3a Drawings of liquid crystal transformation from Otto Lehmann, *Die neue Welt der flüssigen Kristalle* (Leipzig: Akademische Verlagsgesellschaft m.b.H, 1911)

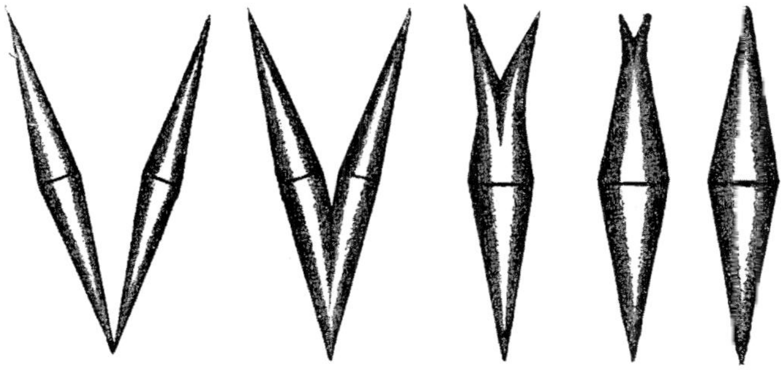

4.3b Drawings of liquid crystal transformation from Ernst Haeckel, *Kristallseelen* (Leipzig: Kröner, 1917)

More important than how these crystals behaved was their appearance. They looked nothing like the hexagonal snowflakes and other symmetrical polyhedra of the nineteenth century, such as the geometric patterns we are used to seeing in the books of Semper, Ruskin, and Viollet-le-Duc. The new crystals of the twentieth century, as seen through Lehmann's microscope, appeared flowing and circular, almost blob-like—*informe*, as one might call them today. While remaining regular and crystalline in pattern, they reproduced an ambient effect in light. They formed complex spider webs, or were filled with oil-like patches expanding in a mucous substance (Fig. 4.4). They appeared to be both soft and solid, rigid and malleable. Had these crystals been discovered in the 1960s, they would have been called psychedelic (and it would then be easier to envisage Haeckel's claim half a century earlier that they had souls).

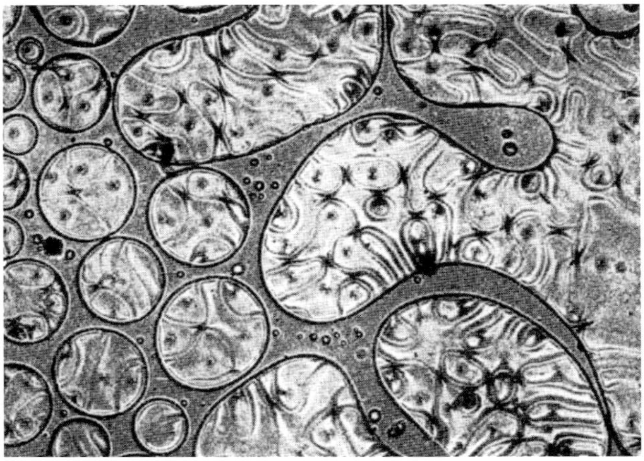

4.4a Microphotograph of liquid crystals from Otto Lehmann, *Die neue Welt der flüssigen Kristalle* (Leipzig: Akademische Verlagsgesellschaft m.b.H, 1911)

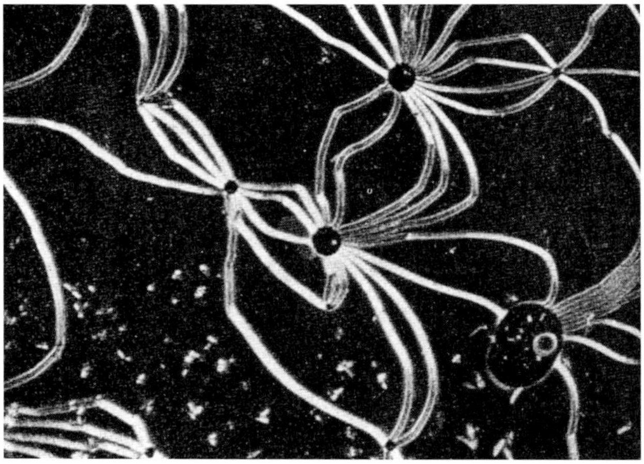

4.4b Microphotograph of liquid crystals from Otto Lehmann *Die neue Welt der flüssigen Kristalle* (Leipzig: Akademische Verlagsgesellschaft m.b.H, 1911)

To demonstrate further the spectacular qualities of his ambient crystals, Lehmann created a scientific film, in which he combined microphotography and animation techniques by montaging several sequences of drawings. Here the animation of crystals became what it always has been: *cinematic*, a matter of projection. Lehmann projected life onto these inorganic bodies and now film and cinema projected that life back. The rotation of the cinematographic machine recreated what the crystallographer called, *das scheinbare Leben* [the "apparent" or "virtual" life] of these material transgressors.[16]

Together with their movement on the screen, Lehmann's crystals demonstrated another form of energy—a type of motion that proved that,

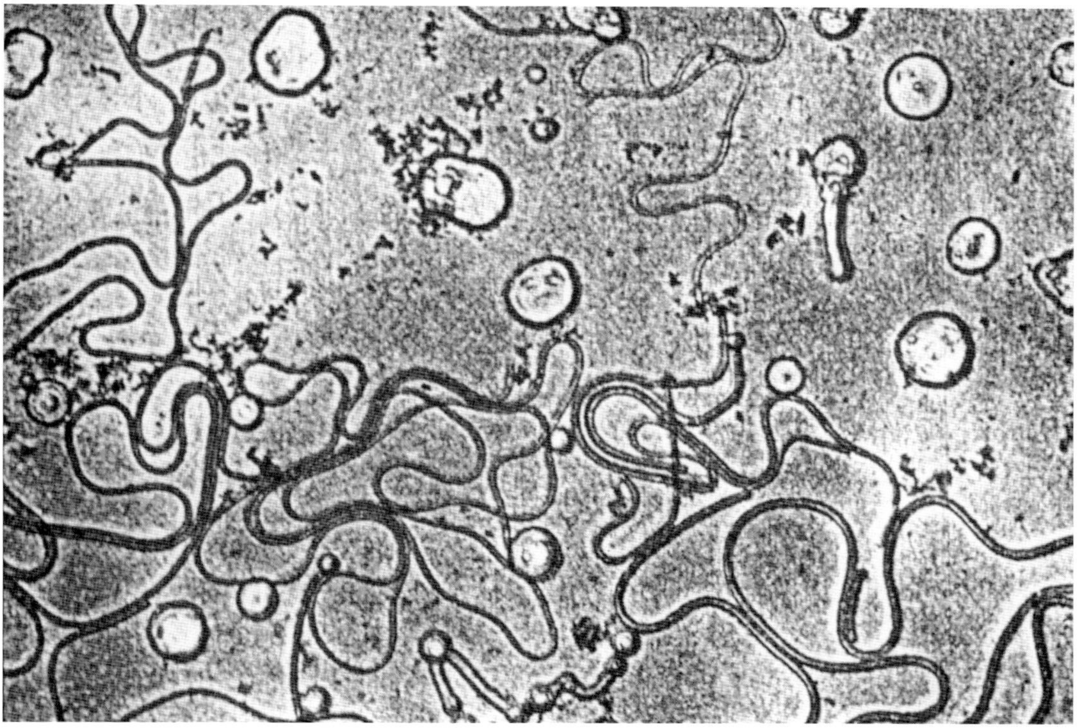

4.5 Micro-photograph of "crystal-worms" from Otto Lehmann, *Die neue Welt der flüssigen Kristalle* (Leipzig: Akademische Verlagsgesellschaft m.b.H, 1911)

beyond the mineral or the nutritive vegetal, these crystals also partook of the animal state. Lehmann discovered that differences in temperature inside the body of several ammonite crystals created certain winding threads that moved in a "snake-like" fashion (Fig. 4.5). These thin twisted tubes, or "snakes" as Lehmann called them, could divide into smaller segments and multiply arbitrarily. When concentrated in one place, they gave the impression of "marine micro-organisms" or *Kristallwürmer* [worms] arrested inside a glass surface.[17] Although by nature parasitical, these "worms" did not erode, but rather enhanced the life of the crystal. Since the snake threads were created by differences in temperature, it meant that the crystals that contained them not only possessed movement, but also feeling and sensation; and, since they had sensation, these crystals therefore also had a soul.[18]

In 1917 Lehmann's mentor, Ernst Haeckel, published *Kristallseelen: Studien über das anorganische Leben* [Crystal Souls; Studies of Inorganic Life], which largely relied on his protégé's texts and illustrations (Fig. 4.6).[19] While reducing the bulk of Lehmann's scientific experiments and measurement tables, Haeckel employed his own philosophy of Monism to expand the more speculative section of *Kristallseelen*. Liquid crystals were part of the larger circle of life—and in fact, of Haeckel's own life: *Crystal Souls* was the revered biophilosopher's last major book, published when he was eighty-three years old. It is as if this notorious career was not only consolidated, but also regenerated by these liquid crystals whose spindles pointed back to Haeckel's original preoccupations with similar transgressive species in nature.

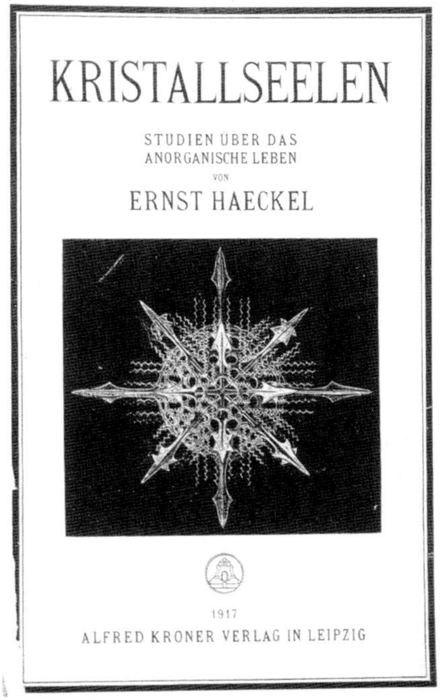

4.6a Book cover from Ernst Haeckel, *Kristallseelen* (Leipzig: Kröner, 1917)

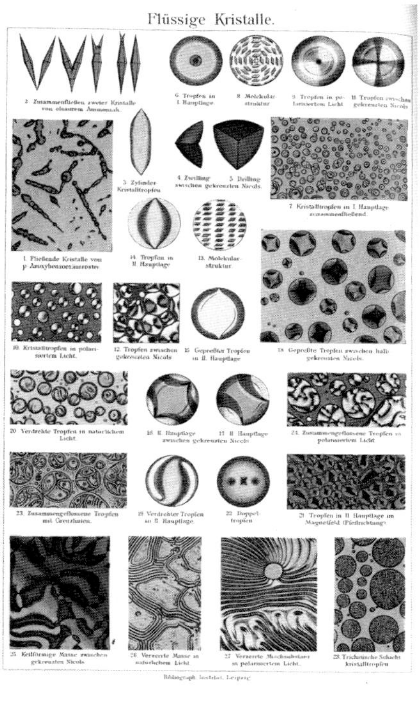

4.6b Frontispiece from Ernst Haeckel, *Kristallseelen* (Leipzig: Kröner, 1917)

Indeed, the illustration of the natural object on the cover of *Kristallseelen* is not one of Lehmann's rheocrystals but one of Haeckel's own radiolarians. Haeckel had first published his well-known studies of radiolarians in the 1860s. The radiolarians were living organisms with crystalline geometry, animals of perfect symmetry and design, their radial symmetry rendered even more perfect by Haeckel's imaginative illustrations (many of these images were later included in Haeckel's widely popular *Kunstformen der Natur* [Artforms of Nature]).[20] The substitution of living crystals by radiolarians on the cover of *Kristallseelen* underlines the correspondence or even the confusion between the two types of ambient organisms. If the radiolarians were crystalline animals, then the rheocrystals were animal-like crystals—the one was the inverted image of the other. Furthermore, since liquid crystals exhibited signs of irritability and movement, it meant they had a soul—a crystal soul—and since they had a soul, they were also living. Lehmann had called them *scheinbar lebende Kristalle* [virtually living crystals], while Haeckel upgraded that to *wirkliches Leben* [real life].[21] The life of crystals was a new chapter in what Hans Vaihinger would call *Die Philosophie des Als Ob* [the philosophy of as if], already omnipresent in early twentieth-century intellectual discourses and now applied by Lehmann to molecular physics.[22] Haeckel's radiolarians and now Lehmann's liquid crystals were the double proof that the distinction between the organic and the inorganic state did not exist. All matter was animate. All substance was one.

This was the main principle of Haeckel's doctrine of *Monismus* [Monism], a philosophical system that embraced science, philosophy, politics, ethics, and religion. All matter had force and energy. In the organic, this force was active; in the inorganic, it was latent yet potent, and much more potent, in fact, than the matter we call living. In his widely translated *Die Welträtsel* [The Riddles of the Universe], subtitled "a monistic view of the universe," Haeckel repeated the principle of evolution he had broached in his earlier study of Anthropogeny:[23] all life originates from the inorganic. All protozoa and protophyta stem from the probiotic inorganic phase of the earth, which is the mother of us all.

This is perhaps the thesis that Nietzsche deployed in an unpublished fragment from 1882 written during the *Gay Science* era, in which the philosopher portrays dead matter as *Mutterschoss* [the maternal bosom]. Nietzsche emphasized that one should celebrate one's return to the inorganic state as a "feast."[24] In light of this, it is easier to understand why Lehmann and Haeckel were mesmerized by the ostensive procreation of rheocrystals. Nietzsche's maternal metaphor for the inorganic sheds a different light on the association of crystals with metaphors of fertilization and pregnancy. Everything moved in a circle: animate crystals reanimated memories of a pre-human inorganic past, but at the same time projected patterns of an equally inorganic future. It was as if the historical implications of Nietzsche's idea of "eternal recurrence" were materialized in the cyclical life of crystals.

In fact, Lehmann's theory of liquid crystals experienced several (after)lives. During the interwar period, scientists disputed Lehmann's claims and argued that these organisms were not crystals but the products of emulsion between two different compounds; thus the entire theory of liquid crystals appeared to vanish. Nothing was heard for two decades; however, new experiments in the 1950s and 60s brought these crystals back to vibrant life mainly because of their benefits in electro-optic applications. Today, liquid crystals are used in a massive number of consumer products, from alarm clocks and wrist-watches to television and computer screens based on Liquid Crystal Display (LCD) technologies.[25] Once invisible, yet now omnipresent: Lehmann's liquid crystals not only survived but triumphed despite the fissures and the "snake worms" in the scientist's original hypothesis.

Inorganic animation

The twelfth volume of Nietzsche's collected works, which contained the posthumous aphorisms of the *Gay Science* epoch, was published in 1901 and was widely read.[26] Though the products of artificial insemination, the children of Nietzsche's inorganic *Mutterschoss* continued to procreate. There were several neophytes who wanted to suckle that hard inorganic breast, and these same Dionysian revelers would be delighted to celebrate their "return to inert matter" as an elaborate "feast."[27] In the domain of German art history, the most celebrated banqueter of the inorganic was Wilhelm Worringer, who coined the phrase "the animation of the inorganic" in his doctoral dissertation *Abstraktion und Einfühlung* [Abstraction and Empathy], first published in1907.[28] Worringer's text is well known and broadly analyzed;[29] therefore I will focus on only one point concerning the illustrations—or rather, the absence of illustrations.

It seems that Worringer abhorred illustrations. He envisioned an art history made only by "sounds or imperceptible tones" and not by "images"; that is, an *abstract* art history, an art history whose very abstraction would be the most concrete illustration of the author's theoretical argument.[30] Thus, with the exception of a Nordic medallion depicting two intertwined serpents on the cover of its 1919 German edition, *Abstraction and Empathy* contained no illustrations in any of its numerous editions. Nevertheless, in the central section of the book, following a discussion of Riegl, Worringer offers a lengthy description of a particular type of ornament. This is the so-called *Bandverflechtungsornament* [Northern interlace or strapwork], which according to the author "dominated the whole North of Europe during the first millennium A.D."[31] Since there are no illustrations, we can only imagine how this ornament might have looked by leafing through the various histories and almanacs of ornament circulating at the time.[32] A good example would be the ribbon frames of medieval Gospel images deriving from Roman tessellated and mosaic patterns, such as the band framework decoration of a miniature of St. Matthew in the St. Cuthbert Gospels (c. 770) in the Munich State Library (Fig. 4.7a).[33] Worringer argues that while in the South such interlaced ornaments became totally abstract and geometric, in the North the same patterns were highly animated. There was a "restless life" inside these abstract loops. The contradiction between the inorganic basis and the animate layering constitutes what Worringer calls *die Verlebendigung des Anorganischen* [the animation of the inorganic] to which Northerners are inextricably attached by an "uncanny pathos":

> In spite of the purely linear, inorganic basis of this ornamental style we hesitate to term it abstract. Rather it is impossible to mistake the restless life contained in this tangle of lines. This unrest, this seeking has no organic life that draws us gently into its movement; but there is life there, a vigorous, urgent life, that compels us joylessly to follow its movements. Thus, on an inorganic fundament, there is heightened movement, heightened expression. Here we have the decisive formula for the whole medieval North. Here are the elements which later on culminate in Gothic. The need for empathy of these inharmonious people does not take the nearest-at-hand path to the organic, because the harmonious motion of the organic is not sufficiently expressive for it; it needs rather that uncanny pathos which attaches to the animation of the inorganic. The inner disharmony and unclarity of these peoples situated far before knowledge and living in a harsh and repellent nature could have borne no clearer fruit. [34]

Worringer's scheme is *not* a dialectical synthesis between the animate and the inanimate, the organic and the inorganic. It has little to do with Haeckel's Monist resolutions. The animation of the inorganic is a permanent reaction, an irresolvable contradiction between two opposite states: abstraction and empathy, fear and attraction, resistance and extension. Like Riegl's basilica, it is both a moving animal and an inert rectangle. Like Lehmann's and Haeckel's fluid crystals, it is both solid and liquid. As Deleuze observed (while paraphrasing Worringer): "It is inorganic, yet alive, all the more alive for being inorganic."[35] The animation of the inorganic transforms what seems to be a material contradiction into a psychological one. It represents the objectification of fear, but also the pleasure we extract from it. Worringer's anxious Northerner allegorizes the quintessential aesthetic subject of modernity: like an agoraphobic, he senses the world in spirals; he vibrates sympathetically with inert matter. Inside the crystalline structure of Gothic cathedrals, we as spectators, according to Worringer, become crystals, our bodies recall our inorganic past when we were still inside Nietzsche's inert *Mutterschoss*.

Worringer's conceptualization of strapwork patterns contains another latent contradiction. While the art historian emphasizes the "purely inorganic framework" of Northern interlace ornaments, the illustrations of actual artifacts from Nordic or Celtic origin tell otherwise. Next to the purely geometric ornaments, there are frames where the abstract lines intertwine with zoomorphic forms or even whole animals, such as rabbits, serpents, and beak-headed monsters (Fig. 4.7b).[36] Historians of ornament have analyzed with the precision of an evolutionist the material transformations taking place in these monstrous decorations. A meandering ribbon turns into the winding trunk of a snake; a thinning line is a snake's tail, while a bifurcating line is

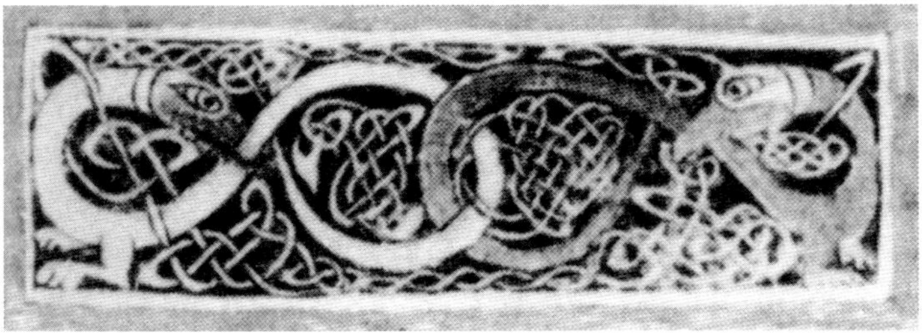

4.7a Band ornament with animal figures. Miniature of St. Matthew, the St. Cuthbert Gospels (detail), from Wilhelm Worringer, *Formprobleme der Gotik* (Munich: R. Piper, 1911)

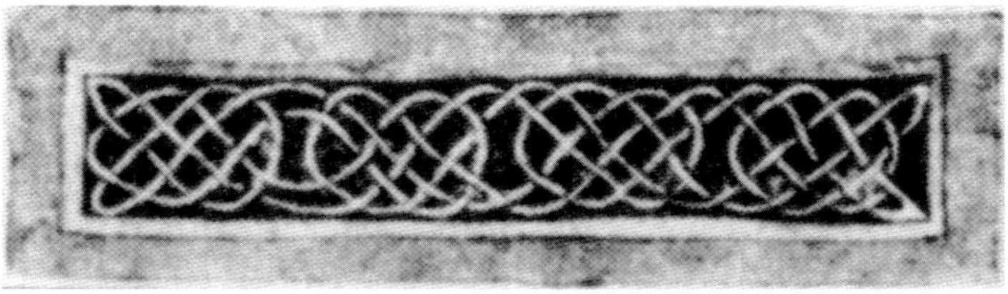

4.7b Band ornament without animal figures. Miniature of St. Matthew, the St. Cuthbert Gospels (detail), from Wilhelm Worringer, *Formprobleme der Gotik* (Munich: R. Piper, 1911)

the clawed foot of a dragon. Every circle becomes an animal head, every dot turns into an eye.[37] The abstract ornament starts gazing back. Every winding line is the question mark of an enigmatic signifier. It is as if the figurative unconscious of Worringer's "inorganic" form of abstraction was belatedly revealing its animal head; just like the subject of the Freudian's unconscious, abstraction has either none or many heads—all of them animal-like.

To be sure, Worringer was familiar with the animal origin of what he misrecognized as abstract patterns, yet he negated this origin. While suppressed from *Abstraction and Empathy*, many of these Nordic zoomorphic ornaments resurfaced among the illustrations selected by the publisher Reinhard Piper for Worringer's next book, *Formprobleme der Gotik* [Form Problems of the Gothic], first published in 1911.[38]

The serpents lurking inside these crystalline ornaments reanimate another visual pattern familiar from the earlier crystallographic studies. I refer to the crystal snakes, the sliding worms created inside liquid crystals, which, as Lehmann showed, moved inside ammonite crystals in a serpentine fashion. Remember that Lehmann attributed the formation of these winding threads to differences in temperature. In a similar fashion, Worringer too would attribute the formation of Gothic abstract tessellated ornament to differences in the *état* or *temperature d'âme*, changes in the psychological temperature created by the migration of the same ornamental motif from the Mediterranean world to Northern European countries.

Yet there are further implicit connections between Worringer's Nordic ornaments and the visual models of contemporary crystallography. Towards the end of his *New World of Crystals*, Lehmann traces certain correspondences between rheocrystals and "non-static" magnet systems. By analyzing the molecular structure of dynamic electromagnetic *Raumgitter* [space-grids], the crystallographer describes the elasticity and deformation that is common in both liquid crystals and certain types of magnets (Fig. 4.8).[39] The models representing the molecular "space grids" of dynamic inorganic matter seem very similar to the types of interlace ornament described by Worringer (Fig. 4.9). There is the same cubic quality transforming the abstract tangle of lines into an energy network. Like interlacing ornaments, the diagonal *Kraftlinien* [force lines] of magnets have the tendency to loop, intertwine and form knots with one another, reinforcing the strength of the space grid. Through the grid, the crystalline iconography makes the transition from ornament to architecture, just as the regular architectonics of modern *Baukunst* was at that time going through its own process of crystallization.

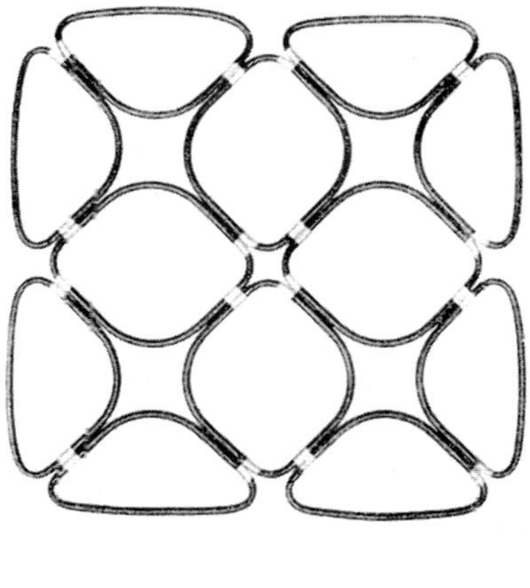

4.8 Model of molecular electromagnetic space grids from Otto Lehmann, *Die neue Welt der flüssigen Kristalle* (Leipzig: Akademische Verlagsgesellschaft m.b.H, 1911)

At this point, we understand that, in his seeming neglect of physiomorphology, Riegl was in fact being infinitely subtle. Morphology still plays a role, yet now formal affinities shift from the external to the internal or molecular level and then extend to an interior psychological space—what Riegl, referring to the early Christian Rotunda, had described as *Innerraum*. Buildings and ornaments transubstantiate into psychograms and then resolidify into blueprints of future architectural formations. Scientific iconography acts as the mediating screen linking the different disciplines of this kaleidoscopic *Gestaltung*, forming an integrated, that is, *Monistic* science of architecture and art.

Monistic art psychology

With the texts of Riegl and Worringer, the discursive circle uniting inorganic biology and the historiographies of art and architecture might appear complete. However, there is another German art historian of the same period, who while less attached to the inorganic, had a marked interest in biological discourses. I refer to Aby Warburg, who throughout his career made use of life concepts in his historiographic practice. While Riegl and Worringer did not have any discernible scientific background, Warburg had studied medicine and perceptual psychology immediately after he completed his studies in art history. Moreover, he was related (through his wife) to Heinrich Hertz, perhaps the most celebrated electrophycisist of the nineteenth century, and the inventor of electromagnetic wave technology. Warburg also personally knew the German embryologist and Neo-Vitalist philosopher Hans Driesch.[40]

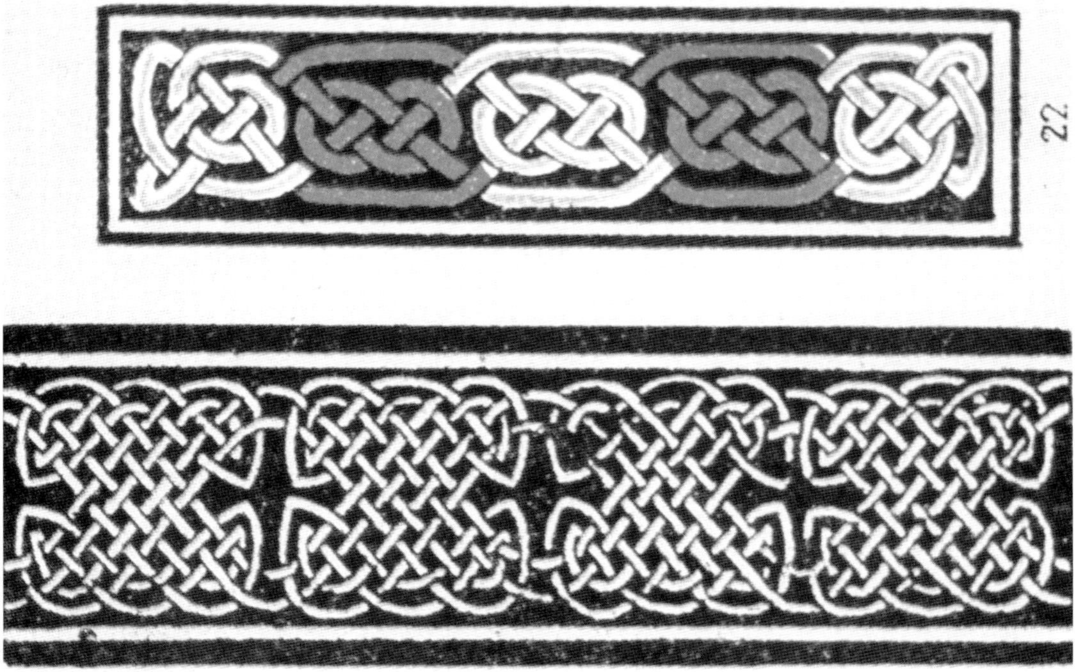

4.9 Celtic ornaments from Owen Jones, *The Grammar of Ornament* (London: Day, 1856)

Warburg's engagement with natural science and philosophy was formative in his conception of art history as an all-encompassing science of culture.

From 1888, when he was still a student in Bonn, until 1903, when he returned from Florence to Hamburg, Warburg was working on a large interdisciplinary project on psychological aesthetics originally titled *Grundlegende Bruchstücke zu einer monistischen Kunstpsychologie* [Foundational Fragments for a Monistic Psychology of Art]. In its original form, the project consisted of 439 dated and enumerated aphorisms, each written on a separate piece of paper and put in chronological order inside a box. In 1901, Warburg revisited the project and, with the help of a secretary, copied all of the aphorisms into two notebooks.[41] While the term "Monistic" appears in the original title of Warburg's project, the words "Monism" or "Monistic" are nowhere to be seen in any of his aphorisms.

Yet both Warburg's library and the dozens of *Zettelkästen* [paper-boxes] filled with his scientific notes include sections on *Naturphilosophie, Lebensphilosophie,* Monism and Vitalism (including an extensive section on Bergson). His library includes several Monistic treatises; apart from Haeckel's bestsellers, there are some lesser-known studies, such as Roberto Benzoni's *Il monismo dinamico* of 1888 and Johannes Schlaf's *Psychomonismus* of 1908, both mentioned in Warburg's scientific notes (Fig. 4.10).[42] Reading the text of his Monistic aesthetics, one understands that Warburg's Monism has little to do with Haeckel's "spiritual" resolutions. It is closer to Benzoni's "dynamism" and Schlaf's "psychism." Warburg creates a dynamic "psychomonism," attempting to compensate between two polarities, such as subject and object,

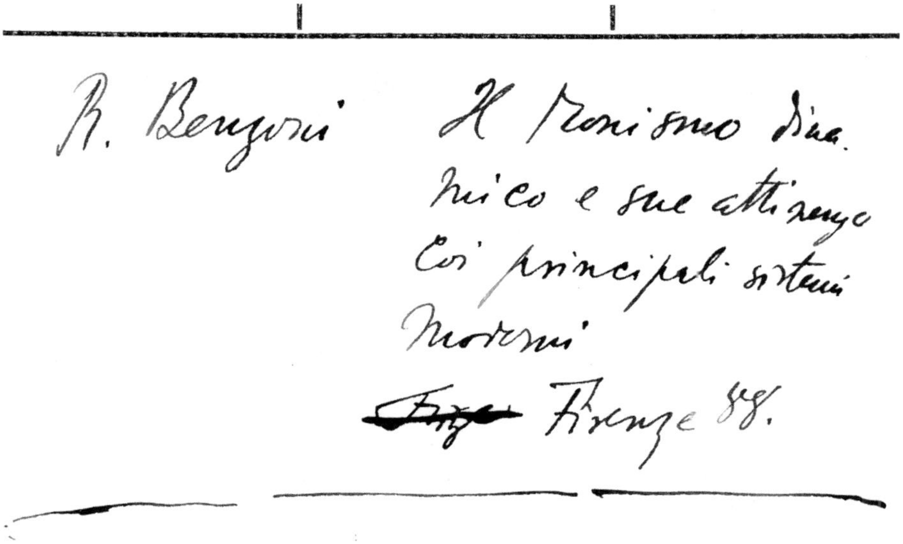

4.10a Aby Warburg manuscript note "Roberto Benzoni, *Il Monismo Dinamico,*" Warburg Institute Archive, Zettelkästen. Photo: The Warburg Institute, London

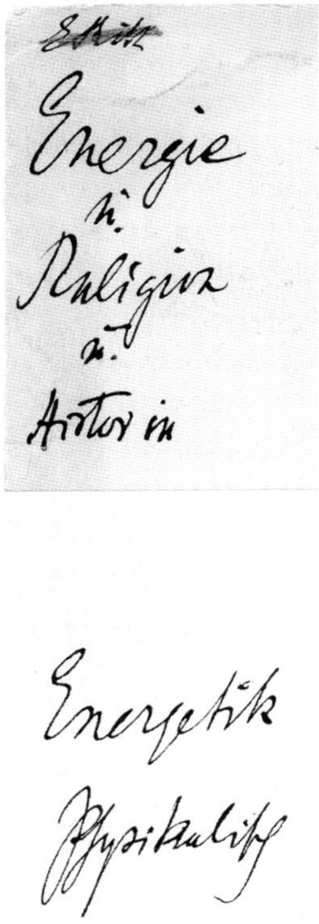

4.10b Aby Warburg, manuscript notes on physics and energy science, Warburg Institute Archive, Zettelkästen. Photo: The Warburg Institute, London

empathy and distance, the identification of magic, and the division of logic. The palindromic movement between these pairs of extremes never reaches equilibrium; it moves perpetually from one condition to the other like a pendulum or a seesaw.[43]

The same idiosyncratic use of scientific terminology applies to Warburg's use of the word *Biologie* [biology], which the art historian frequently employs when referring to an image or an artifact. Here the term has evidently little to do with the life sciences. Following the original etymology of the Greek word, Warburg uses "biology" to denote the discourse of life, or the "life history" of an image such as an emblem, a particular gesture or an iconographic scene. Biology, in fact, here transcends the life limits of an individual artifact and extends to its posthumous legacy—the object's latent existence in cultural memory. So again, as in Haeckel's and Lehmann's inorganic biology, Warburg's art historical biology essentially refers to a form of latent or posthumous life.

Warburg's reconfiguration of "biology" points to the methodological Monism that characterizes his work, which mixes art history, cultural ethnography, evolutionary biology, and natural philosophy into a "Monist"—albeit disparate—science. Warburg envisions science as a funnel: a cone-shaped apparatus concentrating a maximum amount of (intellectual) energy distilled in a minimal surface of interpretation.[44] One point can conduct the whole; one minimal detail may encapsulate an artist, a period, or an entire scientific discipline.

Let us focus on two of these pointed details, which perhaps encapsulate Warburg's Monistic hypotheses. In one of his numerous notes on *Energetik* [energy science], Warburg copies a passage from the *Theory of Energy* by the bio-physicist Georg Helm, which refers to the distinction between kinetic and potential energy.[45] Kinetic energy is associated with movement; potential energy corresponds to "location and method of organization."[46] This is the same form of latent energy recognized by Haeckel in inorganic nature, such as crystals. At the end of his career, Warburg reviewed the entire "thought system" behind his work according to the two types of energy devised by Helm: "Eros and Pathos" was categorized as kinetic energy and "ornament and clothing apparatus" as potential energy.[47]

But in Warburg's art-historical science this "potential" form of energy expands to include living organisms. A note from one of Warburg's better-known influences, the Italian evolutionist and scientist of animal behavior Tito Vignoli, clarifies this.[48] Among the art historian's notes, there is only a single manuscript note on Vignoli's *Mitto e scienza* [Myth and Science], where Warburg copies a brief passage from the book.[49] There, Vignoli distinguishes between two types of animal behavior, described as *statische und dynamische Belebung* [*static* and *dynamic* animation]; Warburg also underlines these two words in his copy of the German edition of Vignoli's book with a red pencil (Fig. 4.11).[50] According to Vignoli, in dynamic animation the animal externalizes its fear with intense cries, movements, and gesticulations. In static animation, the animal in the face of danger stays completely still as

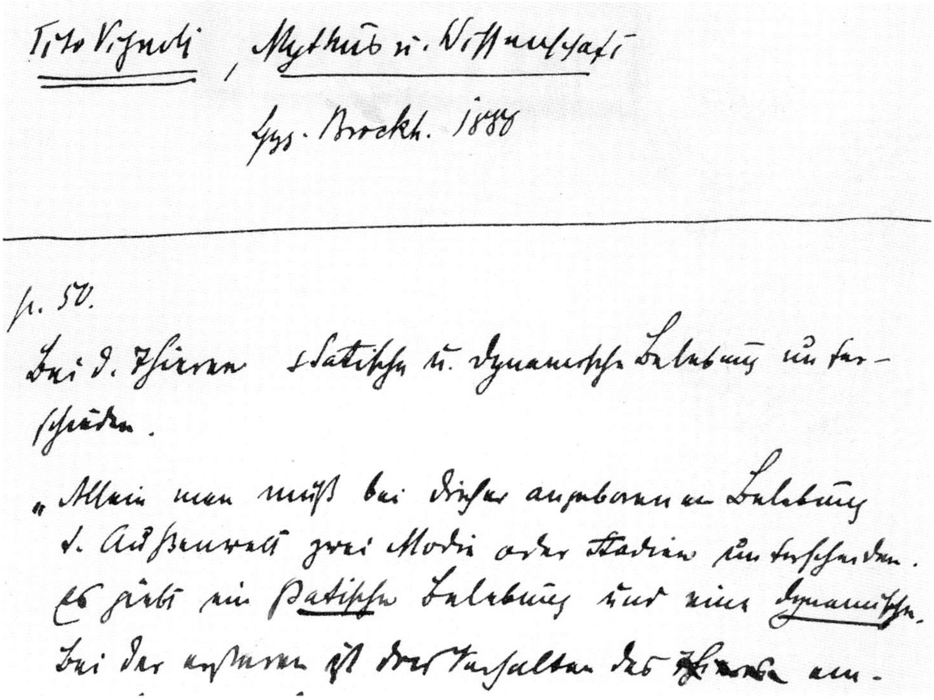

Tito Vignoli, Mythus u. Wissenschaft
Lpz. Brockh. 1880

p. 50.
bei d. Thieren statische u. dynamische Belebung zu unterscheiden.

„Allein man muss bei dieser angeborenen Belebung d. Aussenwelt zwei Modi oder Stadien unterscheiden. Es giebt eine statische Belebung und eine dynamische. Bei der ersteren ist das Verhalten des Thieres an-

4.11a Aby Warburg, note from Tito Vignoli's *Mythus und Wissenschaft* on "statische–dynamische Belebung (static–dynamic animation)," Warburg Institute Archive, Zettelkästen. Photo: The Warburg Institute, London

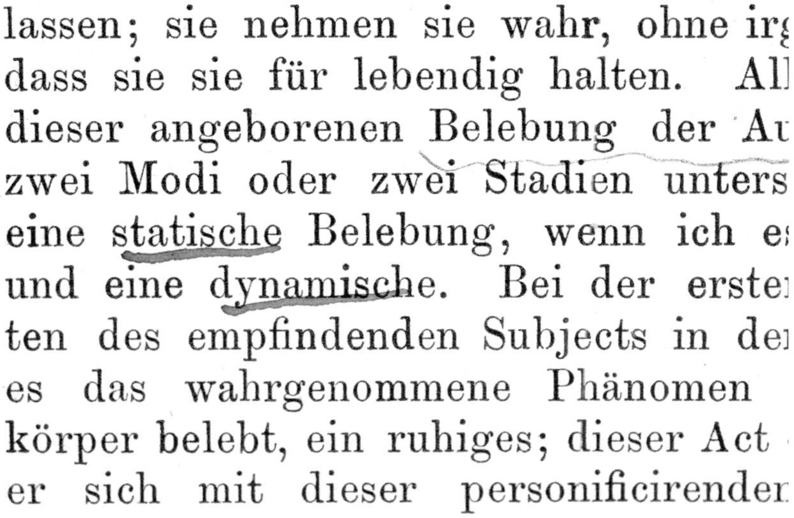

lassen; sie nehmen sie wahr, ohne ir
dass sie sie für lebendig halten. Al
dieser angeborenen Belebung der A
zwei Modi oder zwei Stadien unters
eine statische Belebung, wenn ich e
und eine dynamische. Bei der erste
ten des empfindenden Subjects in de
es das wahrgenommene Phänomen
körper belebt, ein ruhiges; dieser Act
er sich mit dieser personificirende

4.11b The same passage underlined in Warburg's personal copy of Tito Vignoli, *Mythus und Wissenschaft* (Leipzig: Brockhaus, 1880), Library of the Warburg Institute. Photo: The Warburg Institute, London if petrified, yet internally it is extremely agitated by a mortal anguish. It is as if animation here completes a circle: overwhelming excitement leads to petrification, animation causes paralysis. Static animation is another illusive form of the animation of the inorganic, whose "uncanny pathos," according to Worringer, attaches to anxious subjects.[51]

In his own historiography, Warburg employed both pairs of concepts—static and dynamic animation, kinetic and potential energy. The accessories in movement, waving fabrics, and hair of Renaissance nymphs externalized agitation; they activated a dynamic form of animation—what Warburg described as *äussere Beweglichkeit* [external movement]. On the contrary, Orpheus's petrifying gesture, the original model for what Warburg called *Pathosformel* [pathos formula], internalized animation.[52] The gesture freezes the body and transforms animation from dynamic to static. It externalizes movement in a fossilized form. Like Vignoli's petrified animals, the human body in Warburg's iconography turns inorganic, petrified by an extreme level of animation that surpasses its capacity to bear it.

Similar concepts appear in the text of Warburg's *Monistic Psychology of Art*. While the term "Monistic" does not surface in the main text, the term "inorganic" appears several times. In aphorism No. 87 (dated September 14, 1890) we read:

> Clothes are an inorganic extension of the individual, yet they are felt as an organ sensitive to pain—one does not see them, but must consider them in every movement. One grants to things the predicate of unconditional affiliation. The memory image is felt as a bodily member.[53]

The aphorism obviously refers to similar concepts from Warburg's dissertation on the movement of accessories—fabrics and hair—in Renaissance painting, what Warburg described as the representation of *bewegtes Leben* [life-in-movement]. The body appropriates the fabric by transforming it into a living organ. Yet here we learn that not just the fabric itself but also the memory image, that it is transformed into, now becomes a living member. The body is clothed both by fabrics and by memories. The distance between body and memory is erased by means of the fabric that stands between them.[54]

The last aphorism in Warburg's project, written in January 1903, makes a movement from fabric to architecture as the new frame of aesthetic response:

> Approaching/association through subjective mimetic turmoil.
> Distancing through objective architectonic crystallization.[55]

The "near, the subjective, and the mimetic" is here juxtaposed to the "distant, the objective, the architectonic, and the crystalline." We approach by means of "subjective mimesis" and empathetic identification; we withdraw under the auspices of "objective" architecture and abstraction—an argument very similar to the one made by Worringer (after Riegl) a few years later. Considering that it was written in 1903, Warburg's phrase opens up a new perspective for architectural aesthetics. The distancing effect of "architectonic crystallization" erects an ideational partition that shelters the organism from future assaults. A transparent objective division puts an end to the empathetic "turmoil" associated with the Monistic fusions of the past.

Indeed, in 1912, nine years after this last aphorism was written, Warburg revisited his project only to change the title from *Monistic Psychology of Art* to *Pragmatische Ausdruckskunde* [Pragmatic Study of Expression].[56] The "objective" tone of his last aphorism had already announced that change. Like Haeckel's homophagous crystals, the new objective aesthetic devoured the ambient organisms of its own Monist past; one more piece of evidence supporting Haeckel's hypothesis that the "stabile eats the mobile." But this was also a sign that Monism itself, just like the life it described, had by then become latent.

Warburg's reference to the crystallized architectural decorum of modern aesthetics brings us full circle to Riegl's crystalline rotunda and the serenity of its interior space. For both Riegl and Warburg, the crystalline does not signify a type of shape or morphology, but *ambience*. From Riegl's crystalline churches to Lehmann's living crystals, and from Worringer's crystalline ornaments to Warburg's crystallized aesthetics, we witness the evolution of the inorganic from a liquid metaphor to the glacial reality of modernist decorum.

The frenzied dynamograms of Warburg's winding fabrics are now internalized, muted, and fossilized inside the transparent narthex of modern architecture, just like the snake-worms in Lehmann's liquid crystals. The tendrils of Riegl's arabesques and the loops of Worringer's strapwork ornaments have turned into marine plants of a pristine aquarium. Art turns once more into natural history, this time not by the ossifying stylizations of art history, but by the monumentalizing techniques of art and architectural practice.

What we have witnessed in this episodic survey of historiographic and scientific discourses is a process of inorganic evolution, a latent *biology* (as Warburg would call it) of the matter we call inorganic. From Riegl's crystal churches to Lehmann's flowing crystals, and from Warburg's inorganic extensions to Worringer's crystal interlace, we see that the inorganic moves in and with history. It remains mordantly alive in cultural memory, where it transforms from a mental pattern to a physical object and from an identifiable motif into an abstract background—a warped network whose "latent energy" remains hidden until it explodes. A biology of the inorganic traces precisely the trajectory of these periodic explosions.

Postscript: Inorganic afterlife

One of the animate qualities attributed to inorganic matter in the early twentieth century was memory. Mnemo-scientists such as Richard Semon would argue that each chemical alteration left an *engram*—that is, an imprint—that determined the future behavior of matter, whether human tissue, magnet or stone.[57]

Inorganic bodies, too, remembered what happened to them and these memories determined the way this species of matter behaved.[58] But perhaps not only the inorganic has memory, maybe *we* also have a memory of it. Yet psychoanalysis teaches us that next to memory there is also repression—a psychical process through which a subdued idea does not disappear but continues to exist in a latent state. The latent energy of the inorganic attaches to its latent presence in human memory—which might explain its periodic return from oblivion.

One would think that after the infamous "night of broken glass" of 1938, known as *Kristallnacht,* no one, whether a scientist, an artist, or a theorist would ever talk again about crystals—at least not in the same way. In the words of Ernst Bloch, the *Lebenskristall* [crystal of life] became the *Todeskristall* [crystal of death].[59] This is the new mnemonic *engram* embedded by the inorganic on the tissue of Western culture, a sharp "memory-image" that, as Warburg would phrase it, we carry with us as a "bodily member." What we experience today is perhaps not the animation of the inorganic, but the reanimation of this inorganic snakebite by the ferocious descendants of Worringer's Northerners.

Yet the legacy of Lehmann's snake-worms is that the very forces that eroded the crystal also triggered its regeneration. Following its explosion, the historiographic discourse of the inorganic has been the subject of a series of revivals. How else is one to explain the renewed international popularity of Worringer's *Abstraction and Empathy* after World War II? I refer to the time when art historians and artists on both sides of the Atlantic attempted to link Worringer's theory of abstraction with a variety of abstract forms in contemporary art, from the painted rectangles of Rothko to the minimalist sculptures of Tony Smith.[60]

Furthermore, how else, other than as a signal of this "inorganic" form of afterlife, are we to see the inclusion of Lehmann's liquid crystals among the illustrations of one of the most prominent publications of postwar visual culture, György Kepes's *New Landscape in Art and Science* first published in 1956 (Fig. 4.12)?[61] Here, Lehmann's images of blob-like and spider crystals (as well as Haeckel's radiolarians) mingled with the biomorphic furniture and molecular structures of post-World-War-II total design, such as the Eames's chairs and Buckminster Fuller's geodesic domes. Once more the liquid crystals of Monism were absorbed inside the crystalline decorum of modern architecture and its ambient exhibition halls. It seems as if this *new* landscape in art and science discovered by Kepes was already old—permanently crystallized by the fossilized remnants of the past. Monism was now inversely bracketed under *Mo*-[der]-*nism.*

What these resilient relics show is that the animation of the inorganic is precisely a residue that refuses to be metabolized and yet continues to mutate. It is preserved as an excess energy deposit that stays dormant and periodically reawakens in a "new landscape" or cultural setting. Riegl's crystalline rotundas, Haeckel's living crystals, Worringer's strapwork ornaments, and

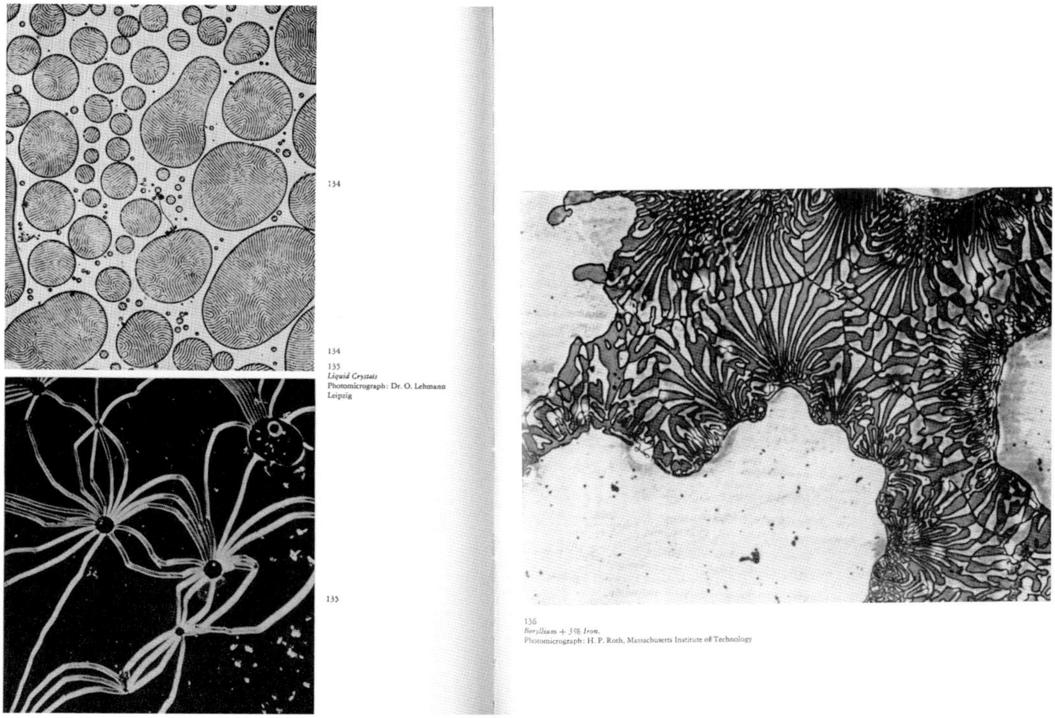

4.12 Page spread from György Kepes, *The New Landscape of Art and Science* (Chicago, IL: P. Theobald, 1956), with photomicrographs of liquid crystals by Otto Lehmann and photomicrograph of beryllium + 3 percent iron by H.P. Roth, The Massachusetts Institute of Technology

Warburg's Monist psychology of art are all part of a new totemic ethnography of Modernist culture—a form of biology as well as an archaeology reanimating the vestiges of modern living space.

Notes

1 Edward Burnett Tylor, *Primitive Culture: Researches into the Development of Mythology, Philosophy, Religion, Language, Art and Custom* (c. 1871), 4th ed. rev. (London: John Murray, 1903); Charles Darwin, *The Descent of Man and Selection in Relation to Sex* (c. 1871) (New York: Appleton & Co., 1873) Vol. 1, 64–65.

2 Following the precedent of nineteenth-century multi-scientists, such as Hermann von Helmholtz and Gustav Theodor Fechner, numerous early twentieth-century researchers performed experiments in both organic and inorganic matter with comparable results. For example, the physiologist Jagadis Chandra Bose, who examined the irritability of plants, would lead research regarding which metals were most suited for telephone receivers and transmitters. See Jagadis Chandra Bose, *Response in the Living and the Non-Living* (London: Longmans, Green, & Co., 1902), *Comparative Electro-Physiology: A physico-physiological study* (London: Longmans, Green, & Co., 1907), and *Researches in the Irritability of Plants* (London: Longmans, Green, & Co., 1912).

3 "Der Centralbau ist der willenlosen Pflanze verwandt, und steht dem Krystallinismus der unorganischen Materie noch näher. Der Längsbau nimmt also auch hier Rücksicht auf das Geistige, wie es im Tiere schon sich äussert zum Unterschied von der Pflanze. Das christliche Culthaus soll vor allem

Innerraum sein." The general title of the lecture series is "History and transition from ancient to modern art" and it was delivered as a course at the University of Vienna during the summer of 1898. This and other manuscript notes from lectures of the same period are published in an appendix of the English edition. See Alois Riegl, *Late Roman Industry*, trans. Rolf Winkes (Rome: Giorgio Bretschneider, 1985), 241 (An. 14, Ms. p. 61). For the original German edition, see Alois Riegl, *Die spätrömische Kunstindustrie nach den Funden in Österreich-Ungarn*, ed. Emil Reisch (Vienna: Österr. Staatsdruckerei, 1927) ; repr. facs. (Darmstadt: Wissenschaftliche Buchgesellschaft, 1964). The German editions do not contain the additional lecture notes.

4 The association of organic forms with curves and inorganic forms with polygonal lines seems to have originated in the work of physiophilosophers in the beginning of the nineteenth century. Lorenz Oken, in his *Elements of Physiophilosophy* (1809–11), writes: "The inorganic is angular, the organic spherical." Quoted in Philip C. Ritterbush, "Aesthetics and objectivity in the study of form in the life science," in *Organic Form: The Life of an Idea*, ed. G.S. Rousseau (London: Routledge, 1972), 43.

5 Riegl, *Die spätrömische Kunstindustrie*, 24 (p. 20 in the English translation).

6 Gottfried Semper, in the "Prolegomena" of his *Style*, also referred to both animals and buildings such as the basilica in terms of the directional axis of movement. See Gottfried Semper, *Der Stil in den technischen und tektonischen Künsten, oder praktische Aesthetik*, Vol. 1 (Frankfurt am Main: Verlag für Kunst und Wissenschaft, 1860), xxxvii, xliii; and also in the recent English translation Gottfried Semper, *Style in the Technical and Tectonic Arts or Practical Aesthetics*, trans. H.F. Malgrave and Michael Robinson (Santa Monica, CA: Getty Research Institute, 2004), 91, 96.

7 For Riegl's references to St. Augustine's texts, see the epilogue "The leading characteristics of the late Roman *Kunstwollen*," in Riegl, *Late Roman Industry*, 223–34.

8 The main text declaring the necessity of a soul as the principle of growth in plants is Thomas Aquinas' commentary on Aristotle's *De Anima*. See *Sancti Thomae Aquinatis in Aristotelis Librum de Anima: Commentarium*, ed. P.F. Angeli and M. Pirotta (Milan: Marietti, 1820), L.ii, 1.vii. For an English translation, see Thomas Aquinas, *A Commentary on Aristotle's De Anima*, trans. Robert Pasnau (New Haven, CT: Yale University Press), 138. For Schopenhauer's references to the "will" in plants, see Arthur Schopenhauer, *The World as Will and Representation*, Vol. II, trans. E.F.J. Payne (New York: Dover, 1958), 294–95. For a more extensive history of the conception of motility in plants for several scientists, including Georges Cuvier, see the chapter "Physiology of Plants" in the fourth edition of Arthur Schopenhauer's *The Will in Nature*, translated into English as *Two Essays by Arthur Schopenhauer* (London: G. Bell, 1889), 281–304. The classic book on the concept of vegetal soul is, of course, Gustav Theodor Fechner, *Nanna oder Über das Seelenleben der Pflanzen* (c. 1848) (Leipzig: L. Voss, 1899) and numerous later editions. See also the psychological studies of plants by R.H. Francé, *Pflanzenpsychologie als Arbeitshypothese der Pflanzenphysiologie* (Stuttgart: Franckh, 1909), and by the same author, *Die Seele der Pflanze* (Berlin: Ullstein, 1924).

9 In the conclusion of *Late Roman Industry*, Riegl refers again to late Roman building in terms of a tree, borrowing from his reading of St. Augustine: "Thus a tree constitutes a unit with its completed individual shape (*de Ordine*, lib.II., c.XVIII, c.I, cl.1017) and no less its individual *anima vegetativa*, to whom it owes its development and movement (growth)." Riegl, *Late Roman Industry*, 227, ft. 119.

10 Alois Riegl, *Stilfragen: Grundlegungen zu einer Geschichte der Ornamentik* (c. 1893) (Berlin: C. Schmidt, 1923). For the English translation, see Alois Riegl, *Problems of Style: Foundations for a History of Ornament* (*Stilfragen*, c. 1893), trans. Evelyn Kain (Princeton, NJ: Princeton University Press, 1992).

11 "The most widely prevalent movement is essentially of the same nature as that of the stem of a climbing plant, which bends successively to all points of the compass, so that the tip revolves. This movement has been called by Sachs 'revolving nutation;' but we have found it much more convenient to use the terms *circumnutation* and *circumnate*." Charles Darwin, *The Power of Movement in Plants* (London: John Murray 1880), 1. See also Charles Darwin, *The Movements and Habits of Climbing Plants*, 2nd ed. rev. (New York: D. Appleton & Co., 1876).

12 Excerpt from Fechner's *Nanna, the Soul of Plants*, translated into English in *The Religion of a Scientist; Selections from Gustav Th. Fechner*, ed. and trans. Walter Lowrie, (New York: Pantheon Books, 1946), 196–97.

13 See Otto Lehmann, *Die neue Welt der flüssigen Kristalle und deren Bedeutung für Physik, Chemie, Technik und Biologie* (Leipzig: Akad. Verlagsgesellschaft m.b.H, 1911). See also Lehmann's later books, which repeat much of the same material yet emphasize the connection with biology: for example, Otto Lehmann, *Die Lehre von den flüssigen Krystallen und ihre Beziehung zu den Problemen der Biologie* (Wiesbaden: Bergmann, 1918).

14 See Ernst Haeckel, *Kristallseelen; Studien über das anorganische Leben* (Leipzig: Kröner, 1917), 27 and frontispiece.

15 See Lehmann, *Die neue Welt der flüssigen Kristalle*, 175; and Haeckel, *Kristallseelen*, 27–28.

16 Lehmann accompanied his film with a new publication titled *Flüssige Kristalle und ihr scheinbares Leben. Forschungsergebnisse dargestellt in einem Kinofilm* (Leipzig: Voss, 1921). There, Lehmann announced that the film was available from Universumfilm-Aktiengesellschaft, Kulturabteilung (Naturwissenschaftliche Gruppe) in Berlin W 9, Köthenerstrasse 43, and could be projected in any cinema theater. Ibid., 4.

17 Lehmann, *Die neue Welt der flüssigen Kristalle*, 268–69.

18 See Lehmann's further references to "crystal worms," with additional photographs, in *Die Lehre von den flüssigen Kristallen*, 492–95.

19 Following the same tactics that would later discredit much of his scientific reputation, Haeckel also made certain minute yet tactical alterations on Lehmann's illustrations, such as coloring several of the plates or changing certain dimensions in some drawings, as for example, the width of the procreating spindle crystals mentioned earlier. Ernst Haeckel, *Kristallseelen; Studien über das anorganische Leben*, 27–28.

20 Ernst Haeckel, *Die Radiolarien. (Rhizopoda radiaria) Eine Monographie*, 4 vols. (Berlin: Reimer 1862–88); and *Kunstformen der Natur* (Leipzig and Vienna: Verlag des Bibliographischen instituts, 1904).

21 Lehmann, *Flüssige Kristalle und ihr scheinbares Leben*, 70.

22 This is a reference by Lehmann to the famous philosophical study by Hans Vaihinger, "The Philosophy of As If" (a book that was also very influential for Aby Warburg and is mentioned in his lecture on the snake ritual). See Otto Lehmann, "Das 'Als ob' in Molekularphysik," in *Ann. D. Philosophie von*

Vaihinger, Vol. 1 (1918), 203; also mentioned in Lehmann, *Flüssige Kristalle und ihr scheinbares Leben*, 70n.

23 Ernst Haeckel, *Die Welträthsel: gemeinverständliche Studien über monistische Philosophie* (Bonn: Strauss 1899). Translated into English as *The Riddle of the Universe at the Close of the Nineteenth Century*, trans. Joseph McCabe (New York and London: Harper & Brothers, 1900). See also Ernst Haeckel, *Anthropogenie, oder, Entwicklungsgeschichte des Menschen: gemeinversthändliche wissenschaftliche Vorträge über die Grundzüge der menschlichen Keimes- und Stammesgeschichte* (Leipzig: Engelmann, 1874); translated as *The Evolution of Man: a Popular Exposition of the Principal Points of Human Ontogeny & Phylogeny* (New York: D. Appleton & Co., 1892).

24 "Vom Leben erlöst zu sein und wieder todte Natur werden kann als *Fest* empfunden werden—vom Sterbenwollenden. Die Natur lieben! Das Todte wieder verehren! Es ist nicht der Gegensatz, sondern der Mutterschoss, die Regel, welche mehr Sinn hat als die Ausnahme: denn Unvernunft und Schmerz sind bloss bei der sogenannten 'zweckmässigen' Welt, im Lebendigen" [11.125]. "Es ist ein *Fest*, aus dieser Welt in die 'todte Welt" überzugehen" [11.70] (emphasis in the original). Friedrich Nietzsche, "Nachgelassene Fragmente Frühjar 1881 bis Sommer 1882," in *Nietzsche Werke Kritische Gesamtausgabe*, ed. Giorgio Colli and Mazzino Montinari, Vol. 5.2 (Berlin and New York: Walter de Gruyter, 1973), 366 and 384.

25 See the online article "History of Liquid Crystals," http://www.lci.kent.edu/lc_history.html#anchor8818 from the website of the Liquid Crystal Institute in Kent State University in Ohio (accessed 12/1/2004).

26 See *Nietzsches Werke*, Zweite Abtheilung Band XII Nachgelassene Werke Unveröffentlichtes aus der Zeit der Fröhlichen Wissenschaft und des Zarathustra (1881–1886) (Leipzig: C.G. Naumann, 1901), 228–29 (aphorisms no. 497–98).

27 For example, the French critic Charles Andler compiled several of Nietzsche's posthumous aphorisms on the inorganic in his intellectual biography of Nietzsche in a section titled "La matière inorganique." There, based on the maternal metaphor "*Mutterschoss*" used by Nietzsche to describe dead matter, Andler writes: "inorganic matter is the maternal bosom" [*La matière inorganique est le giron maternel*]; Charles Andler, *Nietzsche, sa vie et sa pensée*, 6 vols. (Paris: Bossard, 1920–31), Vol. 6, 307. In his "Propositions sur le fascisme" of 1937, Georges Bataille (mis)quotes the same phrase by Nietzsche from Andler's biography as "inorganic matter is the maternal *breast*" [la matière inorganique est le *sein* maternel]. See the special issue of *Acéphale* on "Nietzsche et les fascistes: Une Réparation," *Acéphale* 18 (Paris: January 21, 1937) (fasc. repr. Jean Michel Place, 1995). Some of these notes are translated by Dennis Hollier in *The College of Sociology 1937–39*, trans. Betsy Wing (Minneapolis, MN: University of Minnesota Press, 1988), 79 and 406n.

28 Wilhelm Worringer, *Abstraktion und Einfühlung: Ein Beitrag zur Stilpsychologie*, Inaugural-Dissertation zur Erlangung der Doktorwürde der Philosophischen Fakultät der Universität Bern (Neuwied: Heuser'sche Verlags-Druckerei, 1907). For the English text, see Wilhelm Worringer, *Abstraction and Empathy: A Contribution to the Psychology of Style*, trans. Michael Bullock (c. 1953) (New York: International Universities Press, 1980).

29 See among many others the recent analysis by Siegfried K. Lang, "Wilhelm Worringer's *Abstraktion und Einfühlung*. Entstehung und Bedeutung," in the

critical anthology *Wilhelm Worringers Kunstgeschichte*, ed. Hannes Böhringer and Beate Söntgen (Munich: Fink, 2002), 81–118.

30 On Worringer's opinions about illustrations, see the interview by Ann Stieglitz with Worringer's assistant Dr. Erich Fider regarding the illustrations of the 1919 German edition of *Form in Gothic*; in Ann Stieglitz, "The Reproduction of Agony: Toward a Reception-History of Grünewald's Isenheim Altar after the First World War," *Oxford Art Journal* 12, no. 2 (1989): 87–103.

31 Worringer, *Abstraction and Empathy*, 76.

32 See, for example, Owen Jones's classic handbook *The Grammar of Ornament*, which was translated into German in 1856 with the original plates of the English edition. See Owen Jones, *Grammatik der Ornamente illustriert mit Mustern von den verschiedenen Stylarten der Ornamente in 112 Tafeln* (London: Day, 1856). For more specialized studies of Nordic ornament between the 1880s and 1900s, see note 37 below.

33 Several of the illustrations that the editor Reinhard Piper chose for Worringer's next book, *Form Problems of the Gothic*, show similar ornaments used as frameworks in well-known eighth-century Irish Gospel images from the Bodleian Library in Oxford and the library of St. Gall and Trinity College in Dublin. Wilhelm Worringer, *Formprobleme der Gotik* (Munich: R. Piper, 1911). For the English translation, see *Form in Gothic*, ed. Herbert Read (c. 1927) (New York: Schocken Books, 1957). For Piper's involvement with the illustrations of the book, see Stieglitz, "The Reproduction of Agony."

34 *Abstraction and Empathy*, 76–77 (part of the passage is repeated in a later section, p. 109). For the German text, see *Abstraktion und Einfühlung* (1907), 74.

35 Gilles Deleuze and Félix Guattari, "The Smooth and the Striated" in *A Thousand Plateaus: Capitalism and Schizophrenia*, trans. Brian Masumi (Minneapolis, MN: University of Minnesota Press, 1987), 498–99.

36 For example, all band ornaments from the two sides of the frame decorating the miniature of St. Matthew illustrated in Fig. 4.7 are purely linear, while the two band ornaments at the bottom prominently include snake and rabbit monster figures. Worringer, *Formprobleme der Gotik*.

37 In *Abstraction and Empathy*, Worringer quotes from the essay on Nordic animal ornament by the Danish archaeologist Sophus Müller, *Die Thier-Ornamentik im Norden. Ursprung, Entwicklung und Verhältniss derselben zu gleichzeitigen Stilarten* (Hamburg: Meissner, 1881). Another seminal study on the same topic was the book by Swedish archaeologist Bernhard Salin, *Die altgermanische Thierornamentik. Typologische Studie über Germanische Metallgegenstände aus dem IV. bis IX. Jahrhundert, nebst einer Studie über Irische Ornamentik* (Stockholm: Beckman, 1904). Several of Salin's illustrations were also included by Piper in Worringer's *Form in Gothic*, substantiating further the connection of his abstraction with these hidden animals.

38 See note 33 above.

39 Otto Lehmann, "Flüssige Kristalle und Magnetismus," in *Die neue Welt der flüssigen Kristalle*, 343–67.

40 In fact, Warburg had tried unsuccessfully to procure for Driesch a post in the University of Hamburg in 1917. See correspondence between Warburg and Driesch in the Warburg Archive. For Driesch's embryological theory, see Hans Driesch, *The Science and Philosophy of the Organism: The Gifford lectures delivered before the University of Aberdeen in the year 1907* (London: Black, 1908).

41 All cited material is currently held in the archive of the Warburg Institute (WIA). The box with the aphorisms titled *Ae.[sthetik]* is among Warburg's *Zettelkästen*—the paper-boxes containing his *Wissenschaftliche Notizen* [scientific notes]. The aphorisms are also copied in two sets of manuscript notebooks by Warburg and his assistant, and later transcribed in two sets of typescripts prepared by Gertrud Bing. WIA, III.43.1–3. I am grateful to the former archivist of the Warburg Institute, Dr. Dorothea McEwan, and the current archivist Dr. Claudia Wedepohl for guiding me through the various versions of the manuscript while I was a visiting Getty Fellow resident at the Warburg Institute. All unpublished material is quoted with the permission of the director of the Warburg Institute.

42 Roberto Benzoni, *Il monismo dinamico e sue attinenze coi principali sistemi moderni di filosofia* (Florence: Loetscher & Seeber, 1888). Apart from his writings on Monism, Benzoni had also written on aesthetics. For Warburg's note on Benzoni, see WIA *Zettelkasten* 051/028656. For the other Monistic treatise in Warburg's library, see Johannes Schlaf, *Psychomonismus, Polarität und Individualität; ein offener Brief an Herrn Professor Max Verworn* (Leipzig: Eckardt, 1908). Schlaf was a multi-theorist: his subjects included science, religion, and philosophy (Kant and Nietzsche), and he was also a literary critic and a poet. One should also consider that the first congress of the *Monistenbund* convened by Ernst Haeckel took place in Warburg's native Hamburg in 1911.

43 See Spyros Papapetros, "The Eternal Seesaw: Oscillations in Warburg's Revival," *Oxford Art Journal* 26, no. 2 (2003): 169–76.

44 The "funnel" diagram is based on processes of perceptual psychology. See Aphorism No. 185 from the *Monistic Psychology* dated 30.IV.91. WIA, III.43.3, 74.

45 Georg Helm, *Die Lehre von der Energie (historisch-kritisch entwickelt). Nebst Beiträgen zu einer allgemeinen Energetik* (Leipzig: A. Felix, 1887), 42.

46 "Energetik physikalisch: Kinetische Energie (Bewegungsenergie)—Potentielle [Energie] (Energie d. Lage u. d. Anordnung)," WIA *Zettelkasten* no. 4 ("Historische Synthese") 004/001204.

47 See the relevant note from Warburg's autobiographical sketch quoted in Ulrich Raulff, *Wilde Energien: Vier Versuche zu Aby Warburg* (Göttingen: Wallstein, 2003), 131. Raulff's study contains several references to the connections of Warburg's work with his contemporary energy science.

48 Tito Vignoli, *Myth and Science: An Essay*, translated from the original Italian, c. 1880 (New York: D. Appleton & Co., 1882). For the contemporary German edition see *Mythus und Wissenschaft: eine Studie* (Leipzig: Brockhaus, 1880). On Vignoli's influence on Warburg, see Ernst Gombrich, *Aby Warburg: An Intellectual Biography* (c. 1970) (Chicago, IL: University of Chicago Press, 1986), 216–17.

49 WIA *Zettelkasten Ae.[sthetik]*.

50 See the copy of Vignoli's *Mythus und Wissenschaft* in the library of the Warburg Institute, 50.

51 For a comparative analysis of Worringer and Warburg, see Andrea Pinotti, "Chaos Phobos: arte e pericolo in Warburg, Worringer, Klee," in *Il paesaggio dell'estetica. Teorie e percorsi. Atti del 3 convegno nazionale Universitá di Siena maggio 1996* (Torino: Trauben 1997).

52 See Warburg's lecture on "Dürer and the Italian Antiquity" (1905). For the concept of "accessories in motion," see his dissertation on Botticelli's "Birth of Venus" and "Spring." Both essays are included in Aby Warburg, *The Renewal of*

Pagan Antiquity, trans. David Britt (Santa Monica, CA: Getty Research Institute for the History of Art and the Humanities, 1999).

53 "Kleidungsstücke sind eine unorganische Erweiterung des Individuums, dieselben werden jedoch als schmerzliche Organe gefühlt – man sieht sie nicht, muss aber mit ihnen bei jeder Bewegung rechnen. Man erteilt den Dingen das Praedikat der unbedingten Zugehörigkeit. Das Erinnerungsbild wird als Glied gefühlt." WIA, III.43.1.1, 40.

54 It has not been pointed out by any of Warburg's numerous commentators that, in 1891, the Monist natural philosopher Carus Sterne (the anagrammatic astrological pseudonym of Ernst Krause) published a remarkable book titled *Natur und Kunst* that included an essay titled "*Darstellungen des bewegten Lebens*" [Representations of life-in-movement]. There, Sterne connects the pictorial experiments of painters, such as Raphael, Domenichino, and Velasquez, with the contemporary photographic experiments of Eadweard Muybridge. See Carus Sterne, *Natur und Kunst. Studien zur Entwicklungsgeschichte der Kunst* (Berlin: Allg. Verein für Deutsche Literatur, 1891), 310–20. Furthermore, Sterne was the author of popular works on evolution. See, for example, his *Werden und Vergehen. Eine Entwicklungsgeschichte des Naturganzen in gemeinverständlicher Fassung*, 4th ed. rev. and enlarged (Berlin: Borntraeger, 1900).

55 Aphorism No. 439: "Annäherung/Verbindung durch subjektive mimische Gährung. Entfernung durch objektive architektonische Krystallisation." WIA, III. 43.3.175.

56 See the title page of the first manuscript volume. WIA, III.43.1.1.

57 On the theories of the bio-theorist Richard Semon, whose work was very influential for Warburg's theory of *Mnemosyne*, see Richard Semon *Die Mneme als erhaltendes Prinzip im Wechsel des organischen Geschehens*, 2nd ed. (Leipzig: Engelmann,1908). For the English edition, see Richard Semon, *Mnemic Psychology*, trans. Bella Duffy (London: Allen & Unwin, 1923).

58 This is Haeckel's theory of *Hysteresis* otherwise described as *anorganisches Gedächtnis* [inorganic memory]: that is, the ability of inorganic bodies for customized behavior and repetition of certain qualities. See Haeckel, *Kristallseelen*, 99–100. On the same theme, see the work of the psychologist of matter Walter Hirt, *Das Leben der anorganischen Welt* (Munich: E. Reinhardt, 1914).

59 Bloch reanimates an earlier attack by Lukács on the crystalline aesthetics (and ambivalent politics) of expressionism in his juxtaposition of the *Todeskristall* [Crystal of Death] with the *Lebensbaum* [Tree of Life]. See Ernst Bloch, *The Principle of Hope*, vol. 2, trans. N. Plaice and P. Knight (Cambridge, MA: The MIT Press, 1986), 722.

60 The covers of the post-World War II editions of *Abstraction and Empathy* speak of the "abstractionist" repackaging of Worringer. The snakes on the cover of the early German editions are substituted by a crystalline design on the first German paperback (Munich: R. Piper, 1959) and a Rothko-like composition with a blue rectangle on the cover of the first English paperback (New York: Meridian Books, 1967). For the pairing of Worringer with Tony Smith, see Joseph Masheck, "Crystalline Form, Worringer, and the Minimalism of Tony Smith," in *Building-Art: Modern Architecture under Cultural Construction* (Cambridge: Cambridge University Press, 1993), 143–61.

61 As a former colleague of Moholy-Nagy and teacher at the Bauhaus, Kepes would probably be familiar with theories of animate qualities in crystals by

Raoul Heinrich Francé and other natural philosophers or scientists of the early twentieth century. The anthology edited by Kepes also contained a small general article on crystallography by a chemistry professor. See Kathleen Lonsdale, "Art in Crystallography," in György Kepes, ed., *The New Landscape in Art and Science* (Chicago, IL: Theobald & Co., 1956), 358–59. Lehmann's microphotographs were included in a section on "magnification." See Kepes, 146, fig. 134, 135.

5

Traces of organicism in gardening and urban planning theories in early twentieth-century Germany

David Haney and Elke Sohn

Reform movements in gardening and *Siedlungsplanung* [settlement planning] during the early twentieth century in Germany were marked by a turn away from the picturesque observation of "landscape" as image, towards productive land as the source of human sustenance.[1] The land was thus seen as the basis for practical self-sufficiency, and as functional green space that would no longer be experienced intellectually or contemplatively only. Nature would be physically, sensually, and actively engaged through the body and the senses.

Garden and city were reconceived as a unified, organic whole linking man and nature. They would no longer be seen in isolation, but in interaction with the larger environment in which they were embedded: soil, landscape, and cosmos. A primary reform goal was to integrate garden and city with the environment and the cycle of the elements. "Natural methods" derived from natural science and nature-oriented philosophies were used as models for organic garden and city planning structures.

The *Stadt-Land* (city-country) problematic c. 1900

At the end of the nineteenth century, cities were shaped by the industrialization process, which had massively intensified in Germany in the preceding three decades of the nineteenth century. The city drew people from the land into densely populated centers which did not possess the necessary infrastructure to deal with the influx, resulting in an increase in disease and poverty in German cities. The city was looked on with disdain by many artists and planners fearing that the agricultural base would be "bled dry," with urban growth occurring at the expense of the country. From their perspective, city and country were polar opposites: the city was personified as a "monster," and the country as a "victim." The city stood for international capitalism, which cheapened life and resulted in a dull uniformity. The country, by contrast, was symbolized by the indigenous soil-bound peasant, the farmer, who was the basis of authentic native culture.[2] As in other Western countries, this polarization provided the initial spark for a politically broad spectrum of reform movements that called for a resistance to the prevailing migration from land to city. These movements ranged in approach from explicit anti-urbanism to determined efforts to redesign the city. From the latter perspective, the city was seen as a holistic entity embedded in the surrounding environment. The relationship between city and country was analyzed and concepts formulated to achieve a new, harmonious interplay. The desire to wed *Siedlungen* [outlying settlements] and green spaces in the first decades of the twentieth century was represented by diverse yet programmatically connected terms, such as *Gartenstadt* [garden city], *Stadt-Land-Kultur* [city-land-culture], *Stadtlandschaft* [city landscape], *Stadt-Land-Stadt* [city-country-city].[3]

Landscape, garden, and city as unity

The landscape was not understood as picturesque scenes, but as bounded, geographic districts characterized by topographic, climatic, vegetal, and animal features. Landscape was thus reconceived as region, and the city was brought within this overall context. From the regional perspective, landscape, garden, and city were analyzed as a unified whole, an approach inspired by the natural sciences, which had emerged in the nineteenth century as autonomous disciplines offering new conceptual paradigms.

Texts from the 1850s, including those of Ludwig Büchner, Jakob Moleschott, and Karl Vogt, presented natural scientific methodologies to the public, and the evolutionary theories of Charles Darwin, Ernst Haeckel, and Thomas Huxley popularized biological explanations of societal development.[4] Humankind was placed within an overall order among the animals and considered to belong to nature; its intellectual and cultural products were interpreted against the background of biological necessity. The term *Ökologie* [ecology] was coined to refer to the investigation of naturally determined conditions of existence.[5] At the same time, the conception of a chronological line of development and of permanent progression was evoked through the phrase "the survival of the fittest."

The rural and urban problems that intensified during the end of the nineteenth century were not seen in the light of progress by many contemporaries, but were interpreted instead as "degeneration," resulting from unhealthy, chaotic, and unnatural urban culture.[6] In the subsequent reformulation of Darwin's theory of evolution by natural scientists and nature-oriented philosophers, a series of theories were advanced that were intended to inspire the reform of garden and city, and to strengthen connections between the two.

As an example, theories of "inheritance" were developed based upon earlier concepts proposed by Lamarck. If traits mutated and could be inherited, then this factor played a role in how humankind lived. Healthy nutrition, hygiene, light and air in the dwelling these were some of the themes that were emphasized by reformers. As a parallel development, the philosopher Friedrich Nietzsche invested the human body with new meaning. The soul was no longer a separate manifestation of the divine, instead the human body itself was seen as the source of spirituality.[7] According to this philosophy, a healthy body was a requirement for the healing of the soul. This was to be realized through the physical training of the body in green spaces provided in new garden and city designs.

Based upon his investigations of the biological life of northern Asia, the anarchist and geographer Peter Kropotkin advanced the theory of "mutual aid" as a social impulse in both animals and humans, a phenomenon that Darwin had already noted alongside competition.[8] Kropotkin believed that mutual aid had manifested itself over the course of human history through increasingly large settlements that acted as social organizational forms. While he rejected the metropolis in its contemporary form, he also discussed collective human settlement as being natural and necessary, and a potentially positive expression of the natural law of mutual aid. Kropotkin's ideas were made accessible to German readers through the translations of the anarchist Gustav Landauer, who also introduced his work to the founders of the German Garden City Movement in the early years of the twentieth century.[9]

From country and garden to city

Kropotkin's ideas were interpreted as suggesting that the modern city had its origins in the earliest forms of human gathering. The thesis of the biologist Ernst Haeckel, that the embryonic development of the individual organism mirrors the historical evolutionary process,[10] was also applied by urban theorists to explain the rural origins of the city from both historical-evolutionary and contemporary planning perspectives. They concluded from these analyses that the planning of healthier cities should incorporate agriculture and gardening. The Scottish biologist and city planner Patrick Geddes (1854–1932) illustrated his interpretation of this premise through his "valley section" diagram.[11] He believed that a city could only be understood by analyzing its origins in the underlying rural activities, which in turn had been direct responses to local topographic and climatic conditions. Urban development was thus interpreted as the historic, spatial, and economic progression from agriculture and gardening to large-scale settlement. The region and its corresponding rural activities formed the organizational basis for the city, reflected in the genius loci and the local building culture. The antique temple and the medieval cathedral were interpreted as collective works and architectural focal points in the region. This idea was revived through the "Stadtkrone" [city crown] which had many different architectural manifestations.

This led to further investigation into the characteristics of rural activity and settlement, as well as local environmental conditions. The particular composition of the local soil was postulated as the *Urmaterial* [original material] used by early humans. Humankind was conceived as being an integral part of the cycle of the elements. The biological tenet that particular plant communities had evolved in response to local conditions was applied to human settlement. The farmer's house and garden were thus "original" forms, manifested in unique design expressions for each respective region. In accordance with Neo-Lamarckism, new *Siedlungen* were to be adapted to the environment. The healthy development of humans was bound to the region and its characteristics, not least in respect to agriculture and nutrition, thereby strengthening the importance of regional economy and self-sufficiency. This belief in the interrelatedness of urban settlement and agriculture was incorporated into the full spectrum of political and social reform movements, ranging from conservative and racist, to communist and anarchist.[12]

The special significance given to the environment in urban planning as the source of life in the soil, landscape, and cosmos cannot be understood without considering the Monist world perspective that was widely influential in the years around 1900. Ludwig Büchner, whose writings served as a primary source for Monism, had already rejected every form of dualism between spirit and matter in his work *Kraft und Stoff* [Power and Matter], in 1855. For him, spirit (or God) was nothing other than nature itself. According to Büchner's analyses, humans were biological forms determined by nature. These observations were elaborated into "Monism" by figures such as the biologist Ernst Haeckel (1834–1919), the author Wilhelm Bölsche (1861–1939), the chemist and philosopher Wilhelm Ostwald (1853–1932), and the natural scientist and philosopher Raoul Heinrich Francé (1874–1943). Although a variant of Darwinism, Monism did not accept the understanding that natural form was the expression of causality and mechanical principles of development, but instead advanced the belief that "nature" was animate. Striving to integrate natural science with philosophy, the Monists grounded their beliefs on a radicalized natural-scientific approach: if the spirit that was held to be in humans was not external and god-given, then spirit must already be existent within matter, out of which humans had evolved. Haeckel referred to this as the *kosmologische Grundgesetz* [fundamental cosmological principle] or as *Substanzgesetz* [law of substance].[13]

Monists held that natural law manifested itself in all its appearances, even in the smallest units of matter. Out of these material units was formed the entire cosmos, which possessed spirit in its entirety. One of the greatest proponents of this belief was the physical scientist, psychologist, and philosopher Gustav Theodor Fechner (1801–87), who inspired many artists and planners.[14] In the Monistic sense, the "All" was a continual becoming and dissipation of spirit and matter. The evolution of lower organisms from the living matter of the soil was used to illustrate this metaphysical view.

The *Siedlung* as organism

The Monists directed their attention to the smallest unities and original forms in terms of both historic evolution and individual development: the chemical and physical elements, the monads, the single cells, and the plasmatic cells of animals, plants, and humans. Through the analysis of these natural phenomena, beauty and functionality were read as evidence of original impulses of spirit and design. The increase in intellectuality in higher organisms developed from the division of tasks between conglomerations of cells.

Based on their belief in all-encompassing world laws, the Monists argued that natural and cultural works could be compared on the same basis.[15] Raoul Heinrich Francé went so far as to investigate the city as a manifestation of nature. Already in 1907, using Dinkelsbühl in Bavaria as the basis for his study, he had described the medieval city as a form of natural growth. He thought that, just as with cell combinations in nature, the city was composed of living and organic connections between residents, who were shaped through adaptation to their environmental conditions.[16] The process of amalgamation into complex social organisms was discussed by Francé in terms of increasing levels of culture, life, and spirituality.[17] For his investigations of the city, Francé developed the field of *Kulturbiologie* [cultural biology] as a new "science."[18] He proposed analogies between living creatures and cultural works: both were seen as organisms that were integrated within the cycle of the elements, thus providing further justification for organicism in gardening and urban planning.

The modernization of the garden through the invention of artificial fertilizer, and the reaction of organic philosophy

Perhaps the single most important event marking the entry of gardening into the modern era was the introduction of artificial fertilizer by the German chemist Justus von Liebig in 1842.[19] Agricultural reform did not begin with Liebig, but he was the first to scientifically identify the importance of mineral elements that could be added to the soil to increase plant growth and agricultural production. For Liebig and others who shared his viewpoint, scientific investigation could be applied to practical problems in order to develop new techniques, in this case the use of artificial fertilizer. The methods that he introduced soon gained wide acceptance and were put into use internationally. There were, however, practical and theoretical problems: for example, if the mineral salts in fertilizers accumulated in the soil in too great amounts, this reduced soil fertility.

Before the advent of Liebig's formulation of artificial fertilizer, there was no such thing as "organic gardening" because there was no sense of an alternative, artificial method of gardening to react against. In fact, it was not until the nineteenth century that the words "organic" and "inorganic" took on the respective connotations of biological and non-biological matter. In the antique sense of the term, "organic" was a category referring to organizations of wholes, hence "organisms."[20] The historical development of organic gardening was not just oriented towards improved methods of production, but towards the preservation of the natural processes of the earth as a holistic system. Thus, the concept of organic gardening transcended the discussion of mere gardening technique, becoming a philosophical question as well.

The strongest criticism of Liebig's ideas came not from an agricultural reformer, but from the philologist Jakob von Moleschott, who published a rebuttal to Liebig entitled *Der Kreislauf des Lebens, Physiologische Antworten auf Liebigs Chemische Briefe* [The Cycle of Life: Physiological Answers to Liebig's Letters on Chemistry].[21] In his introduction, Moleschott confessed that he had no specific agricultural knowledge, and that his book did not offer any practical techniques, but more importantly he was rejecting Liebig's worldview. Moleschott claimed that Liebig's concept represented only a "Halbheit" [half-truth] for he only concentrated on one limited factor, the addition of minerals to the soil, without understanding the earth as a unity.[22] He argued that agricultural theory should not be based on an external manipulation aimed only at practical ends, but on the cycle of the elements on earth, which had a spiritual dimension as well. Gardening practice held great significance for Moleschott, for it represented the connection of the human body to the earth. To illustrate his argument, Moleschott noted that the nitrogen or carbon in the reader's body could have once belonged to an African or ancient Egyptian, because of the eternal nature of the cycle.[23] Life forces were organic because they "organized" these elements into biological organisms. The earth itself was a greater extension of this process; he referred to the earth as a "Werkzeug" [tool], a technological metaphor alluding to its functional purpose. He was not arguing for any specific organic gardening techniques, but rather that the cycle of the elements possessed inherent spiritual value, and should be preserved and respected as the source of life on earth. Molleschott's rejection of the ideas of Liebig typified a greater cultural clash between those who believed in the application of technology to serve material progress and increase wealth, and those who turned to theories such as that of the organic as a means of halting what they saw to be the alienation of humankind from the sources of its spiritual being.

Gardening and urban waste

Agricultural theory was also linked to urban design in a pragmatic manner during this period. At the same time that researchers were trying to produce greater yields with less labor in order to feed the growing urban populations as people moved to the cities, engineers were trying to solve the increasing problem of mass urban waste disposal. Because one of the primary issues was the management of the organic elements in agricultural growth, the focus was naturally upon waste, or more directly on human and animal excrement. Liebig was invited by the governing body of the City of London to prepare a report on the possibility of distributing urban waste directly onto agricultural land.[24] He provided detailed analyses on London's yearly waste output, even calculating the minerals that would be provided in the urine resulting from the vast quantity of beer consumed annually.[25] He cautioned, however, that the use of such waste could pose great health hazards, and must be handled with care. In addition, Liebig rejected the suggestion that the Chinese practice of directly collecting human waste could be an alternative to water-borne sewage systems, because European sensibilities would not tolerate the noxious odor. The London report was based on the concept that the elements could be managed as part of a comprehensive, planned system, but this was a means of solving technical problems, not an expression of a philosophical belief in organic wholeness.

Leberecht Migge and organic urban planning

An overall concept of "organic" urban planning as an extension of gardening practice was first proposed in Germany by the garden architect Leberecht Migge (1881–1935) in his booklet *Jedermann Selbst-Versorger!* [Everyman Self-Sufficient!] in 1918.[26] Here, Migge approached the problem of *Siedlungsplanung* [settlement planning] from the perspective of the gardener. Migge was rare among professional gardeners in Germany for expressing the "modern" belief that living conditions could be progressively improved through better technology, while embracing organic gardening technique as a means towards this end. The *Siedlungsplanung* [settlement planning] ideas put forth in Migge's booklet represented a synthesis of the theories of Peter Kropotkin and Raoul Francé. In his book *Fields, Factories, and Workshops*, Kropotkin had argued for smaller, self-supporting communities in which residents could engage in small-scale agriculture and industry.[27] "Everyman" ("Jedermann" in Landauer's translation of Kropotkin) should be able to raise the food he needed to support his family on a small garden plot. "Intensive" agricultural techniques, such as gardening under glass, should be used to maximize production on the smallest plot possible. In *Das Leben im Ackerboden* [Life in the Soil], Francé wrote of the ill effects of the accumulation of toxins in urban soil as the result of the failure to preserve the organic cycle of the elements (Fig. 5.1).[28] According to Francé, urban life was dependent upon food growing, and thus upon this cycle; agricultural and urban living should be conceived as an organic unity from both practical and philosophical viewpoints.

Writing in the period immediately following World War I, when mass hunger was an urgent reality, Migge promised to show how "everyman" could provide for his own nutritional needs through a system of small *Siedlungsgärten* [settlement gardens]. Not only the garden, but the planning of the *Siedlung* itself

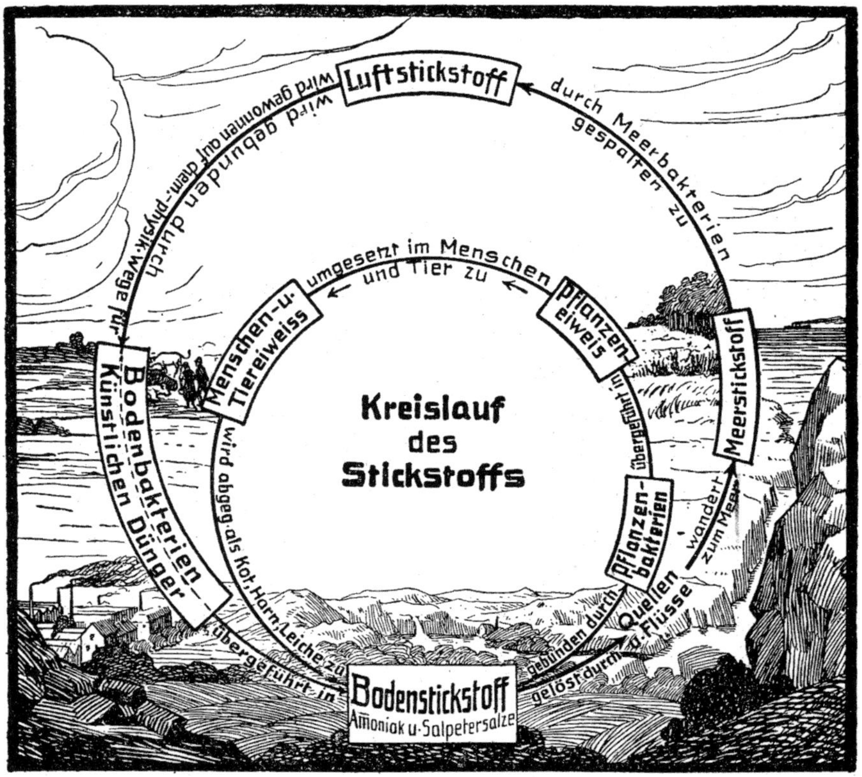

5.1 Raoul H. Francé, "Kreislauf des Stickstoffs" [The Nitrogen Cycle], in Raoul H. Francé, *Das Leben im Ackerboden* (Stuttgart: Franckh'sche Verlagsbuchhandlung, 1922)

was to be based upon gardening practice, "wind, warmth, and water" being primary determinants.[29] The lines of party walls between terraced dwelling units were extended outward to become garden walls to support productive vines and protect the garden from cool, drying winds. The *Schutzmauer* [protective wall] was also a low-tech form of solar collector. In observance of the cycle of the elements, household waste was to be collected in a central composting area, and distributed in the garden after it had aged. Unlike Liebig, Migge enthusiastically reported on the Chinese use of human waste as garden fertilizer, and proposed that each resident collect his own waste from dry toilets.[30] In two later diagrams, Migge illustrated his concept for the reuse of waste on both household and urban scales (Fig. 5.2).[31] In the former, he showed how underground pipes could direct household wastewater directly into the garden, and how solid waste could be aged in special "silos," with a series of drawers for the various stages of decomposition.

The progression in scale from gardening practice to *Siedlungsplanung* was extended to the city as a whole. Migge's first comprehensive large-scale urban plan was produced for the city of Kiel in 1922. In his brochure on the Kiel project, he included diagrams explaining the distribution of water, raw waste, and fertilizer to and from strategic points in the city.[32] Most importantly, he rejected the construction of a water-borne sewerage system in favor of a dry collection system, in which all types of waste would be collected in centralized "dung factories" from which compost would later be redistributed back to private gardens. The city as a whole was to provide for the majority of its nutritional needs, which was thought to contribute to economic stability as well, the concept of self-sufficiency carried to the urban scale. In the context of "Das Neue Frankfurt" [The New Frankfurt] a few years later, Migge prepared a report for the city architect Ernst May in which he put forth similar proposals for the distribution of the resources.[33] Here, however, Kropotkin's theories were also used to argue for a comprehensive urban plan including an outer ring of *Siedlungen* incorporating large commercial gardens, allowing the city to be even more self-sufficient. Inner rings of small, self-sufficient *Siedlung* gardens and a central market building where gardeners' produce could be sold completed the overall planning concept. The last organic urban plan proposed by Migge was for Berlin in 1932, calling for a *Siedlung* to be built next to every sewerage treatment plant on the edge of the city, where the small gardens would receive treated waste directly.[34] He argued that this would reduce transportation costs but he did not acknowledge the fact that many people would find living next to a treatment plant to be less than ideal. This last scheme shows how organic planning ideas could be carried to extremes that were in the end not entirely rational. Despite the fact that none of these plans were fully executed, Migge's ideas were highly influential in German-speaking countries, and his professional colleagues continued to discuss his importance long after World War II.

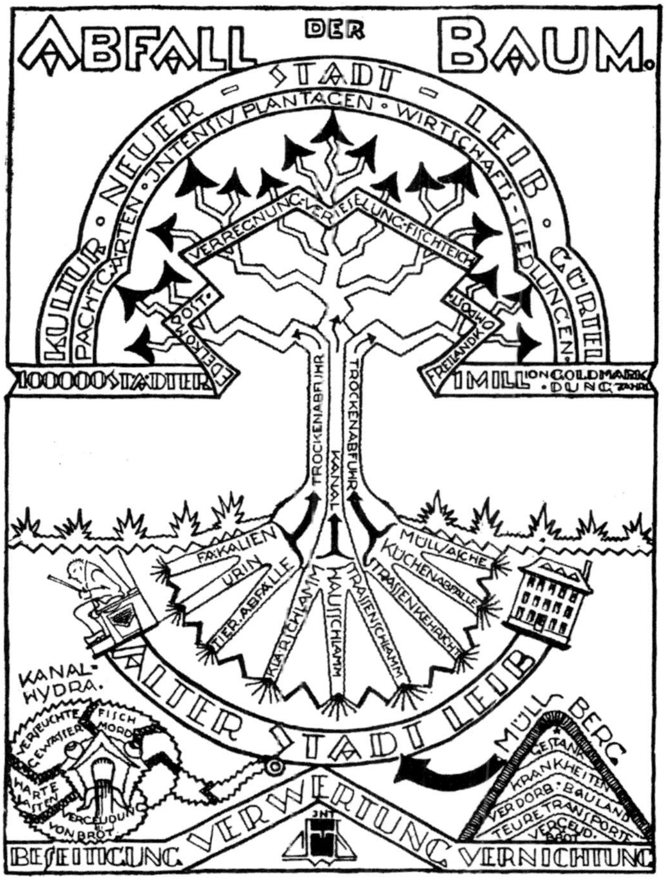

5.2 Leberecht Migge, "Der Abfall Baum" [The Tree of Waste], *Siedlungswirtschaft*, no. 5 (1923): 125

Hans Bernhard Reichow, Hans Scharoun, and the *Stadtlandschaft*

The belief that the *Siedlungsorganismus* [settlement organism] received its sustenance from the land and was integrated into the cycle of the elements, arguably reached its climax in Germany after World War II in the concept of

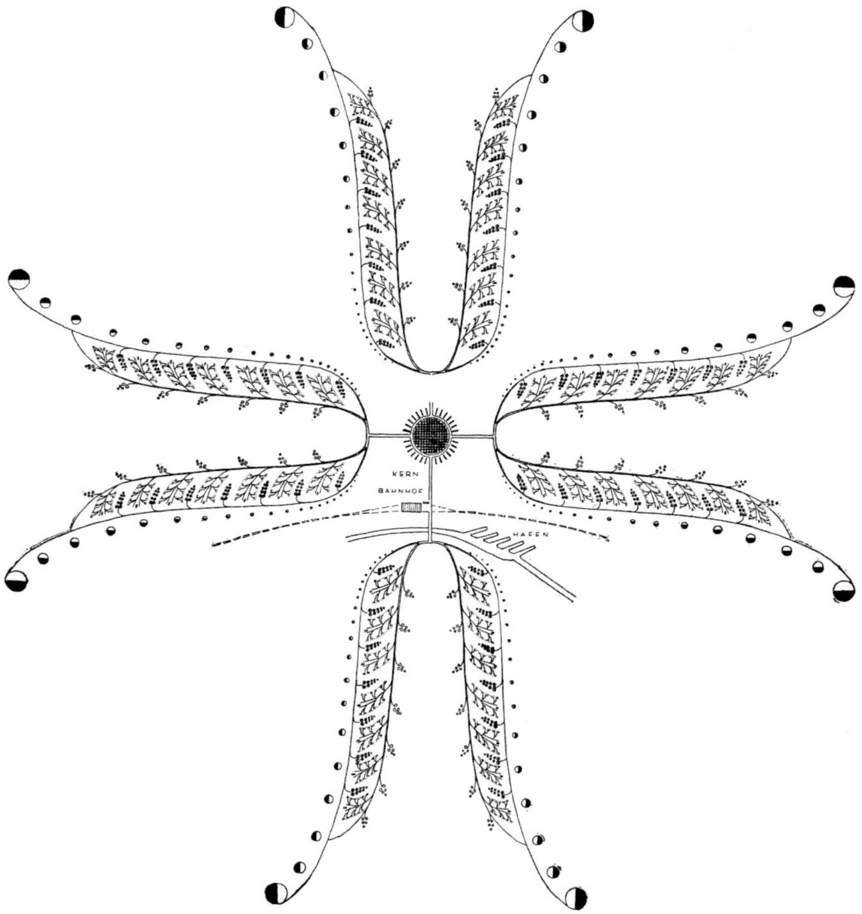

5.3 Hans Bernard Reichow, "Gesamtschema der organischen Stadtlandschaft" [Masterplan of the Organic Cityscape], in Hans Bernard Reichow, *Organische Stadtbaukunst. Von der Großstadt zur Stadtlandschaft* (Braunschweig: Georg Westermann, 1948)

"*Stadtlandschaft*" [city landscape]. The ideas of the architect and urban planner Hans Bernhard Reichow (1899–1974) on this topic culminated in his most important book *Organische Stadtbaukunst: Von der Großstadt zur Stadtlandschaft* [Organic Urban Design: From the Metropolis to the City Landscape]. Reichow was able to carry out numerous post-World War II *Siedlungen* based on these principles, although the term "*Stadtlandschaft*" had been coined earlier during the National Socialist era.[35]

In his book, Reichow cited two Monist theoreticians, Raoul H. Francé and Wilhelm Ostwald. Like Francé, Reichow understood the city as a complex, functional, living organism. He conceived of the individual *Siedlungen* as cells that were the basic planning unit for the "organic urban landscape." The size of each *Siedlung* cell was to be determined by the number of children served by the kindergarten. These cells were self-contained unities providing everything needed by residents, which together with adjoining work districts expressed the identity of the community. Multiple cells together formed a neighborhood (the school community) and multiple neighborhoods composed a district (the cultural and educational community) (Fig. 5.3). With each increase in the scale of

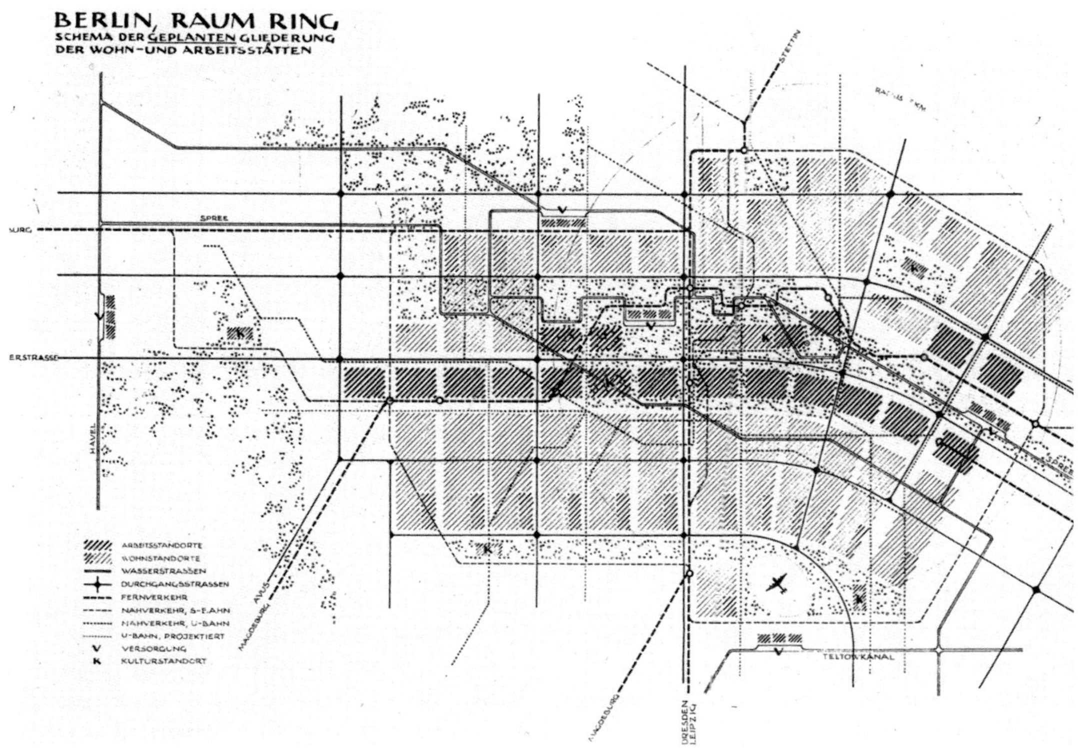

5.4 Hans Scharoun, "Schema der geplanten Gliederung der Wohn- und Arbeitsstätten" [Diagram of the Planned Arrangement of Living and Work Places], in Akademie der Künste Berlin, *1945: Krieg—Zerstörung—Aufbau* (Berlin: Henschel, 1995)

these areas came more public facilities, which were intended as symbols of the community. The *Siedlung* and work units were linked together in rows of linear bands stretching outwards like fingers from the city core into the open landscape. Reichow believed that the landscape as a whole should serve as functional and agricultural green space, in which people actively engaged with nature.[36]

Reichow was by no means the only planner who proposed the idea of *Stadtlandschaft*. Hans Scharoun also argued for it, but from a socialist perspective. In 1945, his collective planning team prepared a reconstruction concept for the city government of Berlin with the title "*Stadtlandschaft*" [city landscape]. Within their vision of a green city, Berlin would transform itself into an agri-industrial *Siedlung* with a 50 percent reduction in population density, while doubling local agricultural productivity.[37] Agricultural and work cells were laid out in linear bands, just as Reichow's had been (Fig. 5.4).

Reichow and Scharoun understood the ideal city units (cells, neighborhoods, and so on) as anatomical structures that in combination formed a universally valid *Stadtorganismus* [urban organism]. However, both planners differentiated the form of each city according to the particular characteristics of the local landscape, thus imparting to each its own identity and giving roots to the community. These concepts were given monumental architectural expression in the schemes of both architects through city halls that served as the *Stadtkronen* [city-crowns] or community centers.

These analogies between biology and urban design cannot be attributed to any particular political orientation because they were utilized by planners with political views ranging from far-left to far-right. Organicism should be understood as a philosophical idea with its own thematic and historical continuity independent of the political and social programs to which it has been applied. Within the field of urban planning, the concept of *Stadtlandschaft* was first conceived in the early twentieth century, with the right-wing conservative planner Reichow sketching out his defining points in a series of publications during the 1930s.[38] On the other end of the political spectrum, Hans Scharoun first illustrated his ideas of the *Stadtkrone* in 1919 in his correspondence with members of the left-wing socialist group of the "Glass Chain." Later, in 1925, he also wrote of the city in terms of a "collective organism" made up of "cells." In fact, the concept of the city as a living organism may be taken as an important feature of modernism. Camillo Sitte, who may be thought of as the father of Modernist city planning in German-speaking countries, had already implied a historical-evolutionary understanding of the city in his writing of the late nineteenth century.

Camillo Sitte

The architect and director of the Staats-Gewerbeschule [State School of Applied Art] in Vienna, Camillo Sitte (1843–1903), traced the historical evolution of urban space and plaza designs beginning with ancient Greek and Roman cities in his most important book, *Der Städte-Bau nach seinen künstlerischen Grundsätzen* [City Planning following Artistic Principles]. He believed that the criteria for modern urban planning could be derived from historical investigations. In the introduction to his book, Sitte referred back to the beauty and vitality of cities on the Greek coast and in Southern Italy, observing that they imitated nature. He emphasized that "in the area of urban planning as well," it is necessary "to learn from the schools of nature and history."[39] Several premises were already embedded within this opening remark alone. Sitte presented the city as a product of natural development, and successful city forms as products of organic and natural growth. Good urban design depended upon the ability to empathize with the existing qualities of the city and to show respect for it as a witness to evolution.

From Sitte's perspective, the spaces and plazas of a city must be allowed to grow in response to essential functions, and the resulting forms must be both beautiful and practical. To illustrate, Sitte observed that the statues in the plazas of antique and medieval cities were arranged in order not to block movement, while at the same time this had a positive artistic effect because they were also removed from the visual axes of monumental buildings.[40] Functional and artistic effects thus coincided. Sitte noted that local conditions changed according to topography and other factors, and thus argued against rigid, formalist urban design principles that were at the time universally applied. He defended the irregularity of old plaza configurations as expressions of historical development and continuous adaptation that had in his words, "originated gradually in *natura*."[41]

Sitte spoke out against the leveling of topography and the regularization of the street plan and analyzed the city as if it were a biological entity whose inherent properties must be respected.[42] Sitte discussed the morphology of the city by using terms such as recurring "types" (or "ur-motifs"), "inheritance," and period-dependent variations ("individuality"), as well as by observing the interplay between parts and whole.[43] Here the idea of the city as organism is already implied: a varying form that developed from a universal anatomy.[44]

Theodor Fischer and Heinz Wetzel

The architect and urban planner Theodor Fischer (1862–1938) was first a professor at the Technische Hochschule [Technical College] in Stuttgart and then, after 1908, in Munich. Fischer taught a whole generation of modern architects and urban planners, including the socialists Bruno Taut and Ernst May, and the conservative Bernhard Reichow. Fischer treated the city as a collective organism with aesthetic and spatial characteristics. The idea of the artwork as organism was taken by Fischer from the theories of Adolf von Hildebrandt, among others.[45] In his architectural work, Fischer sought to connect his buildings with the history of the region to create a sense of cultural continuity. He based this idea largely on the aesthetic association principles of Gustav Theodor Fechner (see the section "From country and garden to city" above).[46] Fischer believed that buildings should be freed from artistic excess and return to simple building forms. To document and analyze traditional regional building types, Fischer and his students traced the evolution of simple, need-based domestic forms, as well as the spatial structure of medieval cities.[47] These studies were also motivated by principles put forward by the English Garden City Movement and realized in the first German garden city of Hellerau near Dresden, designed by the architect Richard Riemerschmidt (1868–1957), a contemporary of Fischer. Many of Fischer's ideas may be directly traced to Monism. This is not surprising since the connection between Monists and urban designers occurred through diverse organizations of the Reform Movement, such as the German Garden City Society, the Deutsche Werkbund (DWB), and the "Brücke" association.[48]

Until 1919, Theodor Fischer worked on his *Sechs Vorträge über Stadtbaukunst* [Six lectures on Urban Design], in which he presented an understanding of urban design through a "practical aesthetic" based on given factors.[49] From Fischer's point of view, form in urban design, whether picturesque or geometric, was a subordinate theme. It developed out of the conditions of the time, and continuously renewed itself.[50] Fischer proposed that urban planning should be returned to the fundamentals of economy, technique (craftsmanship), and landscape. If the practice of urban design observed the real, social needs of the people, then forms would develop logically and naturally. He explained this process in terms of objective, historical development.[51]

Fischer believed that the first architectural need of primitive humans had been for domestic space and, because humans are social beings, their second need was for urban gathering space. The primary expression of the dynamic relationship between community and neighborhood was urban circulation, because it bound humans together. Transportation thus took on special importance in his urban design theory. In this two-part division of settlement patterns into dwelling and path, Fischer saw the reflection of "body and soul" in the urban organism. Within his scheme, the third factor controlling the development of urban design was "nature," to which humans were to adapt themselves with sensitivity.

In respect to transportation, Fischer argued for a network of roadways of different dimensions, from narrow residential lanes to broad commercial streets. In order to provide a basis for the "organic meaning" of transportation arteries, Fischer (as did Reichow later) made analogies to branching phenomena in plants, animals, and naturally accreted old urban structures, using the town of Dinkelsbühl as an example (Fig. 5.5).[52]

Fischer expanded on themes inherent in Sitte's writing, arguing for adaptation to nature by drawing out and heightening the artistic qualities of each landscape. Dominant urban features would thus be created: for example, by building on a hillcrest to emphasize the landscape's character, a result which Fischer referred to as "bekrönende Bauten" [crowning buildings] in a lecture of 1903.[53] He wrote that these types of buildings, "are beautiful because they instill a perfect feeling of purposiveness in us and further, because the uniqueness of the area is captured and elevated to the highest level."[54] The resulting *Stadtkrone* was the monumental representation of the growth of urban culture from rural activities, a commanding presence in contrast to the surrounding sea of houses.

In collaboration with his student Heinz Wetzel, Fischer developed the concept of the "monumentalization of nature." Fischer writes in one of his lectures:

> Everything that nature provides should not be covered up, but be trained and emphasized; heights should be raised, flat areas made more level. The strength of building design lies not in contrasting with nature, but in fusing with it in the highest sense.[55]

Wetzel further developed his master's line of thinking:

> Urban design is the art by which connections are perceived, relations are experienced, valued, and ordered, and which has the capacity to visibly set a scene with what is thus experienced and recognized ... The art of urban design is monumentalized nature, that is, the unique, special appearance of the landscape cast into architectural form. The first step in urban design is to "tear art out of nature" (Dürer), to emphasize the visible in a landscape through intensification ...[56]

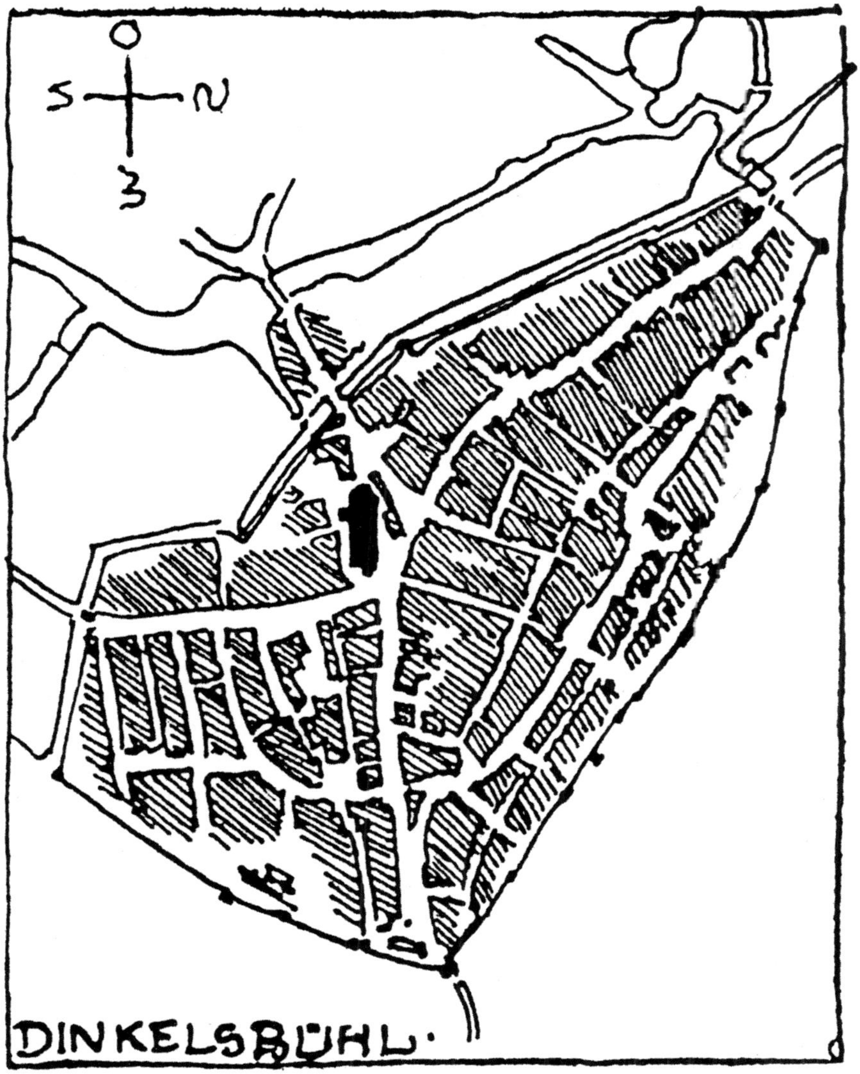

5.5 Theodor Fischer, "Dinkelsbühl," in Theodor Fischer, *Sechs Vorträge über Stadtbaukunst* (Munich, Berlin: R. Oldenbourg, 1920)

Conclusion

The reform of the planning disciplines to arrive at modern methods of garden and city design in the early twentieth century was informed by analogies between natural and artistic works. The integrated conception of the *Siedlung* in respect to the nutritional and formal aspects of the environment (soil, landscape, cosmos) concerned a range of characteristics for the garden and city, according to the perspective of planners of the period. Taken together, they formed a purposeful and living *Siedlungsorganismus* [settlement organism] that supported autonomy, vitality, self-determination, natural growth, cultural improvement, and economic and intellectual rootedness in the region. These analogies drew upon the most recent contemporary discoveries and postulates in the natural sciences and nature-oriented philosophies. This transference of concepts into the planning disciplines was in part quite literal, as in the case of the cycle of the elements, cells as reproductive modules, and the branching principle in the laying-out of streets.

Garden and city as unity would thus be conceived and interpreted through biological and other natural scientific terms. Organicism showed itself as a continuity. In a society ruled by the economy, on the basis of rationality and the domination of nature, the hegemony of natural science cannot be avoided. The advancement of the natural sciences as the basis of modern culture signifies that the highest explanatory powers were attributed to hypotheses drawn from scientific disciplines. In so far as organicism may be understood as an implication of the Modern, it represents a social orientation towards the natural sciences that transcends the spectrum of political views to which it has been attached.

A radical enlightenment thereby tends towards mysticism, Monism being a good example of this. Monism, as part of the free-thinking ideas dating back to the nineteenth century, is to be understood as a factor of modernization in connection with the bourgeois economy.[57] This move was manifested in the retreat from orthodox religious beliefs and the corresponding advancement of the natural sciences. Monism is neither an exceptional case nor a false direction, but the intensification of dogmatic, empiricist natural science (for example, in the radical connection between spirit and matter and resulting theories of animism), reverting to mysticism.[58]

In this sense, the Biocentric represents a continuity within the modern, inclusive of the danger of biological and esoteric ideologies. Against this background, it would be fatal to unequivocally interpret the concepts represented here as precursors of fascist theories—and thus to isolate them as exceptions. If, by contrast, one comprehends the Biocentric as an implication of the modern (in diverse political formulations), then a critical examination, rather than a prohibition, is called for.

Notes

1 The word "*Siedlung*" translates literally as "settlement." It is used to refer to planned housing settlements. These could be either quasi-self-sufficient rural communities or large urban housing estates. The original, dominant idea of the *Siedlung* was that everyone should have their own small garden space for growing vegetables, flowers, and so on. (The plural of "*Siedlung*" is "*Siedlungen*.")

2 See Klaus Bergmann, *Agrarromantik und Großstadtfeindlichkeit* (Meißenheim am Glan: Anton Hain, 1970).

3 On the German *Gartenstadt* [Garden City] see Theodor Fritsch, *Die Stadt der Zukunft: Gartenstadt* (Leipzig, 1896). For the earliest known example of Leberecht Migge's use of the term *Stadtlandkultur*, see a series of articles by Migge published in the journal, *Haus Wohnung Garten,* January 10, May 20 and 22,

October 9, 1920. *Stadtlandschaft*: The term was developed in geography during the 1920s in order to study the mutual influence of city and landscape. It first appeared in a title by Siegfried Passarge, *Stadtlandschaften der Erde* (Breslau: Ferdinand Hirt, 1930). *Stadt-Land-Stadt*: this model was formulated by Martin Wagner in *Die neue Stadt im neuen Land* (Berlin: Karl Bucholt, 1934).

4 Among others see Jakob Moleschott *Der Kreislauf des Lebens* (1852), Ludwig Büchner, *Kraft und Stoff* (1852), and Karl Vogt, *Köhlerglaube und Wissenschaft* (1855).

5 See Ernst Haeckel, *Generelle Morphologie der Organismen* (Berlin, 1866).

6 See Frank Simon-Ritz, *Die Organisation einer Weltanschauung: Die freigeistige Bewegung im Wilhelminischen Deutschland* (Gütersloh: Kaiser, 1997) 46.

7 See Gernot Böhme, *Anfänge der Leibphilosophie im 19.* Jahrhundert; Wolfgang Riedel, "Homo Natura. Zum Menschenbild der Jahrhundertwende," in Kai Buchholz, Rita Latocha, Hilke Peckmann, and Klaus Wolbert, eds., *Die Lebensreform*, vol.1 (Darmstadt: Häusser, 2001).

8 In his article series of the 1890s in *The Nineteenth Century*, Peter Kropotkin wrote the following text: *Mutual Aid: A Factor of Evolution* (London: Heinemann, 1902), translated by Gustav Landauer in 1908 with the German title: *Gegenseitige Hilfe in der Tier- und Menschenwelt*.

9 In 1900 Landauer belonged to the "Friedrichshagener Dichterkreis" [Friedrichshagen Poets' Circle] and was involved in the first land commune and the "Neue Gemeinschaft" [New Community], out of which grew the German Garden City Movement.

10 Haeckel referred to these processes as "ontogenesis" and "phylogenesis." He described this "biogentic principle" in his book, *Generelle Morphologie der Organismen* (1866).

11 See Volker M. Welter, *Biopolis: Patrick Geddes and the City of Life* (Cambridge, MA: MIT Press, 2002).

12 As example of the political spectrum of the land commune movement in the first decades of the twentieth century, see *Ulrich Linse, Zurück, o Mensch, zur Mutter Erde*, (Munich: dtv, 1983).

13 Ernst Haeckel, *Die Welträtsel: Gemeinverständliche Studien über Monistische Philosophie* (1899), rev. ed. (Leipzig: Alfred Körner, 1907) 13.

14 See, among others: Matthias Schirren, "Allbeseelung, Phantastik und Anthropomorphisierung," in Angelika Thiekötter et al., eds., *Kristallisationen, Splitterungen—Bruno Tauts Glashaus* (Basel, Berlin, and Boston: Birkhäuser, 1993).

15 See Raoul Heinrich Francé, *Harmonie in der Natur* (Stuttgart: Franckh'sche Verlagshandlung, 1926). In this text, Francé describes his thesis that, in cultural works (such as the pyramids) and in natural phenomena (such as the interstitial spaces between leaves on plants), the same formal relationships may be found.

16 R.H. Francé, *Streifzüge im Wassertropfen* (Stuttgart: Franckh'sche Verlagshandlung, 1907), 7.

17 Ibid., 13.

18 Francé described the field of "Kulturbiologie" in his book: *München: Die Lebensgesetze einer Stadt* (Munich: Hugo Bruckmann, 1920). He attempted

to show that human physical attributes were connected to local landscape conditions, which were embedded in a greater context of the "Bios."

19 For Liebig's own explanation of his conception of agriculture and chemistry, see Justus von Liebig, *Die Chemie in ihrer Anwendung auf Agricultur und Physiology* (1840), 9th ed. (Braunschweig: Viewig und Sohn, 1876).

20 Georg Germann, "Das Organische Ganzen," *archithese* (1972): 36–41.

21 Jacob Moleschott, *Der Kreislauf des Lebens, Physiologische Antworten auf Liebig's Chemische Briefe*, 2nd ed. (Mainz: Victor und Zahern, 1855).

22 Ibid., 11, 17.

23 Ibid., 85.

24 Liebig, "Letter on the subject of the utiligation [*sic*] of the metropolitan sewage, addressed to the Lord Mayor of London," in Liebig, *Die Chemie*, 88–97.

25 Ibid., 91.

26 Leberecht Migge, *Jedermann Selbstversorger* (Eugen Diedrichs: Jena, 1918, 1919). The two editions vary slightly.

27 Peter Kropotkin, *Landwirtschaft Industrie und Handwerk,* 2nd ed., trans. Gustav Landauer (Berlin-Grünewald: Renaissance Verlag, 1910).

28 Raoul Francé, *Das Leben im Ackerboden* (Stuttgart: Franckh'sche Verlagshandlung, 1922), 42–43, diagram p. 63.

29 Migge, *Jedermann*, 13–17.

30 Ibid., 18.

31 "Der Abfall Baum," *Siedlungswirtschaft*, no. 5 (1923): 125 (repr. here as Fig. 5.2); plumbing diagram, *Siedlungswirtschaft*, no. 1 (1928): 6. *Siedlungswirtschaft* was Migge's own journal, which appeared monthly from 1923 to 1929.

32 Willy Hahn and Leberecht Migge, *Der Ausbau eines Grüngürtels der Stadt Kiel* (Kiel, 1922).

33 "Das Neue Frankfurt" or "DNF" was the title given to Ernst May's comprehensive vision of urban planning and architecture to result in a new way of life. May had previously worked with Migge in Breslau (Silesia), and invited him to Frankfurt am Main to participate in the laying out of the new *Siedlungen* there. May also commissioned Migge to write an urban report on the management of resources: Leberecht Migge, "Grünpolitik der Stadt Frankfurt a.M., Gutachten für die grüne kolonisatorische Entwicklung der neuen Grossgemeinde," no date [c. 1927].

34 Leberecht Migge and Max Schemmel, "Ein Weltstadt kolonisiert! Berlin versorgt sich selbst! Eine Million Berliner siedeln aus!," unpublished report, no date [c. 1932].

35 Reichow was given the opportunity to carry out his concept in one of the few newly founded urban areas in former West Germany: Sennestadt in Bielefeld. Reichow's work was honored through other important projects: He worked as a planner and advisor for "Neue Heimat" and was involved in other large-scale projects such as "Neue Vahr" near Bremen (1956, together with Ernst May) and the garden city of Hohnerkamp in Hamburg (1953). Hans Reichow's concept of *Stadtlandschaft* and its conceptual sources are discussed extensively

in Elke Sohn, "Hans Bernhard Reichow and the concept of *Stadtlandschaft* in German planning," *Planning Perspectives* 18 (2003): 119–46.

36 Hans Bernhard Reichow, *Organische Stadtbaukunst: Von der Großstadt zur Stadtlandschaft* (Braunschweig: Georg Westermann, 1948), 165. "Such ideas lead us from a formerly intensive to a now extensive green planning policy, away from the English park towards the forest and the grove, away from the decorative lawn and flower bed to the city's food-giving landscape, away from the satisfaction of merely aesthetic needs to the fullfilment of general, elemental needs to the establishment of the biologically necessary."

37 See Johann Friedrich Geist and Klaus Küvers, *Das Berliner Mietshaus 1945–1989* (Munich: Prestel, 1989).

38 The concept of the city as *Leistungsorganismus* [controlling organism], which determined the interchange and overall order of city and country/land, was already developed by Reichow in 1932. He drew upon the CIAM guidelines of 1928: H.B. Reichow, "Funktioneller Städtebau," *Monatshefte für Baukunst und Städtebau* 9 (1932): 449–51. Reichow proposed an ideal urban structure in "Der Plan einer Neustadt Antwerpen." Along a green axis, a row of dwelling areas were to radiate outward from a commercial center, making organic growth possible: H.B. Reichow, "Der Plan einer Neustadt Antwerpen," *Monatshefte für Baukunst und Städtebau* 8 (1933): 380–84. In 1936, Reichow drew up his "Allgemeines Schema einer Stadterweiterung," in which bands of *Siedlungen* stretched outward like fingers into the landscape. The city is embedded in the agricultural and horticultural areas that belong to it: H.B. Reichow, "Braunschweigs Grünflächenfrage," *Monatshefte für Baukunst und Städtebau* 7 (1936): 73–78.

39 Camillo Sitte, *Der Städte-Bau nach seinen künstlerischen Grundsätzen*, 3rd ed. (Vienna: Carl Graeser & Co., 1901).

40 Ibid., 26, "Auffallend ist, wie sich bei diesem System die Anforderungen des Verkehres und der künstlerischen Wirkung gegenseitig decken."

41 Ibid., 55.

42 See "Enteignungsgesetz und Lageplan," 1 *Der Städtebau* (1904): 5–8; 2 *Der Städtebau* (1904): 17–19; 3 *Der Städtebau* (1904): 35–37.

43 In *Der Städte-Bau nach seinen künstlerischen Grundsätzen*, Sitte wrote that the open spaces in ancient cities always served the same purpose. The temple and the forum were, for the city as a whole, what the atrium was for the single-family house, a fully outfitted primary room as *Gesamtkunstwerk* and the symbolic representation of the worldview of the community. The ancient forum as "type" was thought by Sitte to have recurred in the designs of more recent cities.

44 Hugo Häring, who influenced Scharoun, introduced this distinction through the terms "Organwerk" and "Gestaltwerk." Thus, cities in particular landscapes were also individualities. See Hugo Häring, "Zwei Städte," *Die Form* 8 (1926). These ideas were based on developments in the natural sciences, such as the comparative anatomy of French natural scientist Baron Georges Cuvier (1796–1832) and the metamorphosis theory of Johann Wolfgang von Goethe (the idea of ur-plants, out of which different varieties developed).

45 Adolf Hildebrand, *Das Problem der Form in der bildenden Kunst* (Straßbourg: Heitz, 1893).

46 See Winfried Nerdinger, *Theodor Fischer. Architekt und Städtebauer* (Berlin: Ernst & Sohn, 1988).

47 Following World War I, the idea of *Heimatschutz* had a strong influence on architects and urban planners. The "Stuttgart School" (H. Wetzel, P. Schmitthenner, P. Bonatz) was based on the teachings of Fischer and acted as the center for this traditional form of modernism. See Wolfgang Voigt, "Die Stuttgarter Schule und die Alltagsarchitektur des Dritten Reiches," in Hartmut Frank, ed., *Faschistische Architekturen* (Hamburg: Christians, 1985).

48 Francé, Haeckel, August Forel, Georg Hirth, members of the "Friedrichshagener Poet's Circle," W. Bölsche, M.H. Baege, B. Wille, and others founded the DMB in 1906. Hirth (editor of the journal *Jugend*) and Forel (psychiatrist) belonged to the Gartenstadtgesellschaft, in which Riemerschmid and Fischer were active. In 1911, Wilhelm Ostwald, then president of the DMB, founded the organization the "Brücke," which was dedicated to international academic exchange. This organization included the DMB, the DWB , and figures who belonged to both—such as M.H. Baege, Peter Behrens, Fritz Hellwag (responsible for the rubric "Die deutsche Werkbundbewegung" in *Das Monistische Jahrbuch* 1913/14, (DWB), Ernst Jäckh (director and later president of the DWB), Hermann Muthesius, Karl Schmidt (director of the Deutsche Werkstätten), and Bruno Wille. "Brücke" itself was an institutional member of the DWB. The same was true for Ostwald, who from 1912 onward, was director of the independent DWB group for color art and developed a color wheel for the DWB. See E. Aigner, *Fünf Jahre Deutscher Monistenbund: Bericht über die Entwicklung der Ortsgruppe München des Deutschen Monistenbundes in den Jahren 1906–1911* (Munich: Mendelsohn Bartholdy, 1911); Joan Campbell, *Der Deutsche Werkbund 1907–1934* (Stuttgart: Klett-Cotta, 1981); *Die Brücke. Mitgliederliste* (Munich: Selbstverlag der Brücke, 1913); Kristiana Hartmann, *Deutsche Gartenstadtbewegung* (Munich: Heinz Moos, 1976).

49 Theodor Fischer, *Sechs Vorträge über Stadtbaukunst* (Munich: Berlin: R. Oldenbourg, 1920), 5.

50 Theodor Fischer, "Altstadt und neue Zeit," Lecture held on September 4, 1928, in Theodor Fischer, *Gegenwartsfragen künstlerischer Kultur* (Munich: Filser, 1947), 23.

51 Theodor Fischer, *Sechs Vorträge über Stadtbaukunst* (Munich and Berlin: R. Oldenbourg, 1920), 5.

52 Ibid., 17.

53 Theodor Fischer, *Stadterweiterungsfragen. Mit besonderer Rücksicht auf Stuttgart* (Stuttgart: Deutsche Verlagsanstalt, 1903), 22.

54 Ibid., 17.

55 Fischer, *Sechs Vorträge über Stadtbaukunst*, 78.

56 Heinz Wetzel, *Stadt, Bau, Kunst: Gedanken und Bilder aus dem Nachlaß*, ed. Karl Krämer (Stuttgart: Krämer, 1978), 36.

57 See Horst Hillermann, *Der vereinsmäßige Zusammenschluß bürgerlichweltanschaulicher Reformvernunft in der Monismusbewegung des 19. Jahrhunderts* (Kastellaun: Aloys Henn, 1976).

58 See Paul Ziche, "Zwischen Fortschrittsglauben und Verzweiflung an der Moderne. Ambivalenzen der Wissenschaftswahrnehmung um 1900," in Buchholz, Latocha, Peckmann, and Wolbert, eds., *Die Lebensreform*.

6

Organic visions and biological models in Russian avant-garde art

Isabel Wünsche

The Russian avant-garde has generally been characterized as a movement closely associated with—or even a result of—the October Revolution of 1917, one that through its organization of proletarian life in industrialized cities would lead to the construction of a new socialist society. The urban, ideological, and utilitarian character of Russian avant-garde art has thus been emphasized and its references to nature mostly ignored or overlooked.[1] Until recently, art historians have also generally viewed Russian avant-garde art as a paradigmatic example of Modernist art and design in the Cubist-Constructivist tradition—this despite early studies by Charlotte Douglas and Christina Lodder. In her 1983 book on Russian Constructivism, Lodder demonstrated that organic principles were at the foundation of the Constructivist designs by Vladimir Tatlin and Petr Miturich;[2] Douglas, in her 1984 essay on modern Russian art, emphasized that the anti-Cubist stances of artists such as Pavel Filonov, David Burliuk, Nikolai Kulbin, Mikhail Matiushin, and even Kazimir Malevich, do not fit into the Cubist-Constructivist line of interpretation.[3]

In this essay, I will focus on the holistic worldviews and organic approaches to art that were particularly dominant among the artists of the pre-revolutionary avant-garde in St. Petersburg, which centered on Nikolai Kulbin's circle of Impressionists and his *Treugolnik* (Triangle) group as well as the artists' group *Soiuz Molodezhi* [Union of Youth]. The physician and artist Nikolai Kulbin, stimulated by recent discoveries in the natural sciences and the development of psychology, proposed that all rules and conventions in the search for new aesthetic possibilities be discarded;[4] between 1908 and 1910, he organized four major art exhibitions, delivered many lectures, and published several articles on his psychological approach to art.[5] Kulbin and the members of his group combined Impressionist and Symbolist modes of painting and placed an emphasis on metaphysical inquiry, mythological motifs, and fantasy.

The Union of Youth arose out of and in opposition to Kulbin's enterprise. Founded in 1910, this rather heterogeneous organization of a dozen young artists focused on "familiarizing its members with modern trends in art; ... developing their aesthetic tastes by means of drawing and painting workshops, as well as discussions on questions of art; and ... furthering the mutual rapprochement of people interested in art."[6] Its members set up a group studio; organized exhibitions, discussions, and dramatic productions; and founded an art library.[7] As Kulbin had done previously, the Union of Youth insisted on recognition of the rightful existence of all artists' groups—an outlook that was reflected in their activities. Stressing artistic individuality and expressive freedom, the organization served as a platform for the renewal of the arts by promoting a wide variety of artistic approaches and stylistic expressions. Less radical in their artistic experiments than their colleagues in Moscow, the members of the Union of Youth were generally post-Symbolist in their orientation—that is, they felt indebted to the Symbolist heritage, but chose to develop in new directions; they promoted the study of the formal aspects of art and the processes of artistic creation while, at the same time, emphasizing metaphysical content. Union of Youth artists were also more attuned to developments in Western Europe; they were closely connected with the Munich art scene and attempted to establish working relations with Scandinavian artists.[8] Rather than a predominant interest in icon painting and Russian folk art that characterized many representatives of the Moscow avant-garde, modern artists in St. Petersburg were more concerned with a wide variety of non-Western artistic expressions, such as African and Oceanic sculpture, Chinese calligraphy and poetry, and Persian and Indian miniature painting.[9]

The early exhibitions of the Union of Youth were shaped by the receptivity and aesthetic liberalism of Vladimir Markov, Iosif Shkolnik, Savelii Shleifer, Eduard Spandikov, and Levkii Zheverzheev, but the final year of the organization's existence was marked by the activities of Mikhail Matiushin and the new stylistic inventions of Pavel Filonov, Kazimir Malevich, and Olga Rozanova. In its final season, 1913–14, the Union of Youth presented Neo-primitivist, Cubist, and Futurist techniques in painting along with spiritual themes and metaphysical concerns; they collaborated with the Hylaea poets David Burliuk, Elena Guro, Velimir Khlebnikov, Aleksei Kruchonykh, Benedikt Livshits, and Vladimir Mayakovsky, and staged theatrical performances of *Pobeda nad soltsem* [Victory over the Sun] and *Vladimir Maiakovsky: Tragediia* [Vladimir Mayakovsky: A Tragedy]. In the end, it was Kulbin, Markov, and Matiushin's interest in humanity's psychological relationship with nature in particular, and their ideas about the creation of art, that pushed the St. Petersburg avant-garde into transrationalism and abstraction and led to the emergence of the Organic School.

Organic principles as the foundation for a new art

Organic concepts have come into play whenever the living form and nature have stood at the center of human inquiry. August Wiedmann defines *organicism* as "a philosophy whose major categories are derived metaphorically from the attributes of living and growing things."[10] In general, organic concepts are based on the conviction that the analytical-reductionist method of describing life phenomena, social structures, and reality as a whole is inadequate because the whole is more than the sum of its parts and the parts of such complex, nonmechanical systems cannot be independently analyzed without destroying their very essence.[11] The universe is thus understood to be a complex, organic whole composed of various functional subunits; the organism is used as a model to describe the overall system and its components. Every organic theory, therefore, views the world as a complex entity of integrated parts, that is, as an organism.

In art, architecture, and design, the term "organic" has been and continues to be used in many ways. It can refer to forms or shapes derived from plant or animal forms found in nature, naturally occurring materials such as wood or clay, as well as assemblies or arrangements of parts that follow principles of self-organization and the purposeful integration of many parts into a greater entity.[12]

From a philosophical viewpoint, an organic worldview reflects a holistic conception of the world, that is, the understanding that the universe is absolute and eternal. There is an emphasis on the natural unity and the interrelationships of all forms of existence in nature: the whole is more than the sum of its parts. Organic models promote the idea that movement is an essential characteristic of nature, preexistent in all forms of being, that it is the overall source of growth, development, continuity, and change in the world process, which leads to the unity of opposites. Organic worldviews are antidualistic, they strive to overcome the dualism of matter and mind so characteristic of Western thought, because they consider both to be different sides of one and the same nature. Organic models profess a harmonious and symbiotic relationship between humans and nature. As an integral part of nature, humans seek not to control nature, but to live in harmony with it. The artist following an organic approach strives for a holistic interpretation of the world and seeks forms that go beyond logic and rational thought into the realm of the subconscious, including empathy, creative intuition, meditation, and mystical experience.

As Caroline van Eck has pointed out in her study on architecture:

> [Organicism in art] is based on the conviction, generally held in artistic theory from antiquity to the end of the nineteenth century, that art should imitate nature, not with the aim of producing perfectly faithful copies but with the aim of creating the illusion of life, of conferring the qualities of living nature upon the products of man, in the hope of effectuating the metamorphosis of dead matter into a living being.[13]

She distinguishes two varieties of organicism: a more general one that is characterized by a concern for a close relationship between art and living nature, expressed by imitation of nature's methods in construction or ornament, and a more restricted form that concentrates on organic unity, aiming to achieve in art a correspondence between the parts and the whole that is modeled on the functional correlations of the parts of living organisms.[14]

The idea of organic growth as a metaphor for the creative process originates in the eighteenth century. The Romantics attributed beauty to nature and thus related the sensation of beauty to the experience of nature. They transferred the qualities of organic nature to the artistic process and compared the imaginative powers of the artist with the creative forces of nature.[15] August Wilhelm von Schlegel maintained that art, "creating autonomously like nature, both organized and organizing, must form living works, which are first set in motion, not by an outside mechanism, like a pendulum, but by an indwelling power."[16] Convinced that there exists in nature a vital, structural, and form-giving principle that gives form and shape to inorganic matter, the Romantics demanded that artists orient their work towards the creative principles of nature.

As can be seen in the root sculptures of Mikhail Matiushin, this metaphor of organic creativity has maintained its appeal well into the twentieth century. Fascinated by the organic processes of plant growth, Matiushin began around 1910 to single out tree roots and branches as the most perfect manifestations of the movement of matter and maintained that organic growth generally expresses itself in curved lines as opposed to the straight line, which is characteristic of inorganic nature and mathematical abstraction.[17] In his 1913 sculpture *First Human Being* from the series *Movement of Roots* (Fig. 6.1), he suggests that nature, through the hidden forces of organic growth, has the power to create living beings. The figures of this series are less artistic inventions than demonstrations of the artist's awareness of organic beauty and his acceptance of nature as the most innovative creator.

Before turning to a discussion of the nature-centric approaches and organic models that can be found in the Russian avant-garde, it is worthwhile to take a closer look at the development of the life sciences that provided the foundation for this process. During the course of the nineteenth century, biology emancipated itself from natural history as well as from medicine and became an independent science focused on the study of living organisms. The research undertaken by nineteenth-century biologists concentrated on problems of form, function, and transformation.[18] Anatomists, histologists, and embryologists studied the appearances and constituent structures of the plant and animal world and were concerned with organic form and the means by which it was brought into being. Concentrating on life functions such as respiration, nutrition, and excretion, physiologists sought to understand the innermost workings of organisms. Evolutionists studying the relationships between living beings and their environments in past and present worlds looked at the transformation of life over vast spans of time.

Prior to the development of ecological and environmental studies, two major explanatory frameworks existed in the field of biology: the mathematical-mechanistic (reductionist) approach and the Vitalist approach.[19] The reductionists relied on René Descartes' dualism, which claimed that all

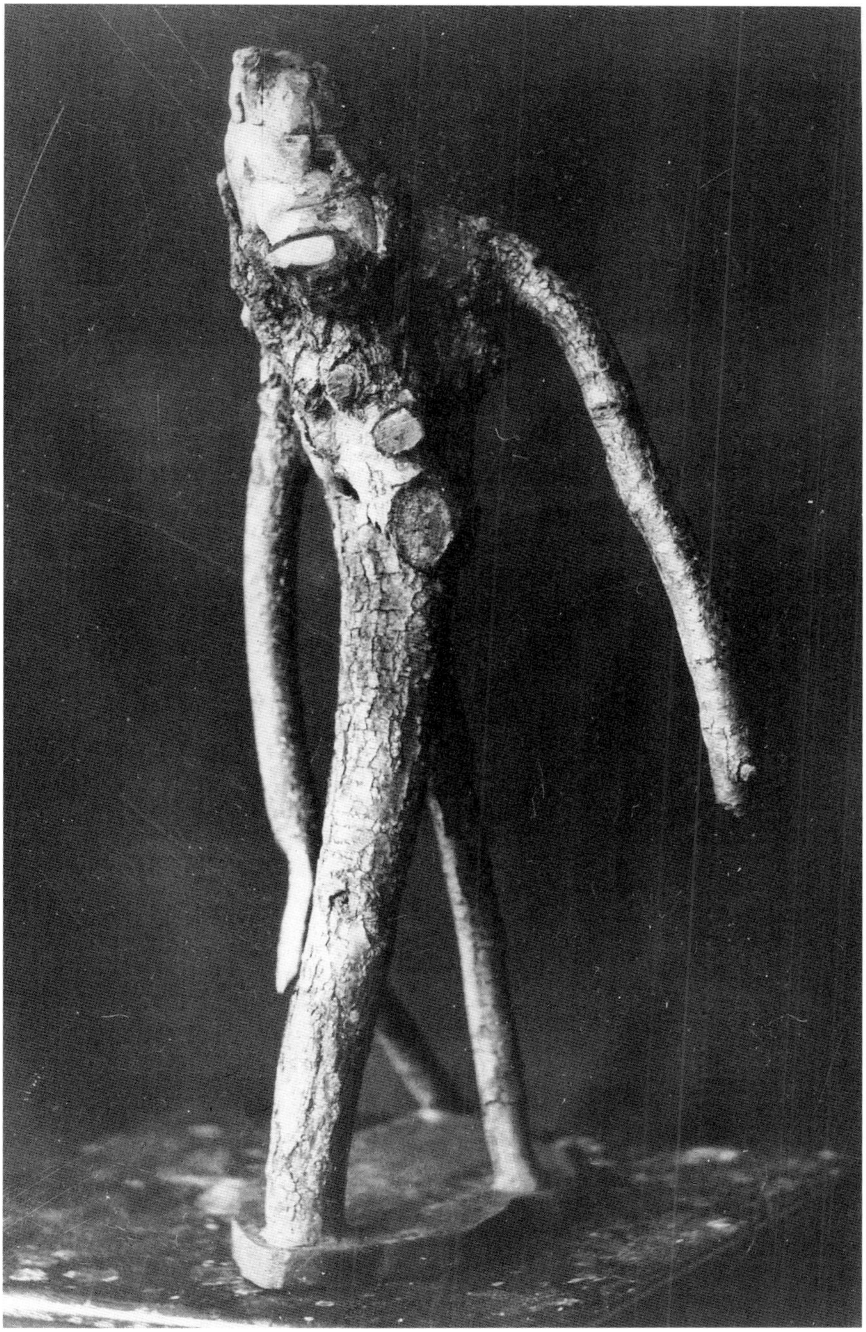

6.1 Mikhail Matiushin, *First Human Being* from the series *Movement of Roots*, 1913. Photograph, A-Ya Archive. Jane Voorhees Zimmerli Art Museum, Rutgers, The State University of New Jersey, 010.003.009. Photograph by Jack Abraham

organisms, with the important exception of humans, were of a mechanistic nature; they believed that ultimately the behavior of all organisms would be mathematically explainable by means of elemental physics and chemistry. The Vitalists offered a countertheory; they maintained that, in contrast to inorganic nature, living matter contains a special vital force or substance that drives all vital processes—one, however, that cannot be explained or investigated using scientific methods.[20] Vitalism played a significant role in biological research during the early decades of the nineteenth century, but reductionism and experimental practice became the driving forces in the development of physiology, embryology, and other branches of biology after 1850. In the last quarter of the nineteenth century, some biologists, among them the brothers R.B. and J.S. Haldane as well as Edmund Montgomery, began to suggest another kind of explanation, called "organicism," which claimed that one did not need to revert to Vitalism to reject the reductionist explanation. They concluded that the processes occurring in a living organism could not be understood through isolated investigation of its parts, but only through investigation into the features of the whole organism and its interaction with the environment.[21] In this context, *organicism* was characterized as

> the dual belief in the importance of considering the organism as a whole, and at the same time, the firm conviction that this wholeness is not something mysteriously closed to analysis, but rather something that should be studied and analyzed.[22]

Generally, biological thought in the nineteenth century was shaped by metaphysics and by methods of contemplation and intuition. In contrast to physics and chemistry, biologists usually began with the observation of natural phenomena rather than experimentation and arrived at their conclusions and understanding of these phenomena first and foremost through using visualization techniques. At the same time, nature-centric or Biocentric worldviews—along with Organicism one must include *Lebensphilosophie, Naturphilosophie,* Neo-Vitalism, and Monism—that were evolving in the natural sciences during the course of the nineteenth century began to be incorporated into the humanities and to shape intellectual and artistic thought.[23] Although differing in various aspects, these philosophies had in common the belief in the primacy of life and the life processes and promoted a harmonious and symbiotic relationship between humanity and nature. Their nonanthropocentric stance led to a paradigm shift in the understanding of the role of humanity, and in particular the role of the artist, who was no longer destined to use nature for his or her own purposes, but rather to work within the parameters of nature and in accordance with its universal laws.

Nature as the artist's model

The St. Petersburg artists variously subscribed to pantheist, Neo-Vitalist, and Monist worldviews. Elena Guro and Nikolai Kulbin were pantheists; they recognized in the universe a living presence, a kind of "soul," whose expression was to be found in the developmental processes of nature. Pavel Filonov held a Neo-Vitalist worldview, according to which the actions of a vital, inner force were responsible for the unity of mind and matter. Mikhail Matiushin was an adherent of Monism, whose followers believed in the oneness of mind and matter and the existence of a unified set of laws underlying nature. The worldviews of these artists were shaped not only by eighteenth-century Vitalism and a Romantic philosophy of nature, but were also directly influenced by the ideas of Jean-Baptiste Lamarck and Charles Darwin, Gustav Theodor Fechner and Wilhelm Wundt, Arthur Schopenhauer, Friedrich Nietzsche, and Henri Bergson.[24]

The artists found confirmation and support for their thinking in the discoveries being made in the natural sciences: the establishment of the cell as the smallest unit of living nature by Matthias Schleiden and Theodor Schwann in 1839, the formulation of the principle of the conservation of energy by Julius Robert Mayer and Hermann von Helmholtz in the 1840s, and new knowledge about the atomic structure of the chemical elements as visualized by Dmitri Mendeleev and Julius Lothar Meyer in the periodic table in the 1860s. Such discoveries served to establish and reinforce the sense that all forms and processes in nature must be interconnected and deepened the artists' understanding and belief in the unity of nature and the world. The shadow cast by these and other scientific developments, including the technological application of phenomena such as electromagnetism, electric light, radioactivity, and X-rays, led to investigations of dynamic and holistic concepts in art. The nature of movement and energy within the structure of the universe; the interrelationship shared by two objects; and the interconnectedness of organism and environment, world and cosmos, mind and matter—these questions gradually became the focus of their inquiries.

The artists viewed humanity as being an integral part of nature and thus were convinced that human existence and human activities had to be guided by the principles and laws of nature. "We cannot conquer nature, for man is nature," wrote Kazimir Malevich.[25] Vladimir Tatlin saw man as "an organic being, consisting of a skeleton, nerves, and muscles;"[26] Nikolai Kulbin saw him as "cells of the body of the living earth."[27] And, as Pavel Filonov maintained, "in the name of the eternal and powerful force that lives within us, the force of the creative that decorated earth, the force of mankind that only recognizes in dying that it leaves its works behind on earth,"[28] they called for and demanded a new, absolute art, one that did not aim to copy nature, but that took its clues from nature and followed natural laws. To achieve this goal, the artist would create original works analogous to the creations of nature; art was the medium by which these newly recognized unities could be acknowledged and expressed.

The artist's relationship to nature was a frequent topic for discussion; art was no longer to be a depiction of visible reality or a reflection of a higher reality, but rather the human equivalent of the creative activities of nature. Natural phenomena involving movement and organic growth would serve as the basis for their artistic concepts and theoretical approaches. The St. Petersburg artists increasingly turned to organic principles and the workings of nature in their search for new artistic forms of expression that would liberate art from realism, rationalism, and mysticism—forms and works of art that were neither elaborations on nor imitations of nature, but rather expressions of a new worldview.

In her essay "Osnovy Novago Tvorchestva i prichiny ego neponimaniia" [The Bases of the New Creation and the Reasons why It Is Misunderstood], published in the third volume of the Union of Youth almanac, Olga Rozanova insisted that the artist must not be a "passive imitator of nature," but rather an "active spokesman of his relationship with her."[29] The problem was with *how* the artist deals with the phenomena of nature and *how* she depicts the visible world, based on her understanding of nature:

> The artist of the past, riveted to nature, forgot about the picture as an important phenomenon, and as a result, it became merely a pale reminder of what he saw, a boring assemblage of ready-made, indivisible images of nature ... Nature [had] enslaved the artist.[30]

Malevich also maintained that the conventional artist had become a "slave of nature" whose creative urge had been trapped inside the real forms of life.[31] He insisted that the modern artist must not imitate the forms and shapes of nature, but instead create his own, new "nature-like" forms.[32] In an analogy to nature's own elemental building blocks of cells and molecules, Malevich began to build up works using simple elements, similar in shape, that would serve as fundamental building blocks for a new world: "[The] forms will live, like all living forms of nature ... Each form is free and individual. Each form is a world."[33]

Filonov insisted that the artist orient his creative activities on the principles of living nature; the various forms of imitation of nature must be replaced by a "scientific, analytical-intuitive naturalism ... [that] examines all the object's predicates, the phenomena of the whole world, [and] the phenomena of human processes seen and unseen by the naked eye."[34] Vladimir Tatlin and Petr Miturich also found inspiration for their constructions in the organic forms of nature. Natural principles formed the basis for all technology, and their investigation, they believed, would lead to alternative, more human forms of technology. Their investigation and use of these natural principles led to the constitutive elements of their "organic constructivism."[35]

During the first quarter of the twentieth century, numerous artists of the Russian avant-garde strove to capture and make visible natural phenomena and universal forces. They searched for new artistic approaches to expressing reality as well as for new, synthetic approaches that could extend the opportunities for artistically apprehending the world. They drew on knowledge from the fields of physics, mathematics, biology, physiology, and psychology—a process that brought art and science into a direct dialogue. The artists linked the immediate observation of nature with scientific knowledge and took an interest in the nature of the human soul and psychophysiological phenomena. Taking as their model the developmental processes, forces, and forms of nature, their aesthetic was informed by pantheist, Neo-Vitalist, and Monist ideas as well as by evolutionary thinking.

The belief in a reality that goes beyond the actual, visible world and the conviction that art could be the medium by which the structures and forces of the cosmos—both visible and invisible, material and immaterial—could be revealed, was shared by many artists of the early Russian avant-garde; these convictions formed the foundation for their approach to art.

Evolutionary thought as a model for artistic development

The holistic approach of the early Russian avant-garde and the artists' search for new forms of art that would reveal the interrelationship of humanity and nature were strongly influenced by evolutionary theory. In early twentieth-century Russia, evolution—predominantly the Lamarckian understanding of "soft evolution," according to which characteristics acquired during the lifetime of the individual could be passed on through inheritance by its offspring—was widely accepted. It was broadly understood that organisms follow a continuous process of development that leads from simple to ever more complex forms in nature.

Charles Darwin's theory of evolution had reached Russia in the 1860s;[36] it was greeted enthusiastically by the Russian Realists. They celebrated its materialist, presumably atheist, and politically radical nature and used it as a tool in their struggle against the dominant idealist philosophy and Orthodox religion. The preoccupation with Darwinism was therefore not restricted to biological laboratories; the new theory also found acceptance in the social sciences and served as a philosophical foundation for the various models of society developed by the Realists and the populists during the 1870s and 1880s.[37]

Yet, despite the generally positive reception of Darwinism in Russia, most adherents of Darwin's theory renounced his analysis as being too strongly influenced by the socioeconomic conditions of capitalism in Britain. Emphasizing the national character of their culture and wanting to distinguish themselves from Western European capitalism, Russian intellectuals rejected natural selection as the mechanism of the evolutionary process and also rejected Darwin's (or rather Herbert Spencer's interpretation of Darwin's) terms "struggle for existence," "competition," and "survival of the fittest" in favor of the idea of "harmony," "cooperation," and "mutual aid"—thus emphasizing the active participation of the organism in its evolution.[38]

Russian scientists and intellectuals viewed the individual organism not as a result of the process of natural selection, but as an agent in the process of its adaptation to its natural environment. Emphasizing the active role the individual played in the process of natural and social development, they postulated a symbiotic relationship between the organism and its environment. The belief in the active participation of each organism in its evolution and the future of the species can be considered to be a general characteristic of intellectual and cultural activities in Russia at the turn of the twentieth century.[39]

Convinced that the development of human society likewise follows the laws of nature, Russian scientists and intellectuals found in Darwin's theory of natural development a parallel in the ongoing "evolution" of human society. By maintaining Jean-Baptiste Lamarck's teleological orientation to a certain degree, and connecting evolutionary theory with the idea of progress in nature and society, they defined progress to be the further development of the species, the intellectual perfection of humanity, and the moral improvement of human society. Scientists, philosophers, and artists of the succeeding generation went on to particularly focus on the question of the ways and means by which one could influence and promote the further development of humanity.

The general acceptance of evolution in Russia also influenced the perception of art and the understanding of the role of the artist. As with nature and society, art was likewise understood to be in a continuous process of development; it was assumed that like all forms in nature, artistic forms too must develop according to the natural law of evolution:

> Evolution in art progresses further and further, for everything in the world moves forward ... Evolution and revolution in art have the same aim, which is to arrive at unity of creation—the formation of signs instead of the repetition of nature.[40]

This idea was closely linked with a fundamental change in the understanding of the role of the work of art itself. As the subject of a never-ending developmental process, the work of art could no longer be understood to be the final product of a unique creative act by the artist. Rather, it was to be regarded as the reflection of a particular developmental stage in the overall process of the creative evolution of humanity. Artists such as Filonov, Kulbin, Malevich, Matiushin, Tatlin, and their contemporaries were convinced that the creative activities of the artist were intimately linked or attuned to the current conditions of human life and development—the artist's output was thus a reflection of the psychophysiological development or evolution of the human body and mind. The work of art as an expression of the human, creative ability became not only a reflection of the human understanding of the world, but also of the stage of humanity's psychophysiological development; it served as a direct link between artistic creativity and human evolution.

Just as natural scientists and intellectuals had linked the dynamic principle in nature and society with a belief in further development and progress, artists and art historians of the time believed that developments in art would likewise follow the principles of natural and social processes, leading them to conclude that art, just as nature and society, was following a path that would inevitably lead toward an increasing level of perfection. Malevich concluded: "The perfection of the world is the perfection of man, of his organism, which changes eternally and renews itself differently; for his construction, his system, is simply a tool by which to conquer the infinite."[41]

The Russian interpretation of Darwinism—based on the idea of harmonious development, the crucial function of cooperation, and a teleological belief in the organism's innate tendency towards perfection rather than in natural selection and the struggle for survival—also redefined the active role of the artist in the process of artistic creation: through his or her creative activities, the artist could not only influence the development of new forms of art, but could also participate in and shape the process of human evolution. No longer someone who studies and then depicts nature or the natural world, the artist now produced work that was instead more a reflection of a particular state in the developmental process of humanity. Each new artistic style became an indication or reflection of a qualitative change in the consciousness of its creator, who, in turn, would induce the work's viewer to adapt to the psychophysiological changes represented. Filonov maintained that the significance of art can be "reduced to its effect on the evolution or revolution of the viewer's intellect, to the emancipation of the artist's or student's creative individuality from the domination of every kind of pseudo-authority, tradition, prejudice and school."[42]

Viewing evolution, then, as a continuous, causal, and progressive natural development from simple forms to complex ones, from the inorganic to the organic, from instinct to conscious behavior, and from the primary sense of touch to the developed sense of sight, artists such as Filonov, Kulbin, Malevich, and Matiushin saw themselves as being at the forefront of a long-term, ongoing process of artistic development; they were convinced that, alongside the development of human perception and cognition, art had arisen in its earliest form out of the primitive pictograms of early cultures and continued to develop, right up to the various -isms of the present. Looking ahead, Malevich wrote:

> We shall see what perfection man [has so far] attained in art and how all the basic instruments of his art must be sharpened, so that his image of the new world is perfect in every aspect. As in the arts of science, so in the creative arts everything that man creates is a detail-element of his general collective picture of the world.[43]

Convinced of the historical significance of their mission, Malevich and his fellow artists began to study and analyze the historical content and methods of depiction found in past artistic styles and forms; their goal was to derive from this study of guiding principles for the ongoing development of art in the present. They found explanations for the great differences in content and style and the various asynchronous pathways of development that art around the world had followed in the differing environmental conditions that had variously shaped and defined the biological and intellectual development of the many peoples and cultures. The perception of the history of art as a more or less continuous pageant of artistic styles, one following the other (if allowing for diversions and parallel developments), offered the artist as well as the viewer the possibility of a historical reception of such work and promoted the understanding of art as being a specific expression of the natural developmental process of the world. The idea of progress and ongoing development toward the attainment of perfection in nature and art included a teleological aspect: the dialectic containment of past artistic achievements within and by the newly arising artistic styles and expressive means of the present. This synthetic interpretation of art history by the avant-garde, with its dialectical emphasis on progression and the containment of the past in the present, found its most pronounced forms of expression in Malevich's theory of the additional element and in Matiushin's interpretation of art history as based on the human perception of space.

Malevich's investigation of the formal features and artistic laws governing the evolution of modern painting led him to realize that each new style or art form introduced a specific formal element that was new. He hypothesized that each further development would bring with it this new aspect, this "additional element," which served to complement or build upon the previous system of painting. He characterized this as taking "the shape of a formula or sign that pointed to the overall context and the unifying building principle of the elements."[44] The theory of the additional element became the foundation for Malevich's pedagogical program of painterly training and education; he used it to define the "specific complex of painterly and formal elements and methods" in Impressionism, Cézannism, Cubism, Futurism, and Suprematism, as well as to explain the transitions from one system of painting to the next.[45] Behind this formal method of stylistic analysis was the belief held by Malevich that a study of the outer—that is, artistic—form could reveal information about humanity's natural and intellectual evolution.

Matiushin traced the development of art according to the evolution of the human perception of space, which, he believed, had already led to the mathematical construction and perspectival representation of three-dimensional space in art.[46] He plotted this development initially from the one-dimensional perception of the point to the line, which established the plane of two-dimensional perception (the horizontal and the vertical). The combination of two-dimensional space of length and volume with the experience of depth, led to the concept of three-dimensional volume and space. With his theory of the progression of spatial perception in art, which he believed had developed hand in hand with sensory perception from primitive to modern humanity, Matiushin identified the ongoing evolution of art as a continuous process, leading from cave painting to Cubism.

The reception and application of evolutionary concepts and thinking in artistic endeavors led to a fundamental change in emphasis: aesthetic concerns were replaced by epistemological questions about the conditions of human perception and the nature of artistic creation. The early Russian avant-garde hoped to find the laws of a new art in nature and in the human psyche; they directed their view inwards. Art and artistic activity no longer centered on the world as objective reality, but rather on the intrinsic value of the artistic means and on the autonomous laws of creative activity and the processes of human perception and knowledge. Traditional themes and pictorial subjects in art were replaced by psychophysiological inquiries that paved the way for a "new Realism" and the emergence of a number of nonobjective art forms, among them Rayonism, Suprematism, and Organic Culture.

Faktura: The living fabric of nature

In their efforts to create a new art, the artists of the Russian avant-garde began to look at and analyze the principles and elementary building blocks of painting, that is, color, form, and texture, as well as their psychophysiological effects upon the viewer. In the course of their artistic experiments with color, form, and material and in their efforts to liberate or extend the human senses, Filonov, Malevich, Rozanova, and Tatlin, looking beyond problems of the application of color and form to the canvas, also began to make use of a variety of natural materials for artistic creation, to explore their physical properties, and to concentrate on questions of texture, material combinations, rhythm, and surface tension.

Color, line, and texture must be viewed as fundamental elements in the development of abstract painting, including that of the Russian avant-garde; all three are referred to extensively in their writings. Wassily Kandinsky wrote that color and line as artistic elements constitute "the essential, eternal and invariable language of painting";[47] David Burliuk characterized line, surface, color, and texture as the main components of pure painting;[48] Larionov, in his Rayonist painting manifesto, stated conclusively that "the laws germane only to painting are: colored line and texture."[49] For Malevich, the essence of a painting—a position previously held by the subject—was in color and texture, "the greatest value in painterly creation."[50] Texture, according to Filonov, was the principle by which the surface of an object is processed and developed, an understanding of "the significance or multi-significance of the surface properties of the object as they interact with the consistency of the material with which the object has been made."[51]

The avant-garde's preoccupation with the basic elements, fundamental principles, and creative processes that constitute the work of art found its reflection in the discussion of *faktura,* a term usually translated as "texture" or "structure."[52] *Faktura* was not a static concept, but its essential qualities were defined and developed further by individual members of the avant-garde from 1913 to the mid-1920s. While *faktura,* as used by the members of the early Russian avant-garde, was characterized by the use of natural materials and a holistic-metaphysical approach to art, it was later adapted by the Constructivists to a strictly materialist ideology and utilitarian orientation in artistic production.[53]

Discussions on materials and processes involved in the creation of the visual arts dominated the first two volumes of the Union of Youth almanac, culminating in Vladimir Markov's 1914 book *Printsipy tvorchestva v plasticheskikh iskusstvakh: faktura* [Creative Principles in the Plastic Arts: Faktura].[54] Markov defines *faktura* as being "a condition of a painting's surface that is perceivable by our eyes and senses."[55] But he also adds that the term can be applied to sculpture, architecture and all other art forms in which the use of color, sound, or some other technique produces a particular sensation in the viewer.[56] *Faktura* was thus a basic principle or quality of art—the specific combination of materials used within the creative process that lead to the sensation experienced when viewing the work of art—and a general property of nature.[57] All artistic creation, whether painting, sculpture, or architecture, was seen as a result of the human desire to use materials. As Markov put it:

> [It] motivates man. Decorating it and working with it give him the ability to achieve all its intrinsic forms and 'noises'—that is what we call *faktura*. Material is the mother of *faktura*. Each newly emerged material can provide new elements from which to create endless new varieties of *faktura*.[58]

Markov analyzed combinations of various materials in nature and in art; organic, mechanic, and aesthetic connections between materials; and the subjection of one material by another or the interactions among several materials.[59] Emphasizing that "it would be a mistake to think that the faktura of a work of art is only achieved through the selected material, the method of its treatment, and its composition," he distinguished between material *faktura* (choice of material, luster, color pigments) and nonmaterial *faktura* (the qualities of lines, color combinations, contrast; the use of tools; and the manner or approach).[60] Markov looked not only at the materials but also at the cultural traditions in which they are used, and the artist's psyche. *Faktura* thus not only contains the purely physical properties of a work of art but is also dependent upon the artist's personality, cultural or national background, and technological abilities and is shaped by the artistic traditions, social environment, and historical conditions in which it is created.

Markov saw *faktura* as a specific Russian cultural-artistic quality that had its foundation in icon painting:

> Let's come back to our icons. Here we also see abundance of materials. We see a painting, surrounded by wrought silver, yet again surrounded by a painting, and then, in turn, by wrought iron; we see icons decorated with paper flowers, beads, towels, with lamps hanging in front of them, with flickering light and covered with soot ... It is as if there is a struggle of the two worlds: the inner, unrealistic world, and the external, perceivable world. Even here these two worlds overlay each other; one world is covering the other; one world is covering and the other one is covered; we achieve mysticism with common *faktura;* in other words, we achieve understanding and perception of new worlds and beauty through their symbolic form.[61]

Markov's notion of *faktura* contains a religious-transcendental dimension;[62] it embodies a holistic approach to artistic creation that was to unite the living fabric of the external, natural world with the spiritual experience of humanity's inner existence.

In Rozanova's 1913 essay "The Basis of the New Creation and the Reasons why It Is Misunderstood," it is once again nature that provides the raw materials from which the artist derives "the distinctive properties of the common material" in order to create "images by means of the interrelation of these properties."[63] She emphasizes that only the modern artist is able to understand and acknowledge "the full and serious importance of such principles as pictorial dynamism, volume and equilibrium, weight and weightlessness, linear and planar displacement, rhythm as a legitimate division of space, design, planar and surface dimension, texture, color correlations, and others."[64] Rozanova considered the incorporation of these new, qualitative principles into artistic practice to be the sign of the arrival of a new era in artistic creation—an era that would see the emergence of a pure and natural art, defined by its own autonomous laws.

Rozanova's emphasis on principles such as dynamism, equilibrium, surface tension, and color relations, reveals a particular concern with energetic qualities—an interest that shaped the work of numerous avant-garde artists during the 1920s and was strongly influenced by the "Energeticist" Monism of Wilhelm Ostwald, whose scientific studies were very popular in Russia at the time. Ostwald's Energeticism, updated and further systematized by Alexander Bodganov in his three volumes on the scientific principles of organization, *Tektologiia* (Tektology),[65] became an underlying paradigm of abstract art in Russia between 1918 and 1924 because it satisfied the need for an art that was based on materialism and scientific principles rather than metaphysics and idealist thought, and thus also responded to the increasing demand that artists needed to create an art that was of social relevance.[66]

Vladimir Tatlin's Material Culture was a direct result of this process, and it was fundamentally shaped by the principle of *faktura*.[67] With his focus on the physical properties and the social function of the work of art, Tatlin married Markov's metaphysical understanding of *faktura* and Rozanova's concern with Energeticist qualities. Working with real materials in real space, his constructions exist as a necessary form in relation to its physical materials and the social context of its use.[68] Paying particular attention to the creation of objects for everyday life, Tatlin demanded that the Material Culture artist "widen the range of our thinking in the area of materials and their relationships, [and look] for the prerequisite for form within the material itself."[69] The artist was encouraged to select materials not only for their physical properties (color, texture, density, elasticity, weight, and strength) but also on the basis of their "natural rhythms" and "energetic potential"; the country's climatic and economic conditions were likewise to be considered.[70]

In his search for new forms in art and design, Tatlin combined his investigations of the various materials and their physical properties with his studies of the structural principles of organic nature and modern technology. Considering organic forms to be the most aesthetic and economical elements in art and technology, he demanded that the artist form his objects in accordance with nature:

> Besides "what", "how" is very important, the organic form is important. For this we take and analyze existing objects, we use technical constructions as models for the forms of everyday objects, and finally, we also use as models the phenomena of living nature. Such are our principal tasks in working on the organization of the new object in the new way of life.[71]

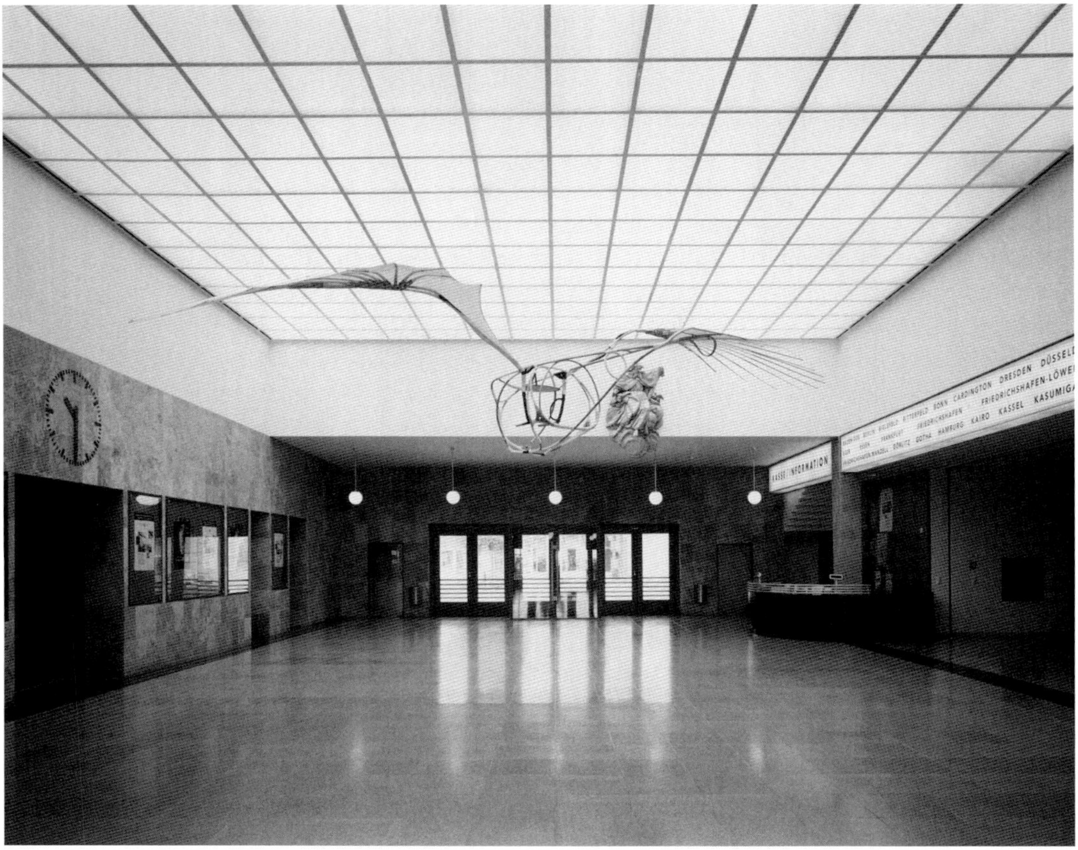

6.2 Vladimir Tatlin, Model of *Letatlin*, 1929–32, reconstruction by Jürgen Steeger, 1991, Zeppelin Museum Friedrichshafen, Technik und Kunst

Tatlin's designs of objects for everyday use during the 1920s and 1930s, among them the bentwood chair, the infant nursing cup, and his glider *Letatlin* (Fig. 6.2),[72] are less shaped by the technological principles of industrial production than they are defined by the application of natural forms and organic processes to technology; they were directly influenced by bionic principles as discussed by Ernst Kapp and Petr Engelmeier in their groundbreaking philosophies of technology.[73] Based on Darwin's biogenetic theory of development and contemporary physiology, Kapp, in his theory of organ projection, developed a technogenetic theory of culture that viewed all tools and weapons as projections and derivations of human organs;[74] Engelmeier, in his philosophical reflections upon the principles of modern technology, looked at technology as a biological and anthropological phenomenon and discussed the role of technology in the history of culture and economy as well as the interrelationships between technology, art, ethics, and other social factors.[75] Thus, for Tatlin, *faktura* meant the acknowledgement of the specific properties of materials as well as the mutual interrelationships of the various materials in a construction that was based on the organizational principles of nature and expressed in the organic form and social function of the object.

Filonov distinguished between two diametrically opposed approaches to art: *kanon i zakon* [canon and law]. *Canon* referred to the externally directed simplification and geometrization of the visible form, such as had been pursued by the Cubists, which, Filonov believed, represented a "biased path of development."[76] *Law*, on the other hand, represented the "organic development of form," working from the inside out. Rather than imposing form from above, this allowed for the development of the forms and structural relationships inherent in the materials.[77] The artist thus did not invent or impose these forms, but rather traced their self-development, from the simplest to the more complex, much in the same way that the internal processes of living nature develop from the initial cell (Fig. 6.3). Filonov's abstractions are abstractions of flowing, curved lines, rather than straight lines.

The distinction that Filonov drew between the Western European and the Eastern art traditions became likewise a matter of canon versus law:

> I define Russian art (in general) as an exclusive variety of European art (in general) because of its specific, textural peculiarities: weight, moisture, spontaneous manner of execution, organic esthetics. These factors indicate that the artist has achieved his goal by inner conviction and not by canon. In this situation the master's spirit dynamically enters the material of the object, dominating the condition of depiction while consciously or unconsciously rejecting the canon.[78]

Filonov contrasted the traditional realism that depicts the momentary perception of an object in a static, nonmoving state with *analytical realism*, the reflection and representation of the various dynamic processes occurring simultaneously within an object.[79]

Use of the term *faktura* likewise picks up on this distinction between Western (European) tradition and the Eastern (Russian) approach. *Faktura*, as an emblem of national culture, encompassed not only the recent developments of the avant-garde, but also the richness and diversity of materials present in all Russian art, from icon painting to the present, an aspect held to be very distinct from artistic developments in Western Europe:

> Generally speaking, it should be noted that contemporary Europe, which has made such major achievements in the field of science and technology, is very poor in regard to the development of the plastic principles bequeathed to us by the past … Europe's scientific apparatus hampers the development of such principles as the principle of weight, plane, dissonance, economy, symbols, dynamism, the leitmotif, scales, etc., etc.[80]

The early Russian avant-garde artists were guided in their approach not by the "rational" pictorial idea, but rather by the perceived nature of the material; the organic qualities and natural laws inherently at work in the material were what determined its use and even constituted the work of art. The principle of *faktura* thus embodied the fundamental difference between East and West in the overall approach to the artistic process; it illuminated the opposition between the Russian focus on the artistic process and the Western European

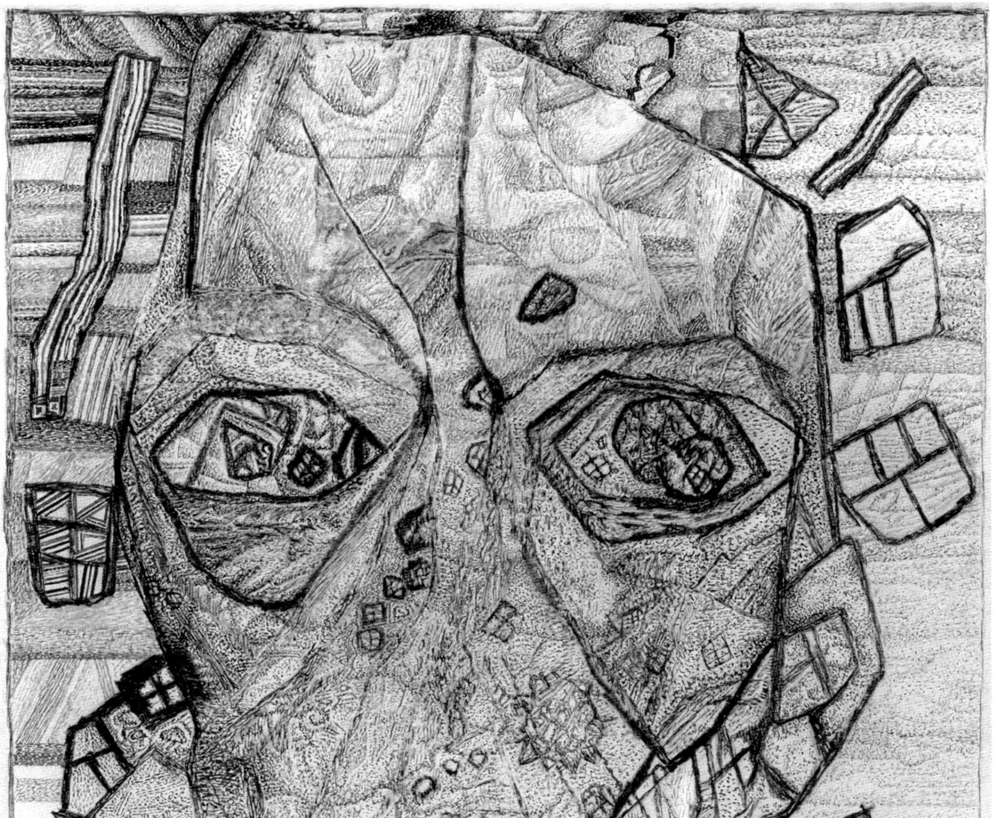

6.3 Attributed to Pavel Nikolaevich Filonov, *Head*, 1925, graphite and watercolor. Jane Voorhees Zimmerli Art Museum, Rutgers, The State University of New Jersey, The George Riabov Collection of Russian Art, donated in memory of Basil and Emilia Riabov, 2003.0788. Photograph by Jack Abraham

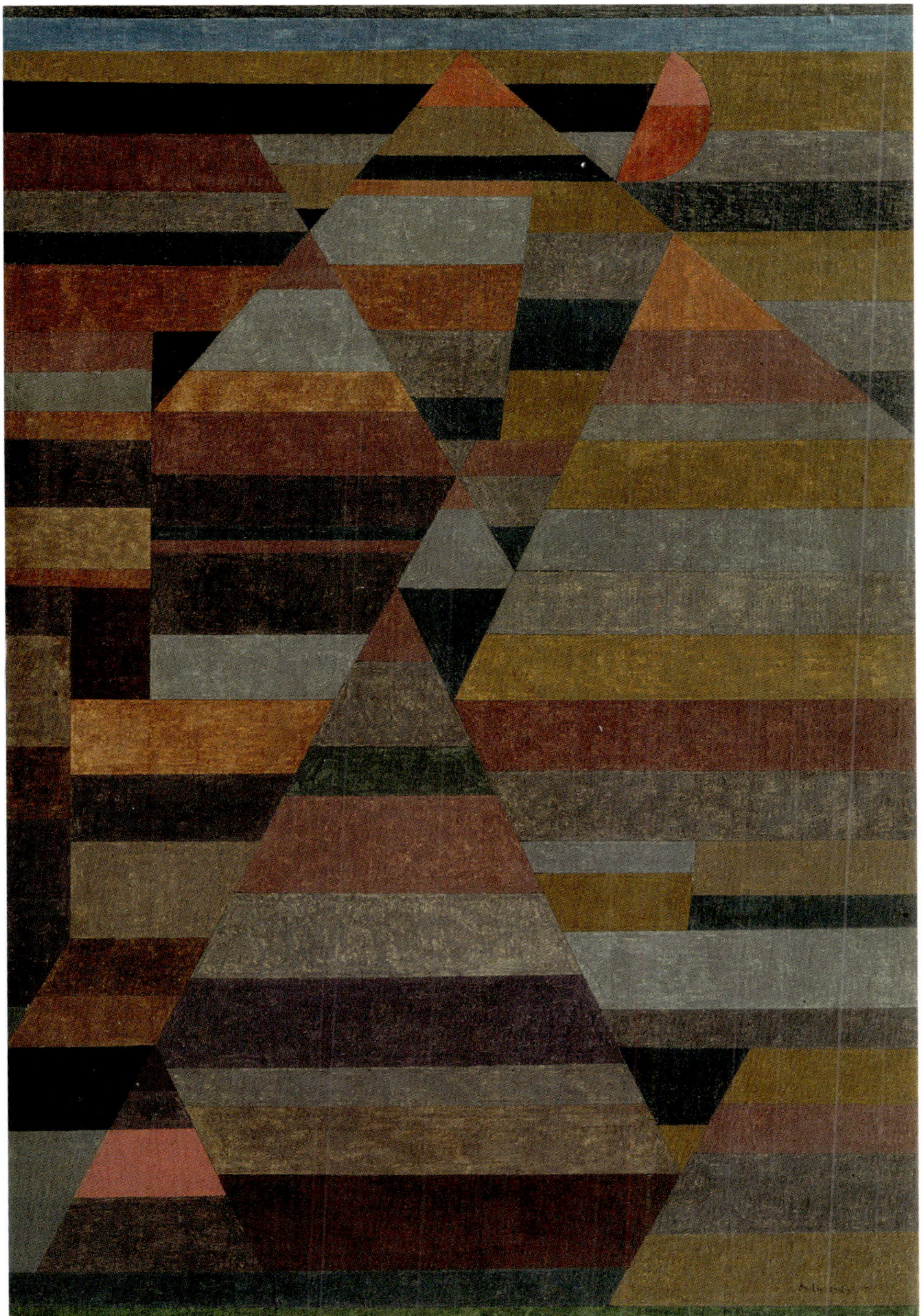

1 Paul Klee, *Nekropolis* [Necropolis], 1929/91, oil on muslin on plywood, 63 × 44 cm. Staatliche Museen zu Berlin, Nationalgalerie, Museum Berggruen, Berlin, Germany. © 2009 Artists Rights Society (ARS), New York/VG Bild-Kunst, Bonn. Photo: Bildarchiv Preussischer Kulturbesitz, Berlin/Art Resource, New York

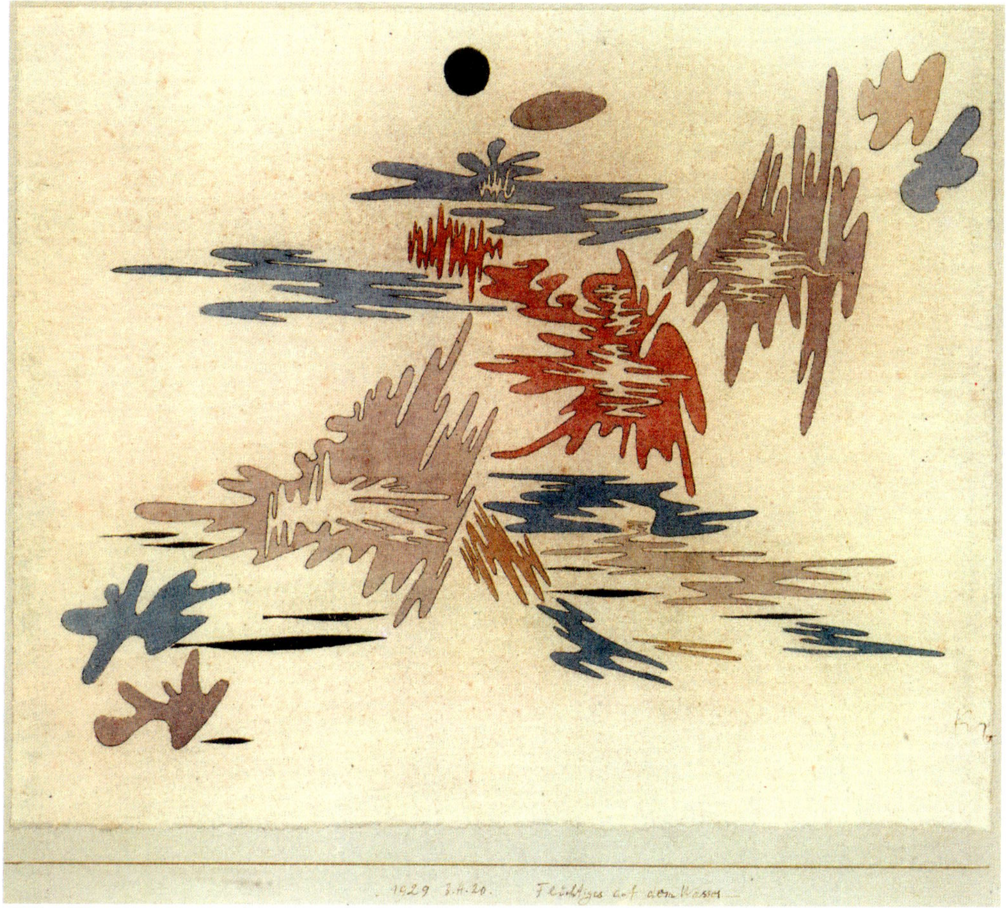

2 Paul Klee, *Flüchtiges auf dem Wasser* [Fleeting on the Water], 1929/32 pen and watercolor on paper on cardboard, 26 × 30.5 cm. Private Collection, Italy. © 2009 Artists Rights Society (ARS), New York/VG Bild-Kunst, Bonn

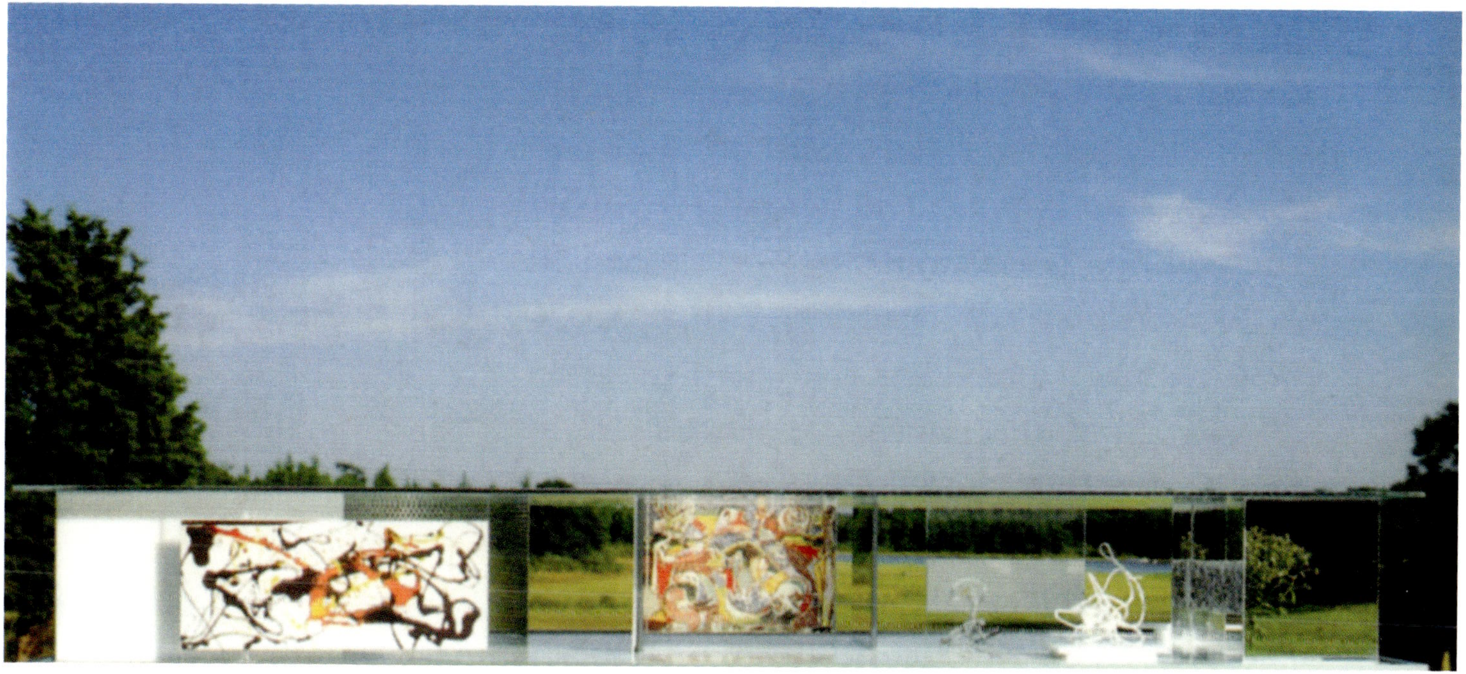

3 Peter Blake, "Ideal Museum" for Jackson Pollock's work, 1949. Original model lost. Replica fabricated by Patrick Bodden, with sculptures by Susan Tamulevich, 1994–95. Reconstructed model in landscape. Made possible by a grant from the Graham Foundation for Advanced Studies in the Fine Arts. Photo: Jeff Heatley. Collection of the Pollock-Krasner House and Study Center, East Hampton, NY

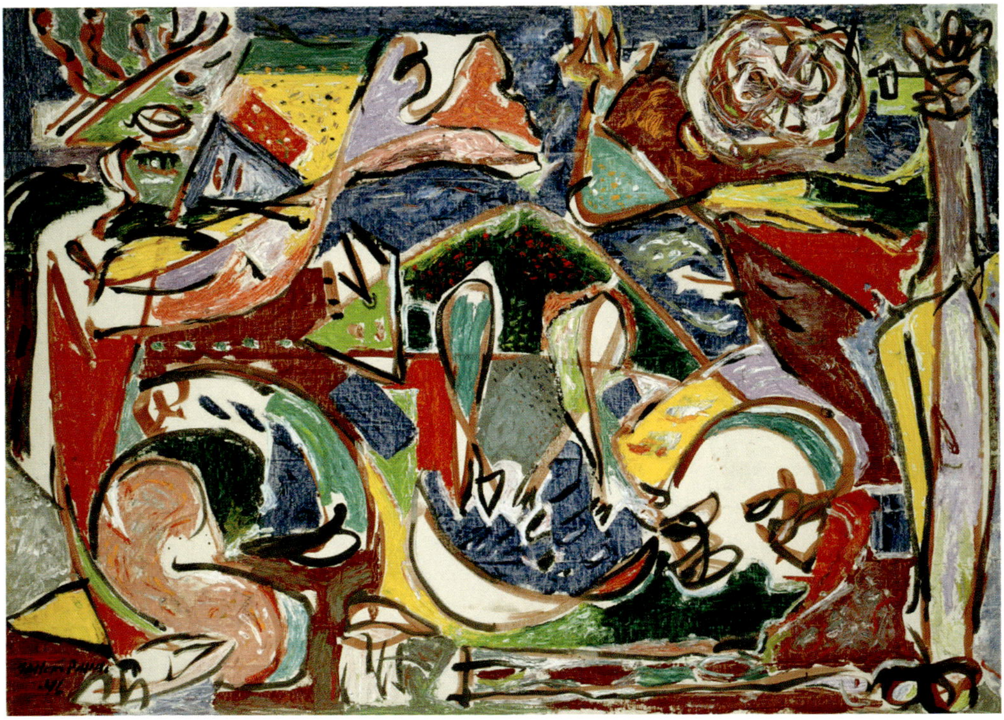

4 Jackson Pollock, *The Key*, 1946, oil on linen, 149.8 × 208.3 cm. Unframed. Through prior gift of Mr. and Mrs. Edward Morris, 1987.261, The Art Institute of Chicago. Photography © The Art Institute of Chicago. © The Pollock-Krasner Foundation/Artists Rights Society (ARS), New York

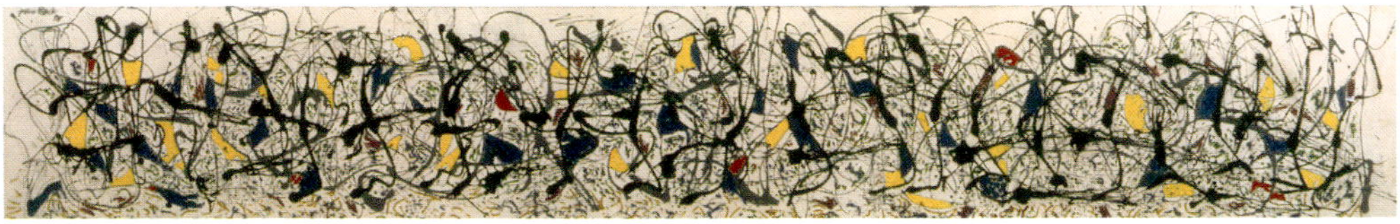

5 Jackson Pollock, *Summertime: Number 9A, 1948*, 1948, oil, enamel and house paint on canvas, 84.8 × 555.0 cm. Tate Gallery, London. Photo: Tate, London/Art Resource, NY. © The Pollock-Krasner Foundation/Artists Rights Society (ARS), New York

focus on the stylistic result of pictorial invention. In contrast to their Western counterparts, the Russian avant-garde placed the autonomous nature (the law) of the artistic material—the principle of *faktura*—above that of artistic innovation. *Faktura* was not to be found in either a stylistic or an expressive effect, but rather in the methods, selection, and treatment of the material throughout the creative process.

Conclusion

The artists of the Organic School of the Russian avant-garde believed that nature was unlimited in its potential and thus a model and never-ending source for artistic creation. They viewed artistic activity not as the passive imitation of nature, but as an active expression of the relationship between the artist and the natural environment, and called for a new, absolute art that did not copy nature, but was instead based on the universal laws, natural forces, and organic principles of nature. Their understanding of the active role of the artist and the crucial position of the work of art in the overall process of human evolution was shaped by evolutionary theory, particularly the Lamarckian tradition of a teleological development toward increasing perfection. Discussing the materials and processes involved in the creation of art and analyzing the elementary building blocks of painting, these artists not only explored the properties of color and form and their psychophysiological effects upon the viewer, but also introduced the principle of *faktura*. They demanded that the artist should not invent new forms, but rather visualize the organic forms, inner movements, and energetic potentials to be found in the natural world and re-establish the harmony between humanity and nature. Emphasizing human creativity and the psychological dimension of art, the artists of the Organic School of the Russian avant-garde viewed art as a means toward self-realization, leading to the unification of art and life, body and soul, humanity and nature.

Notes

1 Ground-breaking publications on the Russian avant-garde include, in chronological order: Camilla Gray, *The Great Experiment: Russian Art, 1863–1922* (London: Thames & Hudson, 1962); *Von der Fläche zum Raum: Russland 1916–24/ From Surface to Space: Russia 1916–24* (Cologne: Galerie Gmurzynska, 1974); John E. Bowlt, ed., *Russian Art of the Avant-garde: Theory and Criticism, 1902–1934* (New York: Viking Press, 1976); Stephanie Barron and Maurice Tuchman, eds., *The Avant-garde in Russia, 1910–1930: New Perspectives* (Los Angeles, CA: Los Angeles County Museum of Art; Cambridge, MA: MIT Press, 1980); *Von der Malerei zum Design: Russische Konstruktivistische Kunst der Zwanziger Jahre/From Painting to Design: Russian Constructivist Art of the Twenties* (Cologne: Galerie Gmurzynska, 1981). With the exception of Alla Povelikhina and Evgeni Kovtun's studies of the work of Elena Guro and Mikhail Matiushin, it is only since the

publication of *The Great Utopia: Russian and Soviet Avant-Garde, 1915–1932* (New York: Guggenheim Museum, 1992) that the existence of the Organic School as an integral part of the Russian avant-garde has been acknowledged.

2 Christina Lodder, "Organic Construction: Harnessing an Alternative Technology," in *Russian Constructivism* (New Haven, CT: Yale University Press, 1983), 205–23.

3 Charlotte Douglas, "Evolution and the Biological Metaphor in Modern Russian Art," *Art Journal* 44, no. 2 (Summer 1984): 153–61.

4 Nikolai Kulbin, "Garmoniya, dissonans i tesnyya sochetaniya v iskusstve i zhizni" [Harmony, Dissonance, and Close Combinations in Art and Life], in *Trudy vserossiskogo s''ezda khudozhnikov v Petrograde, dek. 1911–ianv. 1912* [Works of the All-Russian Artists' Congress in Petrograd, Dec. 1911–Jan. 1912] (St. Petersburg, 1911), 1:39.

5 The exhibitions he organized were: *Modern Trends in Art*, St. Petersburg, April 26–May, 1908; *The Impressionists-Triangle*, St. Petersburg, March 9–April 12, 1909 and Vilna, Lithuania, December 26, 1909–January 20, 1910; *Triangle*, St. Petersburg, March 19–April 14, 1910. His publications include *Studiia impressionistov. Kniga 1-aia* [Studio of the Impressionists. First Book] (St. Petersburg: Izd. Nibutkovsky, 1910) and *Svobodnaia muzyka. Primenenie novoi teorii khudozhestvennogo tvorchestva k muzyke* [Free Music. The Application of a New Theory of Artistic Creation in Music] (St. Petersburg 1909).

6 *Ustav obshchestva khudozhnikov "Soiuz molodezhi"* [The Statute of the Artists' Society "Union of Youth"], February 2, 1910, in Russian State Archive of Literature and Art (RGALI), f. 336, op. 5, ed. khr. 4, l. 4. English in Jeremy Howard, *The Union of Youth: An Artists' Society of the Russian Avant-Garde* (Manchester: Manchester University Press, 1992), 46.

7 Between March 1910 and January 1914, the Union of Youth held seven exhibitions, organized several debates on modern art, and published three edited volumes with essays by its members and contributions by Hylaea poets. For a full account on the activities of the organization see Howard, *Union of Youth*.

8 Nikolai Kulbin and Wassily Kandinsky were in close contact and, in December 1911, Kulbin read the Russian version of Kandinsky's treatise *On the Spiritual in Art* at the All-Russian Congress of Artists in St. Petersburg. See John E. Bowlt and Rose-Carol Washton Long, *The Life of Vasili Kandinsky in Russian Art: A Study of "On the Spiritual in Art"* (Newtonville, MA: Oriental Research Partners, 1980). Vladimir Markov and Eduard Spandikov were both fluent in German and in touch with the Blue Rider group in Munich. They planned to publish a translation of Wilhelm Worringer's 1907 dissertation *Abstraktion und Einfühlung* [Abstraction and Empathy] in the Union's almanac, but the publication did not materialize. See Howard, *Union of Youth*, 120–21. In 1910, Pavel Filonov, Josif Shkolnik, Savelii Shleifer, and Eduard Spandikov went to Finland and Sweden to meet with Scandinavian artists and to invite them to their 1911 exhibition; in 1913 the Union again pursued "a broader union with Finnish and Swedish artists" in order to include the newest trends in Northern art in their upcoming exhibition and also planned to have it travel to Helsingfors [Helsinki]. See Howard, *Union of Youth*, 57, 86, 156.

9 Vladimir Markov's publications included *Iskusstvo ostrova paskhi* [The Art of the Easter Islands] (St. Petersburg: Soiuz molodezhi, 1914), *Svirel kkitaya* [The Chinese Flute] (St. Petersburg: Soiuz molodezhi, 1914), and *Iskusstvo negrov*

[African Art] (Petrograd: Narkompros, 1919). The first and second volumes of the Union of Youth almanac of 1912 included Chinese poetry, an article on Persian art by Varvara Bubnova, and illustrations of Chinese art as well as Persian and Indian miniatures.

10 August Wiedmann, "The Organic Theory of Art," in *Romantic Art Theories* (Henley-on-Thames: Gresham Books, 1986), 91.

11 For general reference, see David Bohm, "Fragmentation and Wholeness," *The Structurist* 11 (1971): 7–18; Eli Bornstein, "Toward an Organic Art: Ecological Views of Man/Nature," *The Structurist* 11 (1971): 59–68; Anna Bramwell, *Ecology in the Twentieth Century: A History* (New Haven, CT: Yale University Press, 1989); Götz Großklaus and Ernst Oldemeyer, eds., *Natur als Gegenwelt: Beiträge zur Kulturgeschichte der Natur* [Nature as Counterworld: Contributions to the Cultural History of Nature] (Karlsruhe: Loeper, 1983); Donna Jeanne Haraway, *Crystals, Fabrics, and Fields: Metaphors of Organicism in Twentieth-Century Developmental Biology* (New Haven, CT: Yale University Press, 1976); Hilde S. Hein, *On the Nature and Origin of Life* (New York: McGraw-Hill, 1971), 54–70; David Pepper, *The Roots of Modern Environmentalism* (London: Croom Helm, 1984); D.C. Phillips, *Holistic Thought in Social Science* (Stanford, CA: Stanford University Press, 1976).

12 Annette Voigt, "Die Natur des Organischen—'Leben' als kulturelle Idee der Moderne" [The Nature of the Organic—"Life" as Cultural Idea in Modernity], in *Spielarten des Organischen in Architektur, Design und Kunst* [Variations of the Organic in Architecture, Design, and Art], ed. Annette Geiger, Stefanie Hennecke, and Christin Kempf (Berlin: Reimer, 2005), 37.

13 Caroline van Eck, *Organicism in Nineteenth-Century Architecture: An Inquiry into Its Theoretical and Philosophical Background* (Amsterdam: Architectura and Natura Press, 1994), 18.

14 Ibid., 20.

15 Wiedmann, "The Organic Theory of Art," 89–100.

16 August Wilhelm von Schlegel, "Vorlesungen über schöne Litteratur und Kunst" [Lectures on Literature and the Fine Arts] (1801–02), in *Deutsche Litteraturdenkmale des 18. und 19. Jahrhunderts* [German Monuments of Literature of the 18th and 19th Centuries], ed. Bernhard Seuffert (Heilbronn: Gebr. Henninger; Stuttgart: Göschen, 1884), 17:102. English in Philip C. Ritterbush, *The Art of Organic Forms* (Washington, DC: Smithsonian Institution, 1968), 18.

17 Alla Powelichina, "Michail Matjuschin—Die Welt als organisches Ganzes," in *Matjuschin und die Leningrader Avantgarde* (Karlsruhe, Stuttgart-Munich: Oktogon, 1991), 26–27. See also: Yevgeny Kovtun, "Matiushin's Roots," in *Devoted to the Russian Avant-Garde* (St. Petersburg: Palace Editions, 1998), 24–25.

18 William Coleman, *Biology in the Nineteenth Century: Problems of Form, Function, and Transformation* (Cambridge: Cambridge University Press, 1977).

19 See Hein, *On the Nature and Origin of Life*.

20 Guido Cimino and Francois Duchesneau, eds., *Vitalism from Haller to the Cell Theory: Proceedings of the Zaragoza Symposium, XIXth International Congress of the History of Science* (Florence: Leo S. Olschki Editore, 1997).

21 J.S. Haldane, "Life and Mechanism," *Mind* 9 (1884): 31–38; Edmund Montgomery, "The Unity of the Organic Individual," *Mind* 5 (1880): 326. See also Phillips, *Holistic Thought in Social Science*, 21–29.

22 Ernst Mayr, *This Is Biology: The Science of the Living World* (Cambridge, MA: Belknap Press, 1997), 20.

23 Maike Arz, *Literatur und Lebenskraft: Vitalistische Naturforschung und bürgerliche Literatur um 1800* [Literature and Life Force: Vitalist Natural Science and Bourgeois Literature] (Stuttgart: M. & P. Verlag für Wissenschaft und Forschung, 1996); Eva Barlösius, *Naturgemäße Lebensführung: Zur Geschichte der Lebensreform um die Jahrhundertwende* [Living a Life Appropriate to Nature: On the History of *Lebensreform* at the Turn of the Twentieth Century] (Frankfurt am Main: Campus, 1997); Monika Fick, *Sinnenwelt und Weltseele: Der psychophysische Monismus in der Literatur der Jahrhundertwende* [World of the Senses and the World Soul: Psychophysiological Monism in Literature at the Turn of the Twentieth Century] (Tübingen: Max Niemeyer, 1993); Anne Harrington, *Reenchanted Science: Holism in German Culture from Wilhelm II to Hitler* (Princeton, NJ: Princeton University Press, 1996); Gunter Martens, *Vitalismus und Expressionismus: Ein Beitrag zur Genese und Deutung expresionistischer Stilstrukturen und Motive* [Vitalism and Expressionism: A Contribution to the Genesis and Meaning of Expressionist Style Formations and Motives] (Stuttgart: W. Kohlhammer, 1971); Paul Ziche, ed., *Monismus um 1900: Wissenschaftskultur und Weltanschauung* [Monism around 1900: Scientific Culture and Worldview] (Berlin: VWB, 2000).

24 Russian artists and intellectuals were well acquainted with Johann Wolfgang von Goethe's morphological studies and his aesthetic concept as well as with Friedrich Wilhelm Schelling's natural philosophy. See Charlotte Douglas, "Beyond Reason: Malevich, Matiushin, and Their Circles," in *The Spiritual in Art: Abstract Painting, 1890–1985*, ed. Maurice Tuchman and Judi Freeman (exhib. cat.) (Los Angeles, CA: LACMA, 1986; New York: Abbeville, 1986), 185–99. On the influence of the ideas of Jean-Baptiste Lamarck and Charles Darwin, Gustav Theodor Fechner and Wilhelm Wundt, Arthur Schopenhauer, Friedrich Nietzsche, and Henri Bergson, see the following sections of this chapter.

25 Kazimir Malevich, "On New Systems in Art" (1919), in *K.S. Malevich: Essays on Art, 1915–1928*, ed. Troels Andersen (Copenhagen: Borgen, 1968), 1:87.

26 Vladimir Tatlin, "Khudozhnik–organizator byta" [The Artist as an Organizer of Everyday Life], *Rabis* [Rabis], no. 48 (November 25, 1929): 4. English in Larissa Alekseevna Zhadova, ed., *Tatlin* (New York: Rizzoli, 1988), 267.

27 Nikolai Kulbin, "Znachenie teorii iskusstva" [The Meaning of Art Theory], in *Studiia impressionistov* [Studio of the Impressionists] (St. Petersburg: N. I. Butkovskaia, 1910), 8–9.

28 Pavel Filonov, *Intimnaia masterskaia zhivopistsev i risoval'shchikov "Sdelannye kartiny"* [Intimate Workshop of Painters and Draftsmen, "Made Pictures"], Leaflet, 1914. German in Jürgen Harten and Jewgenija Petrowa, eds., *Pawel Filonow und seine Schule* [Pavel Filonov and His School] (exhib. cat.) (Düsseldorf: Städtische Kunsthalle, 1990; Cologne: DuMont, 1990), 70.

29 Olga Rozanova, "Osnovy Novago Tvorchestva i prichiny ego neponimaniia" [The Bases of the New Creation and the Reasons Why It Is Misunderstood], *Soius molodezhi* [Union of Youth] 3 (March 1913): 15. English in John E. Bowlt, ed., *Russian Art of the Avant-Garde: Theory and Criticism, 1902–1934* (New York: Viking, 1976), 105.

30 Rozanova, "Osnovy Novago Tvorchestva i prichiny ego neponimaniia," 16. English in Bowlt, *Russian Art of the Avant-Garde*, 105.

31 Kazimir Malevich, *Ot kubizma i futurizma k suprematizmu: Novyi zhivopisnyi realism* [From Cubism and Futurism to Suprematism: The New Painterly

Realism] (Petrograd, 1915). English in Andersen, *K S. Malevich: Essays on Art*, 1:19–41, and Bowlt, *Russian Art of the Avant-Garde*, 116–35.

32 Malevich, *Ot kubizma i futurizma k suprematizmu*, in Andersen, *K.S. Malevich: Essays on Art*, 1:24–25, and Bowlt, *Russian Art of the Avant-Garde*, 123.

33 Malevich, *Ot kubizma i futurizma k suprematizmu*, in Andersen, *K.S. Malevich: Essays on Art*, 1:38, and Bowlt, *Russian Art of the Avant-Garde*, 133–34.

34 Pavel Filonov, "Deklaratsiia 'Mirovogo rastsveta' " [Declaration of "Universal Flowering"], *Zhizn iskusstva* [Life of Art]) (Petrograd) 20 (May 1923): 14. English in Nicoletta Misler and John E. Bowlt, eds., *Pavel Filonov: A Hero and His Fate* (Austin, TX: Silvergirl, 1983), 168.

35 Lodder, "Organic Construction," 205–23.

36 Starting in 1861, Charles Darwin's evolutionary theory was discussed in Russia. The Moscow plant physiologist Sergei Rachinsky published the first complete edition of the book *On the Origin of Species* in 1864 and the radical writer Dmitri Pisarev reviewed it in the journal *Russkoe slovo* [Russian Word]. Darwin's 1871 book *Descent of Man* was published in three different Russian editions the same year. For further reference, see Loren R. Graham, *Science in Russia and the Soviet Union: A Short History* (Cambridge: Cambridge University Press, 1993), 56–76; Daniel P. Todes, *Darwin without Malthus: The Struggle for Existence in Russian Evolutionary Thought* (New York: Oxford University Press, 1989); Alexander Vucinich, *Science in Russian Culture 1861–1917* (Stanford, CA: Stanford University Press, 1970), 104–8, *Darwin in Russian Thought* (Berkeley, CA: University of California Press, 1988), and "Russia: Biological Sciences," in *The Comparative Reception of Darwinism*, ed. Thomas F. Glick (Austin, TX: University of Texas Press, 1972), 227–68.

37 See Graham, *Science in Russia and the Soviet Union*, 56–76; Vucinich, *Science in Russian Culture, 1861–1917*, 273–97, and *Darwin in Russian Thought*, 330–69.

38 Nikolai Chernyshevsky criticized Darwinism because an evolution based on "competition" and "struggle," seemed to justify violence. See Graham, *Science in Russia and the Soviet Union*, 64–65. Nikolai Danilevsky, in his 1885–89 book *Darvinizm: Kriticheskoe issledovanie* [Darwinism: A Critical Study], used Darwin's evolutionary theory as a basis for a fundamental critique of the nature of Western European science that he criticized as deeply materialist, atheist, and intellectually superficial. He complained that Darwin had replaced the teleological principle in nature with the principle of chance and the "struggle for existence" as mechanisms of natural selection and contrasted Darwin's "chaotic" natural cause with the gradual unfolding of the highest "intellectual principle" as universal natural law. See Graham, *Science in Russia and the Soviet Union*, 70; Vucinich, *Science in Russian Culture 1861–1917*, 276. Ilya Mekhnikov attempted to replace "natural selection" with a number of other factors; in the Lamarckian tradition, he spoke of inheritance of acquired characteristics, particularly the organism's inner "special tendency to perfection." See Todes, *Darwin without Malthus*, 92. Nikolai Nozhin considered not "struggle for existence," but "cooperation of similar individuals" as the source of biological and social evolution. See Vucinich, "Russia: Biological Sciences," 250. The well-known anarchist, Peter Kropotkin, saw "cooperation" as the driving force of the evolutionary process where Darwin had placed "competition" within the species. See Graham, *Science in Russia and the Soviet Union*, 62–70; Todes, *Darwin without Malthus*, 123–42. Promoting the principle of "mutual aid" as universal natural law, he wrote in his 1902 book *Mutual Aid*: "Sociability is as much a law of nature as mutual struggle." Even the orthodox Darwinist Kliment Timiriasev,

who published the books *A Short Sketch of the Theory of Darwin* and *Charles Darwin and His Theory*, preferred "harmony" over "struggle" and interpreted Darwin's "natural selection" as a natural method to achieve harmony. See Todes, *Darwin without Malthus*, 159–65; Graham, *Science in Russia and the Soviet Union*, 66–68; Vucinich, *Science in Russian Culture 1861–1917*, 129–33.

39 See Isabel Wünsche, *Harmonie und Synthese: Die russische Moderne zwischen universellem Anspruch und nationaler kultureller Identität* (Harmony and Synthesis: Russian Modernism between Universal Aspirations and National Cultural Identity) (Munich: Wilhelm Fink, 2008), 101–5.

40 Malevich, "On New Systems in Art," in Andersen, *K. S. Malevich: Essays on Art*, 1:94.

41 Ibid., 1:103.

42 Pavel Filonov, *Osnovnye polozheniia analiticheskogo iskusstva* [The Basic Tenets of Analytical Art], manuscript, 1923, Russian State Archive of Art and Literature (RGALI), f. 2348, op. 1, ed. khr. 10. English as Pavel Filonov, "The Basic Tenets of Analytical Art" (1923), in Misler and Bowlt, *Pavel Filonov*, 146.

43 Malevich, "On New Systems in Art," in Andersen, *K.S. Malevich: Essays on Art*, 1:87.

44 Kazimir Malevich, Leningrad State Archive for Literature and Art (LGALI), f. 244, op. 1, ed. khr. 69, l. 21, cited in Irina Karassik, "Das Institut für künstlerische Kultur (GINChUK)" [The Institute of Artistic Culture (GINKhUK)], in *Matjuschin and die Leningrader Avantgarde* (Matiushin and the Leningrad Avant-Garde), ed. Heinrich Klotz (exhib. cat.) (Karlsruhe: Badischer Kunstverein, 1991; Stuttgart-Munich: Oktogon, 1991), 42. See also Evgenii Kovtun, "Publikatsii Malevicha O teorii pribavochnogo elementa v zhivopisi" [The Publications of Malevich. about the Theory of the Additional Element in Painting], *Dekorativnoe iskusstvo* [Decorative Art] 11 (1988): 33–41.

45 The charts of the formation of the additional element in the various styles of modern painting are published in Troels Andersen, ed., *Malevich* (exhib. cat.) (Amsterdam: Stedelijk Museum, 1970), 115–33.

46 Michail Matjusin, "Opyt khudozhnika novoi mery [The Experience of an Artist of the New Dimension], in *K istorii russkogo avangarda* [The Russian Avant-Garde], ed. Nikolaj Chardziev (Stockholm: Almqvist and Wiksell International, 1976), 159–87.

47 Wassily Kandinsky, "Soderzhanie i forma" [Content and Form], in *"Salon 2." Mezhdunarodnaia khudozhestvennaia vystavka org. V. Izdebskim* [Salon 2. International Art Exhibition organized by V. Izdebsky] (exhib. cat.) (Odessa, 1910–11), 15. English in Bowlt, *Russian Art of the Avant-Garde*, 22.

48 David Burliuk, "Kubizm" [Cubism], in *Poshchechina obshchestvennomu vkusu* [A Slap in the Face of Public Taste] (Moscow, 1912), 98. In English as David Burliuk, "Cubism (Surface—Plane)" (1912), in Bowlt, *Russian Art of the Avant-Garde*, 73.

49 Larionov, "Luchistskaia zhivopis," 84. English in Bowlt, *Russian Art of the Avant-Garde*, 96.

50 Malevich, *Ot kubizma i futurizma k suprematizmu*. English in Bowlt, *Russian Art of the Avant-Garde*, 123.

51 Filonov, *Osnovnye polozheniia analiticheskogo iskusstva*. English in Misler and Bowlt, *Pavel Filonov*, 147.

52 For a general account of *faktura*, see Yve-Alain Bois, "Malevitch, le carré, le degree zero," *Macula* 1 (1976): 28–49; Margit Rowell, "Vladimir Tatlin: Form/Faktura," *October* 7 (Winter 1978): 83–108.

53 On the role *faktura* played in Russian Constructivism and production art of the 1920s and 1930s, see Lodder, *Russian Constructivism*, 94–105; Benjamin H.D. Buchloh, "From Faktura to Factography," *October* 30 (Autumn 1984): 82–119.

54 Markov, "Printsipy novago iskusstva" (pt. 1), 1: 5–14 and (pt. 2) 2: 5–18; Rozanova, "Osnovy Novago Tvorchestva i prichiny ego neponimaniia," 14–22; Vladimir Markov, *Printsipy tvorchestva v plasticheskikh iskusstvakh: faktura* [Creative Principles in the Plastic Arts: Faktura] (Petrograd, 1914).

55 Markov, *Printsipy tvorchestva v plasticheskikh iskusstvakh*, 1.

56 Ibid.

57 Ibid., 25.

58 Ibid., 2.

59 Ibid., 1–12.

60 Ibid., 7.

61 Ibid., 59–60.

62 Buchloh, "From Faktura to Factography," 87.

63 Rozanova, "Osnovy Novago Tvorchestva i prichiny ego neponimaniia," 14. English in Bowlt, *Russian Art of the Avant-Garde*, 103.

64 Rozanova, "Osnovy Novago Tvorchestva i prichiny ego neponimaniia," 20. English in Bowlt, *Russian Art of the Avant-Garde*, 108.

65 Aleksandr Bogdanov, *Tektologiia. Vseobshchaia organizatsionnaia nauka* [Tektology: The Universal Science of Organization], 3 vols. (Berlin, Petersburg, and Moscow: Grzhebin, 1922).

66 Charlotte Douglas, "Energetic Abstraction: Ostwald, Bodganov, and Russian Post-Revolutionary Art," in Bruce Clarke and Linda Henderson, eds., *From Energy to Information: Representation in Science and Technology, Art, and Literature* (Stanford, CA: Stanford University Press, 2002), 76–94.

67 Rowell, "Vladimir Tatlin: Form/Faktura," 83–108.

68 Ibid., 85–86.

69 Tatlin, "Khudozhnik–organizator byta," 4. English in Zhadova, *Tatlin*, 266–67.

70 Vladimir Tatlin, "Problema sootnosheniia cheloveka i veshchi: Ob'iavim boinu komodam i bufetam" [The Problem of the Relationship between Man and Object: Let Us Declare War on Chests of Drawers and Sideboards], *Rabis* [Rabis], no. 15 (April 14, 1930); 9. English in Zhadova, *Tatlin*, 268.

71 Tatlin, "Khudozhnik–organizator byta," 4. English in Zhadova, *Tatlin*, 267.

72 Lodder, *Russian Constructivism*, 210–17.

73 The works of both authors were used in theoretical instruction at the VKhUTEIN in Moscow, where Tatlin taught at the Dermetfak [Wood and Metalwork Department] and the Ceramics Department from 1927 to 1930. Particularly Engelmeier's four-volume *Filosofiia tekhniki* [Philosophy of Technology] (Moscow, 1912) was a standard work at the time.

74 Kapp compared, for example, the iron-steel constructions of bridges as derived from bone structures, the railroad as an externalization of the circulatory system, and the telegraph as an extension of the nervous system. See Ernst Kapp, *Grundlinien einer Philosophie der Technik. Zur Entstehungsgeschichte der Cultur aus neuen Gesichtspunkten* [Foundations of a Philosophy of Technology: On the History of Culture from a New Viewpoint] (Braunschweig: Westermann, 1877).

75 Petr K. Engelmeier, "Is Philosophy of Technology Necessary?," *Journal of the Moscow Polytechnic Society* (1929): 36–40, as cited in Carl Mitcham, *Thinking through Technology: The Path between Engineering and Philosophy* (Chicago, IL: University of Chicago Press, 1994), 28.

76 Pavel Filonov, "Kanon i zakon" [Canon and Law] (1912), Institute of Russian Literature (IRLI), f. 656. See Kowtun, "Einige Termini der analytischen Kunst," 94.

77 Filonov, "Kanon i zakon," in Kowtun, "Einige Termini der analytischen Kunst," 94.

78 Filonov, "Deklaratsiia 'Mirovogo rastsveta' ", 14. English in Misler and Bowlt, *Pavel Filonov*, 169.

79 Filonov, *Osnovnye polozheniia analiticheskogo iskusstva*. English in Misler and Bowlt, *Pavel Filonov*, 147.

80 Markov, "Printsipy novago iskusstva" (pt. 1), 1: 7, 11. English in Bowlt, *Russian Art of the Avant-Garde*, 26–28.

7

Biocentrism and anarchy: Herbert Read's Modernism

Allan Antliff

What is at stake when we consider Biocentrism in art from a political perspective? Can such art contribute to our emancipation from material want and social oppression? Among anarchism's historical proponents, English art critic Herbert Read stands out as one who addressed this issue head-on just before the advent of World War II. Then the stakes were, indeed, very high. Read was defending two much maligned modernist tendencies, abstraction and Surrealism. And he was raising the issue of Modernism's revolutionary role in the struggle for a free and just society.

It seems appropriate, then, that Read in 1939 should publish his most succinct statement on abstract art in the Surrealist *London Bulletin*. Read wrote that abstractionists were concerned with "certain proportions and rhythms inherent in the structure of the universe which govern organic growth." "Attuned to these rhythms and proportions," the artist created "microcosms which reflect the macrocosm." Rejecting "an exact presentation" of "the external world" he tapped into "archetypical forms which underlie all the casual variations" in nature. By way of example, the article was illustrated with an untitled abstract painting by Piet Mondrian and a sculpture, *Two Forms* (1937), by Barbara Hepworth. Both expressed tendencies in abstraction toward, on the one hand, an exploration of nature's geometric structures and, on the other, its organic materiality. What united them was a shared Vitalism. The aesthetics of abstract art expressed the living cosmos held, "not in a grain of sand," but "in a block of stone or a pattern of colours."[1]

So far so good, but Biocentrism was not confined to the art object. Read also framed art's social function in these terms by adjudicating what kind of art was desirable on the basis of its amenability to the anarchism of the natural scientist and geographer, Peter Kropotkin. On this basis, he brought not only abstract art but also Surrealism under the umbrella of Biocentrism, and defended both against British Communist Party assertions that realism was the only revolutionary art form. Which is to say that Read's support for

Biocentrism in art was bound up with his anarchism, and the dilemma of being an anarchist at a time when Communism dominated the leftist landscape.

In his edited collection of Kropotkin's writings, published in 1942, Read outlined anarchism's political program: a society where the needs of everyone would be met through a system of decentralized self-governance and a socialized economy. Whereas Marxists argued the centralized state could serve as a means of realizing socialism, Kropotkin argued the state was an authoritarian institution that would undermine economic egalitarianism and repress the social freedoms that were fundamental for progressive development.[2] The state, therefore, had to be abolished at the same time as capitalism. Both generated social conflict that went against humanity's collective interest.

In the course of developing his argument, Kropotkin extrapolated, from nature, fundamental laws that pertained to humanity's evolution.[3] He posited that the natural world tended toward a condition of dynamic equilibrium, in which each species spontaneously adapted to its environment and, in so doing, contributed to the makeup of the ecology as a whole. Nature was dynamic because as species evolved and new ones came into being the conditions of equilibrium changed. The well-being of nature, therefore, lay in the spontaneous development of species and ever increasing diversity in the ecological makeup.

The prime force in nature was "mutual aid"—"the universal law of organic evolution."[4] Kropotkin observed that the vast majority of species thrive because of spontaneous patterns of cooperation that also permeate interspecies relationships. Humanity was nature's most social animal and amongst us the practice of mutual aid had attained the greatest development. This gave rise to cooperative modes of social organization and ethical ideals such as altruism and the desire for justice founded on the principle of equal rights for all.[5] It was in humanity's species interest, therefore, to increase cooperation and to cultivate correspondingly harmonious relationships with the environment.[6] Anarchism was the best means of achieving this, since its non-authoritarian political structures and socialist economy would allow "new forms of production, invention, and organization" to evolve freely for the collective benefit.[7] An anarchist society, wrote Kropotkin, would

> not be crystallized into certain unchangeable forms, but will continually modify its aspect, because it will be a living, evolving organism; no need for government will be felt, because free agreement and federation can take its place in all functions.[8]

Such a society would grow and develop spontaneously, with mutual aid as the guarantor of progressive, as opposed to regressive, development. This would mark it as a healthy social system, as opposed to capitalism, where these conditions did not prevail. Kropotkin argued unhealthy ecosystems degenerated due to imbalances in their makeup caused by the excesses of a dominant species, natural disasters, or some other calamity. In the natural world, harmony was a provisional adaptation subject to constant modification to be maintained and when it was lost, an ecosystem entered into a state of crisis. Thus the health of nature was not predetermined: nor was society's.[9]

And so we return to art. Read's compendium of Kropotkin's writings closes with a chapter on "Art and Society" in which Kropotkin wrote, "*Art* is, in our ideal, synonymous with creation." The artist invented new forms which were powerful and expressive, but "only when cities, territories, nations or groups of nations" adopted the free order of anarchism would art become "an integral part of the living whole."[10] Produced by individuals from every walk of life and rooted in community diversity, art would spread and flourish in painting, sculpture, architecture, and the everyday environment. "Bound up with industry" it would transform "everything that surrounds man, in the street, in the interior and exterior," into "pure artistic form."[11]

It followed, therefore, that "the cause of the arts" was "the cause of revolution."[12] Ideally, Read suggested, the social function of the artist was to express the innermost impulses of the mind in such a way as to contribute to the material organization of life.[13] However, this purely subjective adventure into the unknown could only flourish if there was social and economic liberty for the artist to develop and evolve.[14] And these conditions could only be realized in a classless, anarchist society.

How, then, did abstract art and Surrealism figure in his anarchist program? Read addressed this question through a critique of, on the one hand, the condition of art under capitalism and, on the other, its role under state dictatorship. In the same essay where he identified the cause of art with revolution, Read outlined capitalism's fundamental hostility towards artists. In England, capitalism had created a culture that favoured mass conformity over originality of expression. Furthermore, art had no social value and was regarded at best with indifference.[15] "All over the world" capitalism was spreading "its net of debauchery, its standardization of taste, its imposition of material values."[16] But in England, where the system began, the damage was almost terminal. Sensibility was dead, and the only criterion of judgment was convention to "a standard imposed by manufacturers" in a quest to maximize profit.[17] The English lacked "social freedom" and consequently "the public good, the common-wealth" had been "subordinated to the private good, private wealth."[18] A chaos of styles and utilitarian products completely devoid of aesthetic quality was the result.[19] Beset by continuous disruption the aesthetic instinct, which should be a factor in all aspects of social life, had fallen into precipitous decline.[20]

Capitalism fragmented the social organism and repressed artistic activity in the process, but it was not the only social system hostile towards artistic freedom. Soviet Communism and Fascism were equally damaging, as they subordinated all aspects of society, including the arts, to the central control of the state.[21] Neither recognized that the imaginative expression was a fundamental human need.[22] Instead art was treated instrumentally.[23] Communists celebrated the achievements of socialism while the Nazis idealized nationalism, "but the necessary method" was the same. Both movements demanded "rhetorical realism, devoid of invention, deficient in imagination, renouncing subtlety and emphasizing the obvious."[24] By way of explanation, Read speculated this shared denigration could be traced back to Hegel's characterization of the arts as a primitive form of knowledge founded on sensation. As humanity progressed, Hegel argued, "this primitive mode of thought or representation was to be superseded by the intellect or reason." Art would then be "put away like a discarded toy." Thus Marx, who accepted the relegation of art's function to "the childhood of mankind," treated it as a residual feature of the evolving "ideological superstructure." Read also detected a latent debt to Hegel in Fascism's elevation of the idea over sensation and its concomitant "rational and functional interpretation of art" which reduced the artist to "a subordinate and slavish" role.[25]

A brief examination of Nazi art and the art promoted by Communists in the Soviet Union and the United Kingdom will enliven Read's critique. Hans Schmitz-Wiedenbrück's *Workers, Farmers and Soldiers* (c. 1940), communicates its message in a realist style following the Nazi dictum that national art be understandable to the masses. The painting's theme is racist collectivism. Germany is subdivided into spheres of productivity, with war-making at its apex. The "East Germanic" worker has a "passive and obedient" temperament. The farmer is a "Phalian" type whose disposition tends toward the "lethargic." And the soldiers are "leaders" because they are "pure nordic."[26] Similarly, Soviet artist Arcadi Platsov's *Collective Farm Festival* (1937) depicts ideological themes in a "socialist realist" style so as to "arouse a revolutionary relationship to reality."[27] Under a sunny sky, symbolic of the bright future, Stalin gazes over prosperous peasants who are enjoying the fruits of socialism in one country, including ownership of a combine harvester. The banner, flanked by a five-pointed star and Soviet flag, reads "Living has gotten better, living has gotten merrier." This slogan, coined by Stalin in 1933, by and in large set the tone for how life in the Soviet Union was depicted during the era of the five-year plans.[28]

The Soviet program also set the pace for the type of art promoted by the British Communist Party in the Artists International Association, the *Left Review*, and other journals.[29] "New realism" was the term coined by one of the party's leading critics, Anthony Blunt, to describe this art. "New realist" artists were sympathetic with "the progressive sections" of the proletariat and expressed Communist-inspired themes of class struggle.[30] Viscount Hastings's *Historic Growth of the British Labour Movement*, completed in 1935, is a textbook example of the style. The central figure, modeled on a Welsh miner, depicts "the worker of the future." Flanked by Marx and Lenin, he pulls down "the economic chaos of the present." Smaller groupings on the left and right represent the British labour movement's origins and current composition.[31] Epic murals like this, according to Blunt, were harbingers of the coming "new culture."[32] On this basis Blunt attacked Read's position in *Art and Society* that art could not thrive in the Soviet Union.[33] Blunt approvingly summarized the Soviet policy in art with a quote from Lenin, who told Clara Zetkin that under Communism,

> Every artist has a right to create freely according to his ideals, independent of anything. Only, of course, we Communists cannot stand with our hands folded and

let chaos develop in any direction it may. We must guide this process according to a plan and form its results.[34]

Let us return, then, to Read's position on what made art revolutionary. Like Blunt, he also opposed Fascism, but he did so in the name of an organic politics of anarchism. And this was the basis for his defense of abstract art and Surrealism. Whereas Blunt tossed these "bourgeois" movements in the dustbin, Read argued that aspects of both were integral to the only type of post-capitalism worth fighting for, namely anarchism. Abstract art was both individualist and universal because it expressed formal qualities derived from "the physical structure of the world" and in sympathy with "the psychological structure of man."[35] These "biological structures" fell outside the development of human history, since they were "constant factors in life."[36] There was a historical explanation why Gabo and others expressed themselves using pure form. Hostile toward capitalism, Fascism, and Communism, they sought "to escape into a world without ideologies" through art. In other words, abstract art entailed a politics of resistance. However, its revolutionary import lay not in the present, but in its potential to infuse the man-made environment with nature's universal aesthetic qualities. The role of abstract art was to remain "inviolate, until such time as society will once more be ready to make use of ... the universal qualities of art—those elements which survive all changes and revolutions."[37]

As for Surrealism, in *Art and Society*, published in 1937, Read observed that the movement's goal was to unify our psyche with our social life in recognition that, at present, there was a profound lack of "organic connection" between the two. Surrealism sought to restore this unity through the overthrow of capitalism and this marked it as a transitional art movement.[38] However, in *Poetry and Anarchism*, Read predicted artists would continue creating art attuned to the unconsciousness, inspired as they would be by the "natural freedom" permeating an anarchist society.[39]

And here we arrive at the crux of the matter. An anarchist society would be liberating because the order it generated would be founded upon the free creativity of its participants. Consequently, whereas Communists and their Fascist counterparts sought to impose social order by repressing spontaneous development, anarchists such as Read refused any totalizing schema enforced from above in favor of freedom in every realm, including the arts. The precondition of freedom under anarchism was Communism without authoritarianism, an organic society in which art could evolve unceasingly in accord with the impetus of its creators. On this basis, Read regarded abstractionist and Surrealist Modernists as amenable to anarchism because they refused closure—this guaranteed they would infuriate authoritarians of whatever stripe. That said, the challenge for such Modernists—and Read as well—was to carve out an engaged role for art in a specifically anarchist struggle against capitalism, Communism, and Fascism. On the eve of World War II, that was the most pressing issue of all.

Notes

1 Herbert Read, "An Art of Pure Form," *London Bulletin* no. 14 (1939): 8–9. Mondrian distilled features in nature down to their unchanging "essence." A tree, for example, would be reduced to a basic geometric structure then rendered abstractly. In this way, he imagined he was creating a universal artistic language that prefigured the rise of a new spiritual consciousness destined to bring about the unification of humanity: Charles Harrison, Francis Frascina, and Gill Perry, *Primitivism, Cubism, Abstraction: The Early Twentieth Century* (New Haven, CT: Yale University Press, 1993), 225–26. Similarly, Barbara Hepworth wrote that her sculptures were emotional projections that "radiate the intensity of the whole." Abstracted from nature, these "living" forms embodied "universal" aesthetic qualities. However, there is no indication she shared the spiritual-political orientation of Mondrian: Barbara Hepworth, "Untitled Statement," *Unit 1* (London: Cassell: 1934), 19–20.

2 Herbert Read, "Introduction," in Peter Kropotkin, *Kropotkin: Selections from his Writings*, ed. Herbert Read (London: Freedom Press, 1942), 14–15.

3 On Kropotkin's Biocentrist anarchism see Brian Morris, "Kropotkin's Metaphysics of Nature," *Anarchist Studies* 9 (2001): 165–80. Regarding the Marxist interpretation of our relationship to nature, Read was certainly aware of the Communist application of dialectics across the full spectrum of inquiry, from human psychology to the molecular development of plants, during the 1920s and 1930s. V. Adoratsky's widely reprinted primer, *Dialectical Materialism*, for example, included an entire chapter on "The Dialectics of Nature and Human Development": V. Adoratsky, *Dialectical Materialism: The Theoretical Foundation of Marxism-Leninism* (New York: International Publishers, 1934). Frederick Engels was the first to apply dialectics to nature; see Frederick Engels, *The Dialectics of Nature* (reprint New York: International Publishers, 1940). Kropotkin regarded dialectics as an antiquated methodology and ascribed to the scientific "inductive-deductive method"; Kropotkin, *Kropotkin: Selections*, 119–20.

4 Kropotkin, *Kropotkin: Selections*, 131.

5 Ibid., 123.

6 Ibid., 124.

7 Ibid., 114.

8 Ibid., 131.

9 See Morris, "Kropotkin's Metaphysics of Nature," 168.

10 Kropotkin, *Kropotkin: Selections*, 144–45.

11 Ibid, 146.

12 Herbert Read, "Why We English Have No Taste," in *Poetry and Anarchism* (New York: MacMillan, 1939), 40. The essay was originally published in the French journal *Minotaure* no. 7 (June 1935): 67–68.

13 Read, "Essential Communism," *Poetry and Anarchism*, 45; and Herbert Read, *Art and Society* (London: William Hienemann, 1937), 95.

14 Read, "The Importance of Living," *Poetry and Anarchism*, 125.

15 Read, "Why We English Have No Taste," 36.

16 Ibid., 39.

17 Ibid.

18 Ibid.

19 Read, *Art and Society*, 128.

20 Ibid. Elsewhere Read wrote that art could only realize its social potential in a post-capitalist "communal type of society, where within one organic consciousness all modes of life, all senses and all faculties, function freely and harmoniously." Read, "Why We English Have No Taste," 40.

21 Read, "Poets and Politicians," *Poetry and Anarchism*, 23.

22 Ibid., 25.

23 Ibid., 25. Read refers to the "intellect" in art.

24 Ibid., 25–26. Reflecting on the arrival of exiled European artists in the United Kingdom in early 1939, Read observed that in the Soviet Union "art is no longer allowed to be individual and spontaneous; it too must contribute to the collective effort." "Great art has been produced under similar circumstances" he continued, "but only when, as in the Middle Ages, the collective effort had a spiritual aim. When the aim is materialistic—and slogans apart, the whole energies of the USSR are bent on increasing the general level of industrial production—then art is an irrelevance." Herbert Read, "In What Sense 'Living'?" *London Bulletin* 8–9 (Jan.–Feb. 1939): 7.

25 Read, "Poets and Politicians," 24–25.

26 Bertold Hinz, *Art in the Third Reich* (New York: Pantheon, 1979), 114.

27 I am paraphrasing Maxim Gorki cited in Matthew Cullerne Bown, *Socialist Realist Painting* (New Haven, CT: Yale University Press, 1998), 143.

28 Stalin's declaration was adopted as the official slogan of the Stakhanovite (shock-worker) movement at the first all-Union Congress of Shock-Workers in 1935. In 1933 Gorki, writing in the journal *Soviet Art*, also referred to this slogan while instructing artists to depict Soviet "joy." "Our pictures should be joyous, infectious," he wrote. "They should contain more smiles"; Maxim Gorki cited in Bown, *Socialist Realist Painting*, 143.

29 In his study of the Artists International Association (AIA), founded in 1933, Tony Rickaby notes that British Communists invited alliances with progressive artists under the umbrella of the AIA's anti-fascist, anti-war popular front platform (adopted in 1935). However, within the AIA, Communist-oriented artists organized into groups—the Hogarth Group, the Euston Road School, the British Communist Party Artists' Group—and party critics such as Anthony Blunt, A.L. Lloyd, Aleck West, and Francis Klingender continued to promote realism while attacking Surrealism and abstraction. Tactically, then, the AIA was a means of drawing independent artists into an organization where they might be "worked on" more effectively; Tony Rickaby, "Artists' International," *History Workshop*, 6 (Autumn 1978): 154–68.

30 Anthony Blunt, "Art Under Capitalism and Socialism," in *The Mind in Chains: Socialism and the Cultural Revolution*, ed. C. Day Lewis (London: Frederick Muller, 1937), 115. Blunt, who was art critic during the 1930s for the Communist-oriented *Spectator* magazine and the British Communist Party's theoretical journal *Left Review*, was also a recruiter for the Soviet spy network in the United Kingdom. In 1939, he was appointed to London University as reader in the history of art attached to the prestigious Courtauld Institute. He went on to serve as art adviser to the Monarchy and surveyor of the Royal art collection. Blunt was knighted in 1956.

31 This is Viscount Hastings's description of his mural in the *Daily Mirror* 10 (October 1935), cited in Morris and Radford, *AIA: The Story of the Artists International Association: 1933–1953* (Oxford: Museum of Modern Art, 1983), 15.

32 Anthony Blunt, "The Realist Quarrel," *Left Review* (April 1937), cited in Lynda Morris and Robert Radford, *AIA*, 16.

33 See Read, *Art and Society*, 133.

34 Blunt, "Art Under Capitalism and Socialism," 122.

35 Herbert Read, "The Nature of Revolutionary Art," in *The Politics of the Unpolitical* (London: Routledge, 1946), 126. This essay was originally published as "What is Revolutionary Art?" in *5 On Revolutionary Art*, ed. Betty Rea (London: Wishart and Co., 1935).

36 Ibid.

37 Ibid., 127.

38 Read, *Art and Society*, 120. "The vitality of art," wrote Read, depended on "the free operation of the unconscious forces of life." Ibid., 123.

39 Ibid.

Organicism among the Cubists: The case of Raymond Duchamp-Villon

Mark Antliff

In the opening pages of her book *The Originality of the Avant-Garde and Other Modernist Myths* (1985), Rosalind Krauss singled out the organicist metaphor as a key—and reprehensible—Modernist myth.[1] According to Krauss, art historians immersed in modernist assumptions draw an analogy between the work and its maker, and organicist tropes link art forms to characteristics of the human organism.[2] In her structuralist critique of organicism, Krauss dismissed any notion that a work of art possessed an integral essence, relatable solely to inspiration or conceived of as the product of "stylistic" evolution. Rejecting the organic metaphor, Krauss defined art as a structural form, a system of differences devoid of a positive essence or "origin." Citing the example of Pablo Picasso's Cubist collages, Krauss replaced organicist metaphors with those derived from Ferdinand de Saussure's structuralist linguistics, arguing that the "continual transposition between negative and positive form" in Cubist collage instituted a "systematic play of difference" wherein "no positive sign could exist without the eclipse or negation of its material referent."[3] On this basis, Krauss concluded that the rhetoric of organicism, and its art historical correlate in the realm of biographical explanation, could not account for the structuralist dimension of Picasso's collage aesthetic.

In recent years this structuralist methodology has dominated the study of Cubist collage,[4] but scholars have yet to consider the role of organicist metaphors in the art and art criticism of the so-called "Puteaux Cubists," most notably the painters Albert Gleizes and Jean Metzinger, and sculptor Raymond Duchamp-Villon.[5] In this essay, I will show that the Modernist tradition rightly associated with organicism contained within it forces that problematize closure and break open the closed model,[6] since the hegemony of this discourse within Modernism is itself a myth. In particular, the alliance of these artists to the philosophy of Henri Bergson (1859–1941) spawned a debate within Cubist circles over whether the decorative arts could embody the organicist precepts they associated with Bergson's philosophy.

Analysis of the organic metaphors that permeate the art criticism of Duchamp-Villon and his colleagues serves to undermine Krauss's overly simplified conception of Cubist aesthetics, which singles out Picasso as the only Cubist of his generation who problematized organic form.[7] I shall argue that the Cubist debate over aesthetic closure is best analyzed in light of the Bergsonian critiques of modernism and organicism developed by such figures as the philosopher Gilles Deleuze and literary critic Frank Kermode. Both writers drew on Bergson's thought in mounting their arguments: Kermode from the standpoint of existentialism and phenomenology; Deleuze within the context of post-structuralism. Kermode and Deleuze claim that Bergson's analysis of organicism anticipated contemporary critiques of Modernism; I would argue that the Puteaux Cubists simultaneously embraced Bergsonian paradigms, and failed to fully grasp the implications of a philosophy that ultimately transcended the "closure" usually imputed to organicist conceptions. Since Duchamp-Villon's aesthetic is central to this discourse, I will begin by analyzing his pronouncements before considering the schism that emerged between Duchamp-Villon and his Cubist colleagues over the organicist import of the decorative arts.

Duchamp-Villon's essay of 1916 titled "Kinds of Awareness of Artistic Creation" stands as testimony to his immersion in Bergson's organicist philosophy.[8] Fundamental to Duchamp-Villon's definition of creativity in that text is a concept of perceptual awareness, garnered through our ability to "know objects and bring them to life." This desire to know objects, states the sculptor, "entails a judgment and a choice whose reasons are neither reasoned nor reasonable," but are instead "intuitive" and "more certainly effective."[9] This "effective" or "intuitive" experience of the object allows the artist to take "possession of [the object] to the extent of identifying himself with it." The result of this artistic intuition will be a "fusion of thought with the object thought about."[10] Having "lifted a corner of the veil"[11] in grasping this intuition, the artist then attempts to give form to this experience in the guise of a painting, sculpture or architectural design.

This distinction between reason and intuition, and the relation of intuition to one's ability to identify with an object, iterate some of the most basic tenets of Bergson's philosophy—often echoing Bergson's own metaphors—as outlined in his *Laughter* (1900) and "Introduction to Metaphysics" (1903). In the latter text, Bergson had distinguished between intellectual and intuitive forms of knowledge; further, he had defined intuition as "the sympathy by which one is transported into the interior of an object in order to coincide with what there is unique" about it.[12] In *Laughter,* Bergson had privileged artists as among those who possessed a special capacity for entering into intuitive experience with the world, for intuition "has lifted the veil" of our pragmatically oriented intellect to reveal to artists "the subtlest movements" of nature's "inner life."[13] Clearly Duchamp-Villon and Bergson share the same metaphysical premises, for both philosopher and artist claimed that intuition alone can "lift the veil" of reason and allow artists to merge with an object and know it from within.

Intuition, to quote Bergson, follows "the logic of the imagination that is not reason,"[14] and it is this alogical state alone that allows us to act creatively.

"The life of the imaginative person," argues Duchamp-Villon, "is no more than a series of newly articulated states of consciousness," and as the product of such states the work of art "can be judged only as a whole since it represents the entire development of the Self."[15] In this passage, Duchamp-Villon's Bergsonian assumptions cause him to declare art the product of "vital" processes. Art mirrors the temporal evolution of its creator; it is a complete manifestation of an artist's creative development up to a given moment in time. Moreover, these art objects are both self-contained, yet interconnected since "they complete themselves by giving birth to each other, and no one can predict how they will appear." Even before an intuition is developed into a sculpture or painting, Duchamp-Villon's artist "is already looking among his effective riches ... for the image that will permit him to develop it." This is because each creative act produces "original feelings" implanted in the stream of temporal consciousness like "seeds to be cultivated." Thus, while "in the course of finishing a work, [the artist] already begins the following one, sometimes only in his mind, sometimes by sketching it." With the completion of a sculpture, "all is harmony," and "the human being is, for an instant, in a state of equilibrium."[16] Though the object is now a closed, organic form, the creative act that spawned it, lives on in human consciousness. And the accumulation of such acts in experience constitutes "those reserves" that will inspire new acts, and new art objects. In short, aesthetic closure is never complete, since each work is related to every other product of creative intuition. Duchamp-Villon noted that, "in coming to life," each work "will inscribe itself in time, and the creator will want to believe that this curve is going to be as long as possible." "It cannot be otherwise," he added," since at this time he is mustering all the powers of his being and its infinite possibilities." As the product of creative activity each sculpture is "like a ripe fruit" that "can no longer remain attached to the tree that bears it."[17] That Duchamp-Villon practiced what he preached is evident in works such as his *Pastorale* of 1910 (Fig. 8.1), which, to paraphrase the sculptor, "gave birth" to his *Torso of a Young Man* (1910) (Fig. 8.2). As William Agee and George Heard Hamilton have pointed out, the bodily posture of the running male in *Pastorale* is virtually repeated in the pose of his fragmented and more geometrified *Torso of a Young Man* of the same year.[18]

This freedom to create form in one's own image is then linked by Duchamp-Villon to the "effective" or intuitive capacities of the artist. In his 1911 notes on Cubism, he addresses the issue in the following manner:

> Today the violent discussions which accompanied the appearance of Cubism are the same which disturbed our fathers in the great days of Impressionism; they recur every time remarkable personalities must assert themselves ... the feeling for art arises from the encounter in the work of two personalities, the artist's and the spectator's ... there is a violent collision between the one's conventional learning and the other's spontaneity. But the effective presence of the creator in his work is the indication of the proof of its value.[19]

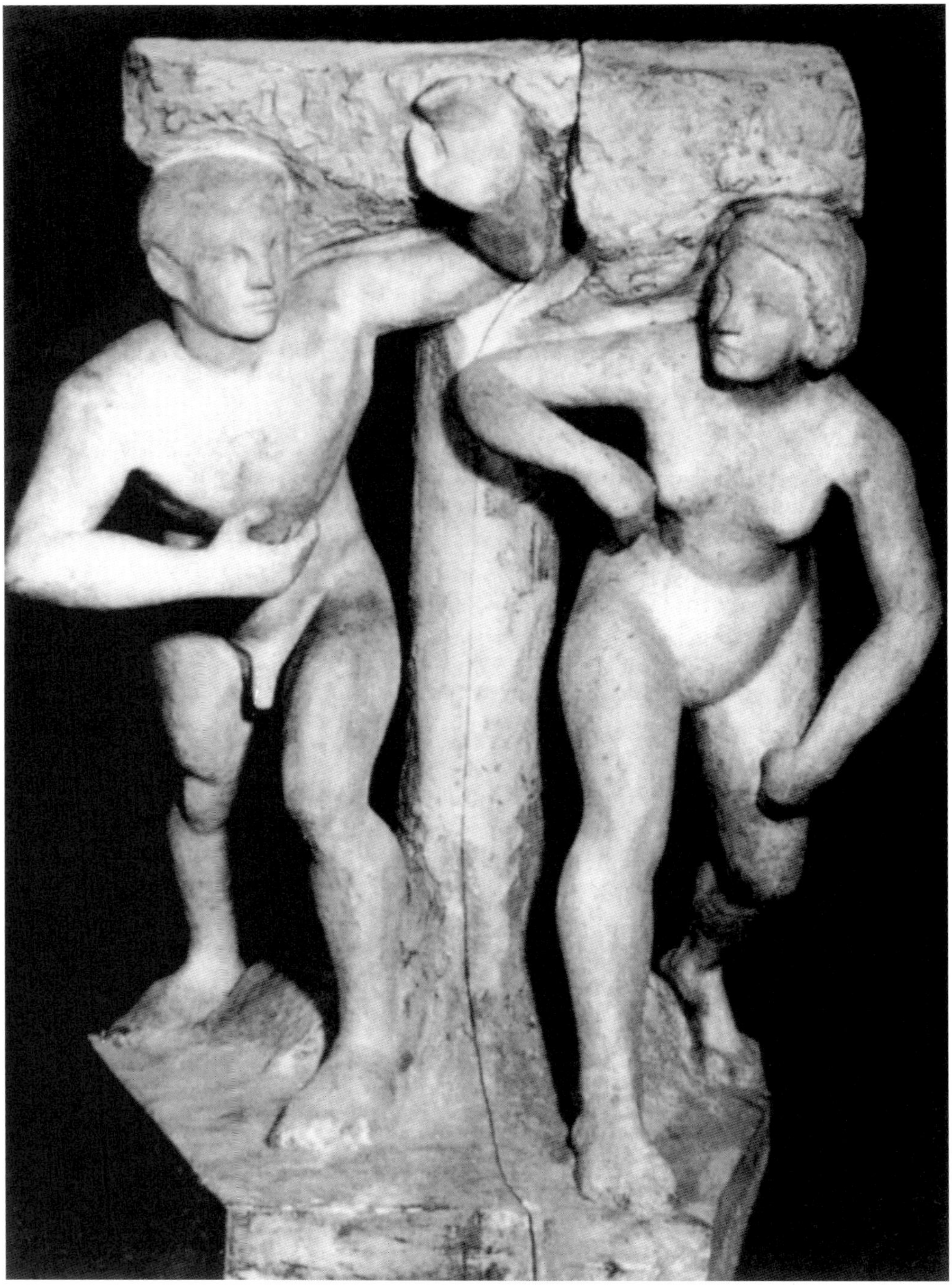

8.1 Raymond Duchamp-Villon, *Pastorale,* 1909–10, plaster, 145 × 130 × 115 cm. Musée des Beaux-Arts, Rouen, France. Photo: Réunion des Musées Nationaux/Art Resource, NY

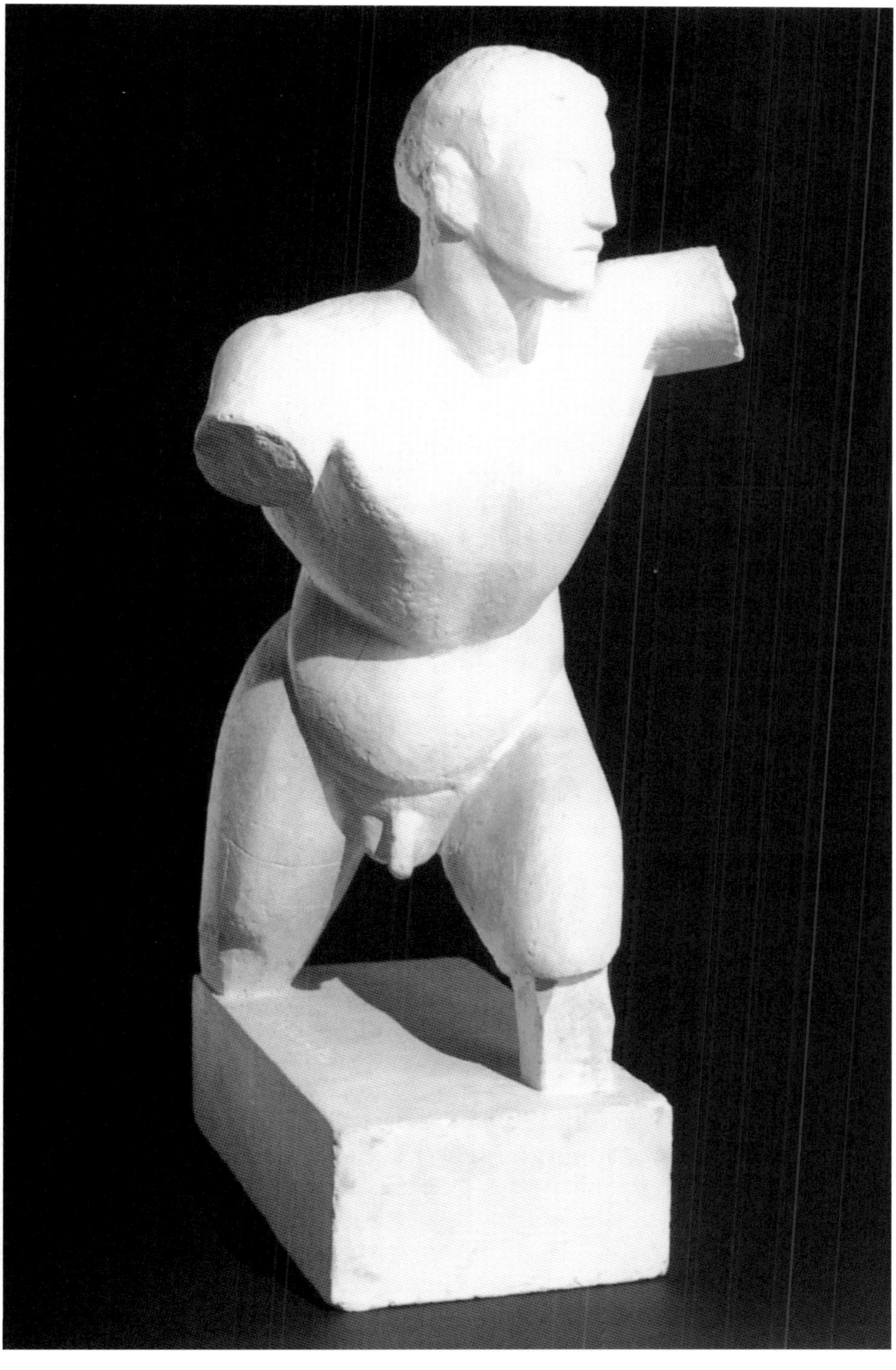

8.2 Raymond Duchamp-Villon, *Torso of a Young Man*, 1910/cast 1912, plaster, 60.5 × 33.7 × 33.3 cm. Hirshhorn Museum and Sculpture Garden, Smithsonian Museum, gift of Joseph H. Hirshhorn, 1966. Photo: Lee Stalsworth

Like Gleizes and Metzinger in their co-authored book *Du Cubisme* (1912), Duchamp-Villon chastises the public for being the slave of past artistic conventions.[20] Ironically, an artist's ideal audience is composed only of other artists who share the same intuitive capacities and are thus able to discern the true "value" of a given work.[21] In an elitist and self-congratulatory vein, Duchamp-Villon numbered himself among the select few who, as the Cubists' creative equals, were able to discern "the effective presence of the creator" in their works: "That's exactly why I could, at the beginning and without knowing them, be attracted to the Cubist painters, and that is why little by little I could understand their aesthetic and better appreciate it."[22]

In short, Duchamp-Villon and his Cubist colleagues justified their aesthetic innovations by declaring them to be the product of their *durée*, and thus in line with the creative élan of past innovators. For the Puteaux Cubists, this meant that artists could combine pictorial conventions forged in the past with innovations keyed to an artist's dynamic *durée*.[23] Such thinking led Duchamp-Villon and others to adapt the imagery of past artists to their own stylistic innovations, thus effecting a mixture of old and new artistic conventions. For instance, I would argue that the side-long glance and gesture of modesty evident in the pose of Duchamp-Villon's 1914 *Seated Woman* (Fig. 8.3) is related to the defensive posture of Susanna in works such as Rubens's *Susanna and the Elders* of 1620, which in turn is modeled after Greek statues of *Aphrodite*.[24] In this reading, the crossing of the figure's left arm over her breasts, combined with her crouching posture, would be an act of modesty in response to an onlooker whose presence is suggested by her glance to the side. Duchamp-Villon has taken a figural arrangement devised by other artists and revised it, this time through his geometrification of form and the chromatic and reflective treatment of the sculptural surface.[25] Just as Rubens in his day adapted a Greek prototype to his own unique style, Duchamp-Villon has utilized Cubist innovation to radically revise the conception of both Rubens and the Greeks. In keeping with a Bergsonian and Cubist paradigm, the novel form of *Seated Woman* is nothing more than the most recent example in a long line of aesthetic innovations, each of which inspired its successor. Similarly, Duchamp-Villon in his facade for the Maison cubiste could combine the elements of an eighteenth-century hôtel[26] while he subsumed highly abstract sculptural reliefs within a bay window and portal modeled after Gothic precedents in his 1914 project for a dormitory.[27] In so doing he remained true to the innovative *élan vital* animating the traditional and the modern.

This organicist vocabulary, however, led Duchamp-Villon to depart from his Cubist colleagues in assessing the merits of decorative aesthetics in painting, sculpture, and architecture. In his 1912 reply to a questionnaire on the deteriorating condition of Jean-Baptiste Carpeaux's *La Dance* (1869) at the Opera, Duchamp-Villon faulted the sculptor and architect for not interrelating the sculptural group with its setting.[28] "Seen from a distance," stated Duchamp-Villon, "the work must live as a decoration through the harmony of volumes, planes, and lines."[29] Not only does the decorative in

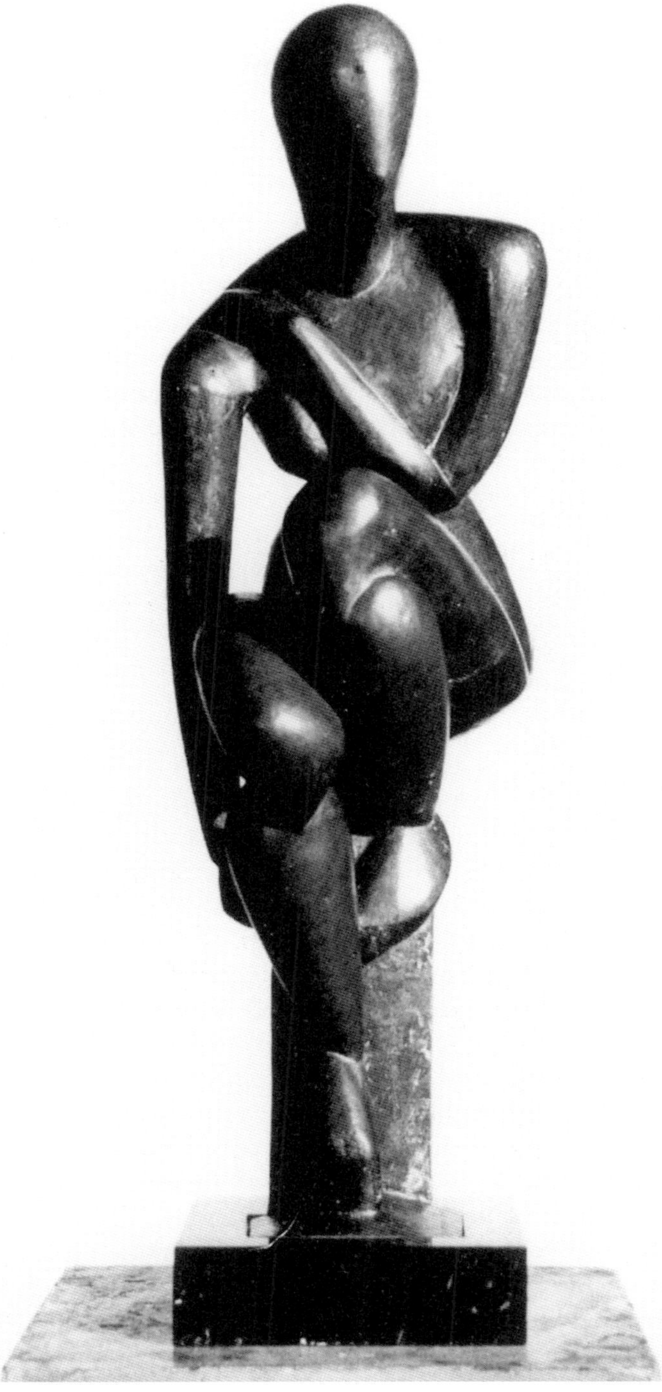

8.3 Raymond Duchamp-Villon, *Seated Woman*, 1914, bronze with black marble pedestal and base, height 65.4 cm. Yale University Art Gallery, bequest of Katherine S. Dreier for the Collection of the Société Anonyme these passages stand for the integral relation of a sculpture to its setting, but that interrelation is organicized by means of a "harmony of volumes, planes and lines" that allow the work to "live as decoration." Harmonic *durée*—the rhythmic interrelation of volumes, planes and lines of both sculpture and monument—serves to transform the sculpture and its setting into a vivified, "living" form. Duchamp-Villon called on architects to conceptualize the man-made environment in terms of "synthetic lines, planes, and volumes which shall, in their turn, equilibrate in rhythms analogous to those that surround us."[30] As we have seen, equilibrium is achieved when a product of creative activity is resolved into a harmonious whole by way of rhythm: in this manner it exists as a living organism. These concerns influenced his later projects, most notably his dormitory design for a college in Connecticut (Fig. 8.4). In a letter of 1914 to his friend Walter Pach, Duchamp-Villon wrote about the decorative program:

> Take, for example the dormitories. I inscribe into each decorative space a frame, whose form must be repeated in various positions at each level. In this frame a small sculpture (bas relief above the doors and below the windows, parts easily visible, of small people or animals: at the top, of compositions purely sculptural without subject). You feel well what variety of aspect one can obtain by this means, without, for all that, the sculpture exceeding the lines of the building, all the while keeping to itself its freedom in the interior of each medallion, or lozenge, or circle, or triangle, etc. etc. Moreover that creates a principle for the whole college, and must give to it a unity of conception, so difficult to obtain. Besides, these means are one of the secrets of Gothic variety.[31]

Referring to the sculptural motifs in another letter, Duchamp-Villon noted his pleasure in finding those "which have their origin in life, no matter how abstract the realisation may appear."[32] In keeping with his notion of unity through variety, Duchamp-Villon imbedded each sculptural design for the Gothic façade in an ellipse; further, the sculpture signified the stellar firmament, with the upper level representing the planets, the middle level the stars, and the lowest level the moon and its rays.[33] As sculptures these motifs are self-contained, organic entities; yet they are tied together through their rhythmic arrangement on the façade. Since these elliptical frames allude to the trajectory of stellar bodies in their travel through space, they are another sign for *durée*. In effect the organic rhythm of each sculptural relief becomes a musical variation within a cosmological harmony of the spheres, which contributes to the rhythmic structure of the building as a whole. Bergson had in fact broached a similar topic, claiming that the coordinated activity among individuals melded them into "a single organism" governed by a "musical theme" composed of "variations."[34] Artists, too, reportedly perceived the musical theme animating life when they entered into intuitive sympathy with a given subject. Perhaps Duchamp-Villon's "unity" through "Gothic variety" was an attempt to reconcile the seeming paradox of respecting the autonomy of a sculptural motif while claiming it to be part of a larger decorative whole. As one rhythm in an overall theme of variations, each sculpture could be

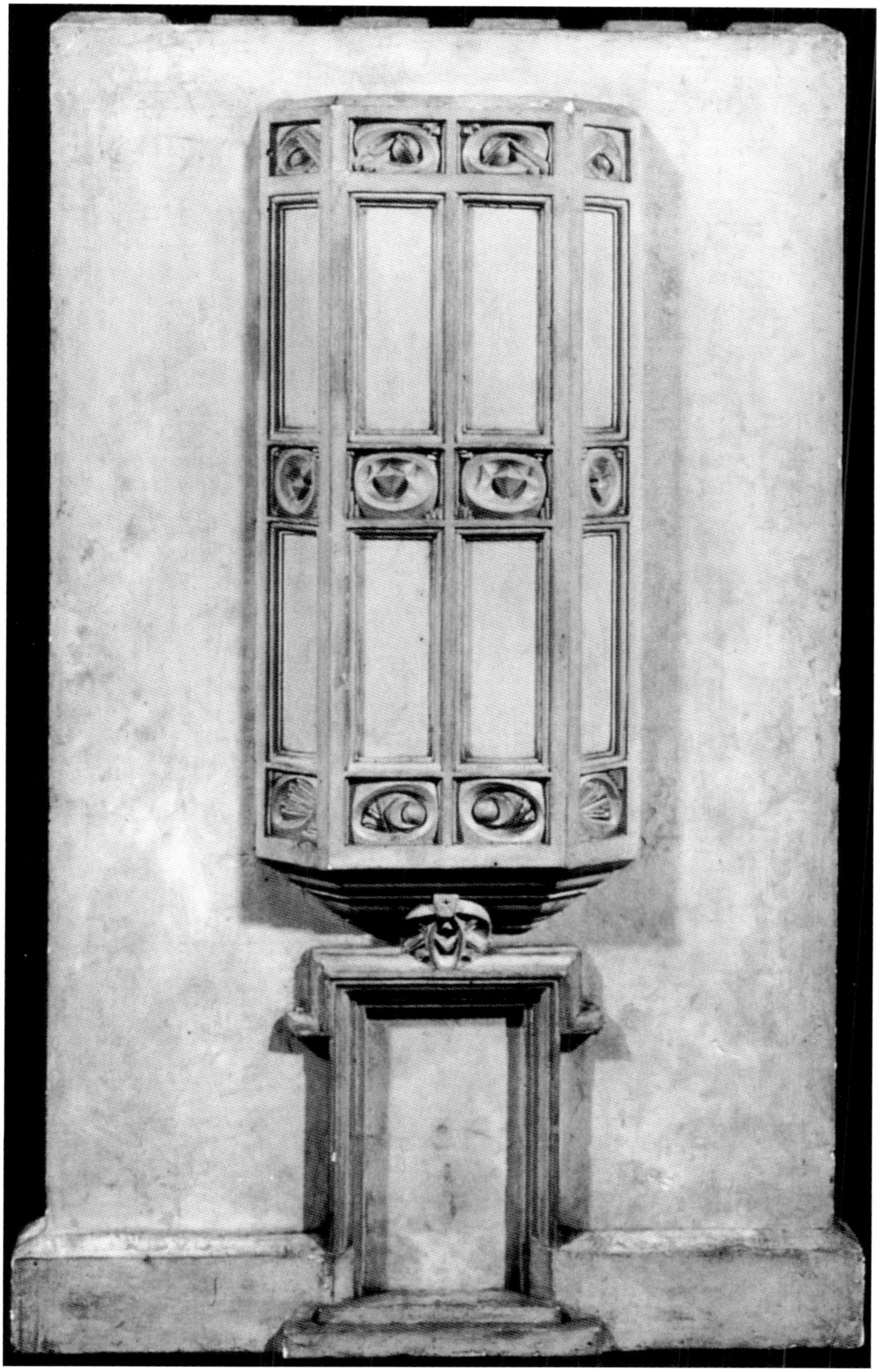

8.4 Raymond Duchamp-Villon, *Project d'architecture*, 1915, plaster maquette, 56 × 33.5 cm. Philadelphia Museum of Art, purchased with the gifts (by exchange) of the Salander-O'Reilly Galleries, Inc., and Mr. and Mrs. Charles C.G. Chaplin, 1987

replaced without compromising its internal rhythm or that of the decorative whole. To paraphrase Bergson, if a sculpture were removed, the façade "would no longer be the same sonorous whole, it would be another, equally indivisible."[35]

Duchamp-Villon's organicism differed dramatically from that of his Cubist colleagues who rejected the decorative altogether. To fully understand that difference we must return to Bergson's writings, to study his conception of the "intensive" and "extensive," as it relates to the rhythm of *durée*, the mixture of time and space that constitutes living form. Referring to the life force animating the universe, Bergson noted that all material forms resolve into changes in rhythmic tension and energy, what he called "qualitative movement." Our duration has its own determined rhythm, and since all movements possess a rhythm "it is possible to imagine many different rhythms which, slower or faster, measure the degree of tension or relaxation of different kinds of consciousness, and thereby fix their respective places on the scale of being."[36] Thus changes in kind and changes in degree interrelate, for within each qualitative kind of consciousness is a certain quantitative degree of "tension" or "extension." In Bergson's cosmology, matter itself possesses a latent consciousness, taking its place as the slowest rhythm on the scale of being, and the rhythmic tension of a being is a function of the degree of freedom inherent in its activity. As the most distended form of *durée*, matter moves at the slowest and most regular of rhythms. As the lowest degree of mind—"mind without memory" to use Bergson's phrase—matter "does not remember the past," and thus "repeats the past unceasingly, because, subject to necessity, it unfolds a series of moments of which each is the equivalent of the preceding moment and may be deduced from it." Since "its past is truly given in its present," matter comes closest to fulfilling the intellectual vision of a time composed of measurable and mutually juxtaposed moments.[37] Freedom is related to "intensity" or contraction, lack of freedom comes to the fore to the extent that this durational tension becomes "expanded" or relaxed. One of the primary tasks Bergson set himself in *Creative Evolution* was to show "how the real can pass from freedom to mechanical necessity by way of inversion."[38] For Bergson, the dichotomy separating free action in the universe from activity of a near-mechanical type had its psychological equivalent in our mental states of attention or relaxation, of intuitive or intellectual modes of thought.

Such ideas are clearly operative in *Du Cubisme*, Metzinger's and Gleizes' most significant aesthetic statement. According to the authors of *Du Cubisme*, it is such "differences of intensity" that serve to distinguish their intuitively inspired canvases from those of their peers.[39] Gleizes and Metzinger's self-proclaimed ability to discern their inner *durée* and transpose it into the "intensive" rhythm of their paintings means that their art has an emotional profundity lacking in the "shallow" production of other artists. Like Bergson, they associate the sensation of depth with the intensive manifold of duration and its absence with an extensive or intellectualized conception of the manifold.[40] Thus, having discerned the rhythm of a Cubist canvas, the beholder will be led "little by little, toward the imaginative depths where burns the light of organization."[41] The "intensity" of a Cubist canvas thus has an internal luminosity, indicative of its status as an organism "with its own raison d'être."[42] For this reason the intensive rhythms of a Cubist painting have little in common with the decorative rhythms one finds in a fresco. According to Gleizes and Metzinger, it is only the restricted format of easel painting that allows artists to express the "complex rhythm" indicative of "depth" and "duration," while large-scale fresco, on the other hand, forces the artist to simplify that rhythm and thus impose an intellectual (and non-vital) framework on art. As a result, rhythm is divorced from its diachronic, durational origins and is instead made to serve a "synchronic vision" that would convert it into an extensive phenomenon composed of "simple," uniform patterns. Denuded of duration, a decorative aesthetic fails to embody the "sobriety" associated with Cubism; it conveys "charm," or even worse, creative "impotence."[43] Thus, duration in *Du Cubisme* is associated with depth of feeling and has its physical analog in rhythmic extensity, exemplified by the volumes created through *passage* and the multiple views the Cubists identify as an intuitive treatment of space.[44] According to the authors of *Du Cubisme,* a decorative work is a mere "organ" that is "incomplete" when removed from its intended setting, whereas an easel painting is a self-contained "organism" that can be moved about "with impunity."[45]

Duchamp-Villon, by contrast, asserted that his sculptural reliefs could exist both as autonomous, organic wholes, and as rhythmic voices in a larger decorative chorus. To his mind, the rhythm of a decorative ensemble does not become overly "simple" or extensive by virtue of the surface covered. As a result it retains its organic, living quality, and each sculpture in an ensemble is an organism subsumed within the larger collective rhythm of a new organism. Thus, in his sculptural contribution to André Mare's decorative ensemble at the 1913 Salon d'automne (1913) (Fig. 8.5), Duchamp-Villon designed four sculptures whose shallow space made them continuous with the wall surface. Lacking the volumetric depth Gleizes and Metzinger thought crucial to the expression of intensive duration, the relief format of these sculptures was attuned to the planarity of Roger de la Fresnaye's adjacent panels.[46] Gleizes and Metzinger, on the other hand, would never reduce the volumetric rhythms of their canvases to meet such decorative demands, for to do so would be to convert an intensive rhythm into its extensive counterpart. No longer animated from within, a painting would be "animated only by the relations established between it and the given objects"[47] that made up the decorative ensemble. Extensively directed, the rhythm would become simple rather than complex, more quantitative than qualitative. It would be devoid of the intensive rhythm of an artist's creative élan, and thus lack organic form.

This debate over the nature of organic form has larger implications when we consider its relation to the post-structuralist critique of organic "closure." Jacques Derrida, for instance, has highlighted the inherent contradictions in modernists' neo-Kantian attempts to define what is internal or external to a

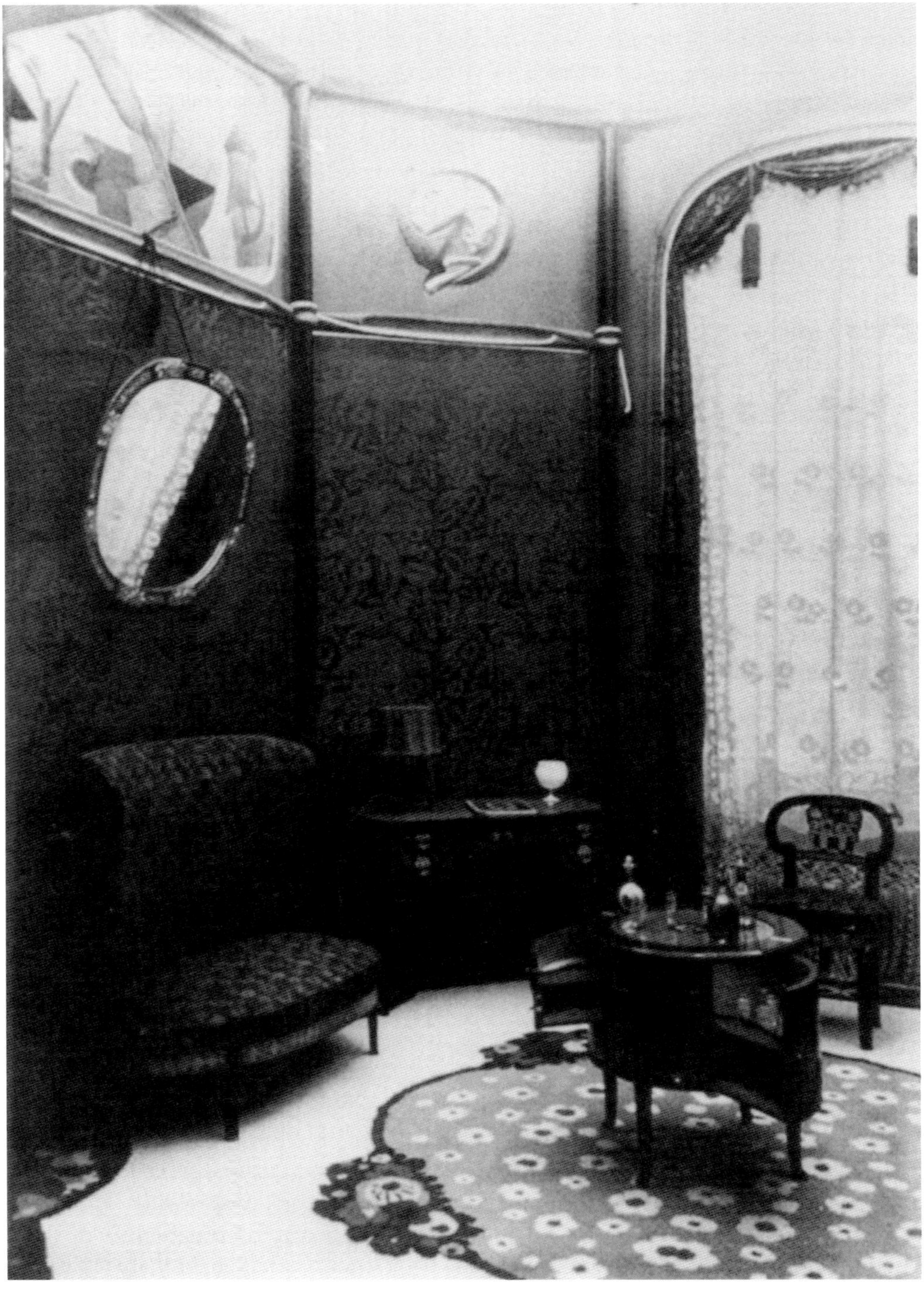

8.5 Raymond Duchamp-Villon, *Boudoir*, Salon d'automne, Paris, 1913. Collection Michèle Mare, Centre Georges Pompidou, Paris painting by way of organic form, and the untenable dismissal of a painting's "boundary" as "supplementary frame of reference."[48] However, critics have also noted that a rebuttal of aesthetic closure exists within the modernist project itself,[49] and it is in this regard that Bergsonism has come to the fore. Thus, for writers like Frank Kermode, the degeneration of fiction into myth that comes with theories of aesthetic and temporal closure is everywhere matched by a "Bergsonian" awareness that such closure is itself a fiction and that the radical heterogeneity of time belies any suspension of change. For Kermode, there are "two modernisms"—an existentialist modernism that celebrates temporal flux and respects our status as temporally finite beings, and one "which will end democracy and all the 'Bergsonian' attitudes to time and human psychology" in order to impose a "closed authoritarian society" (Kermode cites the example of fascism's organicist myths) on its Bergsonian adversaries.[50] Kermode's attack on organic closure arises from an abhorrence for any totalizing system that would repress the idea of change, and thus deny the historicity of our world.[51] Bergson even has his advocates within the post-structuralist camp, most prominently in the anti-Hegelian philosophy of Gilles Deleuze.[52] Bergson, states Deleuze, regarded all life forms as non-closed, biological systems, which meant that the world itself "is always in the process of becoming, developing, coming into being or advancing, and inscribing itself within a temporal dimension that is irreducible and nonclosed."[53] Elsewhere Deleuze notes that the actualization of time in the guise of varying kinds of consciousness had its origins in a virtual time made up of degrees of tension.[54] When Bergson calls upon us to enter into an intuitive relation with the world, he is, in fact, asking us to move from the realm of the actual to that of virtual time, in order to grasp the rhythmic tension of the universe as a whole, prior to any act of organic division.

It is through this theory of closure that the critique of modernism outlined above can be related to that of avant-guerre Cubism. By adopting Bergsonian paradigms the Cubists were faced with the problem of defining an aesthetic frame for a notion of *durée* which, ideally, could never be subjected to closure. Duchamp-Villon addressed this very issue in his interpretation of the diachronic and synchronic interrelation of his sculptures: as an organic form each work was enclosed in its rhythmic equilibrium, yet in the durational life of the artist's imagination each sculptural discovery prefigured another. Duchamp-Villon could claim that his sculpture was both closed and open; in a condition of physical being and of durational becoming in the artistic imagination. In similar fashion, the synchronic arrangement of sculptures in a decorative ensemble allowed both for their organic integrity and their ability to meld into the greater organic form that constitutes the decorative program. Thus, Duchamp-Villon differed from his Cubist colleagues, who denied that a synchronic opening of closure could take place without compromising the organic properties of a given sculpture or painting.

However, with respect to the public's reception of their art, the Cubists did not utilize Bergsonism to avoid closure, they simply argued over how closure was to be achieved. The ability to create organic form was the basis on which these Cubists proclaimed their creative superiority over a public who lacked the capacity for intuitive insight. By inscribing *durée* within organic form, the artist's intuition was contained within the frame, and remained inaccessible to any beholder lacking in artistic imagination. The autonomy of art was therefore part and parcel of the superiority of the artist, and Bergsonism failed to release the Cubists from authoritarian assumptions. In sum, I would argue, in contradistinction to Kermode, that there are not only "two Modernisms"—one Bergsonian, the other authoritarian—but "two Bergsonisms," one open, and the other organically closed to the radical implications of Bergsonian *durée*.

Notes

1 Rosalind Krauss, *The Originality of the Avant-Garde and Other Modernist Myths* (Cambridge, MA: MIT Press, 1985), 1–6.

2 Ibid., 4.

3 Ibid., 32–37.

4 See for instance, Yves Alain Bois, "The Semiology of Cubism," in Lynn Zelevansky, ed., *Picasso and Braque: Pioneering Cubism* (New York: Museum of Modern Art, 1992), 169–208; Rosalind Krauss, "The Motivation of the Sign," in Lynn Zelevansky, ed., *Picasso and Braque: Pioneering Cubism* (New York: Museum of Modern Art, 1992), 261–86; Richard Shiff, "Picasso's Touch: Collage *Papier Collé*, Ace of Clubs," *Yale University Art Gallery Bulletin* (1990): 38–47; Christine Poggi, *In Defiance of Painting: Cubism, Futurism, and Collage* (New Haven, CT: Yale University Press, 1992) 31–57; and Francis Frascina, "Realism and Ideology: An Introduction to Semiotics and Cubism," in *Primitivism, Cubism, Abstraction: The Early Twentieth Century*, eds. Charles Harrison, Francis Frascina, and Gill Perry (New Haven, CT: Yale University Press, 1993), 89–183. Patricia Leighten has critiqued Krauss's analysis of Cubism in an essay on Cubist collage and the political import of structuralist and Bakhtinian discourse. See Patricia Leighten, "Cubist Anachronisms: Ahistoricity, Cryptoformalism, and Bussiness-as-Usual in New York," *Oxford Art Journal*,17, no. 2 (1994): 91–102.

5 In my book devoted to the impact of the thought of Henri Bergson on the Parisian avant-garde, I analyzed the organicist rhetoric of the Cubists Gleizes and Metzinger, and their deployment of that Modernist trope in their defense of the movement. In that volume, I charted the debate—between various artistic and political factions over what constituted organic form and elucidated the ideological implications of this discourse of aesthetic "immediacy." By revealing the extension, on the part of various Bergsonians, of organicist metaphors to encompass historicist narratives concerning the development of—for instance, the French race (in the case of Gleizes), or of a particular class (as in the Futurists' organicist definition of proletarian consciousness)—I charted conflicting attempts to constitute organic form in Modernist discourse. And by revealing the social determinants informing avant-garde conceptions of organic form, I was able to demystify that notion and undermine its self-declared (and hegemonic) pretensions to the condition of the "natural" sign. See Mark Antliff, *Inventing Bergson: Cultural Politics and the Parisian Avant-Garde* (Princeton, NJ: Princeton University Press, 1993).

6 My methodological approach is indebted to that of literary critic Murray Krieger. See Murray Krieger, *A Reopening of Closure: Organicism Against Itself* (New York: Columbia University Press, 1989), 1–5.

7 Aside from claiming that Picasso's collage aesthetic alone could be analyzed in structuralist terms, Krauss makes a sweeping assertion that all other Modernists had an unproblematic relation to the organicist assumptions outlined above. In this context, Krauss singles out Picasso's collage as operating "in direct opposition to modernism's search for perceptual plenitude and unimpeachable self-presence." Krauss, *The Originality of the Avant-Garde and Other Modernist Myths*, 38. The structuralist terms of Krauss's division are also taken up by Christine Poggi who maintains that the collage aesthetics of Georges Braque and Juan Gris—in contrast to that of the "Structuralist" Picasso—are relatable to debates within Puteaux Cubist circles over neo-Kantian and Nietzschean notions of "conception and vision," which signaled a more "traditional" search for the plenitude of "a true means of representation." See Christine Poggi, "Braque's Early Papiers Collés and the Certainties of *Faux Bois*," in Lynn Zelevansky, ed., *Picasso and Braque: A Symposium* (New York: Museum of Modern Art, 1992), 129–49, and Poggi, *In Defiance of Painting*, 93.

8 See Raymond Duchamp-Villon, "Variations de la connaissance pendant le travail d'art" (1916), trans. in George H. Hamilton and William Agee, *Raymond Duchamp-Villon, 1876–1918* (New York: Walker & Co., 1967), 120–25. Agee, in his preface to the 1916 essay, notes that the essay is "eclectic in its sources, which range from symbolist aesthetics to Bergson."

9 Duchamp-Villon, "Variations de la connaissance pendant le travail d'art," 120.

10 Ibid., 121.

11 Ibid., 123.

12 Henri Bergson, "Introduction to Metaphysics," in *The Creative Mind*, trans. M.L. Andison (New York: Littlefield, Adams & Co., 1965, rpt. 1975), 161.

13 Bergson, *Laughter*, in *Comedy*, trans. Wylie Sypher (Baltimore, MD: Johns Hopkins University Press, 1956; rpt. 1983), 160.

14 Ibid., 87.

15 Duchamp-Villon, "Variations de la connaissance pendant le travail d'art," 123.

16 Ibid.

17 Ibid., 122.

18 For a discussion of this interrelationship, see Hamilton and Agee, *Raymond Duchamp-Villon*, 14 and 45–47; Agee also relates Duchamp-Villon's *Decorative Basin* (1911) to the earlier *Pastorale* (1910), in ibid., 55. Similarly, Daniel Robbins has noted that the triangular forms that mark the joining of calves with knees in Duchamp-Villon's *Seated Woman* (1914) are repeated in the nodal intersections of the *Great Horse* of 1914 and *Doctor Gosset* of 1918. For Robbins' analysis of these related sculptural elements, see Daniel Robbins, "The *Femme Assise* by Raymond Duchamp-Villon," *Yale University Art Gallery Bulletin* (Winter 1983): 22–31.

19 Raymond Duchamp-Villon, "Manuscript Notes" (1911), trans. in Hamilton and Agee, *Raymond Duchamp-Villon*, 111.

20 In that text, Gleizes and Metzinger attribute the public's hostility to Cubism, to the mediating effect of past artistic conventions on their perceptual faculties and imaginative consciousness. As a result the public expected artists to

slavishly imitate past artistic techniques, when, in fact, "imitation is the only error possible in art; it attacks the law of time." That temporal "law", defined in Bergsonian terms meant that every artist should emulate the heterogeneity of his own internal *durée*, by subjecting past traditions to innovative revision. See Albert Gleizes and Jean Metzinger, *Du Cubisme* (1912), trans. R.L. Herbert, in *Modern Artists on Art* (Englewood Cliffs, NJ: Raven Press, 1964), 3. For a fuller analysis of this aspect of Cubist theory, see Mark Antliff and Patricia Leighten, *Cubism and Culture* (London: Thames & Hudson, 2001), 111–35.

21 The Cubists even applied this criticism to their artistic rivals among the avant-garde. For example, having declared his own art to be the product of "intuition," the Cubist Henri Le Fauconnier, in an essay of 1912, went on to condemn the royalist and symbolist Emile Bernard as one who "hates intuition" and thus "cannot appreciate the qualitative differences" of works "which often seem to be on the same plane for vulgar spirits." See Henri Le Fauconnier, "La Sensibilité moderne et le tableau," in *Moderne Kunstkring (Cercle de l'Art moderne). Catalogue des ouvrages de peinture, sculpture, gravure* (Amsterdam: Musée Municipal, 1912), 26.

22 Duchamp-Villon, "Manuscript Notes," 1911, trans. in Hamilton and Agee, *Raymond Duchamp-Villon,* 111.

23 Thus, Metzinger could praise Le Fauconnier's *L'Abondance* of 1910–11 for its "indispensible mixture of certain conventional signs with new signs." See Jean Metzinger, "Cubisme et tradition," *Paris-Journal* (18 August, 1911). These "unknown elements" were the novel means by which the Cubist unites representational content to durational form. This paradigm had profound implications with regard to the relation of tradition to innovation in Cubist praxis. "We will even willingly confess," state Gleizes and Metzinger in *Du Cubisme*, "that it is impossible to write without using clichés, and to paint while disregarding familiar signs completely." For this reason, they add, "it is up to each one to decide whether he should disseminate them throughout his work." See Gleizes and Metzinger, *Du Cubisme*, 15.

24 Agee has related the "shifting equilibrium between movement and repose" in *Seated Woman* to "the tenuous balance of Michelangelo's *Madonna and Child*" in San Lorenzo, but the absence of a child in Duchamp-Villon's sculpture, and the similarity between her deportment and that of the *Capitoline Aphrodite* or Rubens' *Susanna*, suggest a sexualized theme . For William Agee's relation of *Seated Woman* to Michelangelo's sculpture, see Hamilton and Agee, *Raymond Duchamp-Villon*, 83.

25 Agee has rightly compared the figure to a studio mannequin used to study human movement and anatomy. See Hamilton and Agee, *Raymond Duchamp-Villon*, 83.

26 See Nancy J. Troy, *Modernism and the Decorative Arts in France: Art Nouveau to Le Corbusier* (New Haven, CT: Yale University Press, 1991), 92–93; and Hamilton and Agee, *Raymond Duchamp-Villon*, 65–69 for a discussion of Duchamp-Villon's façade.

27 For a discussion of the dormitory project and its relation to the Cubists' politicized embrace of the Gothic, see Antliff, *Inventing Bergson*, 106–34; and Antliff and Leighten, *Cubism and Culture*, 119–29. Marcel Duchamp later noted that Duchamp-Villon's interest in the Gothic led him to make frequent trips to Chartres cathedral during the pre-war years. See Hamilton and Agee, 59–60. For an analysis of the Cubists promotion of the Gothic in light of French architectural theory, see Kevin Murphy, "Cubism and the Gothic Tradition,"

in *Architecture and Cubism*, ed. Eve Blau and Nancy J. Troy (London: MIT Press, 1997), 59–76.

28 Duchamp-Villon, "Réponse à une enquête au sujet de La Dance de Carpeaux à l'Opéra," *Gil Blas* (17 September, 1912); trans. in Hamilton and Agee, *Raymond Duchamp-Villon*, 113–14.

29 Duchamp-Villon, "Manuscript Notes" (1911), trans. in Hamilton and Agee, *Raymond Duchamp-Villon*, 113–14.

30 Duchamp-Villon, "Excerpts from a letter to Walter Pach," 16 January, 1913, in *Jacques Villon, Raymond Duchamp-Villon, Marcel Duchamp* (exhib. cat.) (New York: The Solomon R. Guggenheim Museum, 1957), n.p.

31 Duchamp-Villon, "Sur un projet de décoration d'un collège dans le style gothique," Letter to Walter Pach dated 17 March 1914, reproduced in Walter Pach, *Raymond Duchamp-Villon, Sculpture (1876–1918)* (Paris: Huebsch, 1924), 20.

32 Duchamp-Villon,"Letter to Walter Pach," 14 May, 1914, in ibid., 21.

33 Duchamp-Villon, "Sur un projet de décoration d'un collège dans le style gothique," Letter to Walter Pach dated 17 March 1914, reproduced in Pach, *Raymond Duchamp-Villon, Sculpture (1876–1918)*; quoted in Hamilton and Agee, *Raymond Duchamp-Villon*, 80.

34 Henri Bergson, *Creative Evolution* (1907), trans. A. Mitchell (New York: Henry Holt & Co., 191; rpt. 1944), 183.

35 Henri Bergson, *Time and Free Will. An Essay on the Immediate Data of Consciousness* (1889), trans. F.L. Pogson (New York: Harper & Row, 1910; rpt. 1959), 104.

36 Ibid., 275.

37 Ibid., 297.

38 Bergson, *Creative Evolution*, 258.

39 Gleizes and Metzinger, *Du Cubisme*, 13.

40 See my discussion of Bergson's association of depth with *durée* in Antliff, *Inventing Bergson*, 65–66. For an analysis of the difference posited by Bergson between intensive and extensive manifolds, see the chapter titled "The Philosophy of Intensive Manifolds," in T.E. Hulme, *Speculations: Essays on the Humanism and the Philosophy of Art* (London: Routledge & Kegan Paul, 1924; rpt 1987), 171–214.

41 Gleizes and Metzinger, *Du Cubisme*, 5.

42 Ibid.

43 Ibid.

44 See my discussion of the Cubist and Bergsonian notion of extensity as combining space and time through rhythm in Mark Antliff, "Bergson and Cubism: A Reassessment," *Art Journal* (Winter 1988): 341–49; and Antliff, *Inventing Bergson*, 12–13, 43–53, 100–101.

45 Gleizes and Metzinger, *Du Cubisme*, 5. A similar paradigm is evident in Henri Le Fauconnier's "La Sensibilité Moderne et le Tableau," in which he praised the rise of oil painting and decline of fresco, because the former medium captured "qualitative value," "fertile form," and was therefore divorced from the "flat, ornamental style" that typified "decorative" fresco painting. See Le Fauconnier, "La Sensibilité Moderne et le Tableau" (1912), 17–18.

46 As Germain Seligman notes, the matte-like tones utilized by de la Fresnaye in his two panels for Mare's ensemble were meant to emphasize the flat and thus decorative surface of the works, whose status as decoration is also signaled by their uniform size and related subject matter. Whereas the *Arrosoir* dealt with the active theme of gardening, its counterpart, *Mappemonde*, focused on intellectual pursuits, signified by the globe, violin, and surrounding books. Duchamp-Villon's reliefs also had a unified theme in their animal subjects and uniform dimensions. See Germain Seligman, *Roger de la Fresnaye* (London: New York Graphic Society, 1969), 38, 166; and Hamilton and Agee, *Raymond Duchamp-Villon*, 72–75.

47 Gleizes and Metzinger, *Du Cubisme*, 5.

48 See Derrida's analysis of the permeability of the boundary between the work of art (ergon) and the frame (Parergon) in Jacques Derrida, *The Truth in Painting* (Chicago, IL: University of Chicago Press, 1987).

49 For instance, Martin Jay has charted a bifurcation within Modernism between those who would embrace Form and its attendant ocularcentrism, and an "antiformalist impulse in modern art, which can most conveniently be identified with Georges Bataille's *informe*." See Martin Jay, "Modernism and the Retreat from Form," in *Force Fields: Between Intellectaul History and Cultural Critique* (London: Routledge, 1993), 147–57.

50 Frank Kermode, *The Sense of an Ending: Studies in the Theory of Fiction* (Oxford: Oxford University Press, 1967), 57, 110–11, 118, 120–22, 178. I agree with Kermode that rhythm "implies continuities and ends and organisation" (118) and share his contention that Bergson related rhythm to *durée* in his conception of time as organic and meaningful: time in Bergson is related to *kairos* rather than *chronus* (ibid., 57, 178). However, I differ with Kermode in his contention that Bergsonians are invariably prepared to regard temporal closure as fictional, or that all Bergsonists were politically progressive. In my view, Bergson's followers in the Cubist and Futurist movements violated the philosopher's intentions by subsuming Bergsonian *durée* within mythic conceptions of racial evolution or aestheticized violence. For a discussion of these issues, see the chapter titled "The Politics of Time and Modernity," in Antliff, *Inventing Bergson*, 168–84.

51 On Kermode's application of political analogies in his attack on organic closure, see W.J.T. Mitchell, *Iconology: Image, Text, Ideology* (Chicago, IL: University of Chicago Press, 1986), 96–98. In a similar vein, Murray Krieger has recently noted that "Bergson charges the work of art to represent in a perceptible form the elusive temporal blur that denies form," and that this "call for a form always in the process of disrupting its own pretension to closure" rendered imperfect the analogy posited by New Critics "between the divine Book of Books and the individual earthly book on which the optimistic side of organicism depended." Murray Krieger, *A ReOpening of Closure: Organicism Against Itself* (New York: Columbia University Press, 1989), 42–43.

52 On Deleuzes' debt to Bergson, see Paul Douglass, "Deleuze and the Endurance of Bergson," *Thought* (March 1992), 47–61; Michael Hardt, *Gilles Deleuze: An Apprenticeship in Philosophy* (London: University of Minnesota Press, 1993); and Gillian Rose, *Dialectic of Nihilism* (Oxford: Oxford University Press, 1988), 87–108.

53 Gilles Deleuze and Félix Guattari, *Anti-Oedipus: Capitalism and Schizophrenia* (Minneapolis, MN: University of Minnesota Press, 1972), 95–96.

54 See Deleuzes' analysis of virtual temporality in Gilles Deleuze, *Bergsonism*, trans. Hugh Tomlinson and Barbara Habberjam (New York: Zone Books, 1991).

9

Klee's Neo-Romanticism: The wages of scientific curiosity

Sara Lynn Henry

Since my title is provocative, I should like to qualify it in two ways. First, I would like to say that Klee's interest in science was not the only factor that shaped his twentieth-century Neo-Romanticism. There were others—aesthetic, psychological and musical—that transmuted his nineteenth-century roots.

Second, I would say that "wages" can be understood in both a positive and negative sense. On the positive side, Klee gained the ability to abstract nature and yet remain close to and even expand upon its basic principles through his access to scientific knowledge. As discussed by scholars such as Huggler, Haftmann, and Verdi,[1] Klee, like Goethe, wanted to discover *Urformen* and *Ursetzen* [primary forms and principles][2] out of which all related forms develop. Like Goethe, Schelling, and Romantic theory in general, Klee believed that the artist participates in what Schelling termed the "ever-creative original energy of the world."[3]

There is, however, a cautionary side to Klee's access to and freedom to use so much scientific knowledge. His ability to abstractly symbolize and structure nature allowed him to remove himself from a direct, everyday sensory dialogue with its presence. He stood more fully both outside and inside as an organizing mind and as an imaginative play of consciousness. He analyzed, focused, built, and invented according to the principles of nature, as well as according to his own imagination. Romantic painters, though tied to a more mimetic approach to depicting landscape, were, of course, also making choices, arranging, and constructing with the visual material at their disposal. It is also true that Romantic theory, especially as articulated by Goethe, Schelling, and Carus, intimated even greater freedom. But the difference was in the permission, so to speak, that the twentieth-century artist had, to actually penetrate nature, and indeed to structure and restructure it. It was also the greater distance that the twentieth-century artist could go with the reconfiguration of natural subjects through the use of scientific knowledge and the imagination that differentiated them from their predecessors. The result was that Klee sundered the apparent Romantic interrelationship of the human, of nature and of the divine, as found in nineteenth-century visual imagery and theory and with it the relative certainty concerning the place of humans within the whole. Although in a fitful and complex manner, the Romantics maintained a general assuredness of the workings of divine energy and harmony within nature as well as of humans' role as witnesses to and co-participants in the whole. By contrast, Klee's imagery (though less so his theory) is more uncertain, fragile, inward, and confusing in its invocation of the transcendent. Nature, though subject to posited organic, creative forces, is frequently treated with irony and playfulness, and the human is most often imaginatively placed, misplaced, or displaced.[4] Klee's work is symptomatic of a larger trend in mid-twentieth-century art and culture, towards the distancing of the self from a holistic participation in nature. Avant-garde artists tended either to allude to natural principles through the use of abstract, scientific diagrammatic means or to become preoccupied with the vagaries of individual human consciousness, thus disrupting the human–nature continuum so characteristic of Nature Romanticism.

Romantic painters such as Friedrich and Constable did display moments of interest in scientific theory, such as Friedrich's seeming acquaintance with the "geognosy" of his contemporary Abraham Werner,[5] that helped him to shape his images of mountains as embodiments of geological change, or Constable's use of Luke Howard's taxonomy of clouds[6] as an aid to more convincing "skying" of his paintings. But in each case, these artists were clearly concerned with the descriptive and type-form principles of their sources, which they subsequently turned back into a mimetic visualization of nature's appearances.

Klee and other avant-garde artists developed their practices at a different juncture than did the Romantics. Some modern artists became concerned with science's ability to deal with the invisible. They saw how science could cut, measure, and analyze part by part, how it could define abstract types and mathematical principles, and how it could deal with the abstract forces of motion and change.[7] Klee especially had an interest not only in the tangible, visible cycles of nature, but in how such cycles were structured and propelled.

Evolutionary theory prodded Klee further towards the conception of new forms. As he said, "the earth looked different in the past and will look different again," as things must also look different on "different stars."[8] This realization of the continual genesis of new forms gave him a certain freedom, even license to invent new forms, "images of nature's potentialities."[9] For him, science was not a check on accuracy, but rather an opening to freedom and mobility.[10]

In fact, Klee developed a new creative process of "psychic improvisation,"[11] as he called it. He would start with abstract structuring principles, frequently visual analogues to scientific concepts. These he would join with the free play of artistic means to allow forms to develop, bringing his own associations to the resultant configurations. He did this at the time, around 1913 and 1914, when the art world was radically opening up the exploration of the possibilities of abstract and expressive modes. These tendencies in the art world of the time certainly acted as models for his newfound artistic freedom. Klee's images, as a result, became more personal, imaginative and often elusive, though, as he said, they remained committed to "the new natural consciousness" of his times.[12]

In contrast to the more constrained subjectivity that gave rise to Romantic landscape painting, Klee's creative process allowed the free play of the artist's own individual consciousness.[13] His psychic improvisation allowed his mind and spirit to travel great distances, to explore the small nooks and crannies of nature, to spin off into infinity, and to indulge in personal imaginings. This is a flexibility akin to that of the scientific mind that can set the individual free from his everyday moorings in order to explore distant possibilities. The result for Klee was an undermining of the Romantic sense of the scale and place of the human within the everyday landscape. Clark has noted that for the twentieth-century artist nature was both too large and too small because of the new realms opened up by the microscope and the telescope.[14] This awareness has made it difficult for the modern artist to consider the everyday, that is, visible landscape, as the central subject of art and as the measure of place.

Another factor, as much propelled by the new science of psychology as by modern artistic culture, also affected Klee. Like the Expressionists, Dadaists, and the Surrealists, Klee allowed the irrational to erupt into his work. He treated the transformation of motifs with wit, irony, and cock-eyed playfulness, taking a shadowy delight in the fact that for twentieth-century persons there seemed to be few stable verities. This revelation freed him to probe new irrational universes, but it also left him ironically and sometimes bitterly without firm groundings. Klee found himself between the poles of "natural law" and the irrational self.

This essay will explore three aspects of the life of nature[15] as treated by Klee: geological life, the movement of waters, and the phenomena of weather. It will consider the impact of modern geology and meteorology on the structure and iconography of Klee's images; and will contrast the resulting mode of consciousness within his work with that of his Romantic predecessors. In undertaking these tasks, it will serve as a case study of a significant direction in twentieth-century art.

Geological life

In the 1920s, Klee began to delve beneath the external in order to investigate geological structures and processes. This is first seen in his work *Lake Landscape with the Celestial Body* (1920/166) (Fig. 9.1), where hills are structured like stratified rocks woven with fields and forests. During the winter of 1921–22, after he began to teach at the Bauhaus, Klee drew simple diagrams of parallel lines to stand for strata and arrows to show the forces that cause

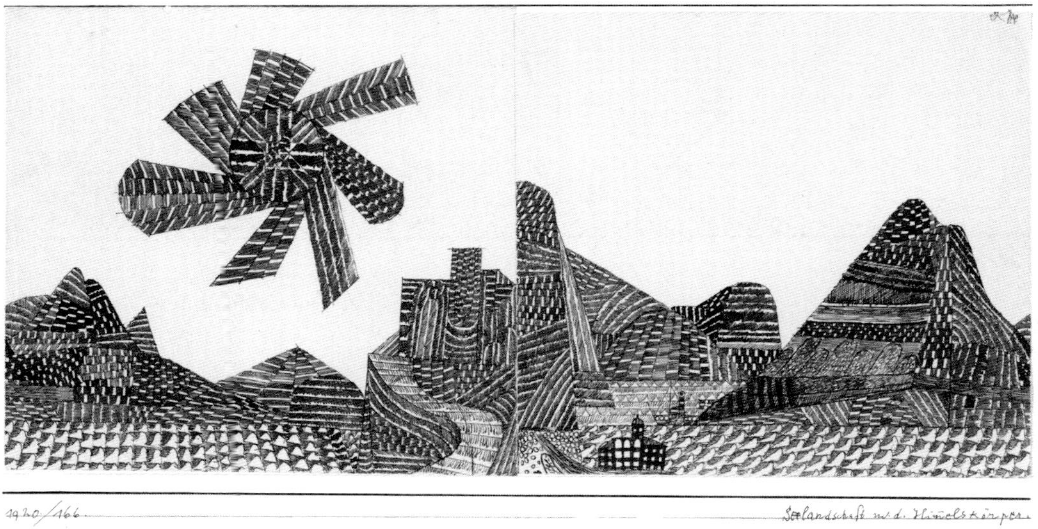

9.1 Paul Klee, *Seelandschaft m. d. Himmelskörper* [Lake Landscape with the Celestial Body], 1920/166, pen on paper on cardboard, 12.7 × 28.1 cm. Zentrum Paul Klee, Bern, Switzerland © 2009 Artists Rights Society (ARS), New York/ VG Bild-Kunst, Bonn

these layers to suddenly drop into faults or compress upward into the wavy curves of mountain upheaval.[16] These diagrams led directly to his paintings *Mountain Formation* (1924/123) and *Stratification Sets In* (1927/222). In these and related works, he built the forms out of abstract pictorial units analogous to the geological diagrams of natural science texts, where geometric patterns indicate the internal structures of mountains and earth. One can compare Klee's drawings with the diagrams in texts he might have used during his *Literarschule* years (1894–99)—for example, Frey's *Mineralogie und Geologie für Schweizerische Mittelschulen* (Fig. 9.2) .[17]

Scientific insight into these phenomena had developed as early as the seventeenth century, well before the Romantics,[18] but until Klee and Max Ernst in the 1920s, no artists had made such use of geological diagrammatic means. It may well have been the development of abstract art in the early twentieth century that gave the artists the permission, so to speak, to utilize these abstract distillations of scientific knowledge. Another factor was certainly the availability of such diagrams in late nineteenth- and early twentieth-century schoolbooks and in popular scientific literature.

Klee evolved more inventive, complex rocky terrain and mountain structures in his work. Fir trees were shown growing on up-ended stony blocks (*Landscape with Rocks and Firs*, 1929/262) recalling a Romantic image by Ferdinand Olivier, *Rocky Ridge with Fragments*, of 1810. Olivier meticulously rendered the external descriptive detail of gargantuan boulders, deposited seemingly erratically by ancient glaciers. Klee's painting, by contrast, shows activated, sharp rectangles, schematized trees, and cross-hatched energy lines that suggest the very forces of nature at work.[19]

Once set into motion, Klee's abstract strata could form the terraces of *Cult Cities* (1934/141), the interweaving of vertical precipices, in *Cliffs* (1934/138), the wrapping of hillsides as in *Severe Rock Picture* (1927/321), and the high

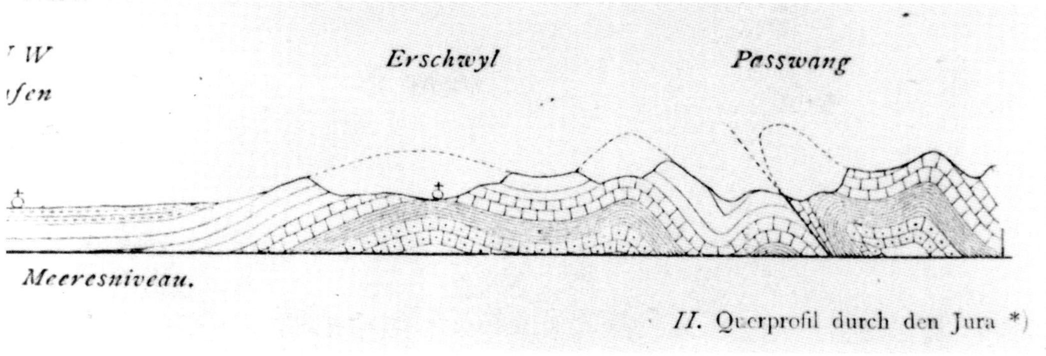

9.2 "Cross Section of the Jura Mountains," from Dr. Hans Frey, *Mineralogie und Geology für Schweizeriche Mittleschulen* (Leipzig: G. Freytag, 1901), 194

peaks of mountains (*Organ Mountain*, 1934/138). They also became intertwined with human structures, creating sylvan edifices (*Forest Architecture*, 1925/251 and *Castle to be Built in the Forest*, 1926/2), a *Rock Temple with Firs* (1926/12), and alpine retreats as in *View of a Mountain Sanctuary* (1926/18). Klee saw this method of layered strata as being analogous to the growth rings of a tree. Hence, there is not only geological layering but also botanical proliferation in his images, along with human building activities. In fact, all are distilled into the same parallel structures![20]

The signs of the human, therefore, are subsumed into those of nature and the signs of nature are structured out of human signs. Such diagrammatic modes of representing periodic change were being employed in late nineteenth- and early twentieth-century studies concerning the variations of morphological structure among species. Though Klee's direct knowledge of books such as D'Arcy Thompson's *On Growth and Form* (1917) has not yet been definitively demonstrated, the parallels are suggestive.[21]

One can compare the presence of the human in Klee's geological imagery to that of the Romantics. The Romantic artist Joseph Anton Koch, for example, in his *The Schmadribach Falls* (1921–22), placed a tiny figure at the base of gigantic snowcapped mountains (Fig. 9.3). Towering cascades descend from the snow melt forming a seething river that ultimately boils across the foreground, strewing rocks left and right and splintering trees. By contrast, Klee's *Castle to be Built in the Forest* (1926/2) is a polite, orthogonal building plan, placed prominently within geometrically ordered fields and foliage, measured as if by the cadences of an architect's calibrated blueprint. In Klee, the nineteenth-century awe before the external forces of nature is replaced by the artist's internal ordered play of conceptual and psychic improvisation.

Several of Klee's landscapes became sets for myth, tragedy, or even parody, as in *Garden for Orpheus* (1926/3), *Destroyed Olympus* (1926/5), *A Prelude to Golgatha* (1926/3–11), and *Barbaric, Classic, Solemn* (1926/69). The human drama became part of the drama of the landscape as was also true in Romantic imagery. But Klee employs satire rather than solemnity. See, for example, his *Destroyed Olympus* (Fig. 9.4) with its tilted, useless classical columns and the half-buried God—be it Zeus or Wotan—who attempts to hurl a missile

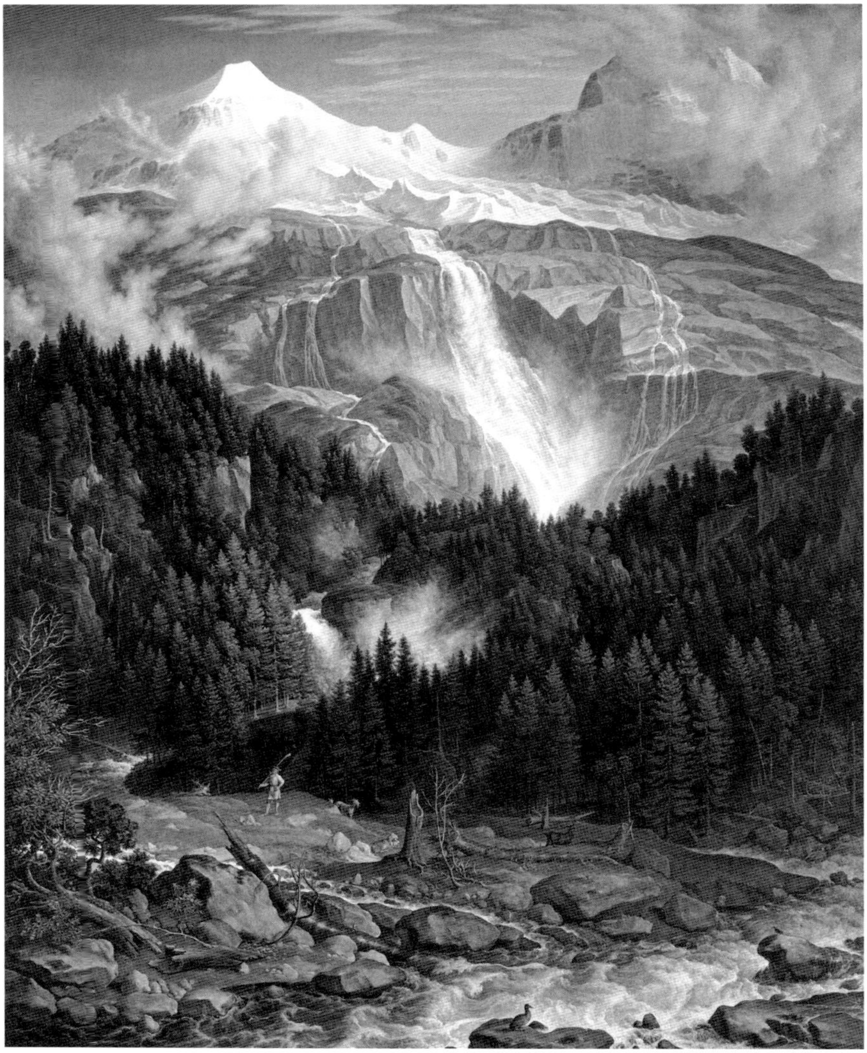

9.3 Joseph Anton Koch, *Der Schmadribachfall* [The Schmadribach Falls], 1821–22, oil on canvas, 131.8 × 110 cm. Neue Pinakothek, Munich, Germany. © Blauel/Gnamm—Arthotek

into the air. This is certainly the twilight of the gods as Geelhaar suggests.[22] Classical and biblical stories do not carry the same weight of authority for modern persons. These myths are no longer the reigning narratives of our era; they have been replaced by those of natural processes and of the self.

Human fate was further layered into the land in several images that Klee created as a result of his trips to faraway places during the late 1920s and early 1930s. He was especially moved by the remnants of ancient civilizations lodged within the landscape. He visited sites in Sicily in 1924 and 1931; he traveled to Elba in 1926 and to Corsica in 1927; he studied prehistoric megaliths in Brittany in 1928; and in the winter of 1928–29, he voyaged to Egypt to see the ancient tombs, temples, and pyramids. In a few instances, Klee drew topographical panoramas that combined the broad sweep of the terrain with notations of towns, mountains, roadways, and passes (for example,

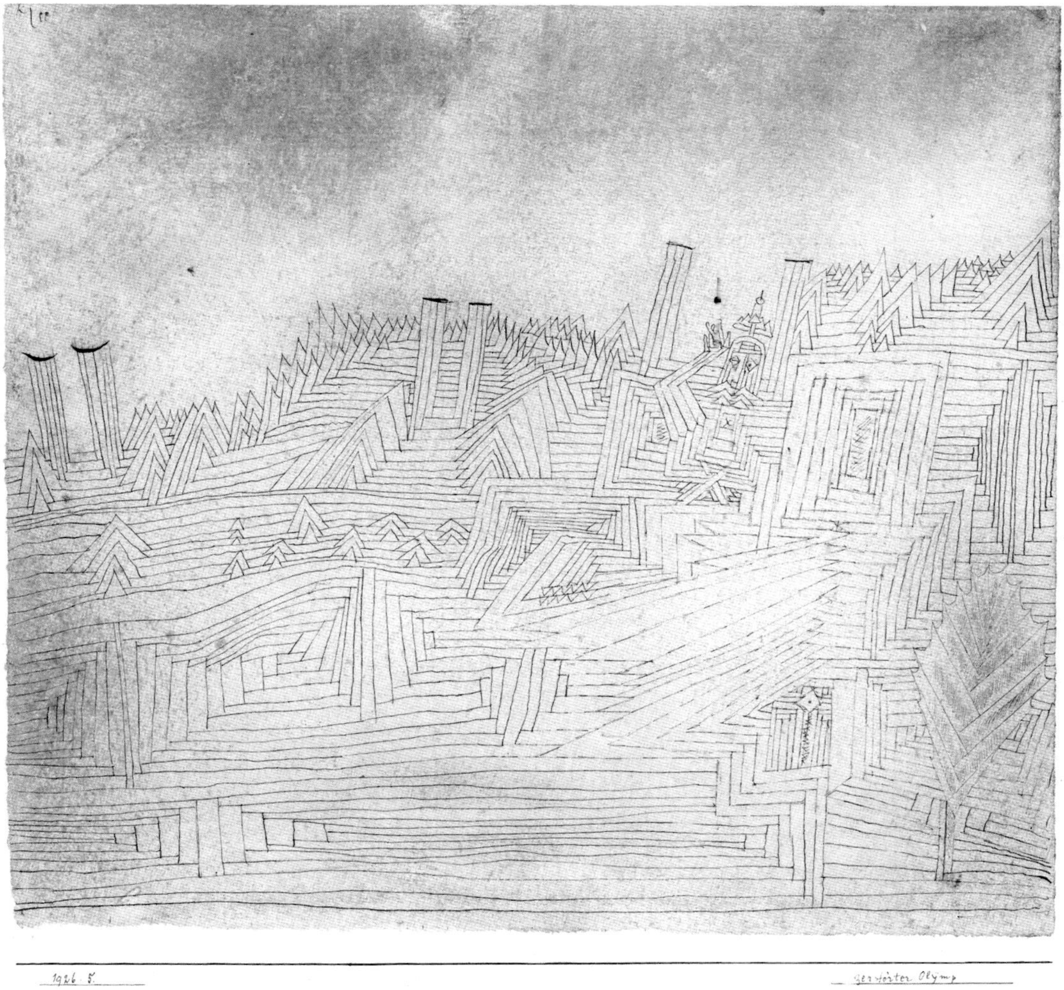

9.4 Paul Klee, *Zerstörter Olÿmp* [Destroyed Olympus], 1925/5, pen and ink and watercolor on paper, on cardboard, 26.2 × 30 cm. Museum Sammlung Rosengart, Luzern, Switzerland. © 2009 Artists Rights Society (ARS), New York/VG Bild-Kunst, Bonn

View of the Mountains by Taormina, 1924/292). These could be transformed into imaginative, rhythmic images of towns, such as *City on Two Hills* (1927/244) and *Chosen City* (1927/238). In the latter work, human structures extend deep into the earth. But these structures are suspended above yet further layers of brown and blue, suggesting even greater geological depths. The constructions also reach into the sky toward a distant sphere populated by similar forms, implying the possibility of intelligence far from Earth—an attitude toward distant spaces very different from that of the nineteenth century (before Jules Verne). Klee's cities have visible connections above and below.

These cities also undergo their own organic cycle of life and death subject to the forces of nature and of humankind. They can be bedecked by flags (*Beflagged City*, 1927/2), traumatized by floods (*Flood Swamps Cities*, 1927; *After the Deluge* 1936/7), or even collapse under the onslaught of adverse forces (*Stricken Town*, 1936/22). Like ancient civilizations, they crumble to

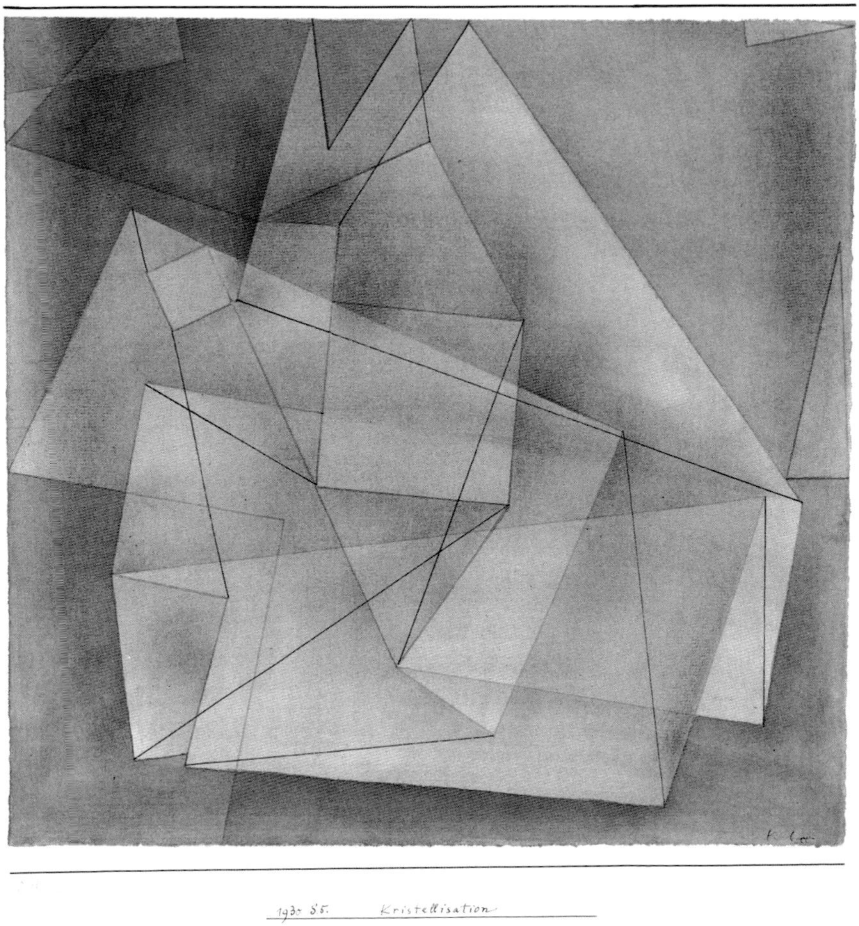

9.5 Paul Klee, *Kristallisation* [Crystallization], 1930/215, pen, watercolour and charcoal on paper on cardboard, 31.1 × 32.1 cm. Zentrum Paul Klee, Bern, Switzerland. © 2009 Artists Rights Society (ARS), New York/VG Bild-Kunst, Bonn

become part of nature's strata. Monuments to the dead are buried in a layered *Necropolis* (1930/57) (Plate 1).

Archaeology becomes confounded with geology. This was especially true in Klee's most striking series of strata landscapes made after his 1928 trip to Egypt. For these works, Klee chose the most elemental geometry to express the ancient monuments set within the severe desert. Compared to a Romantic work such as Hubert Robert's *The Pyramids* of around 1745, in *Necropolis*, Klee allowed for the resonance of both archaeological and geological time by marking the measures of strata from the sky to the earth, from the top of the image to its base. In doing so, however, Klee has omitted even the small place that Robert accords to the human, allowing himself to be what he always wanted to be; a cosmic point of reference.[23] Klee was heir to the Romantic tradition that recognized the transience of all civilization in the face of nature's power. The moralistic scenarios of Cole and Turner, and the images of ruins by Friedrich come to mind in this regard.[24] In contrast to these Romantic depictions, however, Klee's images were removed from a specific time and place, as well as from human action. They leave behind humankind's collective actions, guilt, and conscience, and in doing so they leave behind the last vestiges of Romantic humanism for the sake of universal abstract structures, as if the natural held sway in all realms.

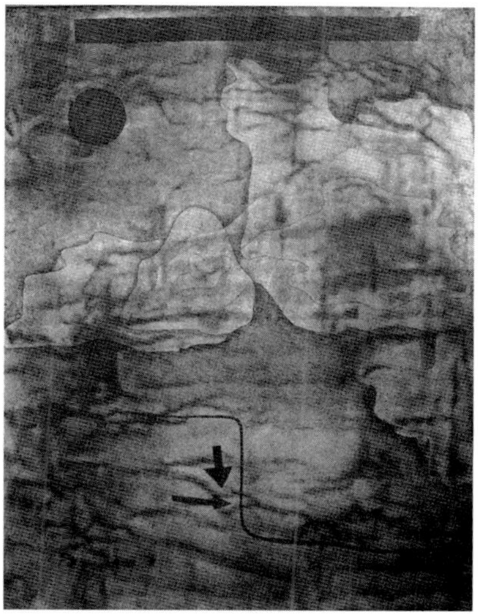

9.6 Paul Klee, *Toter Katarakt* [Dried up Cataract], 1930/184, watercolor on primed canvas, 54 × 44 cm. Private Collection, USA. © 2009 Artists Rights Society (ARS), New York/VG Bild-Kunst, Bonn

Traces of the human are also abandoned in Klee's images of pure geological formation. He structured several images of rock formations and quarries (for example, *Stone Quarry at Ostermundigen*, 1915) that resonated with the crystalline as a visual metaphor. One sees this most vividly in *Rock* of 1929, in which each facet is formed by parallel lines moving out from angled boundaries, each extending, overlaying, and interlocking much as in the process of crystal formation. This linear method had multiple sources for Klee, from etching to Cubism, to his lectures on the elements of form held at the Bauhaus.[25] But the analogy to crystals certainly resulted from his own nature study as evident in the works *Physiognomic Crystallization* (1924/15) and *Crystallization* (1930/215) (Fig. 9.5).

During the 1920s, Klee began to explore natural forms such as the quartz and amber from his own collection of natural objects more directly.[26] He also learned the basic geometry of types of crystals from natural history texts. The type-forms of crystals had been pictured in his own *Gymnasium* [upper school] text[27] and were available in a book that his friend Kandinsky used at this time, Otto Lehmann's *Die Neue Welt der Flüssigen Kristalle* [The New World of Fluid Crystals] (Leipzig, 1911). Klee's structures were not as symmetrical as the pure crystalline forms of his sources but rather manifested the irregularities of processes that can be found in nature and in art. These and related images by Klee reflect the quasi-organic quality of crystalline development discussed by Lehmann:[28] qualities of growth, propagation, and even—following Ernst Haeckel's 1917 book *Kristallseelen*—of latent life and soul! This resonance of Klee's paintings with the writings of Lehmann and Haeckel locates him within the neo-Vitalist ambient of the era. Ever the animist, Klee can also show us an image (*Rock Projection*, 1935/131), that reads at once as a cutaway view of a stony core and a slumbering quadruped.

One painting of Klee's goes beyond the clarity of the crystalline to resonate with the tragic qualities of geological change. His *Dried up Cataract* (1930/184) (Fig. 9.6) shows the poignancy of barren rocks, a burnt-out sun, and a river course that has become a slithering snake—the only creature that could survive in such a hostile environment. This image tacitly restates the more histrionic Romantic theme of crumbling cliffs uprooted trees, and eroding ravines that spoke of the overwhelming power of nature's geological forces, as for example in Friedrich's *Ravine* of 1823. Yet Klee's is a

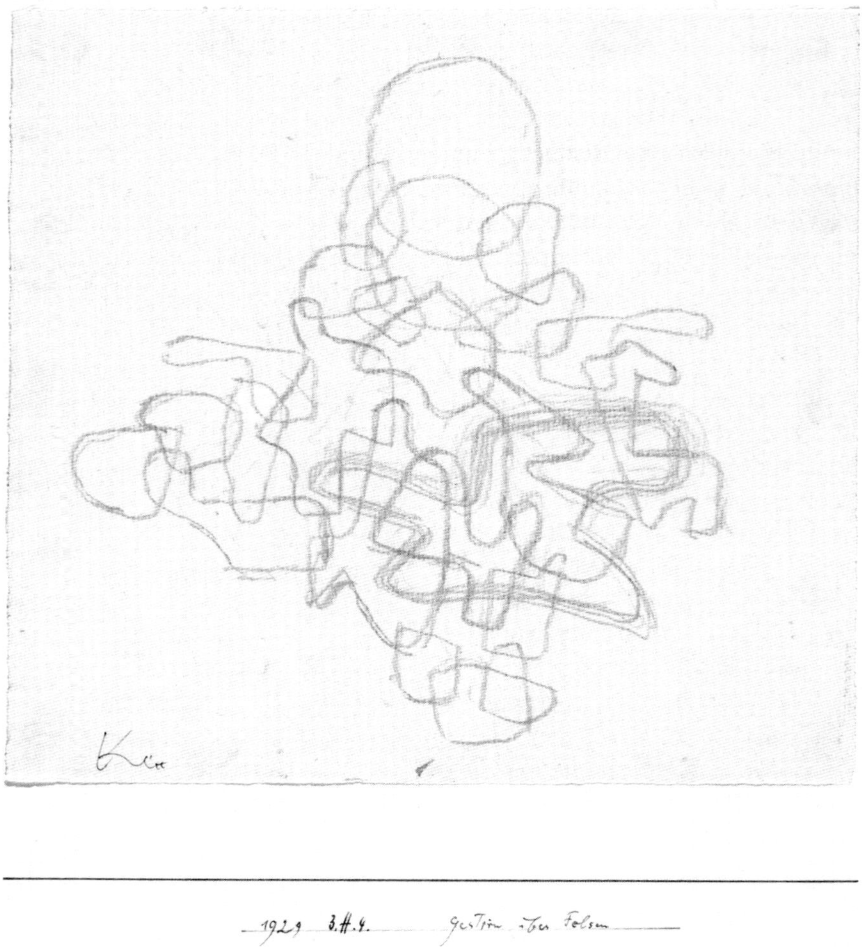

9.7 Paul Klee, *Gestirn über Felsen* [Stars above Rocks], 1929/304, pencil on paper on cardboard, 20.5 × 22.7 cm. Zentrum Paul Klee, Bern, Switzerland. © 2009 Artists Rights Society (ARS), New York/VG Bild-Kunst, Bonn

more pessimistic, more barren view, without the promise of the renewal of life. It is certainly a contrast to the abundance of most Romantic waterfalls (for example, Joseph Anton Koch's *Waterfall* of 1775)[29] which elicit wonder from rustic onlookers. Like his contemporary Max Ernst, Klee could not always support the nineteenth-century belief in organic renewal.[30] Yet on occasion Klee did rise above both human and natural pathos. At the same time as *Dead Cataract*, and related to it, he created several images employing a polyphonic overlay of interpenetrating undulations superimposed on each other.[31] In *Stars above Rocks* the undulations track the essence of hills, brooks, cliffs, clouds, and even stars (Fig. 9.7).[32] The elements interpenetrate, swinging with the life of nature's forces, revealing their identity rather than divergences. Klee felt safe assimilated into a metaphoric natural order.

Rilke, an acquaintance of Klee's whom Klee thought had a sensibility close to his own, had written a poem about the human position between the stars and the rocks (*Evening*, 1902). The poem echoed the ambivalence felt by Klee and by most twentieth-century avant-garde artists when the human was included within the equation of earth and sky. To Rilke, humanity belongs neither fully to stone nor star, nor can persons resolve the dichotomy between these two positions. Klee's answer to this dilemma was to aspire to a transcendent unity that leaves the distinctly human behind. In taking this position, Klee approached the anti-anthropocentric position of early twentieth-century Biocentrically minded thinkers and artists. He considered Rilke to still be an Impressionist with only superficial preparation, whereas he himself pressed more toward "the center."[33]

Water

It was the parts of nature as much as the whole that interested Klee. Unlike the Romantics, who studied individual elements such as clouds, trees, and waters in order to place them within their larger panoramas, Klee analyzed them for their own sake. He was moved by the elusive aspects of nature, such as water, atmosphere, and weather. Romantic artists generally accorded water and sky heroic roles within the drama of panoramic landscapes. As in Turner's *Keelman Heaving Coals by Moonlight* of 1835, lakes and sea could glimmer as sheets reflecting the heavens; they could stretch into the distance as a reminder of the immensity of nature; or they could oppose humans as a sublime adversary. By contrast, Klee's waters and weather elements were more modest, small segments of the larger whole explored for their basic structure and dynamics and animated by natural law. As a geographer might, he analyzed the cycle of a river course for his students. He pictorially plotted its phases using as a model the Reuss River in Switzerland, which he knew well. He described how the waters gather as rivulets in the mountains to form the gentle river of the Urseren valley, how they flow serenely until they abruptly encounter a ravine, crashing down precipitously, and how they dig more and more deeply into the rugged river bed, undermining its banks until whole sections collapse, whipping up an aggressive fury. Then the river calms into a smoother course, opening at a broad mouth as at Lake Lucerne. All of this was a geologically accurate plotting of the phases of a river's cycle as Klee might have seen demonstrated in natural history classes he took at Gymnasium during his youth.[34] He told his students that the forms in this diagram of the river's course resulted from the "history of their origination," thus further confirming his organic model of geological and pictorial transformation.

An awareness of these phases allowed Klee to take small fragments of these typologies and develop their dynamics. Whereas the Romantics and Realists had dealt with descriptive views, Klee thought in terms of cross sections and graphs that modeled the phenomena. He depicted water as rhythmic wave patterns

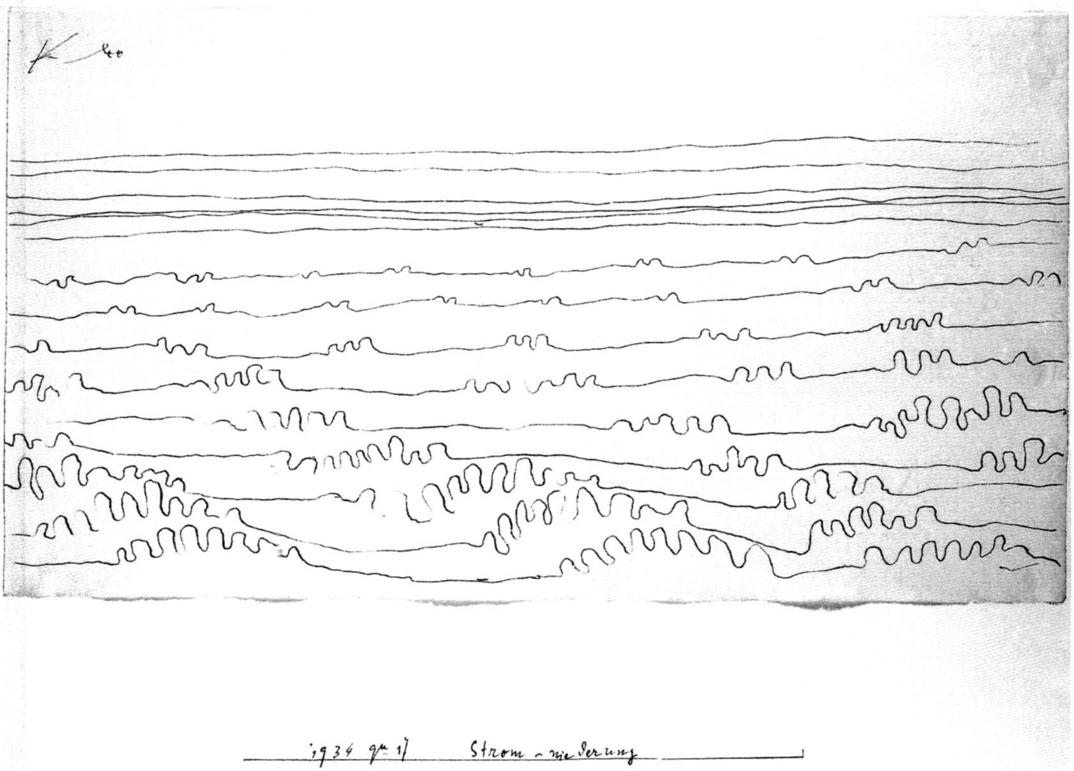

9.8 Paul Klee, *Strom-niederung* [Low-lying River Area], 1934/137, pen on paper on cardboard, 17 × 31.1 cm. Private Collection, Switzerland. © 2009 Artists Rights Society (ARS), New York/VG Bild-Kunst, Bonn

learned from the imprint of air wafting over sand and from the subtle signature of water retreating from the beach,[35] as in *Low-lying River Area* (1939/137) (Fig. 9.3). He also drew on his knowledge of wave phenomena in music, namely the graphing of sound waves by the phonautograph.[36] By using these sources Klee invented a totally new semiology of water depiction. Romantic and Realist painters (for example, Manet's *Alabama and Kearsarge*, 1864) had set down the tonal impression of broken waves and reflected light, approximating the complex phenomena of surface movement.[37] Van Gogh, whose work Klee knew, had used a more linear rendering perhaps inspired by Japanese prints. Klee's solution was closest to the Japanese themselves,[38] who delineated waves either as the overlapping contours of broken waves or as the long continuous parallels of extended rollers. His waves were unique, however, because of what he learned from the scientific imaging of the vibrating sound line. In his images each line could function not only as part of the collective life of the whole, but also as a discrete unit that could be traced from one end to the other, graphing the oscillations, path, variations, and individual personality of each wave. This was a pure, analytic modeling of the phenomenon as compared to the actual criss-cross complexities of real waves. Yet Klee infused his depictions with enough irregularity of rhythm and placement so as to simulate, one might even say, effect, "life." One sees this in *Low-lying River Area* (1934/137), in which each wave line has its own varying number of cresting peaks, changing shapes, and trough-like intervals. Klee could even modulate the turbulence of *Moving Rapids* (1929/236) and of *Untamed Waters* (1934/16) by employing undulating bands of waves that layer, clash, and interweave in invented flows and eddies. Scientific curiosity is not life-denying.

As with all of his signs, Klee's wave lines could take the step from the natural to the supra-natural. In *Play on the Water* (1935/3), the crests and whirlpools suddenly become the cock-eyed face of a water spirit, a play of Klee's imaginative animism.

Weather

Klee's treatment of the atmosphere and its elements of air, wind, rain, and lightning was as logical and inventive as was his treatment of water. He touched on a broad range of motifs encouraged by his basic understandings of meteorology. This science had greatly expanded during the late eighteenth and the nineteenth centuries into areas that stimulated public interest. Up to that time, discoveries had been primarily related to advances in physics and chemistry: for example, the invention of the thermometer and barometer, and studies of the pressure, weight, and components of air. But beginning about 1820 the dynamic patterns of the weather itself began to be studied. Daily weather maps were compiled; thunderstorms, hurricanes, and tornadoes were charted; cloud types were defined; and averages of temperature and pressure were computed. Weather could now be watched, mapped, and predicted. Daily weather maps began to appear in newspapers by 1850.[39] As was done in Gymnasium science classes by Klee's time, atmospheric phenomena could not only be experienced, their constituent elements and mechanisms could now be analyzed.[40]

One of the concepts Klee tried to capture in his art was the simple yet broadly inclusive idea of the atmosphere itself. He created atmospheric shapes that were air/cloud/water-like polyphonic beings that could rise from reflecting waters as in *Fleeting on the Water* (1929/320) (Plate 2). They could also fully levitate as *Air Currents* (1931/111) on angelic wings, and could quiver in free space as in *Atmospheric Group in Movement* (1929/276). Klee's apparitions are shimmery and quixotic, ambiguous as to presence and absence, near and far. One can read in them animated shapes and flights, gestures and pursuits, giving us an elusive aqueous universe with its own reflected sun. The Romantic artist Carl Gustav Carus had characterized reflections of the sky on waters as "truly heaven on earth, "cheerfully or darkly instilling in us a feeling of endless longing."[41] Klee's reflections are a more modern counterpart to Carus'; they give us not so much "heaven" as a strange interjacent world (one among elements of this one) emanating from the artist's own consciousness.

A more complex work plays on ideas originating in ancient astronomy and depicts the full complement of a *Horizon, Zenith, and Atmosphere* (1928/150) (Fig. 9.9) by means of a mathematical construction.[42] In this watercolor Klee

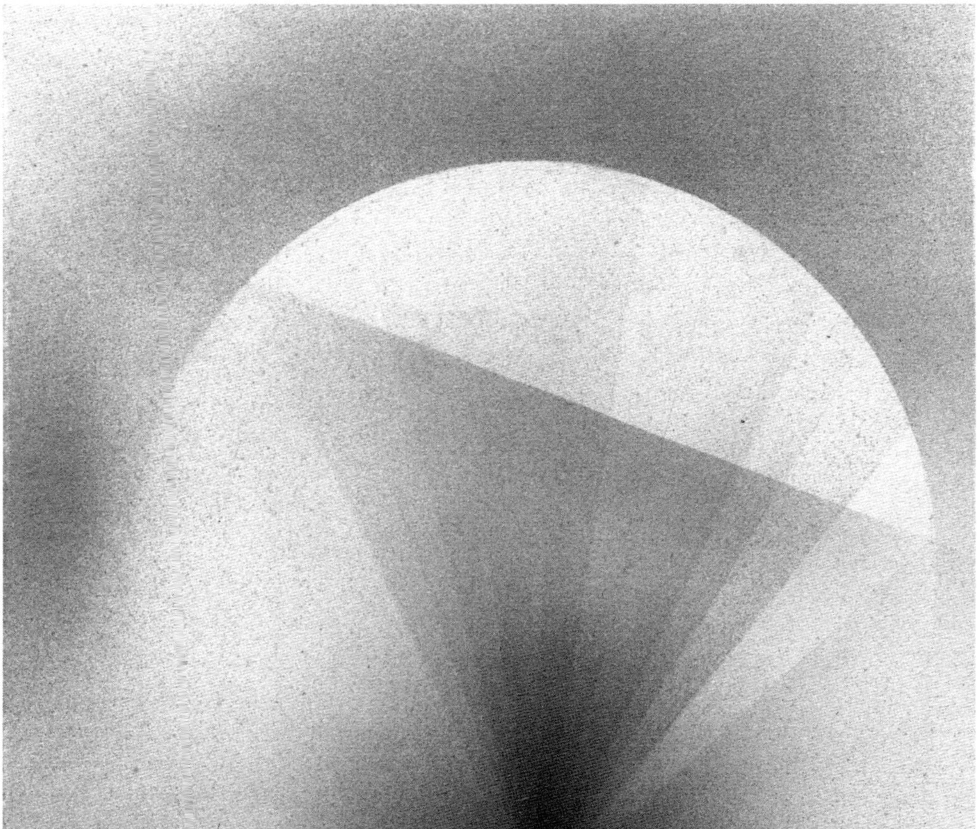

9.9 Paul Klee, *Horizont, Gipelpunkt, und Atmosphäre* [Horizon, Zenith, and Atmosphere], 1925/222, watercolor and pencil with air brush, mounted on board, 37.1 × 27 cm. Solomon R. Guggenheim Museum, New York City, USA, Estate of Karl Nierendorf, by purchase. © 2009 Artists Rights Society (ARS), New York/VG Bild-Kunst, Bonn has formed the highest vault of heaven using a curved azimuth held aloft by atmospheric overlays of airbrushed, brownish tones connoting the Earth's gaseous atmosphere. As early as 1783, Lavoisier had established that the atmosphere is a simple mixture of gases and vapor and that it extends to a height of at least one hundred miles above the earth's surface and then stops, held in place by the Earth's gravitational pull.[43] A diagram used by Klee in his teaching shows that he was aware of this scientific understanding of the atmosphere around the earth, a knowledge that helped to shape his abstract construction.[44]

The processes of rain and lightning informed by a meteorological understanding also became subjects for Klee. Simple falling rain was formed by inverting one of his lacy structures and allowing its delicate lines to fall in gentle rhythmic cadences (*Rain*, 1927/59). *The Danger of Lightning* (1931/139) could cause dark clouds to emit a threatening glow of tension high above mountain peaks or could cause the atmosphere itself to bend and strain as in *Before the Lightning* (1923/150) (Fig. 9.10). Both images suggest the buildup of tension just before lightning cuts through the air and rolls of thunder resound. The latter watercolor, especially, indicates a yet more sophisticated scientific understanding of atmospheric phenomena. We see the buildup of two opposing forces that strain the atmosphere, compressing horizontal lines and pushing apart vertical lines, suggesting the accumulation of electrical energy that will be released by a streak of lightning.[45] This phenomenon was discussed as early as 1890 in German physics and meteorology textbooks and was described in the delightful *Autobiography of an Electron*, published in German translation as *Was ist Elektrizität?*[46] within the "Kosmos" series by the "Gesellschaft der Naturfreunde" [Society of the Friends of Nature]. Both Klee and Moholy-Nagy consulted volumes in this best-selling series of popular scientific texts intended for amateur naturalists.[47] The text for a diagram published in the book shows the result of the exchange of positive and negative electrical charges between one cloud and another and between clouds and the Earth (Fig. 9.11). When the difference in these charges is great enough, it is relieved by a discharge of an electrical current that we call lightning. Both of Klee's electrical storm images suggest the same power and sublimity of nature as Friedrich's *Neubrandenburg* (1817), but the Romantic Friedrich gives us two diminutive human witnesses to the magnificent stormy sky just breaking into light. The figures act as a human grounding in the dark foreground, while their modest scale is mediated by the church tower breaking through clouds toward the light in the middle ground, suggestive of the role of religion. By contrast, Klee gives us only an abstracted graph of meteorological events, albeit on a luminous tonal ground.

The use of the grid as a metaphor for the atmosphere itself in *Lightning Flash* emerges from Klee's employment of grids during 1923 and 1924 as the ground for many of his paintings. It may also have been reinforced by Klee's awareness of the weatherman's "isobars," used by meteorologists to map

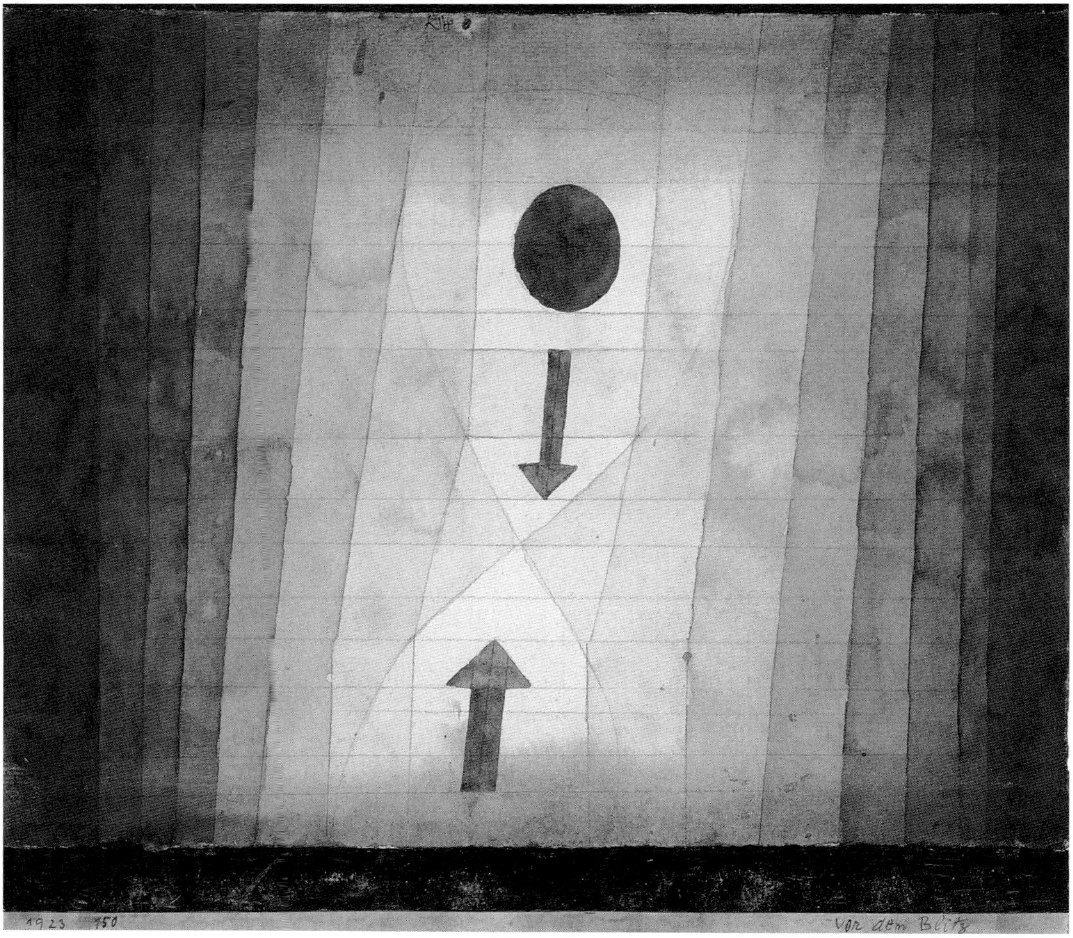

9.10 Paul Klee, *Vor dem Blitz* [Before the Lightning], 1923/150, watercolor and pencil on paper; top and bottom edges with gouache, watercolor, and quill on cardboard, 28 × 31.5 cm. Fondation Beyeler, Riehen/Basel, Switzerland © 2009 Artists Rights Society (ARS), New York/VG Bild-Kunst, Bonn. Photo: Peter Schibili, Basel, Switzerland

variances in air pressure. The concept had been introduced by Alexander von Humboldt as isotherms (temperature lines) in 1817 and was used to plot air pressure on weather maps by 1863. It is interesting that these forms only entered into the artistic expression of a generation that was exposed to them in their youth, a generation whose members were able to translate them into their own abstracted visual diagrams because of shifts in what was acceptable artistic practice during their maturity.

Klee's lightning, once set loose, could be either whimsical or deadly. On the one hand, as in the 1924 work *Fixed Lightning*, lightning could be caught, fixed, and festooned with a flag like a magic tower over a town. On the other, as in *Lightning* (1920/17), it could splinter out of the sky to pierce a prostrate man like a deadly arrow.

Unsettled Weather (1929/343) was also based on meteorological means of diagramming atmospheric phenomena (Fig. 9.12). In this work, Klee symbolically indicated the atmospheric cycle of water with its accompanying weather. The nucleus of this idea is contained in an early poetic observation

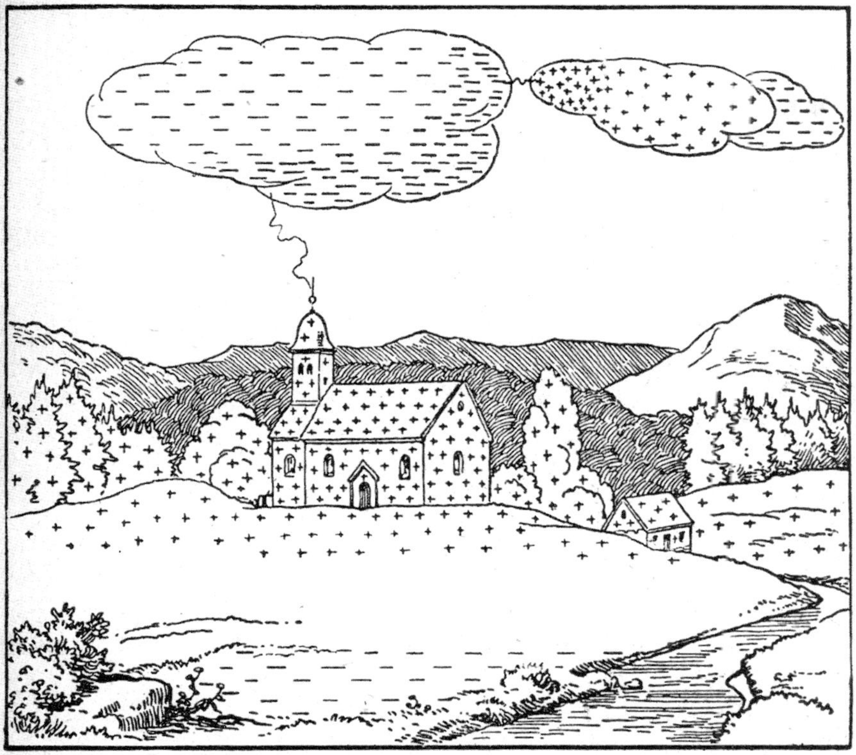

Abb. 10. Die Entstehung des Blitzes. Die mit freien Elektronen (—) geladene Wolke wirkt verteilend (influenzierend) auf eine benachbarte Wolke und auf die Erde, d. h. sie stößt die dort befindlichen Elektronen ab, so daß die Atome elektronenarm (positiv-elektrisch [+]) werden. Wird die Spannung zwischen Wolke und Erde bei immer stärkerer Annäherung sehr groß, so springen die freien Elektronen zur Erde über. Die begleitenden Licht- und Knallerscheinungen, die durch Reibung und Aufprall bedingt sind, nennen wir Blitz und Donner. Ein Ausgleich der Spannung zwischen Wolke und Wolke wird uns meist nur als fahles Aufleuchten und leises, dumpfes Grollen bemerkbar. Wir sprechen dann von „Wetterleuchten".

9.11 "The Origin of Lightning," diagram and text from Charles R. Gibson and Hans Guenther, *Was ist Elektrizität? Erzählungen eines Elecktrons* (Stuttgart: Kosmos, 1919), 31

"The cloud laden with negative electrons causes dispersion within the neighboring cloud and earth; that is to say it repels the electrons found there, so that the atoms become positively charged. When the potential gradient between the cloud and earth become very large, as the cloud nears the earth, then the free electrons leap to the earth."

Klee made in his diary: "A comparison, the sun brews vapors that rise and struggle against."[48] As part of his teaching, by 1923, this observation had developed into a full-blown meteorological diagram of nature's water-cycle in which, as Klee explained, "Water descends from the sky as rain and rises to the sky as vapor, hence I guide the curve upwards and close the circle in the clouds."[49] In *Unsettled Weather,* we can follow this cycle, set on a shimmering ground, from the black arrow to the red aqueous vapor that rises to form a dark storm cloud. Behind and above the cloud a pale sun glows, while below a sickle curve sends down tiny parallel strokes of rain onto a feathery landscape. In spite of the diagrammatic modes of depiction that he employs, the "cosmic ground" is never lost. It is conveyed by his radiant spaces and colored atmospheres, shadowy edges, and corners darkened by mysterious color auras to the point that it seems we are peering into a spherically inflected otherworld, free from the confines of earthly gravity. In *Unsettled Weather* this is accented not only by the pale sun on high but also by a subliminal sun in the lower right, suggesting levitation into free space itself.

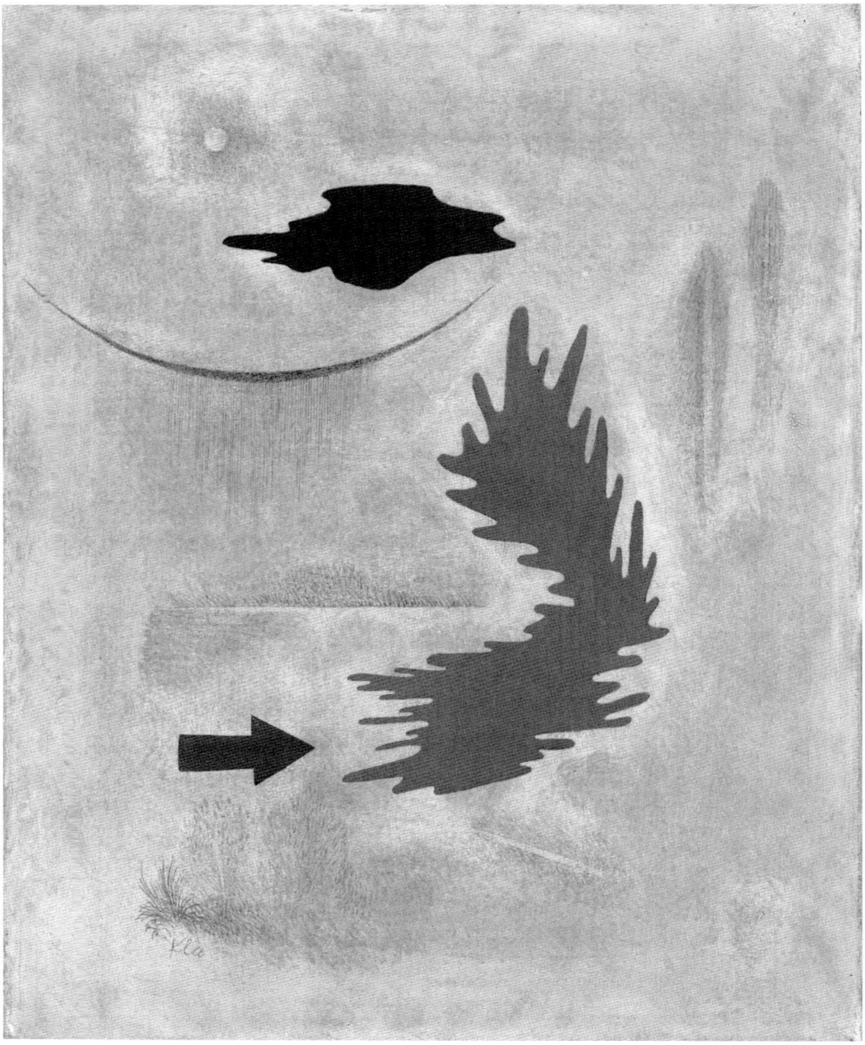

9.12 Paul Klee, *Gemischtes Wetter* [Unsettled Weather], 1929/343, oil and watercolor on muslin, 49 × 41 cm. Private collection, Switzerland. Deposited in the Zentrum Paul Klee, Bern, Switzerland. © 2009 Artists Rights Society (ARS), New York/VG Bild-Kunst, Bonn

Not all of Klee's paintings of the life of the atmosphere were anchored in a natural historical perspective. In several of them he introduced mysterious contradictions, unnatural happenings, and strange spirits. Storm winds could blow violently in one direction while a tree bends in the other (*Storm*, 1929/273), hot winds whisk curtains out of windows (*Fire Wind*, 1923/43), clouds metamorphose into an *Air Chase Scene* (1929/84), and wild circular gusts emanate from an ecstatic flower (*Rose Wind* (1922/202) (Fig. 9.13). Spirit-like forms play in the winds or are perhaps the winds themselves (*Play of the Wind*, 1923/202). These cracks in the natural world give us an opening into Klee's ontology. He wrote that there is a world that "exists between the worlds our senses can perceive ... Children, madmen, and savages can still, or again, look into it. And what they see and picture is for me the most precious kind of confirmation."[50] This "in-between world"

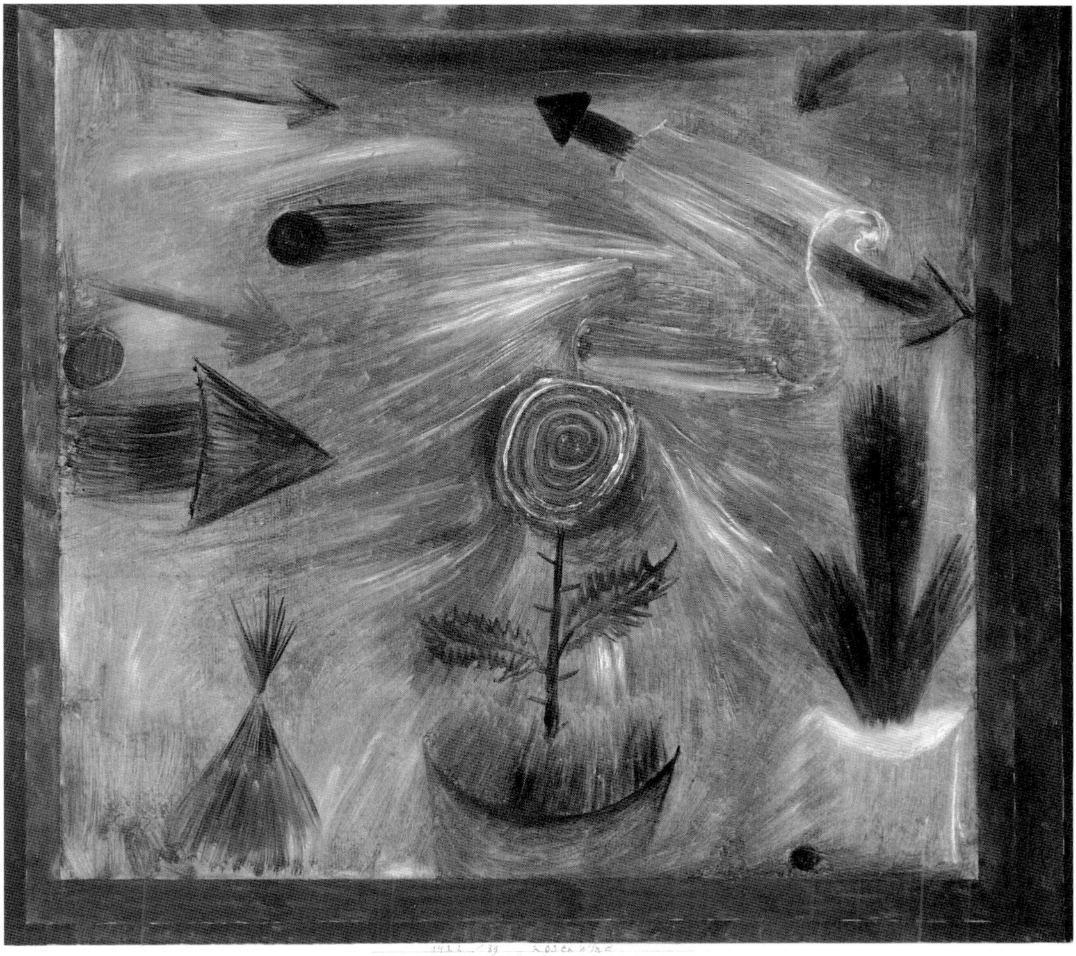

9.13 Paul Klee, *Rosenwind* [Rose Wind], 1922/39, oil on primed paper on cardboard, 38.2 × 41.8 cm. Zentrum Paul Klee, Bern, Switzerland. Livia Klee Donation. © 2009 Artists Rights Society (ARS), New York/VG Bild-Kunst, Bonn

was one of mad possibilities, caprice, and imagination. It places Klee at a juncture different from that of the German Romantic painters, who possessed a more stable view of the relation of humankind to nature and the divine. For the Romantics, the human existed within a tangible, everyday cycle of natural events and personal actions, and through these aspired to a God beyond. Klee, on the other hand, as an early twentieth-century artist inspired by modern science, explored the graphing of the structures and processes of nature. He analyzed components of the whole and perceived abstract rhythms within a living order. Yet there is less certainty about the place of the human. Perhaps this is the modern dilemma. Either the human is coolly subsumed into this transcendent order or exists as a mad play of consciousness against the abstract patterns of the universe.

Notes

1 Klee mentions several writings by Goethe in his diaries, though none of the natural science essays. He notes that he identifies with Goethe: Paul Klee, *Tagebücher 1898–1918*, ed. Wolfgang Kersten (Stuttgart: Teufen, 1988), entry 375. The Kersten edition of Klee's diaries is the critical edition; for the edition edited by his son Felix Klee, translated into English, see *The Diaries of Paul Klee, 1898–1918* (Berkeley, CA: University of California Press, 1964)—entry numbers are the same, Diary entries hereafter referred to as "Diary." Felix Klee stated that Klee had read Goethe's scientific writings (interview with the author, November 24, 1972). Perhaps Klee had seen the study by R. Magnus on *Goethe als Naturforscher* (Leipzig: Barth, 1906). See discussions on Klee and Goethe in M. Huggler, *Paul Klee: Die Malerei als Blick in den Kosmos* (Frauenfeld and Stuttgart: Verlag Huber 1969), 81–84; W. Haftmann, *Mind and Work of Paul Klee* (New York: Praeger, 1967) 154–60; A. Moesser, *Das Problem der Bewegung bei Paul Klee* (Heidelberg: Winter, 1976); and Richard Verdi, *Klee and Nature* (New York: Rizzoli, 1985), 219–26.

2 Terms used in his lectures on "Bildnerische Mechanik oder Stillehre" (1924), unpublished; original and typescript at the Paul Klee-Stiftung, Kunstmuseum Bern, 70, lecture of February 12, 1924.

3 F.W.J. von Schelling, "Über das Verhältnis der bildenden Künste zu der Natur," *Sämmtliche Werke* (Stuttgart, 1860), VII, 291–93. English trans. by J. Elliot Cabot in *Neoclassicism and Romanticism, 1750–1850*, ed. Lorenz Eitner (Englewood Cliffs, NJ: Prentice Hall, 1970), 44.

4 Other scholars have dealt with the Romantic heritage in Klee. David Burnett, "Paul Klee: The Romantic Landscape," *Art Journal* 36, no.4 (summer 1977): 322–26, modestly noted some thematic parallels; Robert Rosenblum, *Modern Painting and the Northern Romantic Tradition* (New York: Harper & Row, 1975), 149–58, placed Klee within the large sweep of the Northern Romantic tradition and inserted only one note of contrast about an early painting as having a more "whimsical and pixilated atmosphere, more appropriate to fairy tales than philosophical speculation", 50. Verdi, *Klee and Nature* (1985), 219–37, richly discussed the rootedness of Klee's theory in Goethe and in the heritage of Romantic "scientific mysticism." O.K. Werckmeister, *The Making of Paul Klee's Career, 1914–1920* (Chicago, IL: University of Chicago Press, 1989), characterized Klee's Romanticism as a form of opportunistic escapism developed in response to the adversities of the World War I period. Glaesemer, who was in conversation with Werckmeister, made a moving and significant defense of the sincerity and profundity of Klee's Romantic view; see Glaesmer, "Klee and German Romanticism," in Carolyn Lanchner, ed., *Paul Klee* (New York: Museum of Modern Art, 1987), 65–81. Glaesemer defined Klee's "cool romanticism" (a term Klee used in Diary entry 951) as an awareness of the tragic split between longing for and the actual attainment of a free mobility toward the infinite, a perception also familiar to earlier Romantic artists. To Glaesemer, Klee encoded his Romantic themes in a distanced sign-like language, which nevertheless shared the earlier view of the totality of things, while still being acutely aware of the polarity between present existence and the transcendent. I would suggest that what was a polarity for the Romantics becomes a rift in Klee.

5 Timothy Mitchell, "Caspar David Friedrich's Der Hatzmann: German Romantic Landscape Painting and Historical Geology," *Art Bulletin*, 66 (Sept. 1984): 452–64.

6 Malcolm Cormack, *Constable* (Cambridge: Cambridge University Press, 1986), 137. Goethe had suggested to Friedrich that he execute a series of cloud studies

based on Luke Howard's classifications. Friedrich rejected this suggestion on the grounds that to do so would undermine the very foundation of landscape painting: Joseph Leo Koerner, *Caspar David Friedrich and the Subject of Landscape* (New Haven, CT: Yale University Press, 1990), 192–93. Such a rejection suggests Friedrich's concern with an experiential approach to nature rather than an intellectual one and, as Koerner notes, the ability of such an approach to point to higher meaning.

7 See especially Verdi's discussion (*Klee and Nature*, 219–30) of the connection of Klee to the morphological studies of Goethe (*Die Metamorphose der Pflanzen*, 1790) and probably to D'Arcy Wentworth Thompson (*On Growth and Form*, 1917). Also my study of Klee's interest in basic principles of physics, Sara Lynn Henry, "Form-Creating Energies: Paul Klee and Physics," *Arts Magazine* 52 (Sept. 1977): 118–21, and "Paul Klee's Pictorial Mechanics—From Physics to the Picture Plane," *Pantheon* XLVII (Jahrgang 1989): 147–65.

8 "Über die moderne Kunst," a lecture given for the Jena Kunstverein in 1924; first published in Bern by Hans Meyer-Benteli, 1945; it is reprinted in German in *Paul Klee, Das bildnerische Denken, Schriften zur Form und Gestaltlehre*, ed. Jürg Spiller, Teil 1 (Basel and Stuttgart: Schwabe & Co., 1956), 92–93; English in *The Thinking Eye. The Notebooks of Paul Klee*, trans. Ralph Mannheim, Charlotte Weidler, and Joyce Wittenborn (New York: Wittenborn, 1961), 92–93; also in *Modern Artists on Art*, ed. Robert Herbert, trans. Paul Findlay (Englewood Cliffs, NJ: Prentice Hall, 1964), 87–88.

9 Felix Klee, *Paul Klee: His Life and Work in Documents* (Berkeley, CA and Los Angeles, CA: University of California Press, 1964), 183, from Lothar Schreyer, *Erinnerungen an Sturm und Bauhaus* (Munich: Albert Langen and Georg Müller, 1956).

10 "... nur im Sinne der Beweglichkeit. Und nicht im Sinne einer wissenschaftlichen Kontrollierbarkeit auf Naturtreue! Nur im Sinne der Freiheit;" from "Über die moderne Kunst," in *Das bildnerische Denken*, 93.

11 Diary, entry 842. Klee wrote "darf ich dann wieder wagen, meine Urgebet der psychischen Improvisation … Hier an einem Natureindruck nur ganz indirect gebunden, kann ich dan wieder wagen, das zu gestalten, was in die Seele gerade belastet." [I may [now] dare to enter my primary realm of psychic improvisation… Here bound only very indirectly to an impression of nature, I may again dare to give form to what burdens my soul]. Klee produced a few improvised works at this referenced time (1908), but this method did not become his predominate mode until 1913 and 1914. See my article "Klee's *Kleinwelt* and Creation," *Print Review* (Fall 1977): 38–49.

12 Felix Klee, *Klee Documents*, from Lothar Schreyer, *Erinnerungen an Sturm und Bauhaus*, 183.

13 In German Romantic painting, the imaginatively symbolic exceptions would be the allegorical studies by Philipp Otto Runge of the *Tageszeiten* [Times of Day]. One should also note that there were cases of freer personal imagination in Romantic writing—for example, in Novalis's fragment "Die Lehrlinge zu Sais" (1797). Sixty drawings by Klee were chosen to illustrate a later English edition of this: Friederich von Hardenberg (Novalis), *The Novices of Sais* (New York: C. Valentin 1949).

14 Kenneth Clark, *Landscape into Art* (Boston, MA: Beacon Press, 1961), 140–41.

15 Klee's interest in the processes and cycles of nature was rooted in Romantic theory, especially as rendered by the writings of Carl Carus (theorist, naturalist

and artist) in his *Neun Briefe über Landschaftsmalerei* (1815–24); the second edition was not published until 1927 in Dresden. Although Klee may or may not have read Carus, he was familiar with Carus' sources—Friedrich, Schelling, and Goethe. Carus had learned from his friend Friedrich, whom he often watched paint; he used Schelling's philosophy to help clarify the works he was seeing; and he dedicated his *Neun Briefe* to Goethe, whom he knew, greatly admired, and about whom he wrote. As Carus explained it, the purpose of landscape painting was not to imitate nature but to resonate with the living whole and to create what he called an "Erlebenbild" or "Picture of the Earth's Life." This, he wrote, could be seen in the sublime immensity of nature, in "the Alps, storms at sea, forests in the mountains, volcanoes, and waterfalls" and also in the quieter times of day and of the year, in "the passages of clouds and all the color-splendor of the sky, the ebb and flow of the sea, the slow but inevitable advancing of the earth's surface, the weathering of naked cliffs, the welling up of the springs, whose waters follow the direction of the mountain chains, are gathered into creeks and finally into streams"—all of these are subjects of Klee's paintings. (*Neun Briefe über Landschaftsmalerei, geschrieben in den Jahren 1815 bis 1824* (Dresden: W. Jess Verlag, 1955), Letter VII and Letter II, 98–99 and 26–27); translation from Elizabeth Gilmore Holt, ed., *From the Classicists to the Impressionists* (Garden City, NY: Doubleday Anchor Books, 1966), 92 and 89. Klee's interest in this heritage was transmuted both by his scientific probing and by the context of early twentieth-century Neo-Romantic Biocentrism, shaped by such thinkers and scientists as Haeckel, d'Arcy Thompson, Ostwald, Driesch, and Lehmann. See Oliver Botar, "Defining Biocentrism," Chapter 1 in this volume; and, for ties to the Bauhaus, see Henry, "Form-Creating Energies", 119, and the present essay. For example, both Driesch (on "Das Unbewusste") and Ostwald (on his "Farbenlehre") spoke at the Bauhaus while Klee was teaching there (information from Ise Gropius guestbook, letter to the author May 8, 1977).

16 Klee's first formalized lectures at the Bauhaus were "Beiträge zur bildnerischen Formenlehre" [Contributions to a theory of plastic forms], winter 1921–22; diagrams were from a lecture of January 22, 1922 on "Verschiedene Bewegungsmöglichkeiten … Irdische und kosmische Beispiele" [Different possibilities of movement … Earthly and cosmic examples], *Thinking Eye*, 311.

17 Hans Frey, *Mineralogie und Geologie für Schweizerische Mittelschulen* (Leipzig: G. Freytag, 1901), figs. 180 and 194. Klee's own text in Literarschule, *H. Wettstein's Leitfaden für Schweizerische Mittelschulen*, 6th ed. (Leipzig: Verlag der Erziehungsdirektion, 1893), had no related illustrations, but it is most likely that his teacher used supplementary texts, since such "Hülfsmittel" were listed at the back of the book, 521–23. (The citation of the "obligatorisch" Wettstein text was found in the *Lehrmittel-Verzeichnis für Deutschen Mittelschulen des Kantons Bern* (Bern: Buchdruckerei Lack Aeschlimann & Jost, 1899), 4). The seventh edition of Wettstein (Zürich: Verlag der Erziehungsdirektion, 1901), though publication was too late for Klee to have used the book during his school years (1895–99), did have an expanded geology section and some relevant diagrams, which suggests that this was considered part of the course (Wettstein, 7th ed., *II. Teil: Physik und Chemie und Erdgeschichte* had a related diagram of "Gebirgsbildung" [mountain formation], 252.) Klee took an impressive array of natural science courses in Literarschule (1894–1899), as the curriculum from *Jahresbericht über das Städtische Gymnasium in Bern* (Bern: Buchdruckerei Stämpflie & Cie, 1895–99) reveals: Geographie—1895, '96, '97 (including Mathematische Geographie and Lehre von der Atmosphäre); Naturgeschichte: Biology—1895 ,'96 & Geologie & Mineralogie—'97; Physik—1896, '97, '98, '99; and Chemie—'98,'99.

His participation in these courses was verified by the annual registers of students, found at the Staatsarchiv Bern. (Thanks to James Hofmeier for assistance in the archive.)

18 Although there had been useful observations made earlier by ancient Greeks and by Renaissance Italians (including Leonardo), the initial fundamental axioms of stratigraphy were laid out by Nicolas Steno (1631–87).

19 There are references throughout Klee's teachings to energies and movement; see especially the teaching note in *Thinking Eye* regarding "Energien formbildender Natur. Natürliches Wachstum" [Energies of a form-creating nature. Natural growth], 94 and Henry, "Form-Creating Energies."

20 See especially Klee's diagrams and discussion of "Zentral bestrahltes Wachstum … Bei Pflanzen: Teilquerschnittlich wachsend. Längsschnittlich wachsend" [Central radiating growth. Plants: Growing in partial cross section. Growing in longitudinal section] and "Vermittlung zwischen progressiven Bewegungsformen" [Mediation of progressive forms of motion] in *Thinking Eye*, 23 and 34–35. For discussions of Klee's "parallel figuration" and themes, see Christian Geelhaar, *Paul Klee and the Bauhaus* (New York: New York Graphic Society, 1973), 98–106; and Robert Kudielka, *Paul Klee: The Nature of Creation, Works, 1914–1940* (London: Hayward Galleries in association with Lund Humphries, 2002), 103–7.

21 See Verdi, *Klee and Nature*, 229–330.

22 Geelhaar, *Klee and the Bauhaus*, 100.

23 Diary, entry 1008.

24 For example Cole's *Course of the Empire* (1836), Turner's *Tenth Plague of Egypt* (1802), and Friedrich's *Temple of Juno at Agrigentum* (1830) or *Abbey in the Oakwood* (1809–10).

25 Klee's method emerged from his lectures concerned with "strukturale Rhythmen" [structural rhythms] from the most elemental to the more complex (such that they can have the character of an organism—that is, they cannot be divided), *Thinking Eye*, 217–92. He used these repetitive means to structure landscapes and towns as well as "Niedrigere und höhere Individuen" [lower and higher individuals] (259).

26 *Thinking Eye*, Introduction, 24 (in *Das bildnerische Denken*, Introduction, 12) details Klee's collection of amber, crystals, shells, petrified plants, algae, seeds, butterflies, and so on.

27 Klee's Gymnasium text had a schematic illustration of different shapes of lead crystals (Wettstein, *Naturkunde*, 6th ed., 497).

28 In nature, irregularities of truncation and beveling can occur as the result of the slowness of formation and from the absorption of foreign matter. Lehmann considered the seeming organic qualities of inorganic "flowing crystals" as he discussed their growth, propagation, and even latent life and soul (*Die Neue Welt*, 264–312).

29 See also Caspar Wolf, *Der obere Staubbachfall im Lauterbrunntal* (1774–77), Ernst Kaiser, *Gebirgstal* (n.d.), Ferdinand Olivier, *Am Gollinger Masserfall* (1815).

30 For Max Ernst, see his *Entire City* (1935), Kunsthaus, Zurich, among other of his works. Carus had written about the life-states of nature in which destruction can occur amid developing life and a new beginning can occur within decay, such as

"the bursting of fresh buds from half-dead branches" (*Neun Briefe* in Eitner, *Neoclassicism and Romanticism, 1750–1850*, II: 50.

31 This means, as in music, "A composition in simultaneous and harmonizing but melodically independent and individual parts or voices" (*Webster's New International Dictionary* (Springfield, MA: G.C. Merriam Co., 2nd ed., 1939)). Geelhaar discussed the origins and development of this form in Klee's work in *Klee and the Bauhaus*, 29–139. See also A. Kagan's discussion in his book *Paul Klee: Art and Music* (Ithaca, NY: Cornell University Press, 1983), 41–93.

32 Other works are *Gestirn über Felsen* (1929/304), *Berg und Luft, synthetisch* (1930/136), *Bewölktes Gebirg* (1931/266), and *Landschaft/polyphonie* (1931/267).

33 Diary, entry 925, after reading passages of *Buch der Bilder*, which included this poem of Rilke's:

Abend [*Evening*]
The evening slowly changes the attire
held for it by a border of old trees;
You watch: and the lands part company with you,
one heavenward—ascending, one that falls;

and leave you, to neither quite belonging,
not quite so dark as the house that is silent,
not quite so surely conjuring the eternal
as that which turns to star each night and rises;

and leaves you (inexpressibly to disentangle)
your life, fearing, gigantic, ripening, that it
becomes, now circumscribed, now comprehending
alternately stone in you and star.

(From *Buch der Bilder*, first published in 1902; English trans. by M.D. Norton in *The Poetry of Rainer Maria Rilke* (New York: W.W. Norton & Co., 1938), 71.)

34 Klee's diagram and discussion from *Form und Gestaltungslehre. Band II. Unendliche Naturgeschichte* ed. Jürg Spiller (Basel and Stuttgart: Schwabe & Co., 1970), 75; English ed., *The Nature of Nature, The Notebooks of Paul Klee,* vol. 2, trans. Heinz Norden (New York: Wittenborn, 1973), 71–75. The general outline of Klee's explanation resembles the description of "Entstehung der Täler" [Formation of Valleys] in the subsequent text (Wettstein, Naturkunde, 7th ed., 1901, 250–52) to Klee's own class text (6th ed., 1893), suggesting that that was a likely topic for his natural history class.

35 *Nature of Nature,* 48.

36 Klee drew and discussed the wave motion of musical tones in his teachings (*Nature of Nature*, 44–51, lecture Nov. 23, 1923; see related diagrams in *Thinking Eye*, 274–79, lecture Feb. 6, 1922). His diagrams exactly match those of the graphing devices of his day. One device, which he probably used as a schoolboy, was a tuning fork that as it vibrated with sound, produced an image on a soot-blackened plate. This was pictured in the subsequent 1901 edition of his natural studies text (Wettstein, *Naturkunde*, 7th ed., 64–65) and was a likely classroom demonstration during his time. Another method of obtaining sound forms that Klee mentioned was by drawing a violin bow across a thin plate covered with sand (*Nature of Nature*, 44, class Nov. 27, 1923), although the resulting forms do not resemble the continuous waves that Klee used for his waters.

37 Such waters are rolling swells, broken and irregular, crossed by trains of waves from surface winds, the wake of boats, or refracted by the shoreline and sometimes further chopped by "capillary ripples."

38 Klee was familiar with both the work of Van Gogh and of the Japanese. He mentioned Van Gogh in his diaries no fewer than six times, discussing at length Van Gogh's contribution in line (Diary, entries 842 and 899). *Der Blaue Reiter* (1912), published while Klee was a participant in that group, illustrates five Japanese drawings, one perhaps by Hokusai, and pairs a Japanese woodcut with a Van Gogh painting—though none are water images—(*Der Blaue Reiter*, ed. Wassily Kandinsky and Franz Marc, 1912; *Dokumentarische Neuausgabe von Klaus Landheit* (München: R. Piper & Co., 1967), 41, 50, 124, 166, 105, 204 and 205. Jed Perl suggests that Van Gogh himself had learned graphic techniques from Hokusai's sketches: "Van Gogh at the Met," *New Criterion* (Dec. 1984): 33.

39 *Encyclopedia Britannica*, 11th ed. (Cambridge, UK, and New York: Cambridge University Press, 1910), 18: 264–65.

40 Klee most likely studied the movements of weather—temperature, precipitation, barometric pressure—and the phenomena of snow, electricity, and polar lights that were covered in the seventh edition of his Gymnasium textbook (Wettstein, 1901, 107–14 and 145–146); that is, the edition subsequent to the one he used in school.

41 Carus, *Neun Briefe*, 1947, 29.

42 The "zenith" is the highpoint of the sky directly overhead, the highest point of the celestial as viewed from any particular spot. A large arc called the "azimuth" can be drawn through this point, cutting the horizon on either side at right angles.

43 An 1881 encyclopedia states that the exact height of the atmosphere had not yet been determined, although it was clear it must have a limit. It was known to extend out to 100 miles, and perhaps 200, from the observation of meteors (*Chambers Encylcopedia* (Philadelphia: 1881), 1:523). A 1922 encyclopedia agreed and added no new knowledge (*New International Enc*yclopedia, New York: Dodd Mead & Co., 1922), 2:323). It is now known that faint traces of atmosphere extend as far as 500 miles.

44 *Thinking Eye*, 322.

45 Klee may not have known all of the specifics, but the general information (through the work of Wall, Winkler, and Benjamin Franklin in the eighteenth and nineteenth centuries) that it had something to do with the buildup of electrical charges in the atmosphere was common knowledge.

46 See Leopold Pfaundler, *Mueller-Pouillet's Lehrbuch der Physik und Meteorologie*, 9th revised and expanded ed. (Braunschweig: F. Vieweg und Sohn, 1888–90), 3:306–10. (The 1864 edition of this text was on the "list of helpful sources" for Klee's school text (Wettstein, *Naturkunde*, 6th ed., 523); there were over 23 editions of Pfaundler by the mid-1920s). Also see Charles R. Gibson and Hans Guenther, *Was ist Elektrizitaet*? (Stuttgart: Kosmos, 1911), 29–34.

47 Klee owned a book from the Kosmos series, Dr. Karl Weule, *Vom Kerbstock zum Alphabet, Urformen der Scrift* (Stuttgart, 1915); and Moholy-Nagy drew from another Kosmos book, Raoul Francé, *Die Pflanze als Erfinder* (Stuttgart, 1920), for his own *Von Material zu Architektur*, Bauhaus Books, no. 14 (Munich: A. Langen Verlag, 1929).

48 Diary, entry 75.

49 *Nature of Nature*, 93.

50 Felix Klee, *Klee Documents*, from Schreyer, *Erinnerungen an Sturm und Bauhaus*, 183–84.

10

Kandinsky and science: The introduction of biological images in the Paris period

Vivian Endicott Barnett

After Vasily Kandinsky settled in Paris and began to paint again in 1934, his work manifested stylistic and iconographic changes. The artist was then 60 years old; he stayed in France for almost eleven years, until his death there in 1944. During this last decade, Kandinsky completed 144 oil paintings, more than 200 watercolors and gouaches, and about 300 drawings. The late work possesses a unity that sets it apart from what he had done between 1897 and 1933, although it can be related to his earlier work. The complex question of what is new and what is already familiar in Kandinsky's Paris works reveals that new motifs are introduced into his art in 1934. It is generally agreed that during the Paris period Kandinsky's colors changed: he selected new hues, favored pastels rather than primaries, and achieved original and intricate color harmonies. In the summer of 1934, at the time of Kandinsky's first exhibition at the Galerie des Cahiers d'Art in Paris, Christian Zervos wrote: "The influence of nature on his work has never been so perceptible as in the canvases painted in Paris. The atmosphere, light, airiness and sky of the Ile-de-France completely transform the expressiveness of his work."[1]

Other significant changes took place when Kandinsky resumed work in Paris early in 1934. He returned to painting large canvases, he began to add sand to discrete areas of his paintings, and he incorporated biomorphic—even biological—forms into his art. However, these features had been tentatively introduced before or—in the case of the large size of his pictures—had once been prevalent in Kandinsky's work. Thus, it becomes exceedingly difficult to differentiate between innovation and the culmination of earlier tendencies.

Certain biographical facts about the artist clarify the changes that accompanied Kandinsky's relocation to Paris. This was the second time he was forced to leave Germany because of political events. Moreover, Kandinsky and his wife, Nina, had left their native Russia in December 1921 and during the intervening years had lived in Weimar, Dessau, and Berlin. Although he did not move to France until the very end of 1933, the transition from the

Bauhaus in Germany to Paris took place gradually from 1928 to 1934.[2] He took annual trips there during this time, and his work was exhibited at the Galerie Zak in January 1929, at the Galerie de France in March 1930, in the *Cercle et Carré* group show in the spring of 1930, and at the Surrealist exhibition of the *Association Artistique Les Surindépendants* during the autumn of 1933. Following the closing of the Bauhaus in Berlin in July 1933, Vasily and Nina Kandinsky spent time in France and Switzerland: they arrived in Paris on December 21, 1933, and were installed in a new apartment in Neuilly-sur-Seine by the beginning of 1934. Not surprisingly, there is a hiatus in Kandinsky's work between August 1933, when he painted *Development in Brown* (RB 1031) in Berlin, and February 1934, when he resumed work in Paris and titled his first picture *Start* (B 1146).[3]

When Kandinsky began to paint again in 1934, he introduced certain specific and original motifs into his work. By analyzing the images in his pictures, it is possible to determine when new motifs entered his pictorial vocabulary and which forms persist from previous periods. For example, *Graceful Ascent* of March 1934 (RB 1033) retains the geometric and curvilinear imagery as well as the strict hierarchical grid-like structure of his Bauhaus work. However, the pastel hues and delicate nuances of value signal the lightness and sweetness of color he created during the Paris period.

The new motifs the artist introduced in 1934 must be singled out and identified. These forms derive from the world of biology—especially zoology and embryology—and from the work of other artists with which Kandinsky was familiar. In 1934 there is a remarkable incidence in his painting of images of amoebae, embryos, larvae, and marine invertebrates, as well as leaf forms and punctuation marks. By focusing on the period from 1934 through 1937 the new imagery of Kandinsky's late work will be defined and interpreted. Once established, his new iconography is continued and elaborated upon throughout his Paris work.

Although the title *Start*, which Kandinsky gave the first painting he did in Paris, would appear to be an English word, "start" was an international term commonly used in sports.[4] *Start* vividly conveys the fast beginning associated with a race or takeoff. With reference to Kandinsky's resumption of painting after a lengthy hiatus, it seems somewhat ironic but clearly expresses an optimistic beginning. The artist contrasts circular, square, and rectangular forms with four distinctly amoeboid shapes whose amorphousness is immediately remarkable and innovative. In fact, Kandinsky introduced images of amoebas—a simple unicellular form of life—into his paintings in 1934. It is especially significant that this most elemental stage of life is depicted in a work of art titled *Start*. The concurrence of image and meaning cannot be accidental.

He elaborates upon the simple amoeboid form in the canvas *Each for Himself* of April 1934. The central white figures and, to an even greater degree, the watercolor study for it (B 1148), resemble an amoeba in overall shape (including pseudopods) and in internal details such as vacuoles.

Likewise, the figure in the upper right corner possesses decidedly cellular characteristics and vaguely embryonic qualities. Each figure is enclosed in a womb-like shape; in particular, the one at the lower right corner looks like a uterus. Although two of the nine images are amoeboid, others bear striking similarities to drawings by Pablo Picasso and Julio González. Not only are the figures in *Each for Himself* innovative but also the format of the picture is new in Kandinsky's work. By organizing three registers of three figures each in compartmentalized zones, Kandinsky presents the mathematical format that recurs in *Thirty* of 1937 (RB 1074), *Fifteen* of 1938 (B 1223), and *4 × 5 = 20* of 1943 (RB 1162). The simplicity and rigid geometry of the pictorial organization can be found in a coeval painting by Victor Brauner, *Petite morphologie*, where nine figures are arranged in three rows. Brauner's work was shown together with that of Kandinsky at the Surrealist exhibition in the autumn of 1933.

In *Black Forms on White*, which was also painted in April 1934, the black amoeboid shapes shown on a white ground in the center suggest a macrophage. In addition, various forms of primitive life are indicated by the white shapes on black ground in the peripheral zones. Contemporary illustrations of both amoeboid and embryonic forms prove the relevance of biological knowledge to Kandinsky's painting. *Black Forms on White* also contains forms suggestive of elements in blood: two white circles with centers at the left edge can be identified as red cells, the two small amoeboid shapes at the top can be associated with white cells, and the small curved elements at the upper left and lower right corners look like platelets.[5]

The difficulty and the complexity of problems encountered in interpreting Kandinsky's pictures become apparent when *Black Forms on White* is compared with a drawing by Hans Arp published in *Le Surréalisme au Service de la Révolution* in 1933.[6] The curving forms, the large figure with eyes at the right and the overall configuration are amazingly similar in Arp's drawing and this painting of 1934. Did Kandinsky and Arp share common interests in specific biological forms and in natural growth? To what extent did he seek inspiration from science in general and zoology and embryology in particular?

In May 1934, Kandinsky completed the large painting *Between Two*. Here two curving forms face each other; they are defined as sand-covered areas on the canvas and are set off from the red background. The figure on the left bears an overwhelming resemblance to an embryo. The large eye and lateral articulation as well as the definition of specific areas leave no doubt as to the identity of the image and certainly demand explanation. Moreover, the curved form on the right seems embryonic, its curved internal rod resembles a notochord and the adjacent black area can be interpreted as a yolk sac.[7]

The many volumes of the encyclopedia, *Die Kultur der Gegenwart* [Culture of the Present] (published in Leipzig and Berlin), to which Kandinsky referred in his illustrations from the mid-1920s for the book *Punkt und Linie zu Fläche* [Point and Line to Plane], can be found in his library in Paris. Diagrams of human embryos from two volumes in this series provide specific images known to the artist. In addition, the circles on the red background that surround the embryonic form in

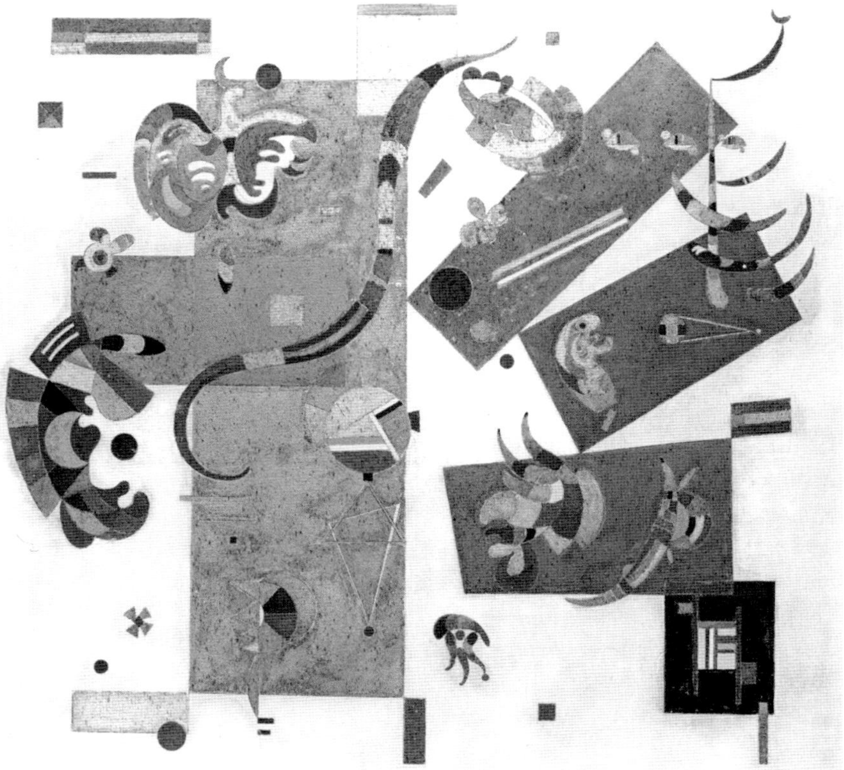

10.1a Vasily Kandinsky, *Monde bleu* [Blue World], 1934, 110 × 120 cm. Solomon R. Guggenheim Museum, New York. © 2009 Artists Rights Society (ARS), New York/ ADAGP, Paris

Between Two resemble the blood cells illustrated in the encyclopedia volume that covers zoology on the page opposite a diagram Kandinsky copied for *Point and Line to Plane*.[8] Even his title, *Entre deux*, alludes to the fact that a new life begins from the union between two people.

The next painting Kandinsky created in May 1934 was *Blue World* (Fig. 10.1a). Although the imagery of *Blue World* is more fanciful and imaginative than that of the preceding work, various embryological and larval forms can be identified. The most obvious embryo is situated to the right of center on an ochre sand-covered rectangle. In addition, the figure at the upper left resembles a fish embryo (Fig. 10.1b) and the curved large-bellied shape on the salmon-colored rectangular zone at the lower right suggests a salamander embryo. Adjacent to the latter in Kandinsky's painting are multicolored segmented creatures that seem to be insects.[9] Moreover, the large blue worm-form in the middle of *Blue World* looks like a nematode. The volume of Kandinsky's encyclopedia devoted to zoology contains all of the scientific diagrams cited as well as related illustrations of insect embryos.[10]

All of the Kandinsky paintings discussed above were exhibited during late May to June 1934 at Zervos's Galerie des 'Cahiers d'Art' in Paris in a small one-man show that took place after Joan Miró's exhibition there and before Max Ernst's.[11] Kandinsky and Christian Zervos first met in 1927, Zervos published Will Grohmann's monograph on Kandinsky in January 1931 and the following year the artist contributed an article to Zervos's publication, *Cahiers d'Art*.

After this exhibition, during the summer of 1934, Kandinsky executed *Relations* (RB 1041) and *Dominant Violet*. In both, he has accentuated precise, pictorial elements by applying fine-textured sand to the canvas and painting over it. The imagery in these pictures derives from the world of nature and relies upon curving lines and whiplash lines. In *Relations* the forms resemble snakes, spermatozoa, worms, and parasites (for example, in the lower left corner) as well as birds. *Dominant Violet* prominently displays a large curving red shape on the right that looks like a nematode. However, the picture's connotations are predominantly those of the deep sea; the large billowing forms look like medusas, jellyfish and related marine invertebrates. Moreover, the shape at the lower right corner distinctly looks like cross-sections of medusas.

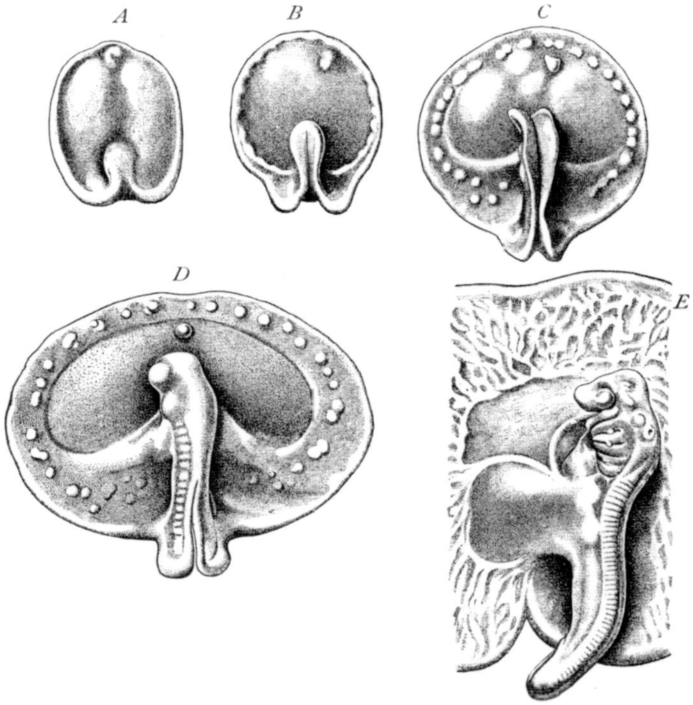

10.1b Fish embryo from *Zellen- und Gewebelehre: Morphologie und Entwicklungs-geschichte. II. Zoologischer Teil (Die Kultur der Gegenwart,* 1913), 358

Kandinsky's predilection for abstractions that originate in natural forms and his fanciful and imaginative stylization of natural forms bring to mind the well-known volumes by Ernst Heinrich Haeckel, *Kunstformen der Natur* [Art Forms of Nature], of which he owned the 1904 edition. Although Haeckel's beautifully colored illustrations belong to an Art Nouveau aesthetic, many reproductions can be linked with Kandinsky's work:[12] for example, one of the many renditions of medusas can be related to *Dominant Violet*. Another plate from *Kunstformen der Natur* that depicts microscopic marine-life (radiolaria) was reproduced in *Cahiers d'Art* early in 1934 and undoubtedly was known to Kandinsky.[13] The images in *Dominant Violet* and other paintings from 1934 to 1935 attest to Kandinsky's awareness of deep-sea life. Among the many clippings Kandinsky saved from magazines and newspapers is part of an article from *Die Koralle* [Coral] by G. von Borkow called "Life Under Pressure: The Unveiled Life."[14] Two illustrations from this article are particularly relevant to *Dominant Violet*: the firola or deep-sea snail resembles the undulating pink form at the upper right and deep-sea fish correspond to many curvilinear elements. Kandinsky's preoccupation with curved lines and his detailed analysis of them in *Point and Line to Plane* clearly indicate that he would have been fascinated by the bright and undulating lines of the deep-sea fish.

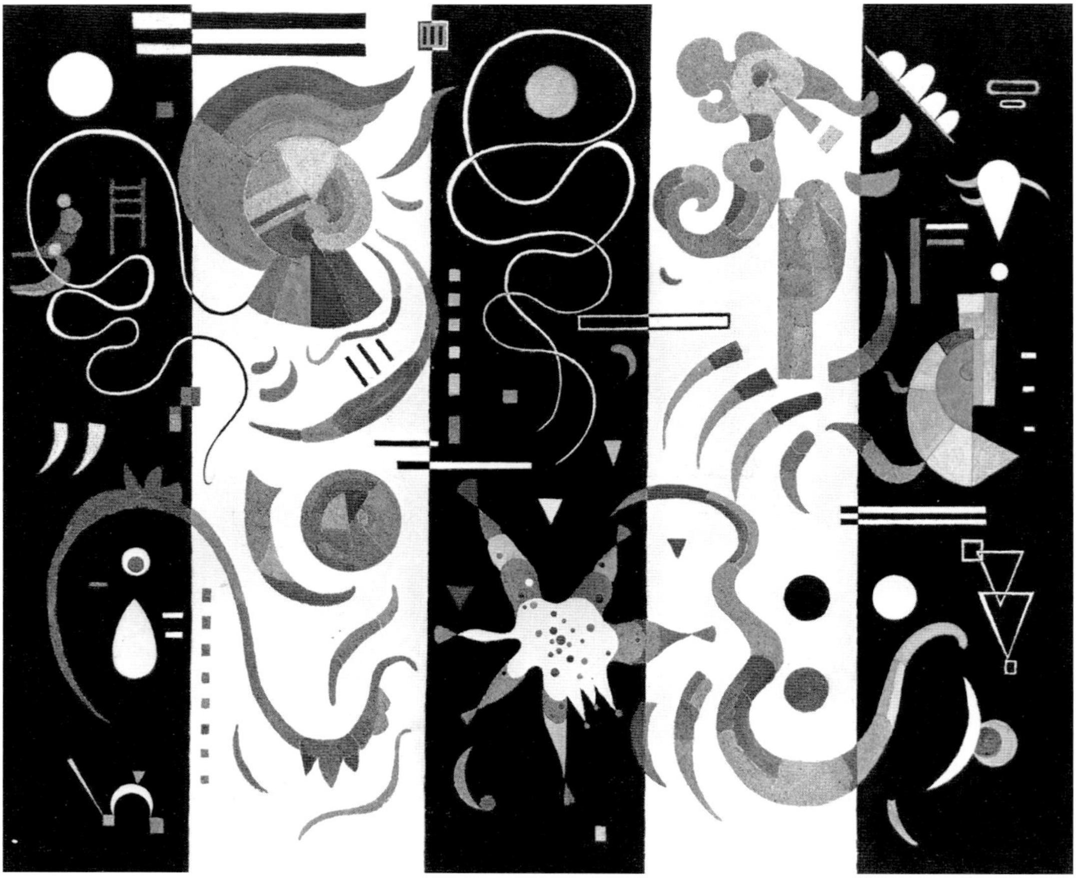

10.2a Vasily Kandinsky, *Striped* [Rayé], 1934, 81 × 100 cm. Solomon R. Guggenheim Museum, New York. © 2009 Artists Rights Society (ARS), New York/ ADAGP, Paris

A greatly enlarged photograph of plankton from von Borkow's article on deep-sea life has relevance to *Division-Unity* (RB 1044), among other pictures. Plankton, brine shrimp, snails, and larval stages of marine life become small, curving motifs that are evocatively and amusingly rendered in Kandinsky's work. Traces of these natural forms can be perceived in *Composition IX* (RB 1064) and *Multiple Forms* (RB 1065), both of 1936, *Sweet Trifles* of 1937 (RB 1077), and *Sky Blue* of 1940.

In the painting *Fragile-Fixed* of September 1934 (RB 1043), a specific leaf-shape enters Kandinsky's vocabulary. It recurs in modified form in *Balancing Act* of February 1935 (RB 1050) and again in *Brown with Supplement* of March (RB 1053). Here the bright green leaves recall the prominent and remarkably similar leaves in the work of Picasso and Henri Matisse. However, the large-scale and stylized outline of Kandinsky's leaves can be traced to another source known to him: Karl Blossfeldt's *Urformen der Kunst* [Original Forms of Art] which was published in Berlin in 1929. Two copies of the book exist in the artist's library. Blossfeldt's photographs consist primarily of flowers and leaves magnified to such a degree that they become abstractions. In June 1929 three such photographs were reproduced in the Parisian journal *Documents*.[15]

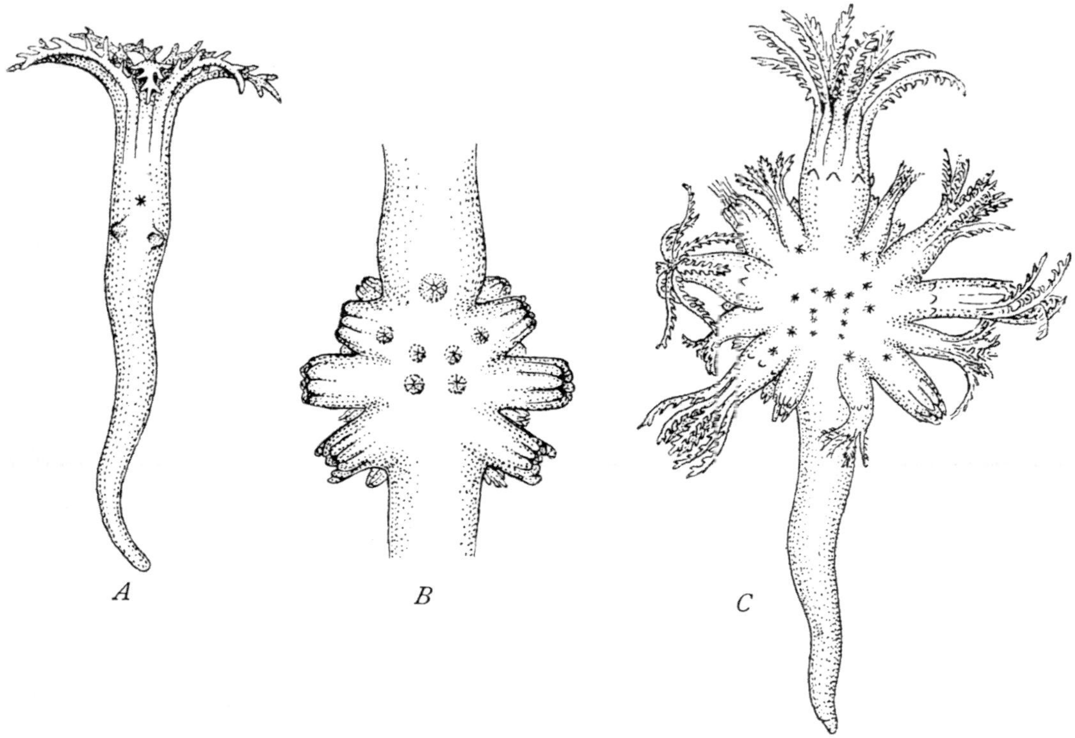

10.2b Sea polyps from *Allgemeine Biologie* (*Die Kultur der Gegenwart*, 1915), 411

Blossfeldt's significance as a photographer, like Haeckel's as an illustrator, lay in his discovery of art in nature.

The last painting Kandinsky did in 1934 exemplifies the richness of his imagery and the invention of his pictorial forms. *Striped* (Fig. 10.2a) unites alternating black and white vertical bands, whiplash lines, and biological forms with similar configurations (snakes, worms, and nematodes), and it juxtaposes birds at the upper left with an exclamation point at the upper right. In the central segment, a red circle at the top contrasts with a star-shaped biomorphic form below. In a preparatory drawing, the distinctive structure of the multi-tentacled form emphasizes the central nucleus and accentuates the many entwining legs—characteristics of an echinoid, a species related to the common five-legged starfish. The depiction of a stage in the growth of sea polyps in the biology volume of Kandinsky's encyclopedia (Fig. 10.2b) recalls the star shape in *Striped*. In the canvas, the distinctions between nucleus and tentacles are preserved and the colorful dots in the center correspond to those in the diagram.

The affinities between Kandinsky's imagery and forms in nature do not, however, preclude references to paintings by other artists. The tentacled, many-legged form articulated most clearly in Kandinsky's drawing brings to mind Miró's spider-like motif as a sign for female genitalia. Comparison of *Striped* and Miró's *Carnival of Harlequin* of 1924–25 reveals not only similarities in specific motifs but also in overall composition. Soon after his arrival in Paris, Kandinsky met Miró and he surely saw the Surrealist's work in exhibitions—such as that at the Galerie des 'Cahiers d'Art' in May 1934—as well as in periodicals. Moreover, *Carnival of Harlequin* was one of several influential pictures by Miró illustrated in the first issue of *Cahiers d'Art* in 1934 (no. I-4), which immediately preceded the issue with Zervos's article devoted to Kandinsky's first Paris pictures. The motifs in such paintings by Kandinsky as *Delicate Accents* of 1935 (RB 1062), *Black Points* (RB 1075), and *Accompanied Center* of 1937 (RB 1079) attest to his familiarity with Miró's work.[16]

During 1934 certain specific signs entered Kandinsky's pictorial vocabulary. The exclamation point makes its first appearance in *Striped*, and a single quotation mark or inverted comma can be discerned at the left edge in *Dominant Violet* and at the bottom center in *Striped*. The latter motif is isolated and accentuated in *Green Accent* of 1935 (RB 1061) and totally dominates *Circuit* of 1939 (RB 1101). The exclamation point recurs in *Rigid and Bent* of 1935 (RB 1063) and *Sweet Trifles* of 1937. These signs had appeared in many works by Miró and Paul Klee. Pictorial signs such as arrows, exclamation points, and apostrophes, as well as numbers and words, functioned as integral parts of Klee's compositions.[17] Kandinsky and Klee were close friends, who worked side by side at the Bauhaus in Dessau from 1926 until 1933, and stayed in contact even after they left Germany. Exclamation points can be found in Klee's pictures produced during the late 1910s and early 1920s, and they become especially prevalent in 1932. Kandinsky was surely familiar with Klee's paintings including exclamation points: *Around the Fish* of 1926, which was reproduced in Grohmann's monograph on Klee in 1929; and *Departure of the Ghost* of 1931, which was illustrated in the same issue of *Cahiers d'Art* including Zervos's article on Kandinsky in 1934.

In comparison with the remarkable innovations made in Kandinsky's work in 1934, the introduction of new motifs subsided during 1935–36. At this time the artist developed and elaborated upon the imagery he had recently invented. Paintings such as *Accompanied Contrast* (RB 1051) and *Two Green Points* (RB 1054) retain images prevalent during the early 1930s, while the style of others—for example, *Two Circles* (RB 1052) and *Points* (RB 1059)—shares similarities with the geometric idiom associated with the Bauhaus period in general. In terms of specific images reflecting an awareness of natural sciences and biomorphic forms, several pictures provide relevant motifs. *Succession* (Fig. 10.3a), which was painted in April 1935, consists of four horizontal registers that contain brightly colored, curving shapes. This format is familiar from the Bauhaus period, specifically from the watercolor *Rows of Signs* of 1931 (B 1052). Although the 1935 canvas and the watercolor share the same composition, the imagery of the Paris picture represents a significant departure from that of his Bauhaus work. The thrust of the curving shapes and the distinctive placement of small circles balanced on these forms in the painting recall an illustration of saccharomyces fungus in Kandinsky's encyclopedia (Fig. 10.3b). A diagram of cells from salamander larvae in another volume of this encyclopedia can also be associated with the dynamic forms in *Succession*. Not only the individual shapes but also their schematic articulation is similar in Kandinsky's painting and the scientific diagrams.

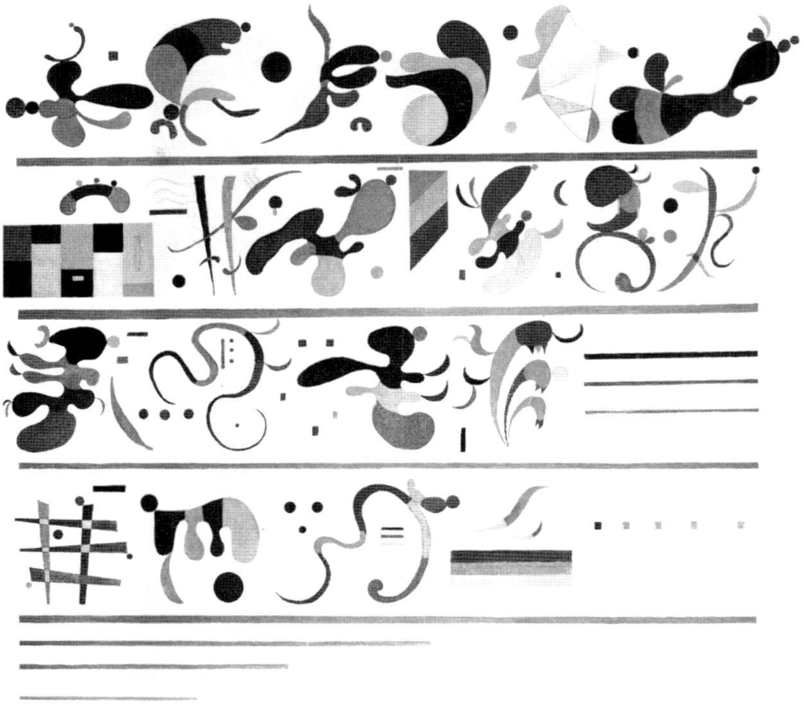

10.3a Vasily Kandinsky, *Succession*, 1935, 81 × 100 cm. The Phillips Collection, Washington DC.

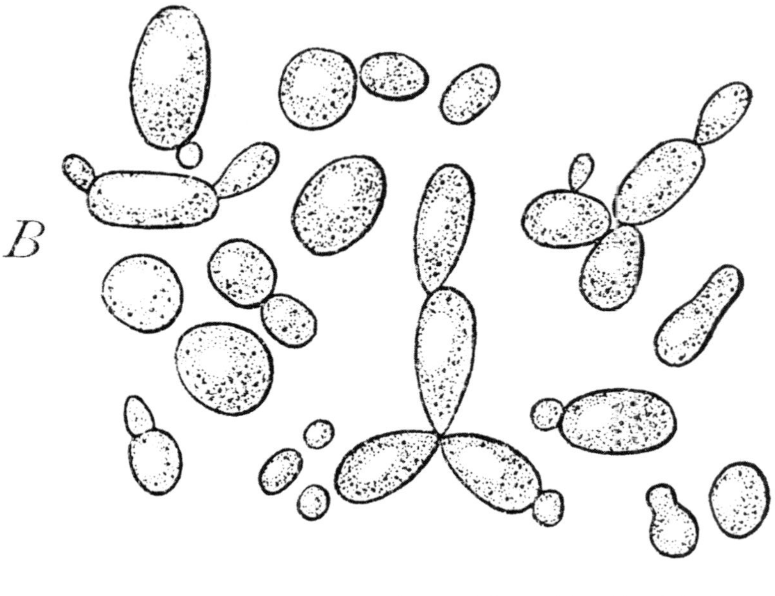

10.3b Saccharomyces fungus from *Zellen- und Gewebelehre: Morphologie und Entwicklungsgeschichte. I. Botanischer Teil*, (*Die Kultur der Gegenwart*, 1913), 74

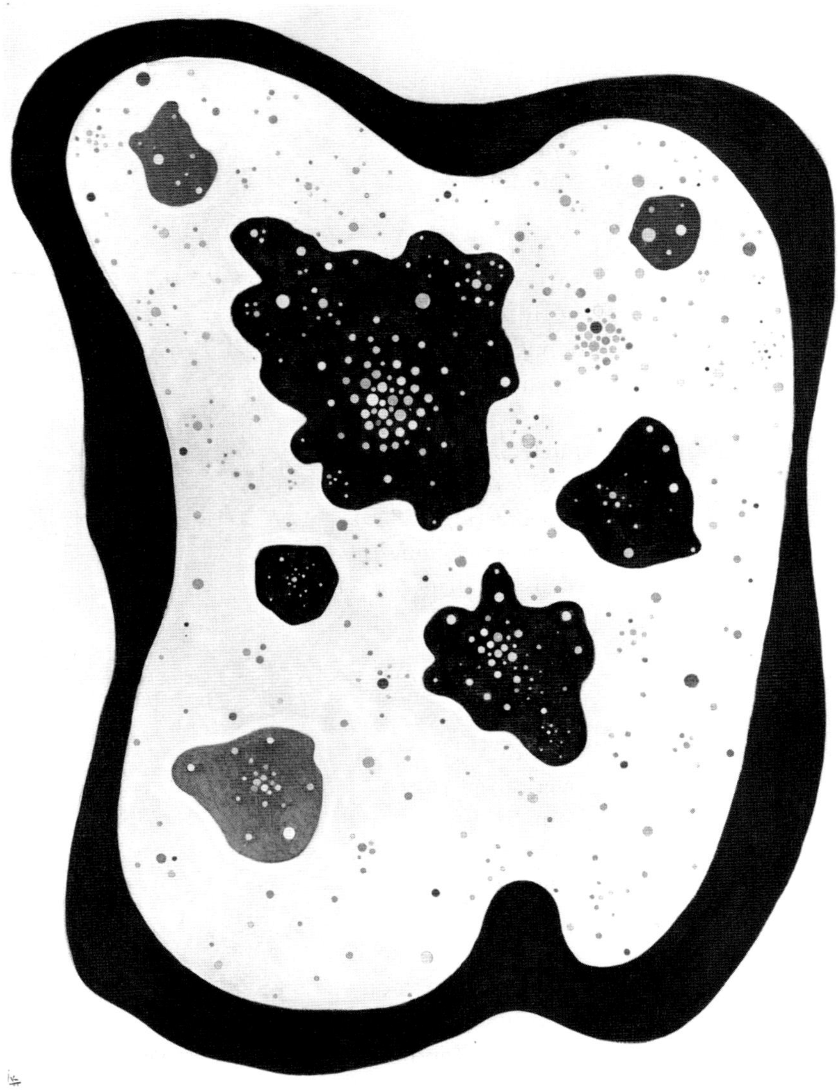

10.4a Vasily Kandinsky, *Environnement* [Environment], 1936, 100 × 81 cm. Solomon R. Guggenheim Museum, New York. © 2009 Artists Rights Society (ARS), New York/ ADAGP, Paris

Several paintings from 1935–36 depict embryos. In *Variegated Black* of October 1935 (RB 1058) three embryonic forms are recognizable: an early stage at the left edge, an adjacent, more clearly identifiable one painted white with a pink eye, and a bright green imaginative variant on the right. In Kandinsky's major canvas *Composition IX*, which was completed by February 1936, an obviously embryonic shape at the upper left is represented together with a yolk sac. Even the pink and white vertical zones can be read as the placental barrier that separates the fetal side from the maternal side. In the central portion of *Composition IX*, there is an ambiguity in the form that resembles both an embryo and a brine shrimp or crayfish.[18] Elsewhere in the painting embryonic images also merge with allusions to brine shrimp and plankton. An exactly coeval picture, *Multiple Forms* (RB 1065), manifests similar embryonic and crustacean images. In a preparatory drawing for it, the depiction of a fish at the upper left (omitted from the final version) resembles the angler fish in Kandinsky's clipping from von Borkow's article in *Die Koralle*. Likewise, the image at the lower corner of *Multiple Forms* is clearly that of a fish.

In another painting, *Environment* from October 1936 (Fig. 10.4a), Kandinsky has depicted an amoeba in greatly enlarged scale. The cell wall is clearly defined; many small multi-colored circles represent the cytoplasm and several colored zones correspond to vacuoles and a nucleus. Moreover, Kandinsky's painting closely resembles an illustration in his encyclopedia (Fig. 10.4b). Of all Kandinsky's works where biological references can be discerned, *Environment* is probably the most direct and obvious.

Sweet Trifles of 1937 is based on rigid bilateral compartmentalization. Within the boxes Kandinsky juxtaposes geometric patterns with biomorphic forms. He places an exclamation point over an earthworm balancing on an imaginatively colored caterpillar and positions an arrow next to a bright blue amphibian perching on a slug. The playfulness and humor of the picture are conveyed by its title, *Bagatelles douces*, and by the exclamation point. On the left side, the articulation of many forms suggests cellular matter; moreover, in the lower right corner the multicellular form distinctly resembles an illustration of the nucleus of an echinoderm in the zoology volume of *Die Kultur der Gegenwart*.

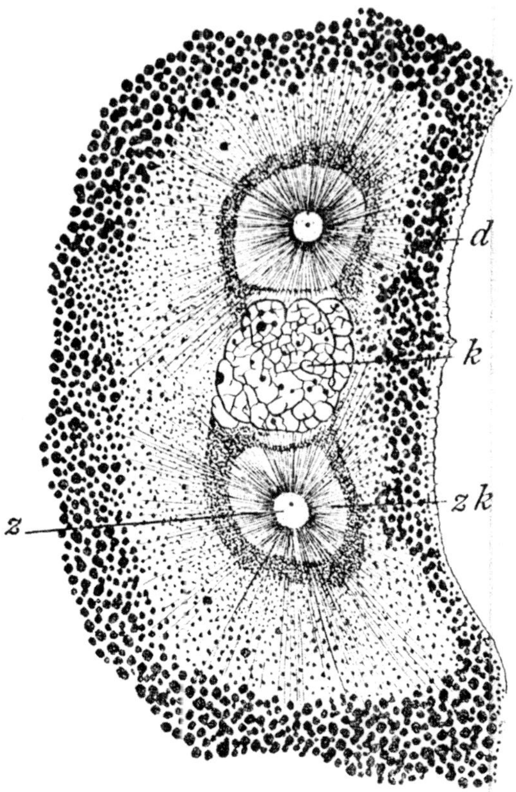

10.4b Cell of worm egg from *Zellen- und Gewebelehre: Morphologie und Entwicklungs-geschichte. I. Zoologischer Teil (Die Kultur der Gegenwart*, 1913), 49

During the summer of 1937, Kandinsky painted *Capricious Forms* (RB 1081), in which the imagery is emphatically biological. Yellow, pink, tan, and green shapes look like sections of soft tissue. Specifically, the forms at bottom center and in the middle at the left edge are clearly recognizable as embryonic; others resemble contemporary illustrations of placental tissue. In a sketchbook containing many preparatory drawings, Kandinsky made a study with colored pencils for *Capricious Forms* which includes a greater variety of hues than the final version and shows an overall pink tonality. In the canvas, red and green circles accentuate the shapes as well as the detailed red, blue, and green linear patterns that articulate distinct layers of tissue.

In April 1938, Kandinsky completed two oil paintings in which there are clear biological references. *Many-Colored Ensemble* contains within an oval center a plethora of small circles that have cellular associations. In addition, there are shapes resembling nematode and annelid worms, a pink bird at the left and an embryonic form at the right. More stylized variations on this embryonic form persist in his work throughout the late 1930s and early 1940s. In *Penetrating Green* from April 1938 (RB 1089), a red sperm is immediately recognizable and is prominently placed in the middle of the composition within a vertical receptacle on a green ground. Two large shapes that vaguely resemble sperm fill the lateral zones. Even Kandinsky's title is expressive of the imagery and leaves little doubt about the meaning.

By 1938 Kandinsky's images become more fanciful, stylized, and even decorative. For example, *Sky Blue* of March 1940 retains biomorphic forms familiar from the first years in Paris, but these are transformed into stylizations of the motifs. For the most part, Kandinsky's paintings, watercolors, and drawings from 1938 and after no longer manifest the overtly zoological and embryological motifs that characterize his work from 1934 to 1937. There are, however, vestiges of biological entities as well as specific biomorphic images. In general, Kandinsky does not depict embryonic forms after 1938; however, the exceptions—*An Intimate Celebration* of 1942 (RB 1139) and *Brown Impetus* of 1943 (RB 1152)—refer back to *Blue World* and *Variegated Black*. Another painting from 1943, *Circle and Square* (RB 1153), shows four figures with clear sexual references; the representation of phallic images is indisputable.

In addition to the visual evidence which has been described at length, there is substantial physical evidence and significant documentary proof to link images in Kandinsky's art with scientific illustrations in his encyclopedia. In preparation for *Point and Line to Plane*, which was published in 1926, he executed a pencil drawing with the inscription *"Lockeres Bindegewebe von der Ratte"* [loose connective tissue of the rat] and also specified the source, *"D. Kult. d. Gegenw.,"* the volume [*Abteilung IV*^{2}] and page number.[19] It is this volume on zoology that contains by far the largest number of illustrations corresponding to images in Kandinsky's work. In addition to the obvious reference in *Point and Line to Plane*, the artist left traces in his own copy of this encyclopedia volume. Next to page 5, where an amoeba is illustrated, there is a small piece of paper with Kandinsky's handwriting and facing page 234, where an annelid is reproduced, his calling card is inserted as a marker.[20] In the other volume of Abteilung IV^{2}, whose subject is botany, Kandinsky put slips of paper between pages 138 and 139 and between 154 and 155, and wrote on each *"Kreis"* [circle]. The illustration on page 138 depicts the cross-section of a plant stem with many rings of quite uniform circles, while that on page 139 contains rounded shapes of much greater variety in size and configuration. In view of Kandinsky's love for the circle as a formal element as well as the symbolic significance of the motif in his work from about 1922 to 1930,[21] it is not surprising that he would respond to obviously circular forms in his encyclopedia. What is interesting is the way he sees abstract forms of art in nature.

In the volume on general biology, the invitation card to the opening of Kandinsky's exhibition at the Galerie Ferdinand Möller on January 30, 1932, is placed between pages 218 and 219. In addition, inserted in the section on botany in the volumes on physiology and ecology are an invitation to an opening for the *Kreis der Freunde des Bauhauses* [Circle of Friends of the Bauhaus] on January 15, 1932, and an invitation to a Lyonel Feininger exhibition organized by this group the same month. The fact that all three markers date from January 1932 proves that Kandinsky was using his encyclopedia at that time. During the 1920s, volumes of the same encyclopedia were influential for Klee.[22] Moreover, other artists at the Bauhaus were aware of various volumes on science in this series. However, the impact of its biological illustrations—principally from the volume on zoology—becomes apparent in Kandinsky's work only after he moved to Paris.

Likewise, there is evidence that Kandinsky cut the photographic reproductions out of magazines and newspapers during the early 1930s, while he was still at the Bauhaus.[23] The article on deep-sea life in *Die Koralle* appeared in February 1931. Virtually all the press cuttings have captions in German, thus indicating a date prior to 1934. Although most of the specific publications remain unidentified, many of the images are of animals, airplanes, people from non-Western cultures, objects shown under high magnification, and subjects that could generally be characterized as "technology" and "nature". In his Bauhaus teaching notes for the second, or summer semester of 1931, Kandinsky compared art, science, technology, and nature.[24] His list of images to show includes a Mercedes-Benz car, a Junkers airplane, an aerial view, and a giraffe: photographs of the illustrations still exist among the artist's papers. Another very significant clipping shows diatoms arranged within a rigid, bilateral format that resembles the pictorial organization of *Sweet Trifles*. Diatoms—unicellular algae or microscopic plankton found in both fresh and salt water—are recognizable in several of Kandinsky's paintings from the Paris years.

Thus, Kandinsky's interest in scientific and natural phenomena is demonstrated by his treatise *Point and Line to Plane* and by his pedagogical material for the Bauhaus courses. Likewise, his familiarity with volumes of his encyclopedia, *Die Kultur der Gegenwart*, is confirmed by these sources.[25] However, the artist only introduced biological motifs into his work after he moved to Paris. It is relevant, at this point, to consider what natural history and scientific resources were available there in 1934. Although there is no proof that Kandinsky ever visited the Muséum National d'Histoire Naturelle in Paris, its extensive and impressive collections, which were permanently on view in galleries adjacent to the Jardin des Plantes, would have been accessible and instructive. Photographs dating from 1932 to 1935 in the Muséum Archives document the Galerie de Zoologie and the Galerie d'Anatomie Comparée de Paléontologie et d'Anthropologie. The former contained vast numbers of cases filled with all varieties of fish, starfish, crustaceans, shells, and insects.[26] Immediately upon entering the latter, one found thousands of fetal specimens of many species in glass jars, organized according to the embryological development of organs and central systems. The collection of comparative anatomy was founded by Georges Cuvier.[27] It cannot be coincidental that, in one of Kandinsky's encyclopedia volumes, there are obvious signs of perusal (coffee stains) as well as a marker for the pages relevant to Cuvier.[28] It should be mentioned that the Musée d'Ethnographie at the Muséum National d'Histoire Naturelle was closed August 1935 and reopened at the new location at the present Trocadéro on the occasion of the *Exposition Internationale des Arts et Techniques* in 1937.

At Paris, early in 1934, Kandinsky surely became aware of a general interest in science there and he must have perceived even more acutely the current predilection for Surrealist art. The previous autumn, Kandinsky had exhibited with the Surrealists in the annual show organized by the *Association Artistique Les Surindépendants*. By the 1930s there was no longer a strong Surrealist movement in Paris, since various members of the group were by then pursuing different directions. However, Kandinsky encountered several individuals who had been associated with the Surrealist group soon after his arrival: he saw Arp and met Miró in March and he had contact with Max Ernst and Man Ray in June. Kandinsky's paintings such as *Striped* and *Accompanied Center* relate to both biological forms and Surrealist imagery in the work of Miró. To an even greater degree, a correspondence is visible between Kandinsky's pictures and Arp's work, where organic shapes with their sense of vitality and growth are particularly evocative. Images similar to the freestanding biomorphic forms familiar from Arp's sculptures can be detected in Kandinsky's canvases *Composition IX* of 1936 and *Various Actions* of 1941 (RB 1121). Arp's relief *Two Heads* of 1929 closely resembles specific rounded forms in Kandinsky's painting *Dominant Violet*, as well as the encyclopedia illustration depicting the stages in the development of a worm. The congruence of biological forms and Surrealist motifs is striking—and refers to the work of Arp. In fact, it was Surrealism in general and Arp and Miró in particular that probably inspired Kandinsky to introduce biological images into his work in 1934.

Kandinsky's art differs from the work of the Surrealists in several essential ways: it does not delve into the unconscious and it does not concern itself with either mythology or dreams. In his pictures there is no evidence of the influence of Freud and psychoanalysis. Kandinsky never experimented with automatism and did not use accident as a creative method. His work lacks both found objects and collages. Moreover, Kandinsky did not share the Communist political orientation of many Surrealists. Although Kandinsky's correspondence reflects a definite opposition to Surrealism, his published writings are more restrained. In his 1937 essay, "Assimilations of Art," written for an issue of *Linien*, he reveals a relatively moderate position toward forms in nature:

> Therefore, I do not become shocked when a form that resembles a "form in nature" insinuates itself secretively into my other forms. I just let it stay there and I will not erase it. Who knows, maybe all our "abstract" forms are "forms in nature," but … "objects of use?"
>
> These art forms and forms in nature (without purpose) have an even clearer sound that we must absolutely listen to.[29]

While Kandinsky's writings are critical of Surrealism, they say surprisingly little about biological sciences—especially embryology and zoology.[30] The few references in *Point and Line to Plane* and in his Bauhaus teaching notes have already been cited. In the latter, he discusses zoology and equates unicellular organisms (protozoa) with organisms capable of polymorphic development, and thus of becoming "a sum"; and he speaks of protozoa as "original beings."[31] In August 1935, Kandinsky wrote a short text for the Danish periodical *Konkretion*, in which he referred to his earlier published writings and stated that:

> this experience of the "hidden soul" in all the things, seen either by the unaided eye or through microscopes or binoculars, is what I call the "internal eye." This eye penetrates the hard shell, the external "form," goes deep into the object and lets us feel with all our senses its internal "pulse."[32]

Since an explanation or documentation of the embryological and zoological forms in Kandinsky's paintings is absent from his writings, interpretations and meanings proposed for them remain hypothetical. The very fact that embryos are depicted so frequently in Kandinsky's work in 1934 and subsequent years raises questions about his personal life. Early in 1917 the artist, then fifty-one years old, married Nina Andreevskaia, who was very much younger than he. According to all the information known about them, and according to their friends, the couple had no children. After Nina Kandinsky's death, it became known that they had had a son called Volodia, who was born in September 1917 and died in June 1920. This fact remained a complete secret during Vasily's and Nina's lifetimes. Although there is no evidence that events in Kandinsky's life influenced his art, the subconscious effects of personal experiences may have emerged many years after their occurrence. When he was old and relatively isolated in Paris, Kandinsky's awareness of his childlessness may have become increasingly acute.

Approached from an entirely different point of view, Kandinsky's paintings of the Paris period suggest a specific biological and philosophical concept.[33] His apparently conscious effort to create biomorphic forms that simultaneously resemble embryos and marine invertebrates can be related to the "principle of recapitulation," the rule or heuristic maxim that the development of the embryo of each organism passes rapidly through phases resembling its evolutionary ancestors. Thus, it is commonly observed that the human fetus successively takes on fish-like, amphibian, reptilian, and bird-like characteristics before developing distinctly mammalian features. Furthermore, the human embryo shares these stages, which occur during the first several weeks of development, with all mammal embryos. The diagram of comparative embryological development was made after Darwin and supports his theory by showing that successive evolutionary specializations are superimposed on existing structures, and that the earlier stages are vestigially retained.

There are a number of hypothetical reasons why Kandinsky would have been interested in, even intrigued with, the principle of recapitulation, which was extremely popular from 1870 to 1910.[34] While the principle that ontogeny (embryonic development) repeats phylogeny (successive evolution of major zoological groups) antedates Darwinian evolution theory by several decades, the most fruitful application of the principle was as an indirect proof of evolution itself. The person who attempted this proof was Ernst Heinrich Haeckel, who was one of Darwin's most prominent early supporters. Haeckel used the principle to make major advances in linking comparative anatomy to embryology in his area of greatest expertise, marine invertebrates. He also used the principle to postulate the "missing link," Pithecanthropus, between "man and ape". In his fieldwork, Haeckel focused on marine invertebrates—radiolaria, hydras and medusas—the very images prevalent in Kandinsky's Paris pictures. An accomplished draftsman, he was responsible for the illustrations as well as the text in *Kunstformen der Natur*. However, he was most famous for his theoretical work in embryology.[35] Around the turn of the century, Haeckel's fame was such that Kandinsky must have been familiar with his work.[36]

Second, Kandinsky would have been interested in the phylogeny/ontogeny recapitulation principle because of its resemblance to an ancient, spiritually oriented philosophical theme which inverts its order; namely the intellectual or spiritual development of humanity from prehistoric times corresponds to the intellectual and spiritual growth of each individual. Georg Wilhelm Friedrich Hegel's *Phenomenology of Mind* and *Philosophy of History* are founded on this principle and it is prevalent in the work of a variety of nineteenth-century thinkers such as Ralph Waldo Emerson and Herbert Spencer.

Finally, Kandinsky is known to have been familiar with Theosophy and its literature.[37] There is evidence in the writings of H.P. Blavatsky, the founder of the movement, that she and other Theosophists were both acutely aware of and ambivalent toward mid-nineteenth-century developments in natural history and embryology. Although Blavatsky abhorred the materialistic interpretation that Haeckel and Thomas Henry Huxley gave to the recapitulation principle, she cited parallels to it in ancient cabalistic and Vedantic writings. The Theosophists believed that man's spirit governed the whole evolutionary process and that humanity developed from amorphous egg-like creatures through a hermaphrodite stage before becoming sexually differentiated. Thus, the Theosophists came to agree with the most advanced biologists that all life proceeds from a single original germ. However, for Theosophists this germ is not protoplasm but the spirit. Rudolf Steiner lectured extensively on Haeckel and his theories of evolution in relation to Theosophy in 1905–1906 and his text "Haeckel, die Welträtsel und die Theosophie" [Haeckel, the Riddle of the Universe and Theosophy] was first published in *Lucifer Gnosis* no. 31, in 1905.[38] By 1913, when Steiner organized the Anthroposophical Society, the relevant texts had been published in many editions in German and they would later be translated into Russian, French, and English.[39]

In terms of Kandinsky's painting, embryological imagery can be interpreted on multiple levels. First, the embryonic forms are not immediately recognizable: art historians, critics, and viewers in general have been slow to identify even the part of nature from which he derived his motifs.[40] As in the paintings Kandinsky executed in Munich before World War I, the images are hidden and abstracted from reality. When natural forms are shown under great magnification or excerpted from their contexts, their identities are disguised. However, a leaf is still a leaf even though it no longer looks like one. Second, an embryo is not recognizable as an adult member of its species yet it contains implicitly everything that it will become. The genetic makeup of each embryo is a generalized image. At an early stage, it is neither ostensibly human nor individual: it is already an abstraction.

In a note to *Point and Line to Plane*, Kandinsky explicitly connects embryonic and evolutionary development to abstract art:

> Abstract art, despite its emancipation, is subject here also to "natural laws," and is obliged to proceed in the same way that nature did previously, when it started in a modest way with protoplasm and cells, progressing very gradually to increasingly complex organisms. Today, abstract art creates also primary or more or less primary art-organisms, whose further development the artist today can predict only in uncertain outline, and which entice, excite him, but also calm him when he stares into the prospect of the future that faces him. Let me observe here that those who doubt the future of abstract art are, to choose an example, as if reckoning with the stage of development reached by amphibians, which are far removed from fully developed vertebrates and represent not the final result of creation, but rather the "beginning."[41]

Kandinsky's images of amoebas, embryos, and marine invertebrates convey a spiritual meaning of beginning, regeneration, and a common origin of all life. Because of his spiritual beliefs and his ideas on abstract art, Kandinsky would have responded to the meanings of rebirth and renewal inherent in the new imagery of his Paris pictures.

Notes

This text is an abridged version of the essay published in 1985 in *Kandinsky and Paris*, the catalogue accompanying an exhibition at the Guggenheim Museum in New York. I am grateful to Christian Derouet and Jessica Boissel for assisting with my research at the Musée National d'Art Moderne, Centre Georges Pompidou, in Paris. I relied upon several people for their scientific knowledge and appreciate their essential help: Dr. Michael Bedford, Harold and Percy Uris Professor of Reproductive Biology, Cornell University Medical College; Dr. Arthur Karlin, Professor of Biochemistry and Neurology, College of Physicians and Surgeons of Columbia University; Dr. Niles Eldredge, American Museum of Natural History; Dr. Peter H. Barnett and Dr. Eric Wahl. The reader is advised to consult the original version of the essay for full acknowledgements and references.

1 Christian Zervos, "Notes sur Kandinsky," *Cahiers d'Art*, 9e année, nos. 5–8 (1934): 154.

2 Many years earlier, in 1906–07, Kandinsky had lived in Sèvres outside Paris with Gabriele Münter.

3 In the following text, works have been identified by catalogue raisonné numbers: RB refers to Hans K. Roethel and Jean K. Benjamin, *Kandinsky: Catalogue Raisonné of the Oil-Paintings, Volume Two 1916–1944* (London and Ithaca, NY: Cornell University Press, 1984); and B refers to Vivian Endicott Barnett, *Kandinsky Watercolours: Catalogue Raisonné Volume Two 1922–1944* (London and Ithaca, NY: Cornell University Press, 1994).

4 Hugo Moser, *Deutsche Sprachgeschichte,* 2nd ed. (Stuttgart: Schwab, 1955), 177.

5 I am indebted to Dr. Michael Bedford for these observations made in conversation with the author, July 2, 1984.

6 "L'Aire est une Racine," *Le Surréalisme au Service de la Révolution*, no. 6 (May 15, 1933): 33.

7 Observations made in conversation with the author by Dr. Arthur Karlin, May 4, 1984, and by Dr. Michael Bedford, July 2, 1984.

8 See Kenneth C. Lindsay and Peter Vergo, eds., *Kandinsky: Complete Writings on Art* (Boston, MA: G.K. Hall, 1982), vol. II, 630.

9 I would like to thank Dr. Niles Eldredge for bringing this to my attention in conversation, June 4, 1984.

10 *Zellen-und Gewebelehre: Morphologie und Entwicklungsgeschichte. II. Zoologischer Teil* (Berlin and Leipzig, 1913), 258, 269.

11 *Cahiers d'Art*, 9e année, no. 1–4 (1934), opposite p. 11. See also Kandinsky's letter to Josef Albers dated June 19, 1934.

12 Ernst Haeckel, *Kunstformen der Natur* (Leipzig, Wien: Bibliographisches Institut, 1904), pls. 4, 8, 18, 30, 47, 84, 94.

13 Plate 31 was reproduced in *Cahiers d'Art*, 9e année, nos. 1–4 (1934): 100.

14 G. von Borkow, "Leben unter Hochdruck: Die entschleierte Welt der Tiefsee," *Die Koralle*, Jg. 6, Heft II (Feb. 1931): 495–99. Kandinsky also cut out from the same issue an article by L. Schwarzfuss, "Die Zunge ist ja so interessant," with photographs of cats' tongues seen under magnification.

15 *Documents*, no. 3 (June 1929): 165, 167, 168.

16 See Stanley William Hayter, "The Language of Kandinsky," *Magazine of Art* 38 (May 1945): 178–79, for a comparison of *The Carnival of Harlequin* and *Accompanied Center.*

17 See Rosalind E. Krauss, "Magnetic Fields: The Structure," in *Joan Miró: Magnetic Fields* (exhib. cat.) (New York: The Solomon R. Guggenheim Foundation, 1972), 29.

18 See *Zoologischer Teil*, 249.

19 See also *Physiologie und Ökologie: I. Botanischer Teil* (1917), 165, which is reproduced as fig. 73 in *Point and Line to Plane.*

20 The author studied the encyclopedia volumes in April 1984 at the Centre Georges Pompidou.

21 See Will Grohmann, *Kandinsky: Life and* Work (New York: H.N. Abrams, 1958), 187–88; and Vivian Endicott Barnett, *Kandinsky at the Guggenheim* (New York: Solomon R. Guggenheim Museum and Abbeville Press, 1983), 43–44.

22 Sara Lynn Henry, "Form-Creating Energies: Paul Klee and Physics," *Arts* 52 (Sept. 1977): 119, 121. However, according to Felix Klee in conversation with the author, July 19, 1984, the encyclopedia volumes are not among the books that belonged to his father now in his possession.

23 I am indebted to Christian Derouet for this information and for bringing the clippings to my attention.

24 Wassily Kandinsky, *Tutti gli scritti: Punto e linea nel piano, Articoli teorici, I corsi inediti al Bauhaus*, ed. Phillipe Sers (Milan: Feltrinelli, 1973), 283.

25 Ibid., 284, 289, 290.

26 The Galerie de Zoologie has been closed to the public for years, but M. Laissus and Mme Rufino kindly allowed me to see the displays in the galleries in 1984.

27 Karl Baedeker, *Paris and Its Environs* (Paris, 1937), 353.

28 *Abstammungslehre: Systematik, Paläontologie, Biogeographie* (Leipzig and Berlin: Teubner, 1914), 322–23, marker 352–53.

29 Lindsay and Vergo, *Kandinsky: Complete Writings on Art*, 2:803.

30 For example, an early reference to "grown men and embryos" in his discussion of ornamentation in *On The Spiritual in Art* does not have meaning with regard to science (Lindsay and Vergo, *Kandinsky: Complete Writings on Art*, 1:199).

31 Kandinsky, *Tutti gli Scritti*, 290.

32 Lindsay and Vergo, *Kandinsky: Complete Writings on Art*, 2:779.

33 I am grateful to Peter H. Barnett for his assistance, especially on the history of science and philosophy.

34 Ernst Mayr, *The Growth of Biological Thought*, 2nd ed. (Cambridge, MA: Belknap Press, 1982), 471–74.

35 Eric Wahl brought these interrelationships to my attention and assisted me with many research questions.

36 Haeckel (1834–1919) is referred to frequently in several volumes of *Die Kultur der Gegenwart: Allgemeine Biologie, Anthropologie* and *Naturphilosophie*. Two important books on him were published in 1934: Gerhard Heberer, *Ernst Haeckel und seine wissenschaftliche Bedeutung. Zum Gedächtnis der 100. Wiederkehr seines Geburtstages* (Tübingen: Heine, 1934); and Heinrich Schmidt, *Ernst Haeckel: Denkmal eines grossen Lebens* (Jena: Frommann, 1934).

37 See Rose-Carol Washton Long, *Kandinsky: The Development of an Abstract Style* (Oxford: Clarendon Press; New York: Oxford University Press, 1980), chapter 2; Sixten Ringbom, *The Sounding Cosmos: A Study in the Spiritualism of Kandinsky and the Genesis of Abstract Painting,* Acta Academia Aboensis, Series A, Bd. XXXVIII (Abo: Abo Akad., 1970); and Sixten Ringbom, "Kandinsky und das Okkulte," in *Kandinsky und München* (exhib. cat.) (Munich: Prestel, 1982), 85–101.

38 This issue of *Lucifer Gnosis* is not preserved in either the Gabriele Münter- und Johannes Eichner-Stiftung, Städtische Galerie im Lenbauchhaus in Munich or in the Kandinsky Archive, Musée National d'Art Moderne, Paris. The latter possess only one copy of *Lucifer Gnosis* (no. 14, from July 1904).

39 For example, "Haeckel und seine Gegner," "Ernst Haeckel und die Welträtsel," "Die Kämpfe um Haeckels' *Welträtsel,* "Die Kultur der Gegenwart im Spiegel der Theosophie," and "Haeckel, die Welträtsel und die Theosophie."

The best published source is Johannes Hemleben, *Rudolf Steiner und Ernst Haeckel* (Stuttgart: Verlag Freies Geistesleben, 1965).

40 For general references in art-historical literature, see Rose-Carol Washton, *Kandinsky: Parisian Period 1934–1944* (exhib. cat.) (New York: M. Knoedler & Co., 1969), 16–17, and "Vasily Kandinsky: A Space Odyssey," *Art News* 68 (Oct. 1969): 49; and Hans Konrad Roethel, *Kandinsky* (New York: Hudson Hills Press, 1979), 42.

41 Lindsay and Vergo, *Kandinsky: Complete Writings on Art*, 2:628.

11

Pollock's dream of a Biocentric art: The challenge of his and Peter Blake's Ideal Museum

Elizabeth L. Langhorne

Abstract Expressionism invites interpretation both as the end of an anthropocentric tradition of painting that goes back to the Renaissance, and as an attempt to leave that tradition behind in favor of what can be called a Biocentric approach. In different ways, critics such as Greenberg, Fried, and Clark suggest the former. I will address the latter, by considering just one episode in the artistic development of Jackson Pollock, his 1949 collaboration with the architect Peter Blake (1920–2006) in creating a model for an "Ideal Museum."[1]

Greenberg was concerned that in his "all-over" poured paintings Pollock was destroying easel painting.[2] He was right. But in leaving panel painting behind, Pollock was struggling to make, rather than the human subject, "life" or "nature" the center of his art. In this respect, Pollock's abstractions invite discussion of the Schopenhauer- and Nietzsche-indebted aesthetics of the Blaue Reiter group, which still supported the work of an artist such as Hans Hofmann. But just this turn to nature has seemed suspect to a critic like T.J. Clark. Consider his description of a Hans Hofmann painting as kitsch:

> A good Hofmann has to have a surface somewhere between ice cream, chocolate, stucco and flock wallpaper. Its colors have to reek of Nature—of the worst kind of Woolworth forest-glade-with-waterfall-and-thunderstorm-brewing ... It is a picture of their "interiors," of the visceral-cum-spiritual upholstery of the rich ... Take them or leave them, these ciphers of plenitude—they are all that painting at present has to offer.[3]

As Clark recognized, many of Pollock's poured paintings invite a similar response.[4]

Pollock's statement "I am nature"—made to Hans Hofmann in 1942 or 1944—claims the identity of self and nature. Unexamined, it either sounds megalomaniacal or deluded in its quasi-mystic identification with nature.[5] In the modern and postmodern world such "oneness" with nature must be dismissed, so Clark claims, as a false sense of plenitude.[6] But this overlooks

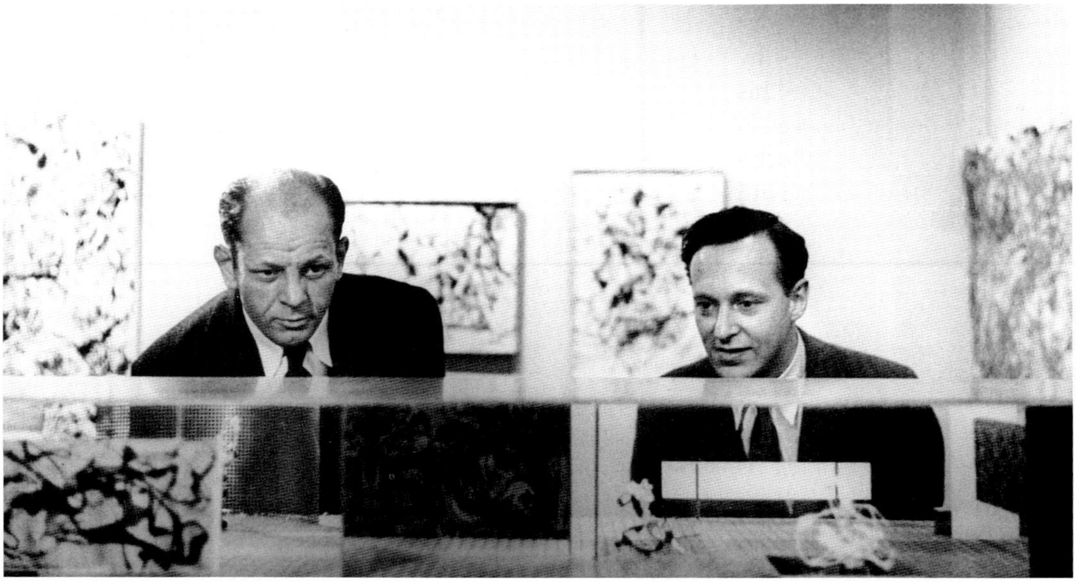

11.1 Jackson Pollock and Peter Blake with model museum designed by Blake, at Pollock's show at Betty Parsons Gallery, 1949. Collection of the Pollock-Krasner House and Study Center, East Hampton, NY

the significance of Pollock's emergent Biocentrism. What is at stake shows itself with special clarity in the project of the "Ideal Museum."

Blake was 28, and had recently been appointed Director of the Department of Architecture and Industrial Design at MOMA, when he met Pollock at a dinner party in East Hampton in the fall of 1948.[7] The two became friends, and when Pollock asked Blake to help hang his second exhibition at the Betty Parsons Gallery in the fall of 1949, Blake told Pollock of a fantasy that he had nurtured ever since that first day in Pollock's studio: "An exhibit of translucency, paintings hanging suspended in the magnificent expanse of landscape out here [at Springs], the landscape penetrating them."[8] According to Blake, Pollock grunted, seemed to get the message, and was interested. Blake continued to explain his wish to exhibit "the paintings between sheets of mirror that would extend the composition into infinity, and that people would walk in among them. Jackson thought a while and said it was a very interesting idea."[9] Blake proceeded to make a model of a flat-roofed, glazed pavilion in the manner of Mies van der Rohe, to show Pollock's paintings "suspended between the earth and the sky, and set between mirrored walls so as to extend into infinity."[10] The model of what would have been a 15.25 meter × 30.5 meter interior was divided by colored reproductions of Pollock's paintings, some taken from a recent article in *Life*.[11] Blake, presumably with Pollock's consent, cropped and played with these reproductions as he needed to fit the scale of the building. Pollock created three small-scale sculptures for the model conceived of as, in Blake's words, "a kind of three-dimensional interpretation of his drip paintings," made of wire dipped in plaster and painted.[12] According to Blake, they were both pleased with the result.[13] The model was displayed in the Betty Parsons exhibition. Unfortunately it disintegrated shortly after the exhibition, and only one of the three sculptures has survived, in a badly damaged state.[14]

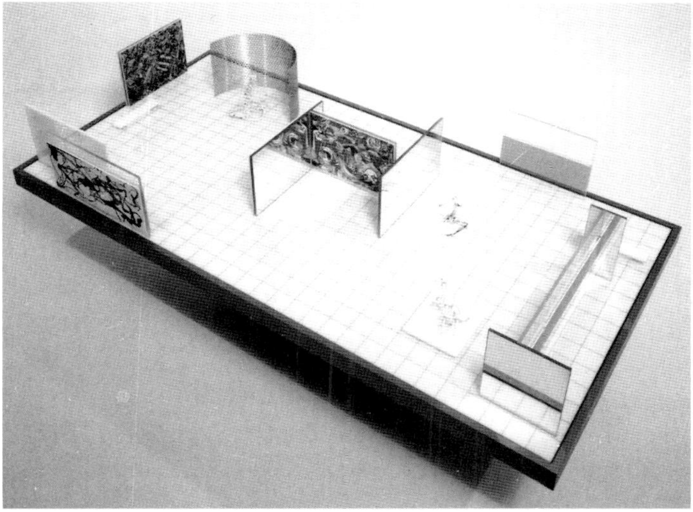

11.2 Peter Blake, "Ideal Museum" for Jackson Pollock's work, 1949. Reconstructed model interior. Photo by Jeff Heatley. Collection of the Pollock-Krasner House and Study Center, East Hampton, NY

The model museum was, however, published by Arthur Drexler in his article "Unframed Space: A Museum for Jackson Pollock's Paintings."[15] This, along with a photograph of Blake and Pollock inspecting the model on display at the Betty Parsons Gallery, were the best visual record of the project until Blake undertook to reconstruct the model in 1994 (Fig. 11.1).[16] The reconstructed model is now displayed at the Pollock House in a bay window looking out to the landscape behind the house. Recently, two photographs of it, one of the exterior facade, the other of the interior plan of the building with the flat roof removed, were republished in Victoria Newhouse's book *Towards a New Museum* (Plate 3 and Fig. 11.2).

In Plate 3, the model is seen directly against the backdrop of what Blake has described as "the wide, horizontal landscape of the inlets just beyond the little shack [referring to Pollock's studio]."[17] Approaching the façade one sees a large poured painting, *Number 24, 1949*, on the far left flush with the wall, and facing, in a startling manner, not inward but outward. The strong orange diagonal moving from the upper left down to the work's center, roughly marked by a large orange circular configuration, leads the eye towards the interior of the building, to *The Key* (1946), which draws us into the center of the entire plan (Plate 4).[18] This painting, done in the spring of 1946, is strongly symmetrical. One of his last figural works before the poured paintings, it is in fact the only painting in the museum containing recognizable figurative imagery. It is also the culmination of Pollock's preoccupation with male and female imagery; note, for example, the curvaceous womb of the figure on the left, and the yellow-tipped phallus of the upright personage on the right.[19] The brown line that joins phallus to womb marks the central horizontal axis of the canvas. Below it Pollock inventories the primary colors, blue, red, yellow, and a central gray area dotted with blue. Above it a striking triangle of the complementary pair dark green dotted with red, establishes an upward thrust reinforced by the outline of the brown diagonal lines. The "thickness" of the green paint contrasts with numerous passages of the exposed canvas, and the range of texture includes the "thinness" of the blues. Pollock thus translates erotic relationship into the interplay of formal elements, of primaries and complementary colors, left and right, up and down, and thick versus thin. Having discovered this "key", Pollock was able in the work that followed to let go of his imagery, to go abstract.

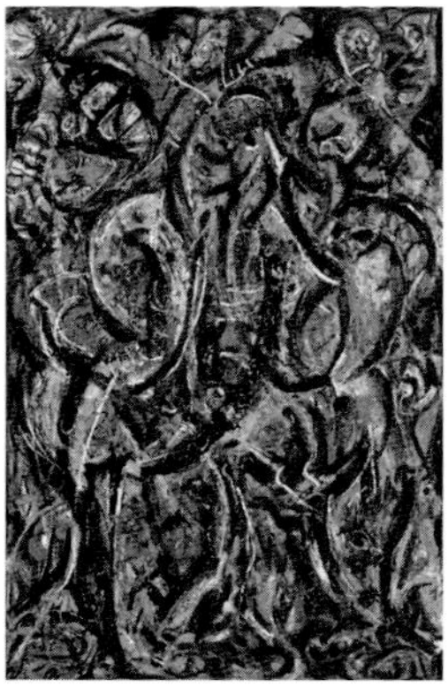

11.3 Jackson Pollock, *Gothic*, 1944, oil on canvas, 215.5 × 142.1 cm. The Museum of Modern Art, New York. Bequest of Lee Krasner 533.1984. Digital Image © The Museum of Modern Art/Licensed by SCALA/ Art Resource, NY. © The Pollock-Krasner Foundation/ Artists Rights Society (ARS), New York

Would Pollock be left with a merely formal achievement, the splendidly "recreated flatness" of a late Cubist canvas?[20] The erotic energies that marked his earlier canvases demand an expanded context, and this is already, as Blake intuited in *The Key*, the context of his relationship to nature. With its color-spaces, more than any other major canvas up to 1946, *The Key* suggests a land- and seascape. Jackson and Lee Krasner had married in October 1945 and moved from New York to the small village of Springs, Long Island. There he had experienced in 1946 his first real country spring since his childhood.[21] Lee Krasner recalls: "He spent hours, sometimes whole days walking around the first spring we were there. He was like a kid, exploring everything."[22] In Springs, Pollock became aware not of being nature, but of being surrounded by nature. "I am nature" became "I am part of nature." Blake as architect dramatizes this opening up. The visitor standing in front of *The Key* finds him- or herself between two large mirrored walls, both at right angles to *The Key*, the one on the right at a narrow remove from the painting, the one on the left abutting it. Even as he establishes a center with *The Key*, Blake counters it. The mirrors extend the painting and the interior to infinity on the horizontal axis.

Tantalized by the illusory space of the baroque mirrors, the viewer wants to explore and find out what is really on the other side of the mirror.[23] As in Mies' Barcelona Pavilion, movement becomes central to the concept of form and space.[24] Taking the most natural turn into the left of the building, one discovers three works conceived as floating "walls": *Gothic* (1944) (Fig. 11.3), *Number 17A, 1948*, and *Number 1A, 1948*. Blake treats the first two as abstractions, not as real objects—tampering with their scale. The already emphatic vertical axis of *Gothic* (1944), in reality 2.14 meters high, is enlarged to what would be close to 3.35 meters. The layered density of *Number 17A, 1948*, with its cluster of three broad, white, diagonal markings in the lower right of the canvas, constitutes an end wall, enlarged from its true 34 inches height. It establishes a left-hand closure to the horizontal breadth of the building. To keep the visitor's physical movement and visual attention inside the structure, Blake uses a curved screen of perforated brass. Here he positions a Pollock sculpture, understood by Blake and Pollock as a three-dimensional interpretation of his poured paintings.

While the three paintings, facing the interior of the left-hand portion of the Ideal Museum, define the axes of architectural space, its height, width, and depth conceived of as walls—each with its distinctive thicknesses and densities—it is Pollock's sculpture that most loudly asserts the interior spatial dimension of these canvases. The sculpture not only literally opens up the layers of poured paint as found in *Number 17A, 1948* into three-dimensional space, but it prepares the visitor for viewing *Number 1A, 1948* (Fig. 11.4). Looking for space within the tensile trajectories of *Number 1A, 1948*, one begins to look at *Number 1A, 1948*, not as a wall, but as a Modernist painting, three-dimensional despite its apparent flatness. The axes of an architectural structure,

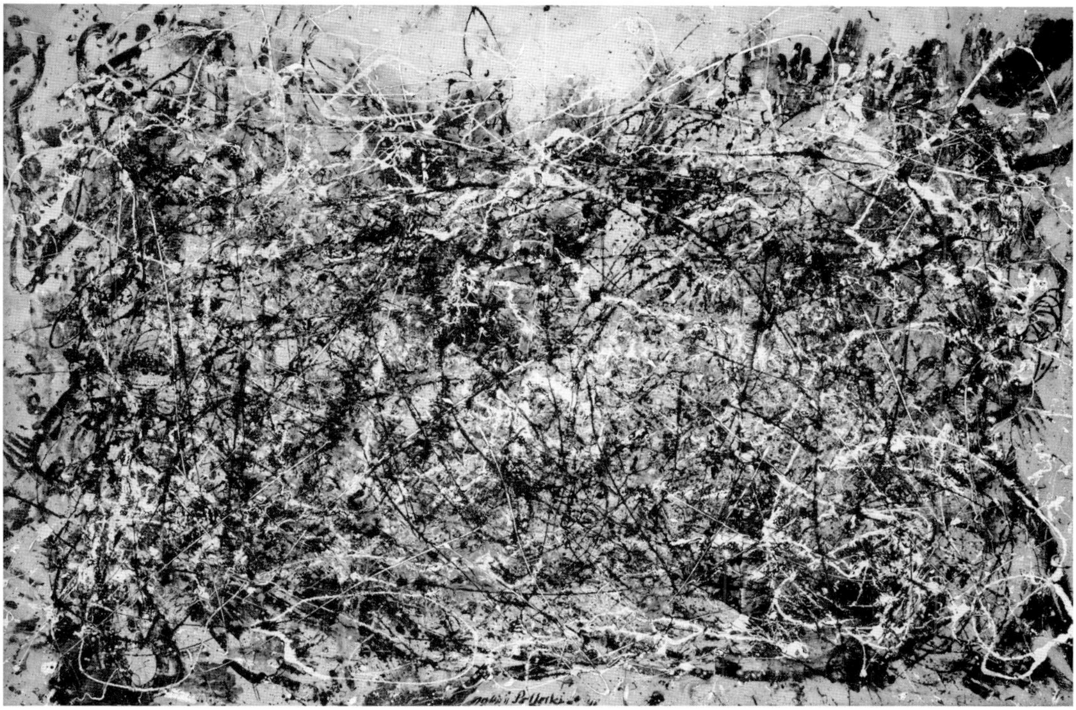

11.4 Jackson Pollock, *Number 1A, 1948*, 1948, oil and enamel on unprimed canvas, 172.7 × 264.2 cm. The Museum of Modern Art, New York. Digital Image © The Museum of Modern Art/ Licensed by SCALA / Art Resource, NY. © The Pollock-Krasner Foundation/ Artists Rights Society (ARS), New York

if you will, are now located within the painting itself: horizontally, vertically, and depth-wise. Blake's installation helps one to experience as pictorially ordered a painting that one might otherwise have experienced as merely chaotic.

As we continue our journey through the Ideal Museum we arrive at the opening to the left of *Number 1A, 1948,* where we finally gain access to a wide view of the landscape beyond. But fully engaged now in the process of looking at Pollock's paintings, we confront the thickness of the paint in *Alchemy*, an early poured painting done in 1947 (Fig. 11.5). The back-to-back placement of *Alchemy* and *The Key* marks Pollock's turn away from the symbolic figural works that had occupied him from around 1941 through 1946, to his adventure with poured abstractions in 1947. Even as we see that Pollock succeeded in transforming this thick paint into the tensile skeins of *Number 1A, 1948*, the difficulty and challenge of his pictorial journey is asserted. By positioning the viewer with his or her back to the transparent wall and the scene outside, Blake rubs the viewer's nose in the dense materiality of the paint that Pollock proposes to transform with a new-found openness to nature.

Blake's continuing use of mirrors in the central tripartite unit of the Museum, this time a plane mirrored on both sides and set at a right angle to *Alchemy* and at a slight remove from it, invites one into the game of pursuing the reflections, of turning the corner to be confronted, not with a painting, but with oneself in the act of looking. No doubt you are startled, much as the "animal-like" sculpture is at your side. I say "animal-like" because of the "head" facing the mirror atop a linear arc curved in such a way as to suggest startled withdrawal.

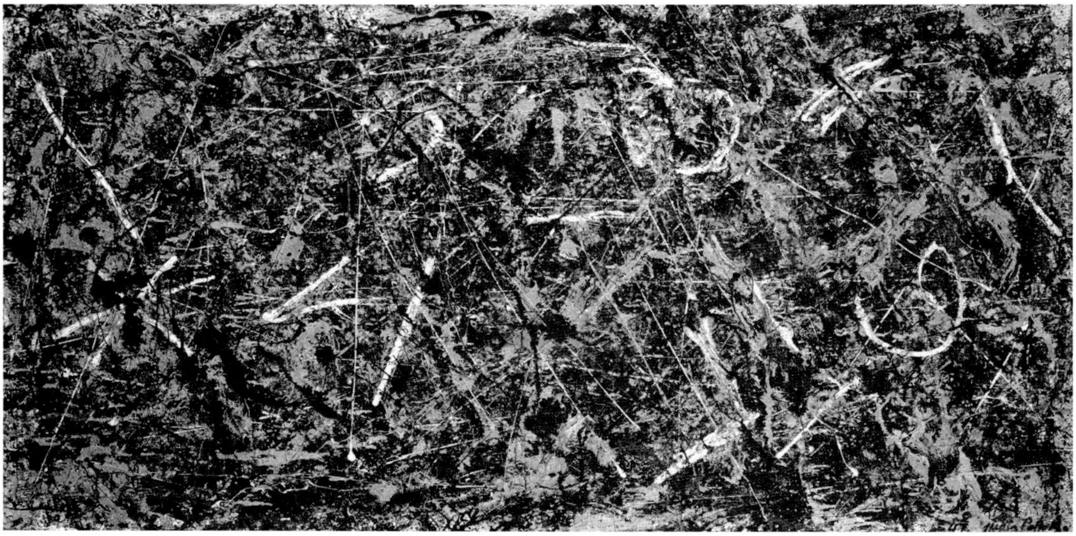

11.5 Jackson Pollock, *Alchemy*, 1947, oil, aluminum, enamel paint, and string on canvas, 114.6 × 221.3 cm. The Solomon R. Guggenheim Foundation. Peggy Guggenheim Collection, Venice, 1976, 76.2553.150. © The Pollock-Krasner Foundation/ Artists Rights Society (ARS), New York

You and "it" are caught between the reflection of *Summertime: Number 9A, 1948* and the loosened rhythms of the actual painting (Plate 5). Turning around in this open space, one might next experience Pollock's third sculpture on a slightly elevated platform, with its upwards spiraling and looping dance of lines spun in space (see Plate 3). The shapes and rhythms of this sculpture are continued on the long (originally 5.5 meters) and horizontal canvas *Summertime,* here suspended in mid-air and defining the far wall of the museum. The potentiality of *The Key* has been released into free play.

In *Summertime,* all the potential movements are put into fluid play at a non-objective level. They engage in a seemingly endless transformative process, as a mark or a color provokes a response, which in turn provokes another response. The erotic tensions between formal oppositions and the primary colors held in crystalline suspension in *The Key,* are released into the dialogue of Pollock's process of painting as liquid gray, then black pours of enamel pigment rhythmically sweep and pulse, in and out, rising up and descending, back and forth, engaging each other and the white ground. This all-over elaboration is continued by means of Pollock's infilling of intersections of the gray and black interlace by discrete areas of blue, yellow, and some red, now caught up in the dancing rhythms, the whole slightly weighted with small speckles of green-blue and brown found along the painting's lower edge. The scale of the surface, originally 84.5 centimeters high, suggests the bodily movements that generate these rhythms. The painted gestures thus become the trace of Pollock's dance in an ever-evolving dialectic guided by an underlying sense of harmonic balancing. The center in *The Key* has evolved into the organizing principle of a moving center in *Summertime.*

As Pollock explained to Robert Goodnough in the May 1951 *Art News*: "My paintings do not have a center, but depend upon the same amount of interest throughout to carry the same intensity to the edges of the canvas."[25] The order that Pollock invokes is not the Aristotelian one of beginning, middle, and end, as Pollock himself lets us know: "There was a reviewer a while back who wrote that my pictures didn't have any beginning or any end. He didn't mean it as a compliment, but it was. It was a fine compliment. Only he didn't know it."[26] *Summertime* presents to us just such a continuous balancing and counteracting of rhythms, seemingly with no beginning and no end. This very quality of endlessness in *Summertime* Blake takes advantage of when adjusting the painting to the design of his Museum, he crops it at either end. But mirrors positioned at right angles to both ends of the canvas extend its emphatically horizontal rhythms to infinity. Looking down the length of *Summertime*, one's attention, following the continuous and infinite extension of the reflection, is propelled out into the landscape and toward the inlet.

To satisfy this directional impulse Blake places another bench to the far side of the mirror at the left edge of *Summertime*.[27] On this bench the visitor's own physical movement through the space of the Museum is transformed into a perceptual feast, a meditative viewing of the landscape itself. To this viewing one brings not just an intense awareness of its dominant horizontality, first acknowledged in *The Key*, but all the freedom achieved in *Summertime*: the eye now disposed to scan the horizon, exploring rhythms up and down, left and right, back and forth, aware of the changing densities of earth, water, trees, sky, and ever-changing shifts in emphasis. *Summertime* was indeed, as Peter Blake realized from the day of his first studio-visit, "the work of someone who understood light and space, and the transparency of the wide, horizontal landscape of the inlets just beyond the little shack."[28]

In this culminating treatment of *Summertime* we begin to realize a "Dream of Space," a phrase that Blake came up with in an imagined conversation with Pollock, responding to an accusation made by Pollock that still rankled some 40 years later:

> In all my years of friendship with Jackson, we rarely talked about art. But one day, out of the blue, he said to me: "The trouble is you think I'm a decorator." I was taken aback—perhaps because he seemed so precisely on target. But the more I thought and think about it, and I still do, some forty years after the fact, the more I think Jackson was wrong: of course I thought his paintings might make terrific walls (after all, architects spend a lot of time thinking about walls). But what his paintings really meant to me from the first day, was something I can only describe as the "Dream of Space"—a dream of endless, infinite space in motion.[29]

Blake's use of a Miesian conception of space in his Ideal Museum further dramatizes the fluid, opening spaces of Pollock's painting.[30] Using the baroque device of mirrors to extrapolate the fluidity between inside and outside spaces found in Mies' building, he explodes the architectural axis of the depth of the building into infinity, simultaneously dramatizing his conviction that Pollock's paintings are "not merely definitions of space, but actually part and parcel of space—floating in mid air."[31] The endless space of *Summertime* partakes of the endless space of the landscape, an extravagant opening to nature and its rhythms. Erotic energies, at first contained within *The Key* and released over time into the pulsing rhythms of poured paint in *Summertime*, now expand into nature. As Blake put it:

> In the four short years between the end of World War II and the publication, in 1949 in *Life* magazine, of a major article on Jackson's work [in which *Summertime* was featured] ... [American painting] had broken away from easel painting and embraced all of space, all of motion, all of action; it was as violent and as passionate and as 'engaged' as life itself.[32]

As an architect, Blake plays upon the tension between the conventions of viewing an easel painting and the explosion of these conventions. He refers the visitor approaching the Museum to Alberti's Renaissance theorization of the pictorial surface as a "window" opening to nature. Notice, for example, the alignment of the central horizontal axis of *The Key* with the actual horizon of the landscape visible through the transparent glass of the building (see Plate 3), the "head" of the abstract sculpture on the right even following the rules of Albertian perspective as it sets the human scale of the model, vis-à-vis the vertical mirrored wall of the far right-hand side of the façade. Next he draws the visitor into the privileged position of the true center of the building, inviting this person to stand still in front of *The Key*, an avowedly Modernist panel painting. But then he quickly proceeds to disorient the visitor in the fluid environment of the Museum, a labyrinth of confusing paintings, further confused by mirrored extensions, and by required rotation around the central unit in which *The Key* is embedded, as in the child's blindfold game of "pin the tail on the donkey." The axial structure that is crystallized in *The Key* with its strong sense of center, left and right, up and down, thick and thin, exfoliates in space over time, as the visitor, forced by the architecture to navigate the spaces that the Pollock paintings define, begins to internalize their axes, densities, rhythms, almost unconsciously.

In his method of showing Pollock's work, Blake does not employ an aesthetic approach that emphasizes the autonomy of individual works and an observer assigned a place before the canvas. Rather his orchestration of space, as he brings the visitor from the relatively confined spaces of the left-hand portion of the museum into the opening spaces of the right, with their sensation of liberation and infinite motion, serves to fully activate the viewer's kinesthetic responses to Pollock's style, now brought to a full realization in *Summertime*. If one were a dancer, one might dance. A famous story recounts how Richard Wagner, listening to Beethoven's Seventh Symphony, wanted to dance it. A poured painting is like a score that invites you to perform it.[33] At this level we perhaps arrive at the idea of a pre-metaphorical expression which teases T.J. Clark. Pollock does want the picture to be put into a new relation to the world, but not another relationship of likeness; he wants some other means of signifying experience: mimesis of nature as an enactment of it.[34]

Blake's Ideal Museum alerts us to the fact that Pollock is leaving behind the optical Renaissance tradition, within which Greenberg, Fried, and most recently Pepe Karmel have wished to place Pollock's art.[35] To the degree that Pollock's mimesis of nature invites the viewer's bodily participation, his art calls us beyond the old anthropocentrism, centered in the viewer as the seeing, knowing subject, to a new Biocentrism. Through our bodies we experience that we are not just thinking subjects or disembodied eyes, but indeed part of larger nature.

Such a Biocentric reading of Pollock's art counters Greenberg's aestheticism and T.J. Clark's reading, which follows in the tradition set by Greenberg. Thus it reopens, from within Modernism, art's role in providing an alternative approach to reality.[36] The dream of an opening to nature embodied in the Ideal Museum offers an alternative to the scientific approach, with its detachment from and sense of control over nature, which underlies the Renaissance paradigm of painting. Instead, it proposes an attitude that is more responsive to and responsible for nature. T.J. Clark sees Pollock's art, in its relation to nature, either as offering a false sense of plenitude of the "Woolworth forest-glade" variety, or, at its best, as script—when after *Number 1A, 1948* and in 1949 Pollock pushes to escape nature towards "anti-nature," towards "a kind of writing ... a script none of us has read before," leaving the body behind.[37] Pollock's collaboration with Blake in the creation of the Ideal Museum points to the difference between Clark's values and Pollock's own willingness to dramatize the opening of his art up to the body and to nature.

In the end Pollock himself betrays such openness. Thus, as in 1950, he chooses plenitude and closure in *One*. That Pollock should find it difficult to experience himself as part of nature and its ongoing rhythms makes him very much an artist of our times. And it is all the more important that he and we should at least dream of it. Nietzsche was such a dreamer. Let me give him the last word:

> The essence of nature is now to be expressed symbolically; we need a new world of symbols; and the entire symbolism of the body is called into play, not the mere symbolism of the lips, face, and speech but the whole pantomime of dancing, forcing every member into rhythmic movement.[38]

Pollock's art, especially as interpreted by Blake's architecture, opens us once again to such an understanding of art and its potential to convey a Biocentric worldview.

Notes

1 Blake variously refers to his model as "a large, somewhat abstract 'exhibit' of his work—a kind of 'Ideal Museum'," and an "Ideal Exhibition" of his work. Peter Blake, *No Place Like Utopia: Modern Architecture and the Company We Kept* (New York: W.W. Norton, 1993), 111.

2 Clement Greenberg, "The Crisis of the Easel Picture" (1948), in *Clement Greenberg: The Collected Essays and Criticism*, vol. 2, ed. John O'Brian (Chicago, IL and

London: University of Chicago Press, 1986), 221–25; and Greenberg, "Review of Exhibitions of Adolph Gottlieb, Jackson Pollock, and Josef Albers" (1949), in ibid., 285–86.

3 T.J. Clark, *Farewell to an Idea: Episodes from a History of Modernism* (New Haven, CT: Yale University Press, 1998), 397.

4 See ibid., 335, 340, 365.

5 See Ellen G. Landau, *Jackson Pollock* (New York: Abrams, 1989), 159, and 259, n. 2. To counter the misconception, "People think he means he's God," Krasner later explained: "He means he's total. He's undivided. He's one *with* nature, instead of 'That's nature over there, and I'm here.'" Quoted in Amei Wallach, "Out of Jackson Pollock's Shadow," *Newsday*, September 23, 1981. For 1944 date, see Bultman, quoted in Jeffrey Potter, *To a Violent Grave: An Oral Biography of Jackson Pollock* (New York: G.P. Putnam's Sons, 1985), 77.

6 Clark, *Farewell to an Idea*, 337, 339, 363.

7 Blake, *No Place*, 110–11.

8 Audiorecording of Peter Blake's lecture, "Unframed Space: Working with Pollock on the 'Ideal Museum'," Pollock-Krasner House and Study Center, East Hampton, NY. A Project of the Stony Brook Foundation, State University of New York, July 30, 1995.

9 Ibid.

10 Blake, *No Place*, 111–12. Blake states his project was based on Mies' 1942 proposal for an *Ideal Museum for a Small City*.

11 Victoria Newhouse, *Towards a New Museum* (New York: The Monacelli Press, 1998), 131. *Number 17A, 1948* and *Summertime: Number 9A, 1948* were illustrated in Dorothy Seiberling, "Jackson Pollock: Is He the Greatest Living Painter in the United States?" *Life*, August 8, 1949.

12 Blake, *No Place*, 112.

13 Blake lecture. Newhouse writes "Jackson Pollock's museum was designed not by the artist but by the architect and critic Peter Blake, though with the artist's approval. Pollock's paintings were such an integral part of the architecture, however, that the museum appears to be as much by him as by Blake." Newhouse, 130.

14 See fig. 1049 in Francis V. O'Connor and Eugene V. Thaw, eds., *Jackson Pollock: A Catalogue Raisonné of Paintings, Drawings, and Other Works*, vol. 4 (New Haven, CT and London: Yale University Press, 1978), 126–27.

15 Arthur Drexler, "Unframed Space: A Museum for Jackson Pollock's Paintings," *Interiors*, 109/6 (1950): 90–91.

16 Replica fabricated by Patrick Bodden, with sculptures by Susan Tamulevich, 1993–94; Newhouse, *Towards a New Museum*, 283.

17 Blake, *No Place*, 110–11.

18 Indicative of the spirit of Blake's "somewhat abstract 'exhibit'," he enlarges *Number 24, 1949* from its original dimensions of 67 cm. x 31 cm. to wall size. No record exists to show how this panel was shown in the Parsons November 1949 exhibition. When later sold, this panel was one of a "triptych" and hung vertically. See O'Connor and Thaw, *Catalogue Raisonné*, vol. 2, 43.

19 This preoccupation is most clear in *Male and Female* (1942), *Male and Female in Search of a Symbol* (1943), *Night Sounds* (c. 1944), *Beach Figures* (c. 1944), *Two* (c. 1945), *The Child Proceeds* (1946).

20 Greenberg, "Review of Exhibitions of Jean Dubuffet and Jackson Pollock" (1947), in *Clement Greenberg: The Collected Essays and Criticism*, vol. 2, 125.

21 Steven Naifeh and Gregory White Smith, *Jackson Pollock: An American Saga* (New York: Clarkson N. Potter, 1989), 516.

22 Naifeh and Smith, Interview with Lee Krasner, ibid.

23 When Blake first saw Pollock's art, he thought of baroque mirrors. "It was a very sunny day and the sun was shining in on the paintings. I felt like I was standing in the Hall of Mirrors at Versailles. It was a dazzling, incredible sight." Blake, quoted in Newhouse, *Towards a New Museum*, 130.

24 About the Barcelona Pavilion Blake wrote that Mies "made space move and transformed it into pure magic." Blake, *No Place*, 55. As Franz Schulze notes of the visitor to the Barcelona Pavilion: "No matter how he visited the pavilion and even if he bypassed the central space, he was obliged to describe a circuitous route." Franz Schulze, *Mies van der Rohe: A Critical Biography* (Chicago, IL: The University of Chicago Press, 1985), 156.

25 Robert Goodnough, "Pollock Paints a Picture," *Art News* 50 (May 1951): 60.

26 O'Connor and Thaw, *Catalogue Raisonné*, vol. 4, doc. 85, excerpt from Berton Roueche, "Unframed Space," *New Yorker*, 5 August 1950, 247.

27 Sitting on the bench, the visitor would also notice to their left the back of *Number 10, 1949* (c. 1949), another long horizontal painting.

28 Blake, *No Place*, 110–11.

29 Ibid., 114.

30 Blake felt that Jackson and Mies shared "a very similar attitude toward the nature of space." Ibid., 112. A further analogy between the space of Mies and Pollock lies in their understanding of an "organic principle of order," Mies' phrase used in his Armour Institute inaugural address. See Peter Blake, *Mies van der Rohe: Architecture and Sculpture* (New York: Penguin Books, 1960), 73.

31 Peter Blake, letter to Francis V. O'Connor, 11 December 1963, quoted in O'Connor and Thaw, *Catalogue Raisonné*, vol. 4, 126.

32 Blake, *No Place*, 116.

33 For Karmel, "Namuth's photographs and films [of Pollock painting] suggest a serious problem with what we might call the kinesthetic reading of Pollock's works—that is, the reading that sees Pollock's lines, splatters, and pools as signs evoking not conventional images but the dancelike movements that created them. The problem is that the kinesthetic sensation evoked by a given mark is often the exact opposite of the movement that actually produced it." Pepe Karmel, "Pollock at Work: The Films and Photographs of Hans Namuth," *Jackson Pollock* (New York: Museum of Modern Art, 1998), 129. In response, I would point out that, no matter how the marks are actually made, the desired rhythms are put into play; these in turn elicit kinesthetic responses.

34 T.J. Clark, "Jackson Pollock's Abstraction," in *Reconstructing Modernism: Art in New York, Paris, and Montreal 1946–1964*, ed. Serge Guilbaut (Cambridge, MA: MIT Press, 1990), 207, 197.

35 See Karmel, "Pollock at Work ," 131–32.

36 See also Belgrad's discussion of mind-body holism and energy field theory as it relates to Pollock. Daniel Belgrad, *The Culture of Spontaneity: Improvisation and the Arts in Postwar America* (Chicago, IL: The University of Chicago Press, 1998), 109–15, 126–27.

37 Clark, *Farewell to an Idea*, 339–40, 314, 365.

38 Friedrich Nietzsche, *The Birth of Tragedy and The Case of Wagner*, trans. Walter Kaufmann (New York: Random House, 1967), 40.

Select bibliography

Allen, Garland E., *Life Science in the Twentieth Century*. New York: John Wiley & Sons, 1975.

Antliff, Allan, *Anarchist Modernism: Art, Politics and the First American Avant-Garde*. London: The University of Chicago Press, 2001.

——, *Art and Anarchy: From the Paris Commune to the Fall of the Berlin Wall*. Vancouver: Arsenal Pulp Press, 2007.

Antliff, Mark, "Bergson and Cubism: A Reassessment," *Art Journal* (Winter 1988): 341–49.

——, *Inventing Bergson. Cultural Politics and the Parisian Avant-Garde*. Princeton, NJ: Princeton University Press, 1993.

——, "Organicism Against Itself: Cubism, Duchamp-Villon and the Contradictions of Modernism," *Word and Image* 12, no. 1 (1996): 22–24.

Arz, Maike, *Literatur und Lebenskraft: Vitalistische Naturforschung und bürgerliche Literatur um 1800*. Stuttgart: M. & P. Verlag für Wissenschaft und Forschung, 1996.

Barlösius, Eva, *Naturgemäße Lebensführung: Zur Geschichte der Lebensreform um die Jahrhundertwende*. Frankfurt am Main, New York: Campus, 1997.

Barnett, Vivian Endicott, *Kandinsky at the Guggenheim* (exh. cat.). New York: Solomon R. Guggenheim Museum; Abbeville Press, 1983.

——, *Kandinsky in Paris. 1934–1944* (exh. cat.). New York: Solomon R. Guggenheim Museum, 1985.

Bauer, Roger et al., eds., *Fin de Siècle. Literatur und Kunst der Jahrhundertwende*. Frankfurt am Main: Vittorio Klostermann, 1977.

Baur, John I.H., *Nature in Abstraction: The Relation of Abstract Painting and Sculpture to Nature in Twentieth Century American Art* (exh. cat.). New York: Whitney Museum of American Art, 1958.

Bayertz, Kurt, "Biology and Beauty: Science and Aesthetics in *Fin-de-siècle* Germany," in Mikulás Teich and Roy Porter, eds., *Fin de siècle and its Legacy*. Cambridge, MA: Cambridge University Press, 1990, 278–95.

Benson, Timothy O., *Expressionist Utopias: Paradise, Metropolis, Architectural Fantasy*. Los Angeles, CA: Los Angeles County Museum of Art, 1993.

Benton, E., "Vitalism in Nineteenth-Century Scientific Thought: A Typology and Reassessment," *Studies in History and Philosophy of Science* 5 (1974): 17–48.

Bergson, Henri, *Matière et mémoire. Essai sur la relation du corps à l'esprit*. Paris: F. Alcan, 1896.

——, *L'évolution créatrice*. Paris: Alcan, 1907.

——, *Creative Evolution*. Translated by Arthur Mitchell. New York: H. Holt & Co., 1911.

——, *Matter and Memory*. Translated by Nancy Margaret Paul and W. Scott Palmer. London: G. Allen & Co.; New York: Macmillan, 1912.

Biederman, Charles. *Art as the Evolution of Visual Knowledge*. Red Wing, MS: The Author, 1948.

Bloch, Ernst, "Über Naturbilder seit Ausgang des Neunzehnten Jahrunderts," in *Literarische Aufsätze*. Ernst Bloch Gesamtausgabe Band 9. Frankfurt/Main: Suhrkamp, 1965: 448–61.

Böhme, Hartmut, "Verdrängung und Erinnerung vor-moderner Natur-Konzepte. Zum Problem historischer Anschlüsse der Naturästhetik in der Moderne." *Kunst Nachtrichten* (Zurich) 24, no. 1 (February 1988): 35–47.

Bölsche, Wilhelm, *Die naturwissenschaftlichen Grundlagen der Poesie. Prolegomena einer realistischen Aesthetik*. Leipzig: Reissner, 1887.

——, *Das Liebesleben in der Natur. Eine Entwicklungsgeschichte der Liebe*. 2 vols. Jena: Eugen Diederichs, 1898–1907.

——, *Weltblick. Gedanken zu Natur und Kunst*. Dresden: Reißner, 1904.

——, *Natur und Kunst*. Dresden: Reißner, 1921.

——, *Love-Life in Nature. The Story of the Evolution of Love*. Translated by Cyril Brown. New York: Albert & Charles Boni, 1926.

Bogdanov, Alksandr, *Tektologiia. Vseobshchaia organizatsionnaia nauka* [Tektology: The Universal Science of Organization]. 3 vols. Berlin, Petrograd, Moscow: Grzhebin, 1922.

Bohm, David, "Fragmentation and Wholeness," *The Structurist*, no. 11 (1971): 7–18

Bois, Yve-Alain and Rosalind Krauss, *Formless: A User's Guide*. New York: Zone Books, 1997.

Bollnow, Otto Friedrich, *Die Lebensphilosophie*. Berlin: Springer, 1958.

Bornstein, Eli. "The Crystal in the Rock," *The Structurist*, no. 2 (1961–62): 5–18.

——, "Creation/Destruction/Creation in Art and Nature," *The Structurist*, no. 7 (1967): 55–63.

——, "Toward an Organic Art: Ecological Views of Man and Nature," *The Structurist*, no. 11 (1971). 59–68.

——, "Art Towards Nature," *The Structurist*, no. 15–16 (1975–76): 142–55.

——, "The Search for Continuity in Art and Connectedness with Nature," *The Structurist*, no. 29–30 (1989–90): 38–43.

——, "Notes on the Mechanical and the Organic in Art and Nature," *The Structurist* no. 35–36 (1995–96): 44–48.

Botar, Oliver. "Ernő Kállai and the Hidden Face of Nature," *The Structurist*, no. 23–24 (1983–84): 77–82.

——, "An Activist-Expressionist in Exile: László Moholy-Nagy 1919–21," in: Belena Chapp, ed., *László Moholy-Nagy: From Budapest to Berlin, 1914–23*. Newark: University Gallery, University of Delaware, 1995, 70–86.

——, "Ernő Kállai and Wilhelm Kolle: Science and Art in Weimar Germany." *Acta Historiae Artium* (Budapest) 42 (1996): 273–77.

——, "Prolegomena to the Study of Biomorphic Modernism: Biocentrism, László Moholy-Nagy's 'New Vision' and Ernő Kállai's Bioromantik." Ph.D. dissertation, University of Toronto, 1998. Ann Arbor, MI: UMI, 2001.

——, "Notes Towards a Study of Jakob von Uexküll's Reception in Early Twentieth-Century Artistic and Architectural Circles," *Semiotica* 134, no. 1–4 (2001): 593–98.

——, "Biocentrism and the Bauhaus," *The Structurist*, no. 43–44 (2003–4): 54–61.

——, "László Moholy-Nagy's 'New Vision' and the Aestheticization of Scientific Imagery in Weimar Germany," *Science in Context: Writing Modern Art and Science* 17, no. 4 (December 2004): 525–56.

——, *Technical Detours: The Early Moholy-Nagy Reconsidered*, New York: The Graduate Center, City University of New York and The Salgo Trust, 2006.

——, "The Roots of László Moholy-Nagy's Biocentric Constructivism," in Eduardo Kac, ed., *Signs of Life: Bio Art and Beyond*. Cambridge, MA: MIT Press, 2007: 315–44.

Bowler, Peter J., *The Eclipse of Darwinism. Anti-Darwinian Evolution Theories in the Decades around 1900*. Baltimore, MD: The Johns Hopkins University Press, 1983.

——, *The Non-Darwinian Revolution: Reinterpreting a Historical Myth*. Baltimore, MD: The Johns Hopkins University Press, 1988.

——, *Reconciling Science and Religion: The Debate in Early-Twentieth Century Britain*. Chicago, IL: The University of Chicago Press, 2001.

Braeunig, Karl, *Mechanismus und Vitalismus in der Biologie des neunzehnten Jahrhunderts*. Leipzig: W. Engelmann, 1907.

Bramwell, Anna, *Ecology in the 20th Century: A History*. New Haven, CT: Yale University Press, 1989.

Brandt, Thomas. "Von der Reduktion zum Wachstum. Vom Wandel geometrischen Formen in den 30er Jahren," in *1937. "... und nicht die leiseste Spur einer Vorschrift"—Positionen unabhängiger Kunst in Europa um 1937*." Düsseldorf: Kunstsammlung Nordrhein-Westfalen, 1987.

Brauer, Fae and Anthea Callen, *Sex, Art and Eugenics: Corpus Delecti*. Aldershot, UK: Ashgate, 2008.

Bredekamp, Horst, "Die Erde als Lebewesen," *Kritische Berichte* 9, no. 4–5 (1981): 5–37.

——, *Darwins Korallen. Die frühen Evolutionsdiagramme und die Tradition der Naturgeschichte*. Berlin: Wagenbach, 2005.

Bromig, Christian, "Biomorphismus oder Anthropomorphismus? Einige kritische Anmerkungen zu Michael Krögers Aufstaz ..." *Kritische Berichte* 19, no. 2 (1991): 92–107.

Buchholz, Kai, Rita Latocha, Hilke Peckmann, and Klaus Wolbert, eds., *Die Lebensreform. Entwürfe zur Neugestaltung von Leben und Kunst um 1900*. 2 vols. Darmstadt: Häusser, 2001.

Bud, Robert, *The Uses of Life: A History of Biotechnology*. Cambridge, MA: Cambridge University Press, 1995.

Burnham, Jack, *Beyond Modern Sculpture. The Effects of Science and Technology on the Sculpture of this Century*. New York: George Braziller, 1968.

Burrow, J.W., *The Crisis of Reason. European Thought, 1948–1914*. New Haven, CT: Yale University Press, 2000.

Burwick, Frederick, ed., *Approaches to Organic Form: Permutations in Science and Culture*. Dordrecht: Reidel, 1987.

——, and Paul Douglass, eds., *The Crisis in Modernism: Bergson and the Vitalist Controversy*, Cambridge, MA: Cambridge University Press, 1992.

Cimino, Guido and François Duchesneau, eds., *Vitalism from Haller to the Cell Theory: Proceedings of the Zaragoza Symposium, XIXth International Congress of the History of Science*. Florence: Leo S. Olschki Editore, 1997.

Clair, Jean, ed., *Cosmos: From Goya to de Chirico, from Friedrich to Kiefer. Art in Pursuit of the Infinite*. Milan: Bompiani, 2000.

—— et al., eds., *L'ame au corps: arts et sciences 1793–1993* (exh. cat.). Paris: Réunion des musées nationaux, 1993.

Clark, John P. and Camille Martin, *Anarchy, Geography and Modernity: The Radical Social Thought of Élisée Reclus*. Lanham, MD: Lexington Books, 2004.

Clark, Kenneth, *Landscape into Art*. Boston, MA: Beacon Press, 1961.

Clarke, Bruce and Linda D. Henderson, eds., *From Energy to Information: Representation in Science and Technology, Art, and Literature*. Stanford, CA: Stanford University Press, 2002.

Cohn, Sherrye, *Arthur Dove: Nature as Symbol*. Ann Arbor, MI: UMI Research Press, 1985.

Coleman, William, *Biology in the Nineteenth Century: Problems of Form, Function, and Transformation*. Cambridge, MA: Cambridge University Press, 1977.

Conti, Christoph, *Abschied vom Bürgertum. Alternative Bewegungen in Deutschland von 1890 bis heute*. Hamburg: Rowohlt, 1984.

Cook, Theodore Andrea, *The Curves of Life: Being an Account of Spiral Formations and their Application to Growth in Nature, to Science and to Art*. London: Constable & Co., 1914.

Crary, Jonathan and Sanford Kwinter, eds., *Incorporations*. New York: Zone, 1992.

Creation: Modern Art and Nature (exh. cat.). Edinburgh: Scottish National Gallery, 1984.

Darwin, Charles, *On the Origin of Species by Means of Natural Selection or the Preservation of Favored Races in the Struggle for Life*. London: John Murray, 1859.

——, *The Descent of Man and Selection in Relation to Sex*. 2 vols. London: John Murray, 1871.

Darwin, Art and the Search for Origins (exh. cat.). Frankfurt am Main: Schirn Kunsthalle, 2009.

De Grood, David H., *Haeckel's Theory of the Unity of Nature: A Monograph in the History of Philosophy*. Amsterdam: B.R. Grüner, 1982.

De Ras, Marion E.P., *Körper, Eros und weibliche Kultur. Mädchen im Wandervogel und in der Bündischen Jugend 1900–1933*. Pfaffenweiler: Centaurus–Verlagsgesellschaft, 1988.

Deleuze, Gilles, *Bergsonism*. Translated by Hugh Tomlinson and Barbara Habberjam. New York: Zone Books, 1990.

Delhomme, Jeanne, *Nietzsche et Bergson*. Paris: Deuxtemps Tierce, 1992.

Dietzsch, Steffen, ed., *Natur, Kunst, Mythos. Beiträge zur Philosophie F.W.J. Schellings*. Berlin: Akademie-Verlag, 1978.

Dominick, Raymond H. III, *The Environmental Movement in Germany: Prophets and Pioneers, 1871–1971*. Bloomington, IN: Indiana University Press, 1992.

Donald, Diana and Jane Munro, eds., *Endless Forms: Charles Darwin, Natural Science and the Visual Arts*. New Haven, CT: Yale University Press, 2008.

Douglas, Charlotte, "Evolution and the Biological Metaphor in Modern Russian Art," *Art Journal* 44, no. 2 (Summer 1984): 153–61.

——, "Energetic Abstraction: Ostwald, Bodganov, and Russian Post-Revolutionary Art," in Bruce Clarke and Linda D. Henderson, eds., *From Energy to Information: Representation in Science and Technology, Art, and Literature*. Stanford, CA: Stanford University Press, 2002, 76–94.

Driesch, Hans, *Die Biologie als selbständige Grundwissenschaft*. Leipzig: W. Engelmann, 1893.

——, *Analytische Theorie der organischen Entwicklung*. Leipzig: W. Engelmann, 1894.

——, *Der Vitalismus als Geschichte und als Lehre*. Leipzig: Barth, 1905

——, *Philosophie des Organischen. Gifford-Vorlesungen, gehalten an der Universität Aberdeen in den Jahren 1907–1908*. 2 vols. Leipzig: W. Engelmann, 1908–09.

——, *The Science and Philosophy of the Organism. Gifford Lectures Delivered at Aberdeen University, 1907–08*. Aberdeen: Aberdeen University, 1908–09.

——, *Leib und Seele. Eine Prüfung des psycho-physischen Grundproblems*. Leipzig: Reinicke, 1916.

——, *Der Begriff der organischen Form*. Berlin: Borntraeger, 1919.

——, *Mind and Body*. New York: MacVeagh, Dial Press, 1927.

——, *Der Mensch und die Welt*. Leipzig: Reinicke, 1928.

——, *Man and the Universe*. Translated by W.H. Johnston. London: Allen & Unwin, 1929.

Eggert, Hartmut, Erhard Schütz, and Peter Sprengel, eds., *Faszination des Organischen. Konjunkturen einer Kategorie der Moderne*. Munich: Iudicium, 1995.

Ellis, Havelock, *The Dance of Life*. London: Constable & Co., 1923.

Engelhardt, Dietrich von, "Naturgeschichte und Geschichte der Kultur in der Naturforschung der Romantik," in Karin Orchard and Jörg Zimmermann, eds., *Die Erfindung der Natur: Max Ernst, Paul Klee, Wols und das surreale Universum* (exh. cat.). Freiburg im Breisgau: Rombach, 1994, 53–59.

Engels, Eve-Marie, ed., *Die Rezeption von Evolutionstheorien im 19. Jahrhundert*. Frankfurt an Main: Suhrkamp, 1995.

Eugster, Konrad. *Die Befreiung vom anthropozentrischen Weltbild. Ludwig Klages' Lehre vom Vorrang der Natur*. Bonn: Bouvier, 1989.

——, "Anthropozentrische und nichtanthropozentrisches Weltbild. Versuche zu Begründungen," *Hestia* (1990–91): 57–74.

Fabre, Gladys, *Abstraction-Creation 1931–1936* (exh. cat.). Paris: Musée d'Art Moderne de la Ville de Paris, 1978.

——, "Art de Synthèse (Synthetic Art)," in *Paris. Arte Abstracto, Arte Concreto, Cercle et Carré 1930* (exh. cat.). Valencia: IVAM, 1990, 396–89.

Faure, Élie, *History of Art: The Spirit of Forms*. Translated by Walter Pach. Garden City, NJ: Garden City Publishing, 1937.

Fechner, Gustav Theodor, *Nanna oder über das Seelenleben der Pflanzen*. Leipzig: Voss, 1848.

——, *Elemente der Psychophysik*. 2 vols. Leipzig: Breitkopf & Härtel, 1860.

——, *Einige Ideen zur Schöpfungs- und Entwicklungsgeschichte der Organismen*. Leipzig: Breitkopf & Härtel, 1873.

Fellmann, Ferdinand, *Lebensphilosophie. Elemente einer Theorie der Selbsterfahrung*. Hamburg: Rowohlts Enzyklopädie, 1993.

Ferry, Luc, *The New Ecological Order*. Translated by Carol Volk. Chicago, IL: The University of Chicago Press, 1995.

Feuerstein, Günter, *Biomorphic Architecture: Human and Animal Forms in Architecture*, Stuttgart and London: Edition Axel Meyers, 2002.

Fick, Monika, *Sinnenwelt und Weltseele. Der psychophysische Monismus in der Literatur der Jahrhundertwende*. Tübingen: Max Niemeyer, 1993.

Fitschen, Jürgen, ed., *Die organische Form: Bildhauerkunst, 1930–1960* (exh. cat.). Bremen: Gerhard-Marcks-Haus, 2003.

Fliess, Wilhelm, "Naturgefühl und Biologie," *Das Tagebuch* 2, no. 37 (September 17, 1921): 1114–17.

Focillon, Henri, *Vie des formes*. Paris: Leroux, 1934.

——, *The Life of Forms in Art*. Translated by Charles B. Hogan and George Kubler. New York: Zone Books, 1992.

Forgács, Éva, "Ernő Kállai: The Art Critic of a Changing Age," *New Hungarian Quarterly*, no. 64 (1976): 174–81.

Foucault, Michel, *The Order of Things: An Archaeology of the Human Sciences*. New York: Vintage Books, 1973.

Foy, James L., *Introduction to Hans Prinzhorn. Artistry of the Mentally Ill: A Contribution to the Psychology and Psychopathology of Configuration*. Translated by Eric von Brockdorff. Berlin: Springer, 1972.

Francé, Raoul, *Die technischen Leistungen der Pflanzen*. Leipzig: von Veit, 1919.

——, *Die Planze als Erfinder*. Stuttgart: Kosmos, 1920.

——, *Zoesis. Eine Einführung in die Gesetze der Welt*. Munich: Franz Hanfstaengl, 1920.

——, *Bios. Die Gesetze der Welt*. Munich: Franz Hanfstaengl, 1921.

——, *Die Welt als Erleben. Grundriss einer objektiven Philosophie*. Dresden: Alwin Huhle, 1923.

——, *Plasmatik. Die Wissenschaft der Zukunft*. Stuttgart: Walter Seifert, 1923.

——, *Harmonie in der Natur*. Stuttgart: Franckh'sche Verlagshandlung, 1926.

——, *Der Organismus. Organisation und Leben der Zelle*. Munich: Drei Masken, 1928.

——, *Welt, Erde und Menschheit. Eine Wanderung durch die Wunder der Schöpfung*. Berlin: Ullstein, 1928.

Freyhofer, Horst H., *The Vitalism of Hans Driesch. The Success and Decline of a Scientific Theory*. Frankfurt am Main, Berne: Peter Lang, 1982.

Frick, Werner and Ulrich Mölk, eds., *Europäische Jahrhundertwende. Literatur, Künste, Wissenschaften um 1900 in grenzüberschreitender Wahrnehmung*. Göttingen: Vandenhoeck & Ruprecht, 2003.

Fuhrmann, Ernst, *Der Sinn im Gegenstand*. Munich: Georg Müller, 1923.

——, *Die Welt der Pflanze*. Berlin: Auriga-Verlag, 1924.

——, *Die Pflanze als Lebewesen*. Frankfurt am Main: Societäts-Verlag, 1930.

——, *Das Wunder der Pflanze*. Berlin: Büchergilde Gutenberg, 1935.

——, *Der Mensch im biologischen Kreislauf der Natur*. Berlin: Siebenreicher Verlag, 1943.

——, *Grundformen des Lebens. Biologisch-philosophische Schriften*. Edited by Franz Jung. Heidelberg: Lambert Schneider, 1962.

Gamwell, Lynn, *Exploring the Invisible: Art, Science, and the Spiritual*. Princeton, NJ and Oxford: Princeton University Press, 2002.

Gaßner, Hubertus, ed., *Élan Vital oder das Auge des Eros. Kandinsky, Klee, Arp, Miró, Calder* (exh. cat.). Munich: Haus der Kunst, 1994.

Gebhard, Walter, *"Der Zusammenhang der Dinge". Weltgleichnis und Naturverklärung im Totalitätsbewusstsein des 19. Jahrhunderts*. Tübingen: Max Niemeyer, 1984.

Geddes, Patrick, *Patrick Geddes: Spokesman for Man and the Environment*. Edited by Marshall Stalley. New Brunswick, NJ: Rutgers University Press, 1972.

Geddes, Patrick and J. Arthur Thomson, *Evolution*. London: Williams and Norgate, 1911.

Geiger, Annette, Stefanie Hennecke, and Christin Kempf, eds., *Spielarten des Organischen in Architektur, Design und Kunst*. Berlin: Reimer, 2005.

Geiger, Annette, "'Form Follows Function' als biozentrische Metapher in der Architektur- und Design-Theorie," in Annette Geiger, Stefanie Hennecke, and Christin Kempf, eds., *Spielarten des Organischen in Architektur, Design und Kunst*. Berlin: Reimer, 2005, 50–67.

Giannachi, Gabrielle and Nigel Stewart, eds., *Performing Nature: Explorations in Ecology and the Arts*. Frankfurt am Main: Peter Lang, 2005.

Giedion-Welcker, Carola. *Contemporary Sculpture. An Evolution in Volume and Space*. New York: Georg Wittenborn, 1955.

——, *Schriften 1926–1971. Stationen zu einem Zeitbild*. Edited by Reinhold Hohl. Cologne: DuMont Schauberg, 1973.

Gienapp, Ruth Anne, "The Monism of Ernst Haeckel." Ph.D. dissertation, Cornell University, 1968.

Glick, Thomas F., ed., *The Comparative Reception of Darwinism*. Austin, TX: University of Texas Press, 1972.

Goethe, Johann Wolfgang von, *Versuch die Metamorphose der Pflanzen zu erklären*. Gotha: C.W. Ettinger, 1790.

Golley, Frank Benjamin, *A History of the Ecosystem Concept in Ecology: More Than the Sum of the Parts*. New Haven, CT: Yale University Press, 1993.

Griffin, David Ray, *The Reenchantment of Science: Postmodern Proposals*. Albany, NY: State University of New York Press, 1988.

Grogin, R.C., *The Bergsonian Controversy in France*. Calgary: University of Calgary Press, 1988.

Großklaus, Götz and Ernst Oldemeyer, eds., *Natur als Gegenbegriff. Beiträge zur Kulturgeschichte der Natur*, Karlsruhe: Loeper, 1983.

Güse, Ernst-Gerhard, ed., *Paul Klee: Dialogue with Nature*, Munich: Prestel, 1991.

Haddon, A.C., *Evolution in Art. As Illustrated by the Life History of Designs*, London: W. Scott, 1895.

Haeckel, Ernst, *Die Radiolarien (Rhizopodaa radiaria). Eine Monographie*. 4 vols. Berlin: Reimer, 1862–88.

——, *Generelle Morphologie der Organismen. Allgemeine Grundzüge der organischen Formen-Wissenschaft*. 2 vols. Berlin: Reimer, 1866.

——, *Natürliche Schöpfungsgeschichte. Gemeinverständliche wissenschaftliche Vorträge über die Entwicklungslehre im Allgemeinen und diejenige von Darwin, Goethe und Lamarck im Besonderen, über die Anwendung derselben auf den Ursprung des Menschen und andere damit zusammenhängende Grundfragen der Naturwissenschaft*. Berlin: Reimer, 1868.

——, *Der Monismus als Band zwischen Religion und Wissenschaft. Glaubensbekenntnisse eines Naturforscher*. Bonn: E. Strauss, 1892.

——, *Monism as Connecting Religion and Science: The Confession of Faith of a Man of Science*. London: Adam and Charles Black, 1894.

——, *Die Welträthsel*. Gemeinverständliche Studien über monistische Philosophie. Bonn: Strauß, 1899.

——, *The Riddle of the Universe*. Translated by Joseph McCabe. New York, London: Harper & Brothers, 1900.

——, *Kunstformen der Natur*. Leipzig, Vienna: Bibliographisches Institut, 1900–1904.

——, *The Wonders of Life. A Popular Study of Biological Philosophy*. Supplementary volume to *The Riddle of the Universe*. Translated by Joseph McCabe. London: Watts & Co., 1904.

Haney, David H. *When Modern Was Green: Life and Work of Landscape Architect Leberecht Migge*. Abingdon, UK: Routledge, 2010.

Haraway, Donna Jeanne, *Crystals, Fabrics, and Fields: Metaphors of Organicism in Twentieth-Century Developmental Biology*. New Haven, CT: Yale University Press, 1976.

——, *Primate Visions: Gender, Race and Nature in the World of Modern Science*. New York: Routledge, 1989.

——, *Simians, Cyborgs, and Women: The Reinvention of Nature*. New York: Routledge, 1991.

Harlan, Volker, *Das Bild der Pflanze in Wissenschaft und Kunst, bei Aristoteles und Goethe, der botanischen Morphologie des 19. und 20. Jahrhunderts und bei den Künstlern Paul Klee und Joseph Beuys*. Stuttgart: Mayer, 2002.

Harrington, Anne, *Reenchanted Science: Holism in German Culture from Wilhelm II to Hitler*. Princeton, NJ: Princeton University Press, 1996.

Harten, Jürgen and Jewgenija Petrowa, eds., *Pawel Filonow und seine Schule* (exh. cat.). Düsseldorf: Städtische Kunsthalle; Cologne: DuMont, 1990.

Hartley, Keith et al., eds., *The Romantic Spirit in German Art 1790–1990* (ex. cat.). Edinburgh: Scottish National Gallery of Modern Art, 1994.

Haydu, George G., "Psychobiology and the Theories of Being and Becoming," *Man and World* 12, no. 4 (1979): 486–97.

Hein, Hilde, *On the Nature and Origin of Life*. New York: McGraw-Hill, 1971.

——, "The Endurance of the Mechanism-Vitalism Controversy," *Journal of the History of Biology* 5, no. 1 (Spring 1972): 159–88.

Helm, Georg, *Die Lehre von der Energie, historisch-kritisch entwickelt. Nebst Beiträgen zu einer allgemeinen Energetik*. Leipzig: Felix, 1887.

Henderson, Linda Dalrymple, *The Fourth Dimension and Non-Euclidean Geometry in Modern Art*. Princeton, NJ: Princeton University Press, 1983.

Henry, Lynn, Sara, "Paul Klee, Nature, and Modern Science: The 1920s." Ph.D. dissertation, University of California, Berkeley, 1976.

——, "Form-Creating Energies: Paul Klee and Physics," *Arts Magazine* 52 (September 1977): 118–21.

Hepp, Corona, *Avantgarde. Moderne Kunst, Kulturkritik und Reformbewegungen nach der Jahrhundertwende*. Munich: DTV, 1987.

Hersey, George L., *The Monumental Impulse: Architecture's Biological Roots*. Cambridge, MA: MIT Press, 1999.

Hildebrand, Adolf, *Das Problem der Form in der bildenden Kunst*. Straßbourg: Heitz, 1893.

Hillermann, Horst, "Zur Begriffsgeschichte von 'Monismus'," *Archiv für Begriffsgeschichte* 20 (1976): 214–35.

——, *Der vereinsmäßige Zusammenschluß bürgerlich-weltanschaulicher Reformvernunft in der Monismusbewegung des 19. Jahrhunderts*. Kastellaun: Aloys Henn, 1976.

Hofmann, Werner, "Ein Beitrag zur 'Morphologischen Kunsttheorie' der Gegenwart," *Alte und neue Kunst* 2 (1953): 63–80.

——, *Zeichen und Gestalt. Die Malerei des 20. Jahrhunderts*. Frankfurt am Main: Fischer, 1957.

——, *Die Plastik des 20. Jahrhunderts*. Frankfurt am Main: Fischer, 1958.

——, *Turning Points in Twentieth Century Art: 1890–1917*. Translated by Charles Kessler. New York: George Braziller, 1969.

Holt, Niles R., "Ernst Haeckel's Monisitic Religion," *Journal of the History of Ideas* 32, no. 2 (April–June 1971): 265–80.

——, "A Note on Wilhelm Ostwald's Energism," *Isis* 61, no. 208 (Fall 1970): 396–89.

Huggler, M., *Paul Klee: Die Malerei als Blick in den Kosmos*. Frauenfeld and Stuttgart: Huber 1969.

Huyghe, René, *Formes et Forces: de l'atome à Rembrandt*. Paris: Flammarion, 1971.

Jackson, Lesley, *The New Look: Design in the Fifties*, London: Thames & Hudson, 1991.

——, *From Atoms to Patterns: Crystal Structure Designs from the 1951 Festival of Britain*. London: Richard Dennis Publications and Wellcome Collection, 2008.

Jain, Elenor, *Das Prinzip Leben: Lebensphilosophie und ästhetische Erziehung*. Frankfurt am Main: Peter Lang, 1993.

Jauss, Hans Robert, "Ursprünge der Naturfeindschaft in der Ästhetik der Moderne," in Heinz-Dieter Weber, ed., *Vom Wandel des neuzeitlichen Naturbegriffs*. Konstanz: Universitätsverlag Konstanz, 1989, 207–25.

Jones, Owen, *The Grammar of Ornament; illustrated by Examples from Various Styles of Ornament*. London: Day & Son, 1856.

Joseph, Lawrence E. *Gaia. The Growth of an Idea*. New York: St. Martin's Press, 1990.

Kac, Eduardo, *Signs of Life: Bio Art and Beyond*. Cambridge, MA: MIT Press, 2007.

Kállai, Ernst (Ernő), "Kunst und Technik," *bauhaus* 2, no. 2–3 (1 July 1928): 3–4.

——, "Rhythmus in Bildern," *Die Weltbühne* 26, no. 41 (October 7, 1930): 553–56.

——, "Zeichen und Bilder," *Die Weltbühne*, 28, no. 38 (June 1932): 444–45.

——, "Bioromantik," *Forum* (1932): 271–74.

——, "Bioromantik," *Sozialistische Monatshefte* 75, no. 1 (January 1933): 46–50.

——, "Kunst und Wirklichkeit," *Forum*, no. 1 (1933): 8–11.

——, *A természet rejtett arca* [The Hidden Face of Nature]. Budapest: Misztótfalusi, 1947.

——, *Művészet veszélyes csillagzat allatt. Válogatott cikkek, tanulmányok* [Art under Dangerous Constellations. Selected articles, studies]. Edited by Éva Forgács. Budapest: Corvina, 1981.

——, *Vision und Formgesetz. Aufsätze über Kunst und Künstler 1921–1933*. Edited by Tanya Frank. Leipzig, Weimar: Gustav Kiepenheuer, 1986.

——, *Schriften in deutscher Sprache, 1920–1925*. Vol. 2 of *Gesammelte Werke/Összegyüjtöt írások*. Edited by Monika Wucher. Budapest: Argumentum Kiadó and MTA Művészettörténeti Kutató Intézet, 1999.

——, *Schriften in deutscher Sprache, 1926–1930*. Vol. 4 of *Gesammelte Werke/Összegyüjtöt írások*. Edited by Monika Wucher. Budapest: Argumentum Kiadó and MTA Művészettörténeti Kutató Intézet, 2003.

——, *Schriften in deutscher Sprache, 1931–1937*. Vol. 5 of *Gesammelte Werke/Összegyüjtött írások*. Edited by Monika Wucher. Budapest: Argumentum Kiadó and MTA Mûvészettörténeti Kutató Intézet, 2006.

Kandinsky, Wassily, *Über das Geistige in der Kunst, insbesondere in der Malerei*. Munich: R. Piper, 1912.

——, *Concerning the Spritual in Art*. Translated and introduced by Michael T.H. Sadler. London: Constable & Co., 1914.

Kapp, Ernst, *Grundlinien einer Philosophie der Technik. Zur Entstehungsgeschichte der Cultur aus neuen Gesichtspunkten*. Braunschweig: Westermann, 1877.

——, *Ludwig Klages. Gesammelte Aufsätze und Vorträge zu seinem Werk*. Bonn: Bouvier Verlag Herbert Grundmann, 1984.

——, "Klages und Prinzhorn," *Hestia* (1986–87): 8–21.

Keitel-Holz, Klaus, *Ernst Haeckel: Forscher—Künstler—Mensch*. Frankfurt am Main: R.G. Fischer, 1984.

Kelly, Alfred, *The Descent of Darwin. The Popularization of Darwinism in Germany, 1860–1914*. Chapel Hill, NC: University of North Carolina Press, 1981.

Kemal, Salim and Ivan Gaskell, eds., *Landscape, Natural Beauty and the Arts*. Cambridge, MA: Cambridge University Press, 1993.

Kepes, György, ed., *The New Landscape in Art and Science*. Chicago, IL: Paul Theobald, 1956.

——, *Structure in Art and in Science*. New York: George Braziller, 1965.

Keshavjee, Serena, ""Natural History, Cultural History and the Art History of Élie Faure," *Nineteenth-Century Art Worldwide*, 8, no. 2 (Fall 2009), online journal.

——, "The Structure of Nature: Natural, Scientific, and Artistic Forms in Nineteenth-Century France," *The Structurist*, 49/50 (2009-2010): 44-50.

Kessler, Charles S., "Sun Worship and Anxiety: Nature, Nakedness and Nihilism in German Expressionist Painting," *Magazine of Art* 45 (November 1952): 304–12.

King, James. *The Last of the Moderns. A Life of Herbert Read*. London: Weidenfeld & Nicolson, 1990.

Kinmont, David, "Vitalism and Creativity: Bergson, Driesch, Maritain and the Visual Arts, 1900–1914," in Martin Pollock, ed., *Common Denominators in Art and Science*. Aberdeen: Aberdeen University Press, 1983, 69–77

Kirk, James Ernest, "Organicism as Reenchantment: Whitehead, Prigogine, and Barth." Ph.D. dissertation, University of Texas, Dallas, 1991.

Klages, Ludwig, *Ausdrucksbewegung und Gestaltungskraft*. Leipzig: Engelmann, 1913.

——, *Mensch und Erde. Fünf Abhandlungen*. Munich: G. Müller, 1920.

——, *Vom kosmogonischen Eros*. Munich: G. Müller, 1922.

——, *Der Geist als Widersacher der Seele*. Leipzig: Barth, 1929–33.

——, *Vom Wesen des Rhythmus*. Kampen auf Sylt: Niels Kampmann, 1934.

——, *Geist und Leben*. Berlin: Junker & Dünnhaupt, 1934.

——, *Der Mensch und das Leben*. Jena: Eugen Diederichs, 1937.

Klee, Felix, *Paul Klee: His Life and Work in Documents*. Berkeley, Los Angeles, CA: University of California Press, 1964.

Klee, Paul, *Pädagogisches Skizzenbuch*. Munich: Langen, 1925.

——, *Das bildnerische Denken. Schriften zur Form- und Gestaltungslehre*. Edited by Jürg Spiller. Vol. 1. Basle: Schwabe, 1956.

——, *The Thinking Eye: The Notebooks of Paul Klee*. Vol. 1. Translated by Ralph Mannheim, Charlotte Weidler, and Joyce Wittenborn. New York: Wittenborn, 1961.

——, *Unendliche Naturgeschichte. Form und Gestaltungslehre. Band II*. Edited by Jürg Spiller. Basle, Stuttgart: Schwabe & Co., 1970.

——, *The Nature of Nature: The Notebooks of Paul Klee*. Vol. 2. Translated by Ralph Manheim. Woodstock, NY: The Overlook Press, 1992.

Klotz, Heinrich, ed., *Matjuschin und die Leningrader Avantgarde* (exh. cat.). Karlsruhe: Zentrum für Kunst und Medientechnologie; Munich and Stuttgart: Oktogon, 1991.

Kluge, Thomas, *Gesellschaft, Natur, Technik. Zur lebensphilosophischen und ökologischen Kritik von Technik und Gesellschaft*. Opladen: Westdeutscher Verlag, 1985.

Kockerbeck, Christoph, *Ernst Haeckels "Kunstformen der Natur" und ihr Einfluß auf die deutsche bildende Kunst der Jahrhundertwende*. Frankfurt am Main: Peter Lang, 1986.

Krause, Erika, "L'influence de Ernst Haeckel sur L'Art nouveau," in Jean Clair et al., eds., *L'ame au corps: arts et sciences 1793–1993* (exh. cat.). Paris: Réunion des musées nationaux, 1993: 342–51.

Krause, Ernst (Carus Sterne), *Werden und Vergehen. Eine Entwicklungsgeschichte des Naturganzen in gemeinverständlicher Fassung*. Berlin: Borntraeger, 1876.

——, *Natur und Kunst. Studien zur Entwicklungsgeschichte der Kunst*. Berlin: Allgemeiner Verein für deutsche Literatur, 1891.

Krauss, Rosalind, *The Originality of the Avant-Garde and Other Modernist Myths*. Cambridge, MA: MIT Press, 1985.

Krieger, Murray, *A Reopening of Closure: Organicism Against Itself*. New York: Columbia University Press, 1989.

Kröger, Michael. "'... gleichsam biologische Urzeichen ...' Die Erfindung biomorpher Natur in Malerei und Fotografie der dreissiger Jahre," *Kritische Berichte* 18, no. 4 (April 1990): 3–87.

Kropotkin, Peter, *Mutual Aid: A Factor of Evolution*. London: Heineman, 1902.

Kudielka, Robert, *Paul Klee: The Nature of Creation, Works, l914–1940*. London: Hayward Galleries and Lund Humphries, 2002.

Kühne-Bertram, Gudrun, *Aus dem Leben—ZUM Leben: Entstehung, Wesen und Bedeutung populärer Lebensphilosophien in der Geistesgeschichte des 19. Jahrhunderts*. Frankfurt am Main: Peter Lang, 1987.

Kukartz, Wilfried, "Ludwig Klages als Prophet der drohenden Umweltkatastrophe," *Hestia* (1982–83): 67–79.

Kull, Kalevi, "Biosemiotics in the Twentieth Century: A View from Biology," *Semiotica* 127, no. 1/4 (1999): 385–414.

Kunst und Naturform (exh. cat.). Basle: Kunsthalle, 1958.

Landmann, Robert, *Ascona—Monte Verità. Auf der Suche nach dem Paradies*. Berlin: Ullstein Sachbuch, 1973.

Laqueur, Walter Z., *Young Germany: A History of the German Youth Movement*. London: Routledge & Kegan Paul, 1962.

Larson, Barbara. *The Dark Side of Nature: Science, Society and the Fantastic in the Work of Odilon Redon*. University Park, PA: Pennsylvania State University, 2005.

Lears, T.J. Jackson, *No Place of Grace: Antimodernism and the Transformation of American Culture 1880–1920*. New York: Pantheon, 1981.

Lehmann, Otto, *Flüssige Kristalle und die Theorien des Lebens*. Leipzig: Barth, 1904.

——, *Die neue Welt der flüssigen Kristalle und deren Bedeutung für Physik, Chemie, Technik und Biologie*. Leipzig: Akad. Verlagsgesellschaft, 1911.

Lenoir, Timothy, *The Strategy of Life: Teleology and Mechanics in Nineteenth Century German Biology*. Dordrecht: D. Reidel, 1982.

——, "General Factors in the Origin of *Romantische Naturphilosophie,*" *Journal of the History of Biology* 11, no. 1 (Spring 1978): 57–100.

Lichtenstern, Christa, *Die Wirkungsgeschichte der Metamorphosenlehre Goethes. Von Philipp Otto Runge bis Josef Beuys*. Weinheim: VCH, 1990.

——, *Metamorphose vom Mythos zum Prozessdenken. Ovid-Rezeption, Surrealistische Ästhetik, Verwandlungsthematik der Nachkriegskunst*. Weinheim: VCH/Acta Humanora, 1992.

Lieber, Hans-Joachim, *Kulturkritik und Lebensphilosophie*. Darmstadt: Wissenschaftliche Buchgesellschaft, 1974.

Lindsay, Kenneth C. and Peter Vergo, eds., *Kandinsky: Complete Writings on Art*. 2 vols. Boston, MA: G.K. Hall, 1982.

Linse, Ulrich, *Ökopax und Anarchie. Eine Geschichte des ökologischen Bewegungen in Deutschland*. Munich: DTV, 1986.

——, *Zurück, o Mensch, zur Mutter Erde*. Munich: DTV, 1983.

Lodder, Christina, "Organic Construction: Harnessing an Alternative Technology," in Christina Lodder, *Russian Constructivism*. London and New Haven, CT: Yale University Press, 1983, 205–23.

Lovejoy, Arthur O., *The Great Chain of Being. A Study in the History of an Idea*. Cambridge, MA: Harvard University Press, 1950.

Lovelock, J.E., *Gaia: A New Look at Life on Earth*. Oxford: Oxford University Press, 1979.

MacGregor, John M., *The Discovery of the Art of the Insane*. Princeton, NJ: Princeton University Press, 1989.

Mainzer, Klaus, "Von der Naturphilosophie zur Naturwissenschaft. Zum neuzeitlichen Wandel des Naturbegriffs," in Heinz-Dieter Weber, ed., *Vom Wandel des neuzeitlichen Naturbegriffs*. Konstanz: Universitätsverlag Konstanz, 1989, 11–31.

Manske, Beate, ed., *Die organische Form: Produktgestaltung, 1930–1960* (exh. cat.). Bremen: Wilhelm-Wagenfeld-Stiftung 2003.

Markov, Vladimir, *Printsipy tvorchestva v plasticheskikh iskusstvakh: faktura* [Creative Principles in the Plastic Arts: Faktura]. Petrograd, 1914.

Marten, Heinz-Georg, *Sozialbiologismus. Biologische Grundpositionen der politischen Ideengeschichte*. Frankfurt am Main: Campus, 1983.

Martens, Günter, *Vitalismus und Expressionismus. Ein Beitrag zur Genese und Deutung expressionistische Stilstrukturen und Motive*. Stuttgart: W. Kohlhammer, 1971.

Mattenklott, Gert. "Nietzsches 'Geburt der Tragödie' als Konzept einer bürgerlichen Kulturrevolution," in Gert Mattenklott and Klaus R. Scherpe, eds., *Positionen der literarischen Intelligenz zwischen bürgerlicher Reaktion und Imperialismus*. Kronberg/Ts.: Scriptor, 1973, 103–20.

——, *Karl Blossfeldt 1865–1932. Das photographische Werk*. Munich: Prestel, 1981.

——, foreword to Ernst Fuhrmann, *Neue Wege*. Hamburg: Ernst Fuhrmann Archiv, 1983, I–IX.

Mayr, Ernst, *The Growth of Biological Thought*. Cambridge, MA: Belknap Press, 1982.

——, *This Is Biology: The Science of the Living World*. Cambridge, MA: Belknap Press, 1997.

McIntosh McHenry, Deni, *Organic Abstraction* (exh. cat.). Kansas City, MI: Nelson Atkins Museum of Art, 1991.

McKnight, Stephen A., ed., *Science, Pseudo-Science, and Utopianism in Early Modern Thought*. Columbia, MO: University of Missouri Press, 1992.

Merchant, Carolyn. *The Death of Nature: Women, Ecology and the Scientific Revolution.* San Francisco, CA: Harper & Row, 1980.

Metamorphose. British Surrealists and Neo-Romantics 1935–55 (exh. cat.). New York: Guillaume Gallozzi, 1982.

Michalski, Ernst, "Die Entwicklungsgeschichtliche Bedeutung des Jugendstils" (1925), in Jost Hermand, ed., *Jugendstil*. Darmstadt: Wissentschaftliche Buchgesellschaft, 1971, 8–26.

Misler, Nicoletta and John E. Bowlt, eds., *Pavel Filonov: A Hero and His Fate*. Austin, TX: Silvergirl, 1983.

Mitcham, Carl, *Thinking through Technology: The Path between Engineering and Philosophy*. Chicago, IL: University of Chicago Press, 1994.

Mölk, Ulrich, ed., *Europäische Jahrhundertwende. Wissenschaft, Literatur und Kunst um 1900.* Göttingen: Wallenstein, 1999.

Moholy-Nagy, László, *Malerei, Photographie, Film*. Munich: Langen, 1925.

——, *Von Material zu Architektur*. Munich: Langen, 1929.

——, *The New Vision*. New York: W.W. Norton & Co., 1938.

——, *Vision in Motion*. Chicago, IL: Paul Theobald, 1947.

Moleschott, Jacob, *Physiologie des Stoffwechsels in Pflanzen und Thieren. Ein Handbuch für Naturforscher, Landwirthe und Ärzte.* Erlangen: Enke, 1851.

——, *Der Kreislauf des Lebens. Physiologische Antworten auf Liebig's Chemische Briefe.* Mainz: Zabern, 1852.

——, *Die Einheit des Lebens*, Giessen 1864.

——, *Die Einheit der Wissenschaft aus dem Gesichtspunkt der Lehre vom Leben*. Giessen, 1879.

Montgomery, David L., "The Myth of Organicism: From Bad Science to Great Art," *The Musical Quarterly* 76 (Spring 1992): 17–66.

Morton, Peter, *The Vital Science: Biology and the Literary Imagination, 1860–1900.* London: George Allen & Unwin, 1984.

Müller, Roland. *Das verzwistete Ich—Ludwig Klages und sein philosophisches Hauptwerk "Der Geist als Widersacher der Seele"*. Frankfurt am Main, Berne: Peter Lang, 1971.

Mundy, Jennifer Virginia, "Biomorphism." Ph.D. dissertation, University of London, 1987.

——, "Form and Creation: The Impact of the Biological Sciences on Modern Art," in *Creation: Modern Art and Nature* (exh. cat.), Edinburgh: Scottish National Gallery, 1984, 16–23.

Nachtigall, Werner, *Konstruktion, Biologie und Technik*. Düsseldorf: VDI, 1986.

Nietzsche, Friedrich, *Werke und Briefe. Historisch-kritische Gesamtausgabe*. 5 vols. Munich: Beck, 1934–42.

——, *Werke. Kritische Gesamtausgabe*. Edited by Giorgio Colli and Mazzino Montinari, Wolfgang Müller-Lauter, and Volker Gerhardt. Berlin: de Gruyter, 1967–.

——, *The Complete Works of Friedrich Nietzsche*. Translated and edited by Oscar Levy. 18 vols. New York: Gordon Press, 1974.

Oken, Lorenz, *Lehrbuch der Naturphilosophie*. Jena: F. Frommann, 1809–11.

——, *Elements of Physiophilosophy*. Translated by Alfred Tulk. London: Ray Society, 1847.

Orchard, Karin and Jörg Zimmermann, eds., *Die Erfindung der Natur: Max Ernst, Paul Klee, Wols und das surreale Universum* (exh. cat.). Freiburg im Breisgau: Rombach, 1994.

Ostwald, Wilhelm, *Vorlesungen über Naturphilosophie*. Leipzig: Veit, 1902.

——, *The Relations of Biology and the Neighbouring Sciences*. Berkeley, CA: Berkeley University Press, 1903.

——, *Malerbriefe. Beiträge zur Theorie und Praxis der Malerei*. Leipzig: S. Hirzel, 1904.

——, *Naturphilosophie*. Leipzig, Berlin, 1907.

——, *Energetische Grundlagen der Kulturwissenschaft*. Leipzig: Klinkhardt, 1909.

——, *Monistische Sonntagspredigten*. Berlin: Dt. Monisten-Bund, 1911.

——, *Die Energie*. 2nd ed. Leipzig: Barth, 1912.

——, *Der energetische Imperativ*. Leipzig: Akad. Verlagsgesellschaft, 1912.

——, *Grundriß der Naturphilosophie*. 2nd ed. Leipzig: Reclam, 1913.

——, *Moderne Naturphilosophie*. Leipzig: Akad. Verlagsgesellschaft, 1914.

——, *Nature Philosophy*. Translated by T. Seltzer. New York: Holt, 1919.

Papanicolaou, Andrew C., *Bergson and Modern Thought: Towards a Unified Science*. New York: Harwood, 1987.

Parkinson, Gavin, *Surrealism, Art and Modern Science: Relativity, Quantum Mechanics, Epistemology*. New Haven, CT: Yale University Press, 2008.

Pataki, Gábor, "'Technoromantik'," in Hubertus Gassner, Karlheinz Kopanski, and Karin Stengel, eds., *Die Konstruktion der Utopie*. Kassel and Marburg: documenta Archiv and Jonas Verlag, 1992, 203–8.

Pepper, David, *The Roots of Modern Environmentalism*. London: Croom Helm, 1984.

Persell, Stuart M., *Neo-Lamarckism and the Evolutionary Controversy in France 1870–1920*. Lewiston: Edwin Mellen Press, 1999.

Phillips, D.C., "Organicism in the Late Nineteenth and Early Twentieth Centuries," *Journal of the History of Ideas* 31, no. 3 (July–September 1970): 413–32.

——, *Holistic Thought in Social Science*. Stanford, CA: Stanford University Press, 1976.

Phillips, Lisa, ed., *Vital Signs: Organic Abstraction from the Permanent Collection* (exh. cat.). New York: Whitney Museum of American Art, 1988.

Pichot, André, *Histoire de la notion de vie*. Paris: Gallimard, 1993.

Pois, Robert A., *National Socialism and the Religion of Nature*. London: Croom Helm, 1986.

Pollock, Martin, ed., *Common Denominators in Art and Science*. Aberdeen: Aberdeen University Press, 1983.

Povelikhina, Alla V., *Organica. The Non-Objective World of Nature in the Russian Avant-Garde of the 20th Century* (exh. cat.). Cologne: Galerie Gmurzynska, 1999.

——, *Organica: New Perception of Nature in the Russian Avant-Gardism of the 20th Century*. Moscow: Moscow Art Centre, 2001.

Prange, Regine, *Das Kristalline als Kunstsymbol. Bruno Taut und Paul Klee. Zur Reflexion des Abstrakten in Kunst und Kunsttheorie der Moderne*. Hildesheim: Georg Olms, 1991.

Prinzhorn, Hans, *Bildnerei der Geisteskranken: Ein Beitrag zur Psychologie und Psychopathologie der Gestaltung*. Berlin: Springer, 1922.

——, *Leib—Seele—Einheit. Ein Kernproblem der neuen Psychologie*, Potsdam: Müller & Kiepenheuer, 1927.

——, *Artistry of the Mentally Ill. A Contribution to the Psychology and Psychopathology of Configuration*. Translated by Eric von Brockdorff. Berlin: Springer, 1972.

Rádl, Emanuel, *The History of Biological Theories, 1905–09*. London: Oxford University Press, 1930.

Railing, Patricia, "'The Machine is no More than a Brush': Morphology of Art and the Machine in Russian Avant-Garde Theory and Practice," *The Structurist*, no. 35–36 (1995–96): 49–56.

Rapaport, Brooke Kamin and Kevin L. Stayton, *Vital Forms: American Art and Design in the Atomic Age, 1940–1960* (exh. cat.). New York: Brooklyn Museum of Art, Harry N. Abrams, 2002.

Read, Herbert, *The Meaning of Art*. London: Faber & Faber, 1931.

——, *Unit 1. The Modern Movement in English Architecture Painting and Sculpture*. London: Cassell & Co., 1934.

——, ed., *Surrealism*. London: Faber & Faber, 1936.

——, *Art and Society*. London: William Heinemann, 1937.

——, "An Art of Pure Form," *London Bulletin*, no. 14 (May 1939): 6–9.

——, *Icon and Idea. The Function of Art in the Development of Human Consciousness*. London: Faber & Faber, 1955.

——, *The Forms of Things Unknown: Essays Towards an Aesthetic Philosophy*. London: Faber & Faber, 1960.

——, *The Origins of Form in Art*. London: Thames & Hudson, 1964.

Reichow, Hans Bernhard, *Organische Stadtbaukunst: Von der Großstadt zur Stadtlandschaft*. Braunschweig: Georg Westermann, 1948.

Richards, Robert J., *The Tragic Sense of Life: Ernst Haeckel and the Struggle over Evolutionary Thought*. Chicago, IL: The University of Chicago Press, 2008.

Riegl, Alois, *Die spätrömische Kunst-Industrie nach den Funden in Österreich-Ungarn*. 2 vols. Vienna: Verlag der Staatsdruckerei, 1901–23.

——, *Stilfragen. Grundlegungen zu einer Geschichte der Ornamentik*. Berlin: Siemens, 1893.

——, *Late Roman Industry*. Translated and annotated by Rolf Winkes. Rome: Giorgio Bretschneider, 1985.

——, *Problems of Style: Foundations for a History of Ornament.* Translated by Evelyn Kain. Annotated by David Castriota. Preface by Henri Zerner. Princeton, NJ: Princeton University Press, 1992.

Ringbom, Sixten, *The Sounding Cosmos: A Study in the Spiritualism of Kandinsky and the Genesis of Abstract Painting*. Åbo: Åbo Akad., 1970.

——, "Paul Klee and the Inner Truth to Nature," *Arts Magazine*, 52 (September 1977): 112–17.

Ritterbush, Phillip C., *The Art of Organic Forms* (exh. cat.). Washington, DC: Smithsonian Institution Press, 1968.

——, "Organic Form: Aesthetics and Objectivity in the Study of Form in the Life Sciences," in George S. Rousseau, ed., *Organic Form: The Life of an Idea*. London and Boston: Routledge & Kegan Paul, 1972, 26–59.

Rosenblum, Robert, *Modern Painting and the Northern Romantic Tradition. Friedrich to Rothko*. New York: Harper & Rowe, 1975.

——, "Resurrecting Darwin and Genesis: Thoughts on Nature and Modern Art," in *Creation: Modern Art and Nature* (exh. cat.). Edinburgh: Scottish National Gallery, 1984, 9–15.

Rousseau, George S., ed., *Organic Form: The Life of an Idea*. London and Boston, MA: Routledge & Kegan Paul, 1972.

Sandmann, Jürgen, *Der Bruch mit der humanitären Tradition. Die Biologisierung der Ethik bei Ernst Haeckel und anderen Darwinisten seiner Zeit*. Stuttgart: Gustav Fischer, 1990.

Schall, Janice Joan, "Rhythm and Art in Germany, 1900–1930." Ph.D. dissertation, University of Texas at Austin, 1989.

Scheler, Max, *Die Stellung des Menschen im Kosmos*. Darmstadt: Reichl, 1928.

——, *Man's Place in Nature*. Translated and introduced by Hans Meyerhoff. New York: The Noonday Press, 1961.

Schelling, Friedrich Wilhelm Joseph von, *Über das Verhältnis der bildenden Künste zu der Natur*. Berlin: Reimer, 1843.

Schenk, Robert and Georg Schmidt, *Form in Art and Nature*. Basle: Basilius-Presse, 1960.

Schlaf, Johannes, *Psychomonismus, Polarität und Individualität; ein offener Brief an Herrn Professor Max Verworn*. Leipzig: Eckardt, 1908.

Schleiden, Matthias Jakob, *Die Physiologie der Pflanzen und Thiere und Theorie der Pflanzencultur*. Braunschweig: Vieweg, 1850.

Schmutzler, Robert, "Der Sinn des Art Nouveau," in Jost Hermand, ed., *Jugendstil*. Darmstadt: Wissentschaftliche Buchgesellschaft, 1971, 296–314.

Schopenhauer, Arthur, *Über den Willen in der Natur. Eine Erörterung der Bestätigungen, welche die Philosophie des Verfassers, seit ihrem Auftreten durch die empirischen Wissenschaften erhalten hat.* Frankfurt am Main: Schmerber, 1836.

Schwann, Theodor, *Mikroskopische Untersuchungen über die Übereinstimmung in der Struktur und dem Wachsthum der Thiere und Pflanzen*. Berlin: Sander, 1839.

Scott, Alwyn, *The Non-Linear Universe. Chaos, Emergence, Life*. Berlin: Springer, 2007.

Semon, Richard, *Die Mneme als erhaltendes Prinzip im Wechsel des organischen Geschehens*. Leipzig: Engelmann, 1904.

——, *Mnemic Psychology*. Translated by Bella Duffy. Introduction by Vernon Lee. London: George Allen & Unwin, 1923.

Shortland, Michael, ed., *Science and Nature: Essays in the History of the Environmental Sciences*. London: British Society for the History of Science, 1993.

Silverman, Debora Leah, "Nature, Nobility, and Neurology: The Ideological Origins of *Art Nouveau* in France, 1889–1900." Ph.D. dissertation, Princeton University, 1983.

——, *Art Nouveau in Fin-de-Siècle France: Politics, Psychology and Style*. Berkeley, CA: University of California Press, 1989.

Simmel, Georg, "The Metropolis and Mental Life" (1903), in Georg Simmel, *On Individuality and Social Forms*. Edited by Donald N. Levine. Chicago, IL: University of Chicago Press, 1971, 324–39.

Smuts, Jan, *Holism and Evolution*. London: MacMillian, 1936.

Spengler, Oswald, *Der Untergang des Abendlandes. Umrisse einer Morphologie der Weltgeschichte*. 2 vols. Munich: Beck, 1919–22.

——, *The Decline of the West. Form and Actuality*. Translated by Charles Francis Atkinson. New York: Alfred A. Knopf, 1927.

Stafford, Barbara, *Body Criticism: Imaging the Unseen in Enlightenment Art and Medicine*. New York: Zone, 1991.

——, *Artful Science: Enlightenment Entertainment and the Eclipse of Visual Education*. Cambridge, MA: MIT Press, 1994.

Steadman, Philip, *The Evolution of Designs: Biological Analogy in Architecture and the Applied Arts*. Cambridge, MA: Cambridge University Press, 1979.

Steinberg, Leo, "The Eye is a Part of the Mind," *Partisan Review* 20, no. 2 (1953): 194–212.

Stokes, Charlotte, "The Scientific Methods of Max Ernst: His Use of Scientific Subjects from *La Nature*," *The Art Bulletin* 62 (September 1980): 453–65.

Taylor, Seth David, *Left-Wing Nietzscheans: The Politics of German Expressionism, 1910–1920*. New York: Walter de Gruyter, 1990.

Thèse, Synthèse, Antithèse (exh. cat.). Lucerne: Kunstmuseum Lucerne, 1935.

Thomas, Richard Hinton, "Nietzsche in Weimar Germany and the Case of Ludwig Klages," in Anthony Phelan, ed., *The Weimar Dilemma: Intellectuals in the Weimar Republic*. Manchester: Manchester University Press, 1985, 71–91.

Thompson, D'Arcy Wentworth. *On Growth and Form*. Cambridge, UK: Cambridge University Press, 1917.

Trotignon, Pierre, *L'idée de vie chez Bergson et la critique de la métaphysique*. Paris: Presses Universitaires de France, 1968.

Tuchman, Maurice and Judi Freeman, eds., *The Spiritual in Art: Abstract Painting, 1890–1985* (exh. cat.). Los Angeles, CA: LACMA; New York: Abbeville, 1986.

Uexküll, Gudrun von, *Jakob von Uexküll. Seine Welt und seine Umwelt*. Hamburg: C. Wegner, 1964.

Uexküll, Johann Jacob von, *Umwelt und Innenwelt der Tiere*. Berlin: Springer, 1909.

——, *Bausteine zu einer biologischen Weltanschauung*. Munich: F. Bruckmann, 1913.

——, *Staatsbiologie (Anatomie—Physiologie—Pathologie des Staates)*. Berlin: Paetel, 1920.

——, *Die Lebenslehre*. Potsdam: Müller & Kiepenheuer, 1930.

Van Eck, Caroline, *Organicism in Nineteenth-Century Architecture: An Inquiry Into Its Theoretical and Philosophical Background*. Amsterdam: Architecture and Natura Press, 1994.

Vattimo, Gianni, *The End of Modernity: Nihilism and Hermeneutics in Postmodern Culture*. Translated and introduced by Jon R. Snyder. Baltimore, MD: The Johns Hopkins University Press, 1988.

Verdi, Richard. *Klee and Nature*. Munich: Zwemmer, 1984.

——, "Botanical Imagery in the Art of Klee," in Ernst-Gerhard Güse, ed., *Paul Klee: Dialogue with Nature*, Munich: Prestel, 1991, 18–31.

Voigt, Annette, "Die Natur des Organischen—'Leben' als kulturelle Idee der Moderne," in Annette Geiger, Stefanie Hennecke, and Christin Kempf, eds., *Spielarten des Organischen in Architektur, Design und Kunst*, Berlin: Reimer, 2005, 36–49.

Vucinich, Alexander, *Darwin in Russian Thought*. Berkeley, CA: University of California Press, 1988.

Waddington, C.H., *Behind Appearances: A Study of the Relations between Painting and the Natural Sciences in this Century*. Cambridge, MA: MIT Press, 1969.

Waenerberg, Annika, *Urpflanze und Ornament. Pflanzenmorphologische Anregungen in der Kunsttheorie und Kunst von Goethe bis zum Jugendstil*. Helsinki: Societas Scientiarum Fennia, 1992.

——, "Das Organische in Kunst und Gestaltung: Eine kurze Geschichte des Begriffs," in Annette Geiger, Stefanie Hennecke, and Christin Kempf, eds., *Spielarten des Organischen in Architektur, Design und Kunst*. Berlin: Reimer, 2005, 21–35.

Wagner, Adolf, *Geschichte des Lamarckismus: Als Einführung in die Psycho-Biologische Bewegung der Gegenwart*. Stuttgart: Franckh'sche Verlagshandlung, [1909].

Warburg, Aby, *The Renewal of Pagan Antiquity*. Introduction by Kurt Foster. Translated by David Britt. Santa Monica, CA: Getty Research Institute for the History of Art and the Humanities, 1999.

Washton Long, Rose-Carol, *Kandinsky: The Development of an Abstract Style*. Oxford: Clarendon Press; New York: Oxford University Press, 1980.

Wedewer, Rolf, "Zur Naturvorstellung Arps," *Pantheon* 43 (1985): 171–78.

Weindling, Paul, "Ernst Haeckel, Darwinismus and the Secularization of Nature," in James R. Moore, ed., *History, Humanity and Evolution: Essays for John C. Greene*. Cambridge, MA: Cambridge University Press, 1989, 311–27.

Weinstein, Michael A., *Structure of Human Life: A Vitalist Ontology*. New York: New York University Press, 1979.

Welter, Volker M., *Biopolis: Patrick Geddes and the City of Life*. Cambridge, MA: MIT Press, 2002.

Whitehead, Alfred North, *Science and the Modern World*. Cambridge, MA: Cambridge University Press, 1927.

——, *Modes of Thought*. New York: MacMillan, 1938.

Whyte, Lancelot Law, *The Unitary Principle in Physics and Biology*. London: Cresset, 1949.

——, ed., *Aspects of Form: A Symposium on Form and Nature in Art*. London: Percy Lund Humphries, 1951.

——, *Accent on Form: An Anticipation of the Science of Tomorrow*. New York: Harper & Brothers, 1954.

——, *The Universe of Experience: A World View Beyond Science and Religion*. New York: Harper & Row, 1974.

Wichmann, Siegfried, *Jugendstil Art Nouveau: Floral and Functional Forms*. Boston: New York Graphic Society and Little, Brown & Co., 1985.

Wiedmann, August, *Romantic Roots in Modern Art*. Old Woking, Surrey, England: Gresham Press, 1979.

——, "The Organic Theory of Art," in August Wiedmann, *Romantic Art Theories*. Henley-on-Thames: Gresham Books, 1986, 89–100.

Wightman, W.P.D., *Science and Monism*. London: Allen & Unwin, 1934.

Williams, John Alexander, *Turning to Nature in Germany: Hiking, Nudism and Conservation, 1900–1940*. Stanford, CA: Stanford University Press, 2007.

Wörner-Heil, Ortrud, *Von der Utopie zur Sozialreform*. Darmstadt: Hessische Historische Kommission, 1996.

Wolberg, Lewis R., *Micro-Art: Art Images in a Hidden World*. New York: Abrams, 1978.

Wolschke-Bulmahn, Jürgen, *Auf der Suche nach Arkadien: Zur Landschaftsidealen und Formen der Naturaneignung in der Jugendbewegung und ihrer Bedeutung für die Landespflege*. Munich: Minerva, 1990.

Woodcock, George, *Herbert Read: The Stream and the Source*. London: Faber & Faber, 1972.

Worster, Donald, *Nature's Economy. A History of Ecological Ideas*. 2nd ed. Cambridge, MA: Cambridge University Press, 1994.

Worringer, Wilhelm, *Abstraktion und Einfühlung. Ein Beitrag zur Stilpsychologie*. Inaugural-Dissertation, Universität Bern. Neuwied: 1907.

——, *Abstraction and Empathy: A Contribution to the Psychology of Style*. Translated by Michael Bullock. London: Routledge & Kegan Paul, 1953.

——, *Formprobleme der Gotik*. Munich: R. Piper, 1911.

——, *Form in Gothic*. Translated and edited by Herbert Read. London: Alec Tiranti, 1957.

Wucher, Monika, "Attribute des Konstruktivismus. Die Ordungsversuche des Ernő Kállai," in Hubertus Gassner, Karlheinz Kopanski, and Karin Stengel, eds., *Die Konstruktion der Utopie*. Kassel and Marburg: documenta Archiv and Jonas Verlag, 1992, 190–95.

Wünsche, Isabel, *Das Kunstkonzept der Organischen Kultur in der Kunst der russischen Avantgarde*. Ph.D. dissertation, Heidelberg University, 1997. Ketsch: Mikroform Dissertation, 1997.

———, "M.V. Matiushin's Organic Culture: Harmonious Development in Nature and Man," in *Studia Slavica Finlandensia*, XVI/2 (1999), 50–64.

——, "Intensifying Perception and Conceptualizing Nature: Organica in European and American Art of the Post-War Period," in *Organica/Organic: The Non-Objective World of Nature in the Russian Avant-Garde of the 20th Century* (exh. cat.). Cologne: Galerie Gmurzynska, 1999, 104–9.

——, "Biological Metaphors in 20th-Century Art and Design," *YLEM Journal: Artists Using Science & Technology* 8, no. 23 (2003): 4–10.

——, "Organische Modelle in der Kunst der klassischen Moderne," in Annette Geiger, Stefanie Hennecke, and Christin Kempf, eds., *Spielarten des Organischen in Architektur, Design und Kunst*. Berlin: Reimer, 2005, 97–111.

——, "Naturerfahrung als künstlerische Methode: Organische Visionen in der Kunst der klassischen Moderne," in Elke Bippus and Andrea Sick, eds., *Industrialsierung und Technologisierung von Kunst und Wissenschaft*. Bielefeld: Transcript, 2005, 86–108.

——, "Lebendige Formen und bewegte Linien: Organische Abstraktionen in der Kunst der klassischen Moderne," in *Floating Forms: Abstract Art Now* (exh. cat.). Bielefeld: Kerber, 2006, 10–22.

——, "Biocentric Modernism: The Other Side of the Avant-Garde," in *Local Strategies. International Ambitions: Modern Art in Central Europe, 1918 –1968*. Prague: Academy of Sciences, 2006, 125–32.

——, "František Kupka: Creation in Nature and Art," *The Structurist*, no. 47–48 (2007–2008): 64–69.

——, *Harmonie und Synthese: Die russische Moderne zwischen universellem Anspruch und nationaler kultureller Identität*. Munich: Wilhelm Fink, 2008.

——, "Wassily Kandinsky und František Kupka: Alternativen zum Kubismus," in *Slavische und nichtslavische Literaturen und Kulturen in Europa—Parallelen, Beziehungen, Zusammenhänge. Die Ost-West-Problematik*. Prague: Academy of Sciences, 2009, 189–210.

Ziche, Paul, ed., *Monismus um 1900: Wissenschaftskultur und Weltanschauung*. Berlin: VWB, 2000.

Index